LANDSCAPE PLANNING
Environmental Applications

LANDSCAPE PLANNING
Environmental Applications

Second Edition

William M. Marsh
University of Michigan, Flint

John Wiley & Sons, Inc.
New York . Chichester . Brisbane . Toronto . Singapore

ACQUISITIONS EDITOR / Barry Harmon
PRODUCTION MANAGER / Katharine Rubin
PRODUCTION SUPERVISOR / Sandra Russell
MANUFACTURING MANAGER / Lorraine Fumoso
COPY EDITOR / Marjorie Shustak
COVER DESIGN / Nina L. Marsh
COVER ILLUSTRATION / Brian Larson

Recognizing the importance of preserving what has been written, it is a policy of John Wiley & Sons, Inc. to have books of enduring value published in the United States printed on acid-free paper, and we exert our best efforts to that end.

Library of Congress Cataloging in Publication Data:
Marsh, William M.
    Landscape planning : environmental applications / William M.
Marsh.—2nd ed.
    Includes index.
    ISBN 0-471-52506-5 (pbk.)
    1. Land use—Planning—Environmental aspects.   2. Landscape
architecture—Environmental aspects.   3. Landscape protection.
I. Title
HD108.6.M37   1991
712—dc20   90-25163
                                                                            CIP

Printed in the United States of America
10 9 8 7 6 5 4 3 2

PREFACE

One of the original objectives of this book was to help bring physical geography, planning, and landscape architecture together around a set of applied problems and environmental issues; in short, to make a more effective integration among land planning, land science, and landscape design. Over the past decade teachers, researchers, practitioners and students together have made appreciable progress toward that objective. Not only have barriers between disciplines become more permeable, but a broader range of fields have become real forces in the landscape movement: architecture, civil engineering, geology, environmental science, forestry, and many others. Happily, students move in somewhat wider, and I hope more rewarding, academic ranges than they did in 1980.

The scope of this edition is considerably broader than that of the first edition. New topics are addressed as individual chapters—namely, landscape dynamics, physiography, groundwater, and wetlands—and many original chapters have been revised substantially to include topics such as sand dune nourishment and stormwater quality. In response to users' comments, the order of the chapters has also been rearranged. New case studies have been added on groundwater planning, urban flooding, habitat planning, and wetland restoration. Charles Woodruff, Jr., Leonard Ortalano, Jon Rodiek, Tom Woodfin, Peter Grenell, David Salvesen, and Ron Abrams contributed these case studies, and their efforts are greatly appreciated.

A word on problem sets and the instructor's supplement. Because instructors like to tailor studio/laboratory problems to their local setting or region, it is difficult to provide setups and data meaningful to a wide range of users in both Canada and the United States. The problem sets for this edition, therefore, are intended to serve as examples or suggestions along with brief discussions of additional ideas for exercises. This material, along with chapters on map reading and remote sensing, can be found in the instructor's supplement; adopters should ask the publisher for the instructor's supplement and feel free to use the material however it best suits their needs.

Many people contributed their time and talent to this edition. Nina L. Marsh, who revised the graphics program, drafted the new illustrations, and worked tirelessly to bring the volume together, deserves special thanks. Thanks are also extended to the reviewers: Donna Luckey of the University of Kansas, Pete Melby of Mississippi State University, Duane Mezga of Michigan State University, and James Segedy of Ball State University. Becky Pettengill typed the manuscript and Barry Harmon of John Wiley & Sons moved the project along to publication. To the hundreds of students in landscape architecture, planning, and geography whom I have had the pleasure to lecture before and work with over the years, goes a final note of gratitude for their patience and questions.

William M. Marsh
Flint, Michigan

CONTENTS

CHAPTER 8
Stormwater Discharge and Landscape Change   115

CHAPTER 9
Watersheds, Drainage Nets, and Land Use   131

CHAPTER 10
Stream Flow and Flood Hazard   145

INTRODUCTION

0.1 BACKGROUND CONCEPT

Virtually every modern field of science makes contributions toward resolving societal problems. In some cases the contributions are not very apparent, even to the practitioners in that field, because they are made via second and third parties. These parties are usually the applied professions, such as urban planning, landscape architecture, architecture, and engineering, which synthesize, reformat, refine, and adapt knowledge generated by scientific and technical investigations.

Geography, geology, hydrology, soil science, ecology, remote sensing, and many other fields hold such a relationship with the various fields of landscape planning. For more than a century, earth and environmental professionals have studied the world's physical features, learning about their makeup, how to measure them, the forces that change them, and how we humans use them. Planning is concerned with the use of resources, especially those of the landscape, and how to allocate them in a manner consistent with people's goals. Thus planning and the environmentally oriented sciences are linked together because of a mutual interest in resources, land use, and the nature and dynamics of the landscape.

0.2 CONTENT AND ORGANIZATION

This book addresses topics and problems of concern to planners, designers, scientists, and environmentalists. The focus is on environmental problems associated with land planning, landscape design, and land use. The coverage is broad, though not intended to represent the full range of existing applications; such a book would be too large and cumbersome for most users. The choice of topics was guided by three considerations. First, the main components of the landscape should be represented—namely, topography, soils, hydrology, climate, vegetation, and habitat. Second, the topics should be pertinent to modern planning as articulated by urban planners, landscape architects, and related professionals, including, for example, stormwater management, slope classification, and wetland interpretation. Third, the topics would not demand advanced training in analytical techniques, data collection, mapping, and field techniques.

The book is organized into two parts. The first part, comprised of Chapters 1, 2, and 3, addresses the roots of environmental planning, the nature of modern environmental problems, regional physiography, and landscape dynamics. The second part, Chapters 4 through 18, deals with environmental topics and problems in landscape planning. Each chapter introduces a problem area, describes its application to planning problems and issues, and illustrates various techniques and methods of analysis.

Chapters 2, 3, 7, and 18 are new to this edition of *Landscape Planning*. Chapter 2 deals with the physiography of the United States and Canada, and Chapter 3 with form–function relationships in the landscape. Chapter 7 addresses groundwater and land use planning, and Chapter 18 covers wetlands and related management issues. The discussions of remote sensing and map reading, which were individual chapters in the first edition, are presented in the instructor's handbook along with various problem sets and studio exercises.

0.3 LANDSCAPE PLANNING, ENVIRONMENTALISM, AND ENVIRONMENTAL PLANNING

The term *landscape planning* is used in this book to cover the macro environment of land use and planning activity dealing with landscape features, processes, and systems. Only three decades ago, the term *land use planning* was generally used for this sort of activity, but today, because of new knowledge, the recognition of new problems, the changing needs of society, and the modern proliferation of specialty fields, several new and alternative titles have emerged.

The environmental crisis of the 1960s and 1970s was brought on by a flurry of concern over the quality of the environment. Much of this concern took the form of a political movement to protect the "environment" from the onslaught of industry, government, and urban sprawl. Loosely translated, "environment" was taken by the movement to mean things of natural origin in the landscape, that is, air, water, forests, animals, river valleys, mountains, canyons, and the like. From this emerged the *environmentalist,* a person who believes in or works for the protection and preservation of the environment. *Environmentalism,* it follows, is a philosophy, a political or social ideology, that implies nothing in particular about a person's training, knowledge, or professional credentials in matters of the environment. Organizations such as the Sierra Club, Greenpeace, and Friends of the Earth practice environmentalism.

The environmental crisis also paved the way for stronger and broader environmental legislation at all levels of government. New types of professional skills were needed to provide various services in connection with environmental assessments, waste disposal planning, air and water quality management, and so on. In response, several new "environmental" fields emerged while many established fields, such as civil engineering and chemistry, developed "environmental" subfields. Taken as a whole, the resultant environmental fields fall roughly under three main headings: environmental science, environmental engineering and technology, and environmental planning.

Environmental planning is a "catch-all" sort of title applied to planning and management activities in which environmental rather than social, cultural, or political factors, for example, are central considerations. The term is often confused with environmentalism and with the preparation of environmental impact studies, but in reality, environmental planning covers an enormous variety of topics associated with land development, land use, and envrionmental quality, including relatively new topics such as toxic waste disposal and the management of wetlands, as well as traditional problems, such as watershed management and planning municipal water supply systems. To some extent, landscape planning is also a term of convenience used to distinguish the activities of what we might call the landscape fields such as geography, landscape architecture, geomorphology, and urban planning from other areas of environmental planning, many of which are more closely tied to environmental engineering and public health.

0.4 THE SPATIAL CONTEXT: SITES AND REGIONS

Because we need to address topics and problems of the landscape that are pertinent to modern planning as articulated by the practicing professional, most material in this book is presented at the site or community scale. Sites are local parcels whose size usually ranges from less than an acre to hundreds of acres, with a simple ownership or stewardship arrangement (individuals, families, or organizations). They are the spatial units of land use planning, the building blocks of communities.

Regions, in the vocabulary of land use planning and landscape design, are variously defined as the geographic settings that house communities, either a single community and its rural hinterland, several communities and the systems connecting them (roads or streams, for example), or a metropolitan area with its inner city, industrial, and suburban sectors. This concept differs from the geographer's notion of a region, which encompasses a much larger area—for example, the Midwest, the Great Plains, or the Hudson Bay region. Many environmental problems have a regional scope (geographer's version)—for instance, acid rain in the eastern midsection of the continent and water supplies for irrigation in the Southwest—but for a variety of reasons, planning programs have generally not been very effective on this scale in North America. Most of our examples of effective or promising planning of the environment are of regional (planner's version), community, or site scales. For the present era, at least, these appear to be the operational scales of most landscape planning efforts.

1

BACKGROUND, PROBLEMS, AND CONTENT

1.1 INTRODUCTION

People have probably engaged in some form of environmental planning as long as organized society has been around. There is ample evidence, for example, that topography and water supply were important considerations in the siting of the Romans' new towns and that the ancient Egyptians devised planning schemes for distributing irrigation water. It is clear, however, that most of the ancients' interests in what we call environmental planning were purely practical, having to do with things like food, water, and defense.

Early attitudes

With few exceptions, prior to the fifteenth century nature itself was given little regard as part of the environment. By far the lowest point in Western civilization's **attitude** toward nature occurred in Europe in the Middle Ages, when it was commonly viewed with suspicion, fear, and ignorance. Forests, for example, were seen as dangerous places haunted with beasts and thieves, and a common person's total familiarity with the landscape would not extend much beyond the village of his or her birthplace. However, with the Renaissance (beginning in the fifteenth century) and the Enlightenment (seventeenth and eighteenth centuries), humans and nature came to friendlier terms. The enlightened mind saw nature as having logic and order, something understandable to humans.

The Romantic movement

In the eighteenth century the concept of nature was extended to include pleasure and the enjoyment of natural things. This marked the beginning of a love affair with the environment, called the **Romantic movement.** With the Romantic movement we find nature given consideration for its own sake and for its beauty, spiritual meaning, and influence on the quality of life. In landscape design a new school of thought, called Landscape Gardening, emerged in England in which the landscapes of rural estates were made to look "natural" by using curved lines in gardens, field edges, and water features (Fig. 1.1). The arts of the Romantic movement also reflect the rise in environmental consciousness; nineteenth-century painting, music, and literature illustrate this awareness especially well with, among other things, bucolic scenes and pastoral moods.

In the United States the first village improvement associations, which began in the 1850s, applied Romantic concepts to communities; they beautified streets, cemeteries, and town squares and promoted laws for the protection of songbirds and the creation of parks. Overall, the Romantic movement can be credited with elevating the concept of nature and the natural environment to the status of an important human value, and this concept forms an important underpinning for modern environmental planning. Indeed, the environmental crisis of the 1960s and 1970s was founded largely around environmental quality and decline as moral issues.

The public health movement

Another development of the nineteenth century also provided an important underpinning for environmental planning: the scientific understanding of the environment's role in **public health.** This understanding came about through the documentation of environmentally sensitive diseases, such as malaria, dysentery, and typhoid fever (Fig. 1.2). It resulted in an improved public and institutional understanding of the relationship between human impacts on the environment (such as the decline in water quality from sewage discharges) and the health and well-being of society. One manifestation of this understanding was the planning and development of municipal sanitary sewers; Chicago's system, built in 1855, was one of the first in North America.

The conservation movement

A third underpinning for environmental planning was the **conservation movement.** It, too, began in the 1800s, growing out of a concern for the damage and loss of land and its resources as a result of development and misuse. Tied to both Romantic and scientific thought, the conservation movement, led by environmental stalwarts

Fig. 1.1 A drawing illustrating Romantic concepts in landscape design of the 1700s in England. Langley Park, Kent, England by Humphrey Repton.

such as John Muir and J. J. Audubon, initiated the national park system; Yellowstone, the first national park, was established in 1872. The movement subsequently led to many other major conservation programs, including the U.S. Forest Service, the Soil Conservation Service, and the Bureau of Land Management, as well as many state and local programs.

The conservation concept also influenced community land use planning in the United States and elsewhere. Conservation-sensitive land use planning in the 1970s adopted an ecological perspective in which uses were assigned to the land according to its carrying capacities, environmental sensitivity, and suitability as a human habitat. Although the conservation concept has been practiced in one form or another for many decades, its application to community development was advanced significantly by Ian McHarg, a landscape designer, who in the 1970s and 1980s promoted the concept of environmental planning as a means of striking a balance between land use and the environment.

The environmental crisis   In the face of rapidly expanding cities, highway development, and a burgeoning industrial sector after 1940, these movements crystallized in **the environmental crisis** of the 1960s and 1970s (Fig. 1.3). Although the environmental crisis is often remembered for protest movements and social upheaval, its most lasting effects are represented by a new body of environmental law, the National Environmental Policy Act, which addresses air quality, water quality, energy, the work environment, and many other areas.

1.2 THE PROBLEM: CHANGE AND IMPACT

Landscape change   The rate at which North Americans have developed this continent is unprecedented in the history of the world. Virtually every sort of landscape has been probed and settled

Fig. 1.2 An illustration from the mid 1800s in London, England, illustrating the sort of conditions that led to the public health movement.

in some fashion, and in the vast woodlands and grasslands of the continent's midsection, scarcely a whit of the original landscape remains. Wholesale transformation of natural landscapes represents only part of the story, however; the introduction of synthetic materials and forms represents the other part.

The age of materialism and economic expansionism has produced a colossal system of resource extraction which, for the United States, reaches over most of the world. At the output end of the system is the manufacture of products and residues of various compositions, many decidedly harmful to humans and other organisms. Both end up in the landscape: steel, glass, concrete, and plastics (in the form of buildings and cities), waste residues (in the form of chemical contaminants in air, water, soil, and biota), and solid and hazardous wastes (in landfills, waterbodies, and wetlands).

Built environments   The landscapes that are ultimately created are essentially new to the earth. Cities, for example, are often built of materials that are thermally and hydrologically extreme to the land, and in structural forms that are geomorphically atypical in most landscapes. It is a landscape distinctly different from the landscapes it displaced and, in many respects, decidedly inferior as a human habitat. The modern metropolitan environment that results tends to be less healthy, less safe, and less emotionally secure than most people desire. Moreover, the very existence of such environments poses a serious uncertainty to future generations owing to the high cost of maintaining both the environment and the quality of human life within them. In addition, their relationship with the natural environment of water, air, soil, and ecological systems is a lopsided one that does not adequately fit our notion of a sustainable balance between an organism and its habitat. Herein lies much of the basis for land use planning, landscape design, and urban and regional planning.

Land use-environmental   The planning problems we are facing today are many and complex, and not all, of
mismatches   course, are tied directly to the landscape. For those that are, most seem to result from **mismatches between land use and environment.** The mismatches are of mainly four origins: (1) those that stem from *initially poor land use decisions* because of ignorance or misconceptions about the environment, as exemplified by the person who unwittingly builds a house on an active fault or unstable slope; (2) those that stem from *environmental change* after a land use has been established, as illustrated by the

Fig. 1.3 Social protest of the environmental crisis of the late 1960s and early 1970s.

property owner who comes to be plagued by flooding or polluted water because of new development upstream from his or her site; (3) those that stem from *social change,* including technological change, after a land use has been established, represented, for example, by the resident living along a street initially designed for horse-drawn wagons but now used by automobiles and trucks and plagued by noise, air pollution, and safety problems; and (4) those that stem from *violations of human values* concerning the mistreatment of the environment such as the eradication of species, the destruction of rainforest, and the alteration of historically valued landscapes (Fig. 1.4).

1.3 THE PURPOSE OF PLANNING

The need   In general, the primary objective of planning is to make decisions about the use of resources. Over the past 20 years, **the need** for land use and environmental planning

Fig. 1.4   Modern environmental protest. Environmentalists of the Greenpeace organization utilize the media in their campaign for environmental protection.

has increased dramatically with rising competition for scarce land, water, biological and energy resources, and the need to protect threatened environments. The problems and issues are diverse in both type and scope, ranging from worldwide issues, such as desertification and misuse of the tropical rainforests, to problems of draining and filling a 2-acre patch of wetland on the edge of a city. In North America, despite the political undertones historically associated with public planning, environmental planning has gained real legitimacy in the past decade, though more as a reactive than a proactive process—that is, more as a system of restrictive (should not) policy than one of constructive (how to) policy.

Decision makers   Who does planning? Actually, professional planners probably do not do the majority of planning. Most of it is done by corporation officers, government officials and their agents, the leaders of institutions, the military, and various other organizations, including citizen's groups. Professional planners (those with formal credentials in planning, or related areas) usually function in a technical and advisory capacity to the **decision makers,** providing data, forecasting futures, defining alternative courses of actions, and structuring strategies for implementation of formal plans. The overall direction of a plan, however, always represents some sort of policy decision—one based on a formal concept of what a company, city, or neighborhood intends for itself and thus will strive to become. These concepts about the future are called *planning goals,* and they are the driving force behind the planning process.

1.4 DECISION MAKING, TECHNICAL PLANNING, AND DESIGN

Three broad classes of activity make up modern planning: decision making, technical planning, and landscape design. The first is that activity related to the decision-making process itself, which is usually carried out in conjunction with formal bodies such as

Decision-making planning

Technical planning

Landscape design

planning commissions and corporate boards. It involves building the methods and means for arriving at planning decisions, formulating plans, and then providing the information necessary for carrying out decisions. Among the tasks commonly undertaken in **decision-making planning** are consolidation of technical studies, definition of relevant policies, articulation of goals, formulation of alternative courses of action, and selection of preferred plans.

The second class of planning activity can be called **technical planning** and it involves various processes and services that are used in support of both decision-making and design activities. It includes environmental inventories, such as soil and vegetation mapping, engineering analysis, such as soil suitability for construction, and assessment of the impacts that proposed land uses may have on the environment. Technical planning is usually carried out by a variety of specialists, including cultural geographers, physical geographers, geologists, ecologists, hydrologists, wildlife biologists, archaeologists, economists, and sociologists, as well as professional planners from urban planning, landscape architecture, and architecture. The line separating decision-making from technical-planning activities is often indistinct, and in most projects the two types of planning merge into one another.

Following the decision-making process and the first wave of technical support studies, we move into the arena of design. **Landscape design** entails the laying out on paper or on the computer screen the configuration of the uses, features, and facilities that are to be built, changed, or preserved by virtue of the decision-maker's decisions. Design may call for additional technical studies, such as soil testing, refinement of maps, and even laboratory analysis. Therefore, the planning processes and the relationship among the three areas of professional activities should not be regarded as a linear sequence but more as an interrelated circuit as is depicted in Figure 1.5. Resolving a

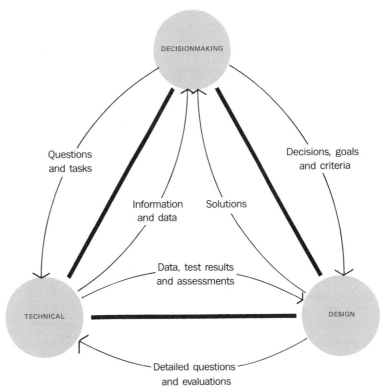

Fig. 1.5 The relationship among the technical, decision-making, and design areas of modern planning.

planning problem usually involves several iterations of the circuit in which a check and balance relationship often emerges among decision makers, technical planners, and designers.

1.5 ENVIRONMENTAL IMPACT ASSESSMENT

NEPA

The use of technical planners or specialists in planning has increased sharply in the past two decades as a result of environmental impact legislation. Indeed, the enactment of the National Environmental Policy Act of 1969 **(NEPA)** is directly tied to the emergence of environmental planning as a formal area of professional practice. This act calls for planners to forecast and evaluate the potential impacts of a proposed action or project on the natural and human environments. Although the act covers only projects involving federal funds (such as sewage treatment systems, highways, and domestic military facilities), NEPA initiated the enactment of more broadly based environmental impact legislation at state and local levels in many parts of the United States. As a whole, the various bodies of impact legislation brought on a flurry of activity in environmental planning in the 1970s and served to establish environmental factors as legitimate considerations in urban and regional planning.

Environmental impact methodology

The basic **environmental impact methodology** can be summarized in five steps, or tasks, that are normally performed sequentially.

- ■ The first is to select variables or factors that are pertinent to the problem, record them in an inventory, and identify their interrelationships.
- ■ The second is to formulate alternative courses of action.
- ■ The third is to forecast the effects (or impacts) of the alternatives.
- ■ The fourth is to define the differences between the alternatives: that is, to specify what is to be gained and lost by choosing one alternative over another.
- ■ The final step is to evaluate, select, and rank the alternatives.

Environmental impact statement

The report prepared from this assessment is called an **environmental impact statement** (EIS). It must identify the unavoidable adverse impacts of the proposed action, any irreversible and irretrievable commitments of resources as a result of the proposed action, and the relationships between short-term uses of the environment and its long-term productivity. In addition, the EIS must include among its alternatives one calling for no action, and this, too, must be subjected to analysis and evaluation.

Conditions and ambiguities

One of the most important and difficult tasks in the EIS process is the third, forecasting the impacts of alternative actions. An *environmental impact* can be defined as the difference between (1) the condition or state of the environment given a proposed action and (2) the condition expected if no action were to take place. Impacts may be direct (resulting as an immediate consequence of an action) or indirect (resulting later, in a different place, and/or in different phenomena than the action). Obviously, forecasting indirect impacts, and their correlative, cumulative impacts (where many factors work in combination to produce change), can be very difficult and is often a source of much uncertainty in environmental assessment. Furthermore, since an impact represents an environmental change, the problem that also arises (as in the case of an action calling for eradicating vegetation that contains both valued and noxious plant species) is that of deciding which are desirable and undesirable impacts and how different impacts should be weighted for relative significance.

1.6 AREAS OF ACTIVITY IN LANDSCAPE PLANNING

Environmental inventory

For planning that deals with the environment, several types of activities have become conventional in the United States and Canada. One of the best known is the so-called **environmental inventory,** an activity designed to provide a catalog and description of the features and resources of a study area. The basic idea behind the inventory is that we must know what exists in an area before we can formulate planning alternatives for it. Among the features consistently called for in environmental inventories are water features, slopes, microclimates, floodplains, soil types, vegetation associations, and land use as well as archaeological sites, wetlands, valued habitats, and rare and endangered species. In the preparation of environmental impact statements, inventories also include an evaluation of the phenomena recorded based on criteria such as relative abundance, environmental function, and local significance. This is supposed to indicate the comparative importance or value of a feature or resource (Fig. 1.6).

Opportunities and constraints

A second type of planning activity is aimed at the discovery of **opportunities and constraints.** This activity is often undertaken after a land use has been proposed for an area but the density, layout, and appropriate design of the land use program are still undetermined. The study involves searching the environment for those features and situations that would (1) facilitate a proposed land use and those that would (2) deter or threaten a proposed land use. Basically, the objective is to find the potential matches and mismatches between land use and environment and recommend the most appropriate relationship between the two. This may involve a wide range of considerations including off-site ones where the site is affected by systems and actions beyond its borders, such as stormwater runoff and air pollution from development upstream and upwind.

Land capability and carrying capacity

Land capability (or suitability) studies are designed to determine what types of use and how much use the land can accommodate without degradation. For areas composed of different land types the objective is to define the development capacity, or **carrying capacity,** of different land units or subareas. Capability studies may also be performed to determine best use, such as open space, agricultural or residential, for different types of land over broad areas (Fig. 1.7).

Hazard assessment

Hazard assessment is a specialized type of constraint study. The objective in hazard studies is to identify dangerous zones in the environment where land use is or would be in jeopardy of damage or destruction. Hazard research has been concerned with both the nature of threatening environmental phenomena, namely, floods, earthquakes, and storms, and the nature of human responses to these phenomena. Zoning and disaster relief planning for hurricane and flood-prone areas, for example, have benefited from hazard assessment at the national, state, and local levels. Another benefit is the emergence of risk management planning as a part of development programs, which involves building strategies and contingency plans for coping with hazards.

Forecasting impacts

Hazard assessment, environmental impact assessment, and constraints studies are all dependent on another activity: **forecasting impacts.** This activity involves identification of the changes called for or implied by a proposed action, followed by an evaluation of the type and magnitude of the environmental impact. The process is a tough one because of the difficulty in deriving accurate forecasts by analytical means. As a result, forecasts of impacts are usually "best estimates," and the significance assigned to them seems to be as much a matter or perspective (for example, engineer versus environmentalist) as anything else. Nevertheless, the *process* is an important one because it often leads to (1) clarification of complex issues and their environmental implications; (2) modification of a proposed action to lessen its impact; or (3) abandonment of a proposed project.

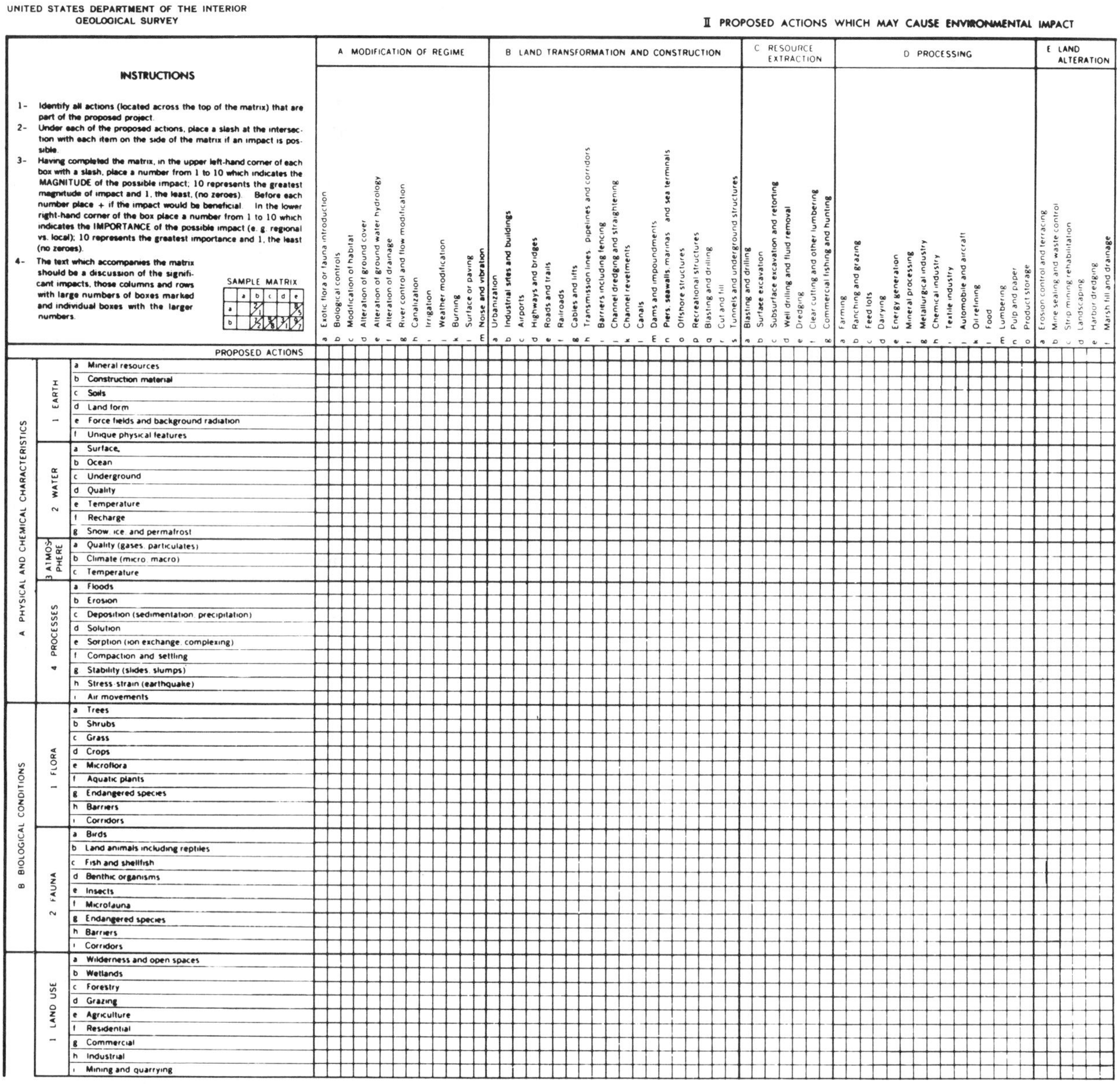

Fig. 1.6 An excerpt from a matrix designed for an environmental inventory. The matrix provides for an evaluation of the magnitude and significance of the impact on a ten-point scale.

Special environments   Analysis and evaluation of **special environments** such as wetlands, unique habitats, and archaeological sites is a rapidly rising area of planning activity. Though logically a part of impact assessment, capability studies, and most other planning activities, special environments have gained increased attention with the enforcement of wetland protection laws, rare and endangered species laws, and similar ordinances relating to prized resources in the environment. The focus of activity to date is overwhelmingly empirical, dealing mainly with field identification and mapping of the feature or organism in question. The results usually center on the question of presence or absence of, for example, a threatened species or a valued habitat, as the basis for deciding whether a proposed land use can or cannot take place in or near the area under consideration.

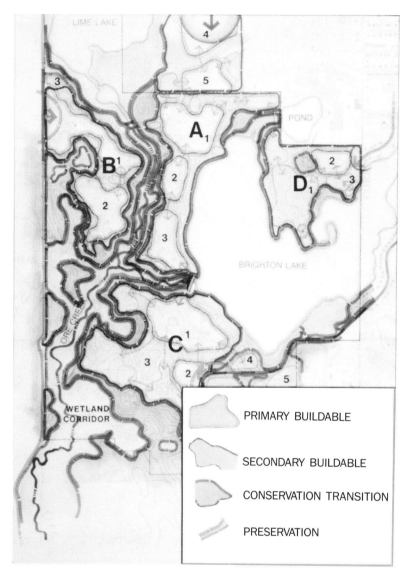

Fig. 1.7 Land capability map for a modern residential development. Land is classed as buildable, transitional buffer, or conservation easement.

Site selection   **Site selection** is a traditional planning problem that incorporates a host of planning activities. Typically, we would begin with a proposed idea for a land use program or an actual program for a facility or enterprise in hand and attempt to find an appropriate place to put it. It often entails no more than an exercise in locational analysis based on economic factors, but in many instances, such as in siting resorts, office complexes, and housing projects, it may also involve environmental factors such as the risk of hazards and the potential for conflict over special environments and features. **Feasibility studies,** on the other hand, begin with a known site and, with the

Feasibility studies   aid of field studies and various forecasting techniques, attempt to determine the most appropriate use for it. Increasingly, planners and developers are interested in learning about a site's limitations based on environmentally protected areas and features, such as wetlands and habitats, as a part of feasibility studies.

Facility planning   **Facility planning** involves siting, planning, and designing installations that are dependent on structural and mechanical systems. Sewage treatment plants, industrial installations, airfields, and health complexes are typical examples. Not many years ago, little consideration was given to environmental matters in facility planning beyond water supply, sewer services, and in some cases, an environmental impact statement. Today, however, environmental analysis and site planning, both onsite and offsite, are given serious consideration as they influence environmental quality, public image and community relations, landscape management, and especially public and worker liability.

Master planning   **Master planning** may include all the planning activities mentioned above, for its overriding aim is to present a comprehensive framework to guide land use changes. Early in the master planning process, goals are formulated relating to land use, economics, environment, demographics, and transportation. Existing conditions are analyzed, and alternative plans are formulated; the alternatives are then tested against goals and existing conditions, and one is adopted. The master plan usually comprises three parts: (1) a program proposal consisting of recommendations, guidelines, and proposed land uses; (2) a physical plan, showing the recommended locations, configurations, and interrelationships of the proposed land uses; and (3) a scheme for implementing the master plan which identifies funding sources, enabling legislation, and how the changes are to be phased over time.

Management planning   Finally, we must consider **management planning.** Although environmental planning is normally associated with the early phases of the planning process, it is becoming apparent that it must also be part of the design, construction, and operational phases of projects. In the construction phase, management plans must be formulated to minimize environmental damage from heavy equipment, material spills, soil eroision, and flooding. Similarly, once construction is over and the land use program is operational, it is often necessary to devise environmental management programs to achieve lasting stability among the landscape, built facilities, and environmental systems such as drainage, airflow, and ecosystems. As with master plans, management plans must be comprehensive to be most effective.

1.7 METHODS AND TECHNIQUES

The methods used in environmental and landscape planning are basically no different from those in other areas of planning. The fact that environmental phenomena are more closely associated with the "hard," or natural, sciences does not mean that this area of planning is necessarily more rigorous than, for example, transportation or land use planning. The differences lie rather in the perspectives, particularly in what components of the plan are given greatest emphasis and in the analytic techniques used to generate data and to test the planning and design schemes.

Data sources   The questions and topics that are the focus of analysis in environmental planning originate in all phases of projects and problems and are of varying complexity and sophistication. In the early phases of a project the emphasis is generally on gathering and synthesizing data and information. Planners often refer to this listing as an environmental inventory, following the language of EIS methodology (see Fig. 1.6). The idea behind the inventory is to learn all we can about the character of a project site and its setting. Although this normally includes field inspection and field measurement, the generation of quantitative data usually are not the primary objectives. Instead, the sources of most data are secondary (published) sources: topographic maps, soils maps, aerial imagery, climatic data, and streamflow records. When detailed field measurement is undertaken early in a project, it is usually in connection with a known or suspected engineering, safety, or health problem, such as soil stability or buried waste, or in connection with policy problems such as wetlands or threatened species. For the most part, the environmental analysis in the early phases of a project is typically not analytic in the scientific sense. That is, it is more concerned with defining distributions, densities, and relations among the various components of the environment than with rigorous testing of cause-effect relationships.

Analysis   Later in the project the process becomes more **analytic** as problems and questions arise relating to formulating and testing planning and design schemes. The techniques employed vary widely. For some problems, quantitative models are used, such as hydrologic models to forecast changes in streamflow and flood magnitudes in connection with land development of a watershed. For others, hardware models are called for, such as wind-tunnel analysis of building shapes and floodflow simulations in stream tanks (Fig. 1.8). For still others, a statistical analysis to test the relationships between two or more variables (such as runoff and water quality) is appropriate.

Generating results from the various data-gathering, descriptive, and analytic efforts does not mark the end of the environmental planner's or designer's responsibility. *Integration*   Ahead lies the difficult task of **integrating** the various and sundry results in a meaningful way for decision making. No calculus has been invented that satisfactorily facilitates such a difficult integration—a dilemma faced in all planning problems. The integration almost always requires some sort of a screening and evaluation to determine the relative importance and meaning of the results. The actual integration is usually a

Fig. 1.8   A hardware model of a portion of the Mississippi River used by the U.S. Army Corps of Engineers to simulate the behavior of floodflows in a partially forested floodplain. The rows of cards produce an effect on flow similar to that of trees.

Displaying results

qualitative rather than a quantitative process and typically centers on a visual (graphic) **display** of some sort. This may be a matrix, a flow diagram, a set of map overlays, or a gaming simulation board. Above all, it is important to understand that the final outcomes are found not in the results of specific procedures or techniques (as we might be led to believe from our experience in a college science laboratory class), but in a less exact and more eclectic process that invariably rests on a decision maker's or decision-making body's perspectives and values concerning the problem as well as on related political and financial agendas.

1.8 THE PLANNING PROFESSIONS AND PARTICIPATING FIELDS

Urban planning

Traditionally, only three fields, namely, urban planning, landscape architecture, and architecture, are recognized for training the professionals who guide the formal planning processes. These fields are focused mainly on the decision-making and design aspects of planning. **Urban planning** has the broadest scope with concern for entire metropolitan areas. Most professional activity in urban planning revolves around decision making in the public sector related to economic development, social programs, land use, and transportation planning. Most urban planners work for planning and related agencies in cities, townships, and counties, although the number working in the private sector has increased in the past two decades.

Landscape architecture

Landscape architecture tends to be more site oriented than urban planning. Landscape arthitecture works with both the natural and built elements of the landscape, seeking to blend the two into workable and pleasing environments. Professional activity covers the full range of settings from urban to wilderness landscapes and includes projects as small as residential site planning and those as large as national park planning. Landscape architects work in both the private and public sectors.

Architecture

Architecture has the narrowest focus in landscape planning, dealing mainly with buildings and their internal environments. Architecture is concerned with the landscape mainly as a setting for buildings and related facilities as well as a source of environmental threats, such as floods and earthquakes, to building stability.

Each decade a growing number of scientific fields participate in planning in North America. The 1970s saw increased participation from geography, geology, biology, chemistry, anthropology, and political science in the formal arenas of planning mainly in connection with environmental assessment and impact activities. The 1980s nurtured the development of technical subfields in response to the increased complexity of planning problems and the need for specialists in areas such as hazardous waste management, groundwater protection, and wetland evaluation and restoration.

Technical subfields

Technical subfields have emerged in both traditional planning fields and the participating sciences. For many of the subfields sponsored by the scientific disciplines there are counterparts, more or less, in the traditional planning fields. Tied together by common research interests, these subfields form an important source of data and information for the decision-making and design processes. In landscape architecture, for example, there are ties with botany, ecology, and geography over issues such as watershed management, habitat planning for urban wildlife, and wetland restoration.

Geography

Both architecture and **geography** are interested in the microclimates of building masses and urban environments. Geography also shares an abiding interest with landscape architecture and planning in remote sensing and computer-aided mapping for land use planning and environmental assessment. In urban planning one of the subfields shared with political science is environmental policy, dealing with the formulation, interpretation, and applications of ordinances.

1.9 SELECTED REFERENCES FOR FURTHER READING

Catanese, Anthony J., and Snyder, James C. *Introduction to Urban Planning.* New York: McGraw-Hill, 1988, 386 pp.

Godschalk, David R. *Planning in America: Learning from Turbulence.* Chicago: APA Planners Press, 1974, 240 pp.

Hargrove, Eugene C. *Foundations of Environmental Ethics.* Englewood Cliffs, N.J.: Prentice Hall, 1989.

Holling, C.S. (ed.) *Adaptive Environmental Assessment and Management.* New York: Wiley, 1978, 377 pp.

Leopold, Aldo. *A Sand County Almanac.* Oxford: Oxford University Press, 1949. (Reissued by Ballantine Books, 1970).

Lynch, Kevin, and Hack, Gary. *Site Planning.* Boston: MIT Press, 1984, 384 pp.

McHarg, Ian L. *Design with Nature.* New York: Doubleday, 1969.

Newton, N.T. Design on the Land: The Development of Landscape Architecture. Cambridge: Belknap Press, 1971

Ortolano, Leonard. *Environmental Planning and Decision Making.* New York: Wiley, 1984.

2

THE PHYSIOGRAPHIC FRAMEWORK

2.1 INTRODUCTION

There is a predictable sameness creeping over the face of the North American landscape. Since the early 1970s, highways, shopping centers, residential subdivisions, and most other forms of development have taken on a remarkable similarity from coast to coast. Not only do they look alike, but modern developments also tend to function alike, including the way they relate to the environment, that is, in the way stormwater is drained, waste disposal is managed, and landscaping is arranged.

Physiographic diversity

We know that this facade of development masks an inherently diverse landscape in North America. If we look a little deeper, it is apparent that **landscape diversity** is rooted in the varied physiographic character of the continent and this, in turn reflects differences in the way the terrestrial environment functions. Does it not seem reasonable then that development schemes should also reflect these differences if they are to be responsive to the environment? Herein lies one of the important missions for environmental planning: to help guide development toward environmentally responsive landscape planning and design schemes that avoid mismatches between land uses and environment.

In this chapter we make a brief survey of the physiographic regions of the United States and Canada. Our purpose is to gain some understanding of the different types of terrain, resources, and environmental conditions that make up the North American landscape. Such understanding is very important for today's landscape professional, not only because we are increasingly called on to deal with problems far beyond our local theaters of operation, but also because many of the environmental phenomena we deal with in planning and design extend well beyond the site or local region. In addition, it is apparent that many of the standardized treatments of the environment are inappropriate for certain physiographic settings.

Physiographic regions

While **physiographic regions** are defined by the composite patterns of landscape features, it is important that we remember that the physiography of any region represents the product of a host of processes that operate at or near the earth's surface. These processes are arranged in various systems characterized by flows of matter driven by energy: drainage systems, climatic systems, mountain-building (geologic) systems, geomorphic systems, ecosystems, and land use systems that overlap and interact in different ways and rates. These systems have developed over various periods of time in North America ranging from hundreds of millions of years in the case of the geologic systems that built the Appalachians and the Rockies to only several centuries in the case of agricultural and urban land use. The physiographic patterns and features we see today represent an evolving picture—at this moment a mere slice of the terrestrial environment at the intersection of the time lines of many forces and systems.

The framework

Generally, regional geology provides a useful **framework** for describing the gross physiography of North America: the Canadian Shield, the Appalachian Mountains, the Interior Highlands, the Coastal Plain, the Interior Plains, the Rocky Mountains, and so on (Fig. 2.1). The geologic structure of each region sets the drainage trends and patterns and in turn the general character of landforms. Added to this is the role of climate as it influences vegetation, soils, runoff, permafrost, and water resources (Fig. 2.2). When we speak of a physiographic region, we are referring to a geographic entity defined by a particular combination of landforms, soils, water features, vegetation, and related resources. Ten major physiographic regions, as follows, are traditionally defined for the United States and Canada, and they are broken down into smaller regions called physiographic provinces.

Fig. 2.1 Physiographic regions of North America.

2.2 THE CANADIAN SHIELD

Geology The Canadian Shield is a large physiographic region in the northcentral part of the continent (Fig. 2.1). It is composed of the oldest rocks in North America (older than a billion years) and is the geologic core of North America. Geologically, the Canadian Shield is extraordinarily complex, with intersecting belts of highly deformed rocks throughout. These rocks have been subjected to not one or two, but many, ancient episodes of deformation. Thus most of the rocks are hard, tightly consolidated, and diverse in mineral composition, including iron ore, nickel, silver, and gold.

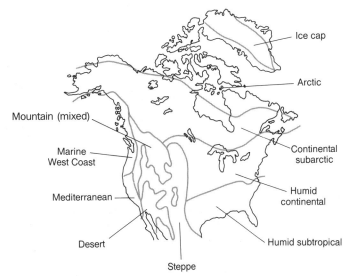

Fig. 2.2 Major climatic zones and of North America.

Most of the Canadian Shield has been geologically stable (relatively free of earthquakes and volcanic activity) for the past 500 million years or so. During that time, erosional forces have worn the rocks down to rough plateau surfaces, in places resembling low mountains in their ruggedness. In addition, large sections of the shield lie at lower elevations and are covered with sedimentary rocks. The largest of these areas—though it does not belong to the Canadian Shield region per se—is the broad interior of the continent stretching from the U.S. Midwest through the Canadian Interior Plains northward to the Arctic Lowlands of northern Canada. Over this vast area the Shield rocks are buried under a deep cover of sedimentary rocks, thousands of feet thick in most places, and hence have essentially no influence on the surface environment.

Glaciation   A significant recent chapter in the long and complex physiographic development of the Canadian Shield was the **glaciation** of North America. Great masses of glacial ice formed in the central and eastern parts of the Shield and, in at least four different episodes in the past 1 to 2 million years, spread over all or most of the region. (The last ice sheet melted from the shield only 6000 to 8000 years ago.) The advancing ice sheets scoured the Shield's surface, removing soil cover and rasping basins into the less resistant rocks.

Local diversity   As a result of this action, much of the Shield was left with an irregular and generally light soil cover interspersed with low areas occupied by lakes and wetlands. When we combine this characteristic with the already diverse surface geology, it is easy to see why the Canadian Shield is one of the most complex landscapes in North America. From the standpoint of landscape planning and design, the Shield presents few easily definable patterns and trends in landforms, drainage, and soils. Variation is typically great even at a local scale of observation; therefore, careful field work is called for in virtually all planning problems.

Bioclimate   The Canadian Shield lies principally in the continental subarctic climate zone, which is marked by fiercely cold winters and short cool summers. A great proportion of the Shield is occupied by a surface layer of permafrost, though the coverage is discontinuous. The vegetative cover is characterized as mainly boreal (northern) forests (spruce, fir, and birch, for example) mixed with wetlands in the more rugged sections and tundra in the northern zone.

Drainage   Throughout much of the Shield are extensive outcrops of barren rock. **Drainage** patterns are very irregular, so much so that the term deranged is used to describe them (Fig. 2.3). Lakes and wetlands are abundant, and freshwater is clearly one of the Shield's greatest resources. Settlement is light, and land use is sparse throughout most of the Shield including the two sections that lie within the United States, the Adirondack Mountains, and the Superior Uplands. Where settlements are found, they are usually related to an extractive economic activity, usually mining, forestry, or fishing. It is, however, an alluring recreational landscape, and it has attracted the development of parks, resorts, and summer homes along the Shield's southern margin.

2.3 THE APPALACHIAN REGION

Overview   The Appalachian Region is an old mountain terrain that formed on the southeastern side of the Canadian Shield several hundred million years ago (Fig. 2.1). Although the Appalachians date from around the same time as the Rocky Mountains, they developed appreciably different terrains. The Appalachians are lower, less angular, and less active geologically. Whether these differences have always existed, or whether they are due to a long period of inactivity in the Appalachians during which erosional forces have worn them down, we cannot say. In any case, the Appalachians are characterized by

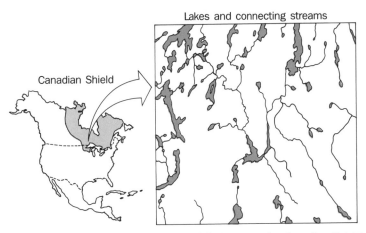

Lakes and connecting streams

Canadian Shield

Fig. 2.3 An example of the complex character of drainage on the Canadian Shield.

rounded landforms that are generally forest-covered in their natural state and rarely exceed 6000 feet in elevation. Unlike the Canadian Shield, major trends and patterns are discernible in the Appalachian Region, making it somewhat easier to deduce general physiographic conditions at the regional planning scale.

Blue Ridge   The Appalachian Region stretches from northern Alabama in the American South to Newfoundland in the Canadian Maritime Provinces. It is subdivided into five provinces on the basis of landforms. The highest and smallest province (in area) is the **Blue Ridge** which stretches in a narrow band from New York to Georgia. It is composed of folded metamorphic rocks, that is, rocks hardened from the heat and pressure of mountain-building. The Blue Ridge is high enough that climate over much of this province is distinctly wetter and cooler, especially in its southern reaches, called the Great Smokey Mountains.

Piedmont Province   East of the Blue Ridge is the **Piedmont Province** of the Appalachians (Fig. 2.4). This province is composed mainly of metamorphic rocks covered by a soil mantle of variable thickness. Although large parts of the Piedmont are fairly level, the surface is best characterized as hilly. From the Blue Ridge, the Piedmont slopes gradually eastward until it disappears under the sedimentary rocks of the Coastal Plain, which borders the Atlantic Ocean. **Drainage** follows this incline toward the Atlantic. Stream *Drainage and settlement* and river gradients are relatively steep, but where they cross onto the Coastal Plain, they decline somewhat and flows become less irregular. For early settlers and traders moving up rivers from the Atlantic, the first fast water (rapids) they would encounter started with the Piedmont. The eastern border of the Piedmont became known as the Fall Line, and on some rivers it became a place of **settlement:** Richmond, Virginia, Raleigh, North Carolina, and Macon, Georgia, are Fall Line cities (Fig. 2.4).

The Piedmont lies principally in the humid subtropical climate of the American South. Soils tend to be heavily leached and generally poor in nutrients. Runoff rates are high, especially where land has been cleared, and surface water supplies from streams are abundant. Early in the development of Southern agriculture, the Piedmont was a favorite area for cotton and tobacco farming, but these activities waned as the soils declined and cotton farming shifted to the Mississippi Valley and later into Texas. Today the rural areas of the Piedmont support a mix of forest and light farming.

Ridge and Valley   The **Ridge and Valley** Province lies west of the Blue Ridge, stretching from middle Pennsylvania to middle Alabama. One of the most distinctive terrains in North America, the Ridge and Valley is characterized by folded and faulted sedimentary rocks

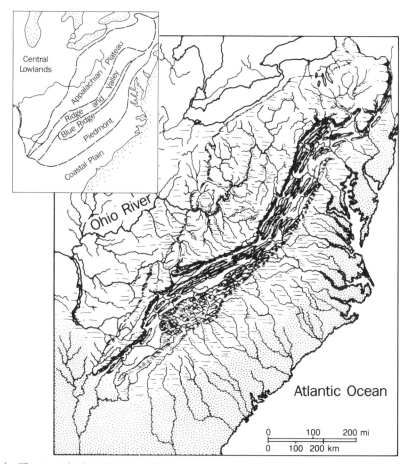

Fig. 2.4   The Appalachian Region of eastern North America including the Blue Ridge, the Piedmont, the Ridge and Valley, the Appalachian Plateau, and the Northern Appalachians.

that have been eroded into long ridges separated by equally long valleys (Fig. 2.5). Ridges and valleys may be more or less continuous for several hundred miles, broken only by stream valleys, called water gaps, or dry notches, called wind gaps (Fig. 2.3).

Drainage   **Drainage** lines generally follow the trend of the landforms, with trunk streams flowing along the valley floors and their tributaries draining the adjacent ridge slopes. But there are notable exceptions, for some of the large rivers in the north, specifically the Delaware, Susquehanna, and the Potomac, drain across the grain of the ridges and flow into the Atlantic. In the southern part of the Ridge and Valley, most streams drain into the Cumberland and Tennessee rivers, which are part of the Mississippi System. Settlements and farms in the Ridge and Valley are concentrated in the valleys where soil covers are heavy and water is abundant. The ridges are traditionally been left mostly in forest, being too steep for much else. However, modern residential and recreation development, attracted to the forests, rugged terrain, and excellent vistas, has pushed its way onto some Appalachian Ridges with varying degrees of success vis-à-vis the environment.

Appalachian Plateaus   West of the Ridge and Valley Province is a section of elevated sedimentary rocks into which rivers have cut deep valleys. This province is referred to as the **Appalachian Plateaus** (Allegheny Plateau in the north and Cumberland Plateau in the south) and extends from western New York to Tennessee. The rocks are flat-lying for

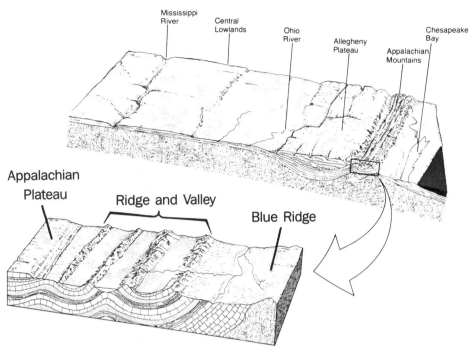

Fig. 2.5 A block diagram of a typical section of the Ridge and Valley Province showing the folded rock formations and related landforms, soils, and drainage.

the most part, and besides the deep valleys and flat-topped uplands, this section is famous for its great coal deposits, considered the largest single reserve of coal in the world.

Coal mining   Where the coal deposits lie close to the surface, the favored extraction method is strip mining. Where the coal is too deep for strip mining, shaft mining is used in which a horizontal tunnel is dug into the exposed end of the formation along a valley wall. Strip mining has produced some of the more serious environmental problems in the United States. Not only are top soil, vegetation, and habitat destroyed, but also the spoils (coal debris and subsoil) are subject to erosion and weathering, resulting in sedimentation and chemical pollution of streams as well as unsightly and unproductive landscapes (Fig. 2.6).

Northern Appalachians   The **Northern Appalachians,** north of New York, are made up of several separate mountain ranges composed principally of crystalline rocks. The most prominent of these ranges are the Green Mountains and White Mountains of Vermont, New Hampshire, and Maine, the Notre Dame Mountains of the Gaspe Peninsula of Quebec, and the Long Range Mountains of northern Newfoundland. (The Adirondack Mountains of northern New York appear to belong to the Northern Appalachians, but they are a southern extension of the Canadian Shield.) The whole of the Northern Appalachians was glaciated, leaving it with abundant rock exposures and a generally thin cover of glacial deposits. These characteristics combined with northern conifer forests and *Drainage*   abundant lakes and wetlands give much of the Northern Appalachians a character similar to the uplands of the Canadian Shield. The lakes have been the focus of the acid rain phenomenon attributed mainly to the sulfur dioxide emissions from power plants and industrial sources fed by coal from the Appalachian Plateau. In addition, this section of the Appalachians borders on the Atlantic Ocean, producing an especially rugged coastline of rocky headlands and deep embayments.

Fig. 2.6   A photograph of a strip mining operation with extensive piles of spoils in the Appalachian Plateaus.

2.4   THE INTERIOR HIGHLANDS

West of the Cumberland Plateau, in southern Missouri and northern Arkansas, lies a small region of low mountainous terrain that closely resembles the Appalachians. This region is called the Interior Highlands, and it is made up of two main provinces: the Ozark Plateaus, whose landforms are similar to the Appalachian Plateau; and the Ouachita Mountains, whose landforms are very similar to those of the Ridge and Valley section except the grain of the terrain is east-west trending (Fig. 2.1).

Ozark Plateaus   The highest elevation in the **Ozarks,** as this area of plateaus is commonly called, lies around 3000 feet; those in the Ouachita Mountains lie close to 4000 feet. Most ridges in the Ouachita Mountains are forested and too steep for settlement; in the Ozarks, however, ridges are often flat-topped and cleared for farming. Ozark stream valleys, on the other hand, are relatively deep and steep sided and, like those in the Appalachian Plateaus, are viewed as attractive places for reservoirs. This opportunity has not escaped the federal government, and today both the Ozarks and the Appalachian Plateaus are laced with reservoirs where forested stream valleys once existed.

2.5   THE ATLANTIC COASTAL PLAIN

The Atlantic Coastal Plain forms a broad belt along the U.S. Eastern Seaboard and the Gulf of Mexico (Fig. 2.1). Geologically, this region is the landward extension of the continental shelf, and consistent with the submarine part of the continental shelf, the Coastal Plain is composed of sedimentary rocks that dip gently seaward. Where these

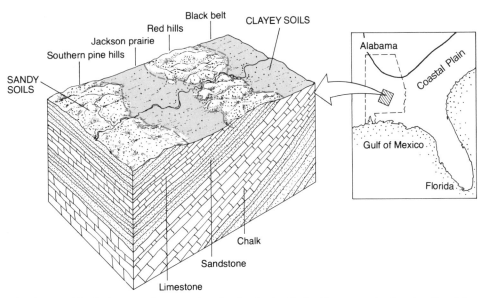

Fig. 2.7 A block diagram showing the dipping bedrock, landforms, and related soils of the Coastal Plain.

rocks outcrop within the Coastal Plain, they are often marked by a band of hilly topography and soils that are compositionally similar to the bedrock (Fig. 2.7). Overall, however, the topographic relief of the Coastal Plain is very modest, and the highest elevations (mainly along the inner edge) reach only 300 feet or so above sea level.

Outer Coastal Plain   Bordering the sea, in the province called the **Outer Coastal Plain,** the land is generally low and wet. Swamps, lagoons, estuaries, and islands are abundant, and these are subject to periodic incursion by storm waves and hurricane surges (Fig. 2.8). Offshore islands, called barrier islands, which are mostly accumulations of wave and current deposited sands, are especially prone to storm damage. However, this has not deterred development, for each year residential and recreational land uses push further onto the barrier islands throughout the Atlantic and Gulf coasts. Some of the largest wetlands in North America, such as the Everglades in Florida, the Great Dismal Swamp of Virginia and North Carolina, and the Bayous of Louisiana, are found in the Outer Coastal Plain.

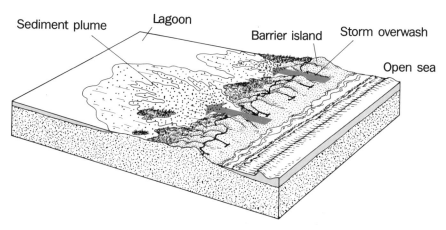

Fig. 2.8 A diagram illustrating the effects of stormwave overwash of a barrier island along the outer Coastal Plain.

Inner Coastal Plain   Inland, on the **Inner Coastal Plain,** the land is generally higher and better drained. In central Florida much of the drainage is concentrated in underground caverns that have collapsed at selected locations to form pits or depressions called sinkholes. The larger sinkholes take on groundwater forming inland lakes, springs, and wetlands. Elsewhere the lowlands of the Inner Coastal Plain are formed by stream valleys. Large lowlands are found along all the major river valleys, and most contain

Mississippi Embayment   large areas of wetland. The largest river lowland is the **Mississippi Embayment,** which stretches from the Mississippi Delta northward to the southern tip of Illinois (Fig. 2.9). To describe this area as a river lowland is somewhat misleading because it comprises many river lowlands, some modern (active) and some ancient (inactive).

Flooding is frequent and widespread in the Mississippi Embayment and the other large river lowlands. The damage it wreaks on property and life is enormous and has

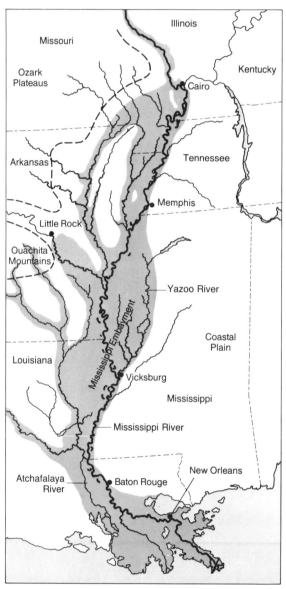

Fig. 2.9 The Mississippi Embayment, a broad lowland formed by the combined deposits, floodplains, and related features of the lower Mississippi and its tributaries.

increased steadily throughout the twentieth century. The cause of the problem is basically twofold: (1) increased development in high-risk areas with the growth and spread of residential population; and (2) engineering (structural) changes made in river channels, which constrict flow and increase the levels of floodwaters in certain locations.

Bioclimate   The Coastal Plain lies almost entirely within the humid subtropical climatic zone. Soils tend to vary from sandy to clayey to organic depending on the underlying bedrock, nearness to the coast, and river valley location. Vegetation patterns tend to follow the patterns of soil and drainage, with pines generally on the sandy higher

Local diversity   ground and trees such as tupelo, gum, and bald cypress in the wet lowlands. In dealing with planning problems in the Coastal Plain, it is important first to differentiate between upland and lowland terrain based on vegetation and soil patterns as well as topographic trends. Next, it is helpful to draw an association between terrain type and the essential processes that operate there, especially in the lowlands, and to understand the risks posed by each, mainly floods, surges, and hurricanes.

2.6 THE INTERIOR PLAINS

The heart of the North American landscape is a broad region of rolling terrain called the Interior Plains (Fig. 2.1). This region is made up of two large provinces, the Central Lowlands and the Great Plains, and one small province, the St. Lawrence Lowlands. All

Geology   three are underlain with sedimentary rocks that are covered with diverse deposits of varying thicknesses. In the Central Lowlands, north of the valleys of the Ohio and Missouri rivers, these deposits are mainly glacial, but in Illinois, Iowa, northern Missouri, Kansas, and Nebraska deposits of rich wind-blown silt, called loess, cover the glacial deposits and are the dominant surface material (Fig. 2.10). Other deposits include sand dunes in northwestern Nebraska and around the Great Lakes, clayey lake beds near the Great Lakes, and river deposits (alluvium) along most stream valleys.

Water resources   The Interior Plains are drained by three major **watersheds:** the Mississippi and its tributaries, which cover most of the region; the St. Lawrence, which drains the Great Lakes Basin; and the Nelson, Churchill, and Mackenzie drainage basins, which drain the Canadian Plains and small portions of North Dakota and Minnesota. Water is generally abundant in the Central Lowlands, especially the Great Lakes area, but it declines westward into the Great Plains as mean annual precipitation falls and evaporation rates rise. River water, fed by runoff from the Rocky Mountains, is locally plentiful in the Great Plains, especially now that many of the large rivers such as the Missouri have been dammed to form large reservoirs. In addition, groundwater is abundant throughout much of the Great Plains: one aquifer, named the Ogalalla, considered one of the largest in the world, stretches from South Dakota to northern Texas. Not surprisingly, agriculture in the Great Plains is overwhelmingly dependent on irrigation and is growing more so each decade.

Soils   **Soils** in the Central Lowlands are extremely diverse, especially in the Great Lakes states and southern Ontario, owing to the extraordinary mix of glacial deposits left there during the last glaciation of the region. Environmental surveys for planning must recognize that soils may vary significantly at the local scale, and sometimes problem soils may be hidden under surface deposits. In the northern part of this region, in the newer glacial terrain, lakes and wetlands are abundant and soils tend to be sandy. Westward, this diverse terrain gives way to a more uniform landscape, the prairies, and farther west, to the Great Plains (Fig. 2.11). In the prairies and plains, the terrain tends to fall into two classes: river lowlands (for example, the floodplains of the Illinois, Mississippi, Missouri, and Iowa rivers), and broad, level, or gently rolling uplands between the river valleys, which make up the bulk of the landscape. Soils on the upland

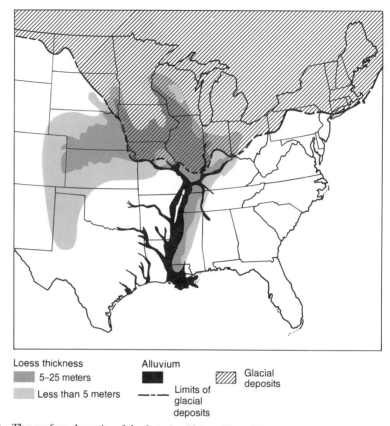

Fig. 2.10 The surface deposits of the Interior Plains. Glacial drift is found north of the Missouri and Ohio rivers. Loess covers the drift in the central Midwest and extends over the adjacent section of the Great Plains.

surfaces have formed in either glacial deposits or loess deposits. Both tend to be very fertile, and with the ample water resources of the region, the Interior Plains has become one of the richest agricultural regions in the world. It has also become a region

Urbanization   of massive **urbanization.**

Superimposed over a large part of this North American heartland are major urban/industrial corridors, such as the one linking Toronto, Buffalo, Cleveland, Toledo, and Detroit. The growth of these corridors in the past several decades has resulted in many serious environmental problems. Prominent among these problems are (1) conflicts between urban and agricultural land uses; (2) misuses and eradication of floodplains, wetlands, and shorelands; and (3) widespread air and water pollution including threatened groundwater resources from buried wastes. The Central Lowlands and the St. Lawrence Lowlands are major sources of acid rain; and water pollution from both point (concentrated outfalls) and nonpoint (geographically diffused) sources are critical in both urban and agricultural areas. The locus of environmental planning and management activity in the Interior Plains tends to fall along the interface between the expanding urban corridors and the surrounding rural landscape.

2.7 THE ROCKY MOUNTAIN REGION

The western border of the Great Plains is formed by the Rocky Mountain front, one of the most distinct physiographic borders in North America. From the Great Plains (at an

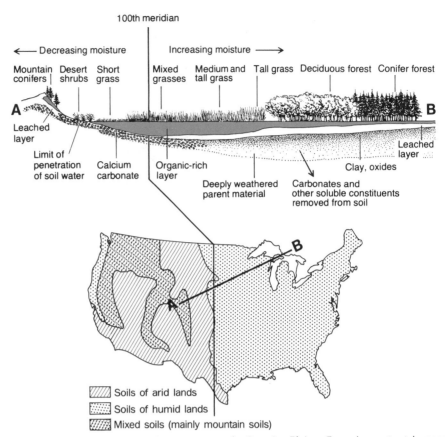

Fig. 2.11 Soil and vegetation changes across the Interior Plains. Organic content increases westward as moisture declines.

elevation around 5000 feet) the terrain abruptly rises 3000 to 6000 feet, and we enter the rugged region of the Rockies. This region stretches from central New Mexico to near the northern border of British Columbia. It is made up of four provinces: the Southern, Middle, and Northern provinces in the United States and the Canadian Province in Canada.

Geology   The Rocky Mountains are considered to be relatively young mountains because they are still active—though many of the rocks are of ages comparable to those in the Appalachians. **Geologically,** they are most diverse in the American provinces, where volcanic, metamorphic, and sedimentary rocks are all very prominent. The highest terrain in the Rockies, which is around 13,000 to 14,000 feet (4000 to 4300 meters) elevation, is found in Colorado, Wyoming, and along the British Columbia/Saskatchewan border. The largest areas of low terrain are the Wyoming Basin (around 5000- to 6500-foot elevation), which is underlain by sedimentary rocks, and the Rocky Mountain Trench, a remarkably long, narrow valley stretching for 500 miles along the western edge of the Canadian Province.

Drainage   Americans have traditionally recognized the Rocky Mountains as the "continental divide"—the high ground that separates **drainage** between the Pacific and Atlantic watersheds. To the Gulf-Atlantic go the Missouri, Platte, Arkansas, Rio Grande, and many other large rivers that rise in the Rockies; to the Pacific go only two large rivers that rise in the Rockies: the Colorado and the Columbia. By contrast, in the northern part of the Canadian Province the Rockies do not form the continental divide. The

Peace River, which drains into Hudson Bay, and the Mackenzie River, which drains into the Arctic Ocean, both rise west of the Rockies in British Columbia.

Bioclimate
Owing to their diverse geology and rugged, high topography, the Rocky Mountains are highly varied in **soils, vegetation,** and **climate.** The American Rockies lie generally in an arid/semiarid zone, but moisture conditions are often quite different from range to range depending on elevation, location, and orientation to prevailing winds and the sun. West slopes usually receive greater precipitation than east slopes because of the prevailing westerly airflow; and south-facing slopes are measurably drier owing to greater solar heating from the southerly exposures. Moisture conditions also improve with elevation, not only because precipitation tends to be greater higher up, but also because evapotranspiration rates are decidedly lower at cooler temperatures. This explains the contrasts in vegetation between the upper and lower parts of mountains. Heavy forests (pines, firs, and spruce, for example) are dominant at elevations between 7500 and 10,000 feet, whereas grasslands or shrub desert are dominant around the mountain base (Fig. 2.12). Above 10,000 feet the landscape is generally treeless and dominated by alpine meadows and snowfields. In the Canadian Rockies, forest elevations are lower, and glaciers and snowfields are more abundant at higher elevations owing largely to the higher (subarctic) latitude of this area.

Land use
Settlement in the Rocky Mountains is light; there are no large cities within the region. (Denver, Salt Lake City, and Calgary lie on the borders of the region.) Most land is publicly owned. In both Canada and the United States, extensive tracts have been set aside as national parks, national monuments, and national forests. Increasingly, landscape planning and management activity are focusing on these tracts as the pressures of recreation use and tourism rise. In addition, mining operations for coal, copper, gold, and other minerals are of great environmental concern locally in both the Rocky Mountains and the next region west, the Intermontane, because of their destructive effects on habitat, scenic resources, and ranch land.

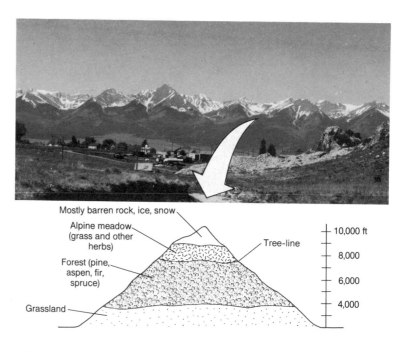

Fig. 2.12   The vertical zonation of vegetation in the Northern Rocky Mountains, a response to climate change with elevation.

2.8 THE INTERMONTANE REGION

Between the southern province of the Rockies and Pacific Mountain Region to the west lies an elevated region of plateaus and widely spaced mountain ranges. There are two major plateaus in this region: the Colorado, which lies at elevations around 6500 feet and is composed of sedimentary rocks; and the Columbia, which lies at elevations around 5000 feet and is composed of basaltic rock. The remainder of the region, about half its area, is the Basin and Range Province (Fig. 2.13).

Basin and Range topography   The **Basin and Range** (also called the Great Basin) is characterized by disconnected, north-south trending mountain ranges formed by faulting and tilting of large blocks of rock. The basins between the ranges are filled with thick deposits of sediment

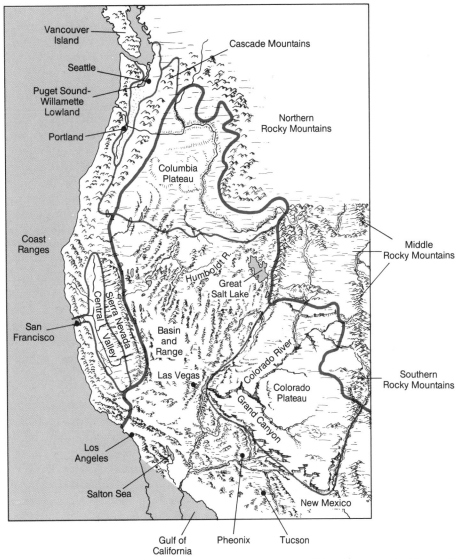

Fig. 2.13 The Basin and Range and Pacific Mountain regions of the western United States. The Grand Canyon lies in the Colorado Plateau. The southern part of the Basin and Range, in Arizona, is experiencing rapid population growth, as is southern California in the Los Angeles metropolitan region.

(thousands of feet deep) eroded from the adjacent mountains. The heavy accumulation of sediment is partially attributed to the region's dry climate, which generates insufficient runoff to support continuous-flowing streams to transport the sediment away. Indeed, the Basin and Range is the only large area of North America with internal drainage, that is, where many streams actually dry up before reaching the sea.

Development   In the past several decades, population has grown tremendously in the southern part of the Intermontane Region, principally in Arizona. This has resulted in both urban and agricultural **development,** which has placed great demands on limited water supplies in this arid region. Groundwater aquifers are being rapidly depleted, and Arizona is being forced to turn to aqueduct systems to transport water into the area.

2.9 THE PACIFIC MOUNTAIN REGION

Along the Pacific margin of North America is a complex region composed of many mountain ranges (Fig. 2.13). This region, known as the Pacific Mountain Region, contains just about every geologic structure and mountain type imaginable, and by virtue of its location on or near major fault zones, it is the most geologically active part of the continent. Earthquakes are commonplace throughout the region, and volcanism is active in the Cascade Range (which contains Mount St. Helens), in the Alaskan Peninsula, and in the Aleutian Islands.

Mountain ranges   Some of the more prominent **mountain ranges** include the Coast Mountains of British Columbia and Alaska, the Sierra Nevada of California, the Cascades of Washington and Oregon, the Coast Ranges of California and Oregon, and the Alaskan Range of southern Alaska. The Coast Mountains and the Sierra Nevada are mostly great masses of resistant granitic rock, whereas the Cascades are basically huge piles of weak (erodable) volcanic material. The Coast Ranges are mainly deformed sedimentary rocks aligned into a series of ridges and valleys paralleling the coast. The Alaska Range, in the northernmost part of the region, is a complex body of mountains built by folding, faulting, and volcanic activity and is the highest range in North America.

Coastal terrain   Unlike the Atlantic Coast, the Pacific Coast lacks a coastal plain. In most places the mountains or their foothills run to the sea where wave erosion has carved a rugged and picturesque shoreline. Owing to ancient sea level changes and geologic uplift of the land, much of the coastline is terraced, that is, characterized by steplike formations. In addition, the coastline is frequently intersected by streams that have cut narrow canyons down to the shore. Sandy beaches with sand dunes are found in the bays and near stream mouths. Accessibility to the coastline is difficult, and development is risky because of slope instability, the limited area suitable for building, and the often fragile character of the ecological environment.

Seismic activity   **Earthquakes** are a threat throughout the entire Pacific Mountain Region. The region is laced with fault lines, many of which have a recorded history of activity. The most active earthquake zones are found in California and Alaska. California is clearly the most hazardous of the two, especially south of the San Francisco Bay area, not only because of the prominent fault systems there (such as the San Andreas), but also because of the massive urban development lying on or near active fault zones. California's urban/suburban population within this area approaches 20 million people.

Two major lowlands are found in the Pacific Mountain Region. The larger of the two is the Central Valley of California, which lies between the Sierra Nevada and the Coast Ranges (Fig. 2.13). The other is the Puget Sound–Willamette Valley lowland which lies between the Coast Ranges and the Cascades in Oregon, Washington, and British Columbia. Both lowlands are floored with deep deposits of sediment washed down from the surrounding mountain ranges over millions of years.

Bioclimate   The **climate, vegetation,** and **soils** of the Pacific Mountain Region are as diverse as its geology. In Alaska and Canada, heavy precipitation in the Coast Mountains—the annual average exceeds 100 inches—nourishes large glaciers at elevations above 6500 feet and great fir forests at lower elevations. These forests extend down the coast into northern California, where redwood forests become the dominant coastal forests. Precipitation declines sharply farther down the California coast, and between San Francisco and Los Angeles the redwoods give way to a scrubby forest, called chapparal. Still farther south, in extreme southern California and the Baja California of Mexico, the chapparal gives way to grass and shrub desert.

Farming and forestry In California, the combination of subtropical climatic conditions and water supplies from mountain streams has produced one of the most diverse and productive **agricultural regions** in the world. Grains, vegetables, grapes, and fruits are grown extensively in the southern two-thirds of the state, mostly with the aid of irrigation. The forest industry traditionally flourishes in the area between San Francisco and the Alaska Panhandle. In this area, as in the Rocky Mountains, public-owned forest and parks occupy large tracts of land in both Canada and the United States.

2.10 THE YUKON AND COASTAL ARCTIC REGION

Yukon Basin South of Alaska's North Slope lies the Brooks Range (and its eastern limb in Canada, the British Mountains), a low, east-west trending mountain range. South of the Brooks Range and occupying the large interior of Alaska and the adjacent portion of the Yukon Territory is the **Yukon Basin.** The Yukon River drains this large basin, flowing westward into the Bering Sea. Fairbanks, the principal city of central Alaska, is located near the center of the Yukon Basin. *Permafrost* is found over most of the Yukon Basin, but its coverage is discontinuous and its thickness highly variable. The landscape of the Yukon Basin is dominated by boreal forests in the south, but northward the tree cover grows patchy and gives way to tundra. The treeless tundra stretches in a broad belt along the entire Arctic Coast.

Arctic Coastal Plain The Arctic Ocean is fringed by a coastal plain similar in topography to the Coastal Plain of southern United States. The **Arctic Coastal Plain,** however, is narrower and more desolate, being extremely cold and locked in by sea ice most of the year. The North Slope of Alaska, now famous for its oil reserves, is part of the Arctic Coastal Plain, as is the MacKenzie River Delta (just east of the Canada-Alaskan border) and the plain that fringes the northern islands of Canada. Virtually the entire Arctic Coastal Plain is underlain by permafrost, which in some areas extends offshore under the shallow waters of the Arctic Ocean.

Bioclimate Climate, permafrost, and ecology are the principal planning considerations of this region. The growing season, which is less than 60 days, prohibits agriculture, and permafrost limits development over much of the region because it leads to infrastructural damage. As one of the last great wilderness reserves on the continent, the tundra is given highest priority by environmentalists for long-term protection of its ecosystems. Conflict over economic development proposals and programs is destined to continue for decades.

2.11 SELECTED REFERENCES FOR FURTHER READING

Atwood, W. W. *The Physiographic Provinces of North America.* Boston: Ginn, 1940.
Bird, J. B. *The Natural Landscape of Canada.* New York: Wiley, 1972.
Birdsall, S. S. and Flovin, J. W. *Regional Landscapes of the United States and Canada.* New York: Wiley, 1985.
Bowman, Isaiah. *Forest Physiography.* New York: Wiley, 1909.

Hunt, C. B. *Natural Regions of the United States and Canada.* San Francisco: Freeman, 1974, 725 pp.

King, P. B. *The Evolution of North America.* Princeton, N.J.: Princeton University Press, 1959.

Leighly, John (ed.). *Land and Life: A Selection from the Writings of Carl Ortwin Sauer.* Berkeley: University of California Press, 1963, 435 pp.

Paterson, J. N. *North America: A Geography of the United States and Canada.* New York: Oxford, 1989, 528 pp.

Thornbury, W. D. *Regional Geomorphology of the United States.* New York: Wiley, 1965.

3

LANDSCAPE FORM AND FUNCTION IN PLANNING

3.1 INTRODUCTION

Life and land

It is no news that we are in serious trouble with the landscape. In North America, there are few places where we have been able to achieve a lasting balance among land use activities, facilities, and environment. Part of the explanation for this state of affairs has to do with the direction of modern urban **life.** In the past generation or two, people have generally lost touch with the **land** and in turn with most traditional knowledge about the way the landscape works. Planning for the use and care of the local landscape is no longer part of personal and family tradition and responsibility. It has to a large extent been relegated to second and third parties and has been transformed into a bureaucratic process made up of inventories, checklists, and permits, which asks for little understanding of the true character of the landscape.

The route to finding the true character of the landscape lies in understanding the way the land functions, changes, and interacts with the life it supports. One of the most fundamental points of understanding is that the landscape is more dynamic than it is static, with forms and features in a continuous state of change. Change is driven by systems of processes that include rainstorms, streamflow, fires, land use, and plant growth, and these processes shape the landscape now as they did in the past. It is increasingly apparent that successful landscape planning must do more than respond to mere shapes and features in the landscape but must respond to the processes themselves.

3.2 ESSENTIAL PROCESSES OF THE LANDSCAPE

One of the prevailing misconceptions about the landscape is that it is made up of features, especially natural features, that date from times and events millions of years ago. This view is especially common for landforms and soils that are typically regarded as products of the geologic past. Therefore, any attempt to understand their origins and development requires special knowledge of ancient chronologies and events. For most landscapes, however, this view is probably not valid.

The present era

By and large, the forms and features we see in the local landscape are the products of the processes that presently operate there. This perspective is important, because it implies that it is possible to understand the landscape according to the workings of the environment in **the present era,** more or less. Using an analogy from medical science, we know that the individual organs in the body have sizes, shapes, and compositions related to their function. As with the organs in the human body, form and function in the landscape go hand in hand. It follows that as the clever physician is able to read basic functional (physiological) problems from changes in organ shape and composition, so the insightful student of landscape can read changes in the functional character of the land from observable changes in landforms, soil, drainage features, vegetation, and so on.

Formative processes

What are the essential or **formative processes** of the landscape? They include waves, wind, glaciers, and runoff; however, there is little question that running water heads the list. This includes all the various forms of runoff fed directly or indirectly by precipitation—namely, overland flow, streamflow, soil moisture, and groundwater. The work accomplished by runoff, measured by the total amount of material eroded from the land, exceeds that of all other formative processes by manifold, even in dry environments. Therefore, we can safely conclude that the landforms we see in most landscapes are mainly water carved, water deposited, or influenced by water in some significant way (Fig. 3.1). Excluded, of course, are landforms in glacial environments and sand deserts, but many of these, too, are influenced profoundly by running water.

Landscape differentiation

The **differentiation of terrain** into various physiographic zones and habitats

Fig. 3.1 Water-carved landscapes. Runoff is the most effective agent in shaping the landscape over most of the earth.

begins with the sculpting of landforms by runoff. As the landforms take shape, different moisture environments emerge such as wet valley floors, mesic (intermediate) hill-slopes, and dry ridge tops. These in turn give rise to different plant habitats and the combination of moisture conditions, vegetation, and surface sediment yields soil. Thus, in our search for fundamental order in the landscape, it is advisable to begin with landforms and drainage. In most instances the remainder of the landscape, vegetation, soils, and habitats, will fall into place once the essential system of landforms and runoff has been worked out (Fig. 3.2).

Form-function concept   If we agree that the landscape represents a basic **form-function** (or process) relationship, then we should be able to deduce a great deal about the processes that operate in it from the forms we can observe. This concept is very important in planning projects. Although we can draw on the results of various scientific studies, we rarely have the time and resources to undertake detailed scientific investigations as a part of

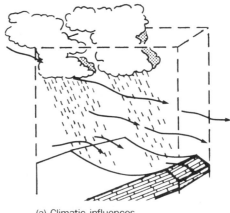

(a) Climatic influences

(b) Development of runoff system and landforms

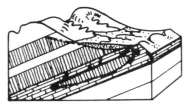

(c) Formation of soil, vegetation and habitat

Fig. 3.2 A schematic diagram illustrating the evolution of soil, vegetation, and habitat in response to the development of drainage and related landforms.

planning projects. That is, we are usually unable to launch studies to generate first-hand data leading to analysis of processes and their effects on the landscape.

Any actions taken as a part of land use planning and design which result in changed forms, such as cut and fill grading, soil preparation, and vegetation alteration, must produce a change in the way the landscape processes work. If certain balances exist on a slope among, for example, soils, the runoff rate, slope inclination, and vegetation cover, then an alteration of one component without appropriate counter alterations in the other three will result in an imbalance. The slope may begin to erode, sediment may accumulate on it, or vegetation may decline. In any case, the problem of maintaining balance in the landscape in the face of physical changes brought on by land use demands that we view the land as a dynamic gameboard rather than a static stage setting. As a rule, our goal in environmental planning should be to guide change in such a way as to maintain the long-term performance of the critical processes and systems of the landscape.

3.3 THE NATURE OF LANDSCAPE CHANGE

There is an old debate in science about the character of change in nature. Does nature change gradually over long spans of time, as traditional evolutionists thought, or does nature change in short bursts, as many earth scientists think? Both views are correct to some extent, but it appears that the second one is more appropriate for the larger features of the landscape such as stream channels, hillslopes, and land use.

Events

The essential processes of the landscape work at highly uneven rates, rising and falling dramatically over time. Each rise or fall in, say, streamflow or wind can be described as an **event.** Each event can be measured in terms of its magnitude, that is, its size such as the discharge of a stream or the velocity of wind. A huge streamflow that produces massive flooding is a high-magnitude event.

Event force

Very significant to our understanding of landscape change is the fact that the **force** exerted on the environment by an **event** *increases geometrically with its magnitude.* This means that to accurately interpret the potential for change (or work) by a force such as wind or running water we must understand, for example, that a threefold-magnitude increase from, say, level 2 to level 6 represents an increase in force as great as 25-fold. This is termed an exponential relationship in which force increases as some power function of event magnitude.

Magnitude-frequency concept

If we examine the relationship between the **magnitude and frequency** of events in the landscape, we will find that almost regardless of the process involved (e.g., streamflow, wind storms, rainfalls, fires, earthquakes, snowfalls, oil spills, car accidents, or disease epidemics) the pattern is basically the same. There are large numbers of small events, much smaller numbers of medium-sized events, and very few large events. The truly giant events, which can render huge amounts of change, are very scarce indeed. As it turns out, the events that do the most work in the long run are not the giants (they are too infrequent) and not the high-frequency events (they are too small even when counted together), but fairly large events of intermediate frequency.

Identifying formative processes

An inherent pitfall of landscape analysis for planning purposes is that we usually have no chance to observe or measure the events that really shape the landscape. For hydrologic and atmospheric processes, these are events, such as a very intensive thunderstorm, a floodflow, or a massive snowfall, which happen perhaps two or three times or less per year. The events we are apt to see on the typical field visit (which are very modest if you go out on a nice day) are usually meaningless in terms of total effectiveness in shaping the landscape. Therefore, unless we are careful we run the risk of grossly misinterpreting how the site actually functions, how its features are shaped, and how things relate to each other. We may be led to infer that the processes we happen to observe are really the essential ones or that it was all shaped so long ago that the processes operating there in this era cannot possibly have anything to do with the site as we see it. Both conclusions would be mistaken.

Relating form to function

How do we avoid the pitfalls of misinterpretation of the landscape? The answer lies in understanding the **form-function relation.** When we describe the forms and features of the landscape, we are actually observing the artifacts and fingerprints of the formative processes (Fig. 3.3). Through insightful field investigation we can deduce which processes at which levels created, shaped, or affected different landscape features.

Stream valleys and channels provide some of the best illustrations of this approach. Studies show that the stream channel is shaped principally by relatively large flows that occur several times a year. These may be floodflows or flows that fill the channel with modest spillover into adjacent low areas. Such flows are capable of scouring the channel bed, eroding outside banks, and causing the channel to shift laterally as is illustrated in Figure 3.3. Bank vegetation may be undercut, and where flows overtop the banks, waterborne debris such as dead leaves is often stranded on shrubs and trees. Taken together, these features serve as markers of flow depths and extent as well as indicators of the distribution of energy and the work accomplished by running water.

Fig. 3.3   A section of the Mississippi River floodplain showing the artifacts (forms and features) left in the landscape as a record of the river's formative processes.

3.4 THE CONCEPT OF CONDITIONAL STABILITY

Whether or not a landscape is stable under the stress of the various forces applied to it depends not only on the strength of those forces, but on the resisting strength of the landscape as well. Resisting strength is provided by forces that hold the landscape together, that is, keep soil from washing away, slopes from falling down, and trees from toppling over. Among the resisting forces—which include gravity, chemical cementing agents, and vegetation—living plants are the most effective in holding the soil in place.

Landscape's critical balance   In most natural landscapes a **state of balance** exists between the driving forces, represented by water, wind, human, and other processes, and the resisting forces. Only when this balance is broken—usually because a powerful event exceeds the strength of the resisting force—is the landscape prone to massive change such as wholesale soil erosion and slope failure. Most landscapes, however, are resistant to breakdown from all but the strongest events. In some places, however, stability is maintained by an

Conditional stability   extremely delicate balance which is conditional on a special ingredient in the environment. That ingredient, such as a mat of soil-binding roots on an oversteepened slope, functions as the stabilizing kingpin in the landscape. If the kingpin is weakened or released, the landscape can literally fall apart under the stress of even modest events.

Recognizing such conditional situations as critical to landscape planning because it is necessary to guide the change brought on by land use without pulling a kingpin and triggering a chain of damaging events. Thus, in evaluating a site for a planning project, it is important to identify features that may be pivotal to overall stability of the landscape. These may not be the most apparent features in terms of size or coverage. Among the conditional, or metastable, features commonly noted are steep, tree-covered slopes, vegetated sand dunes, stream banks made up of erodable sediment, certain wetlands, and groundwater seepage zones.

By way of example, let us illustrate the concept of conditional stability using a forest-covered sand slope in a coastal setting. In an unvegetated state, sand slopes (such as a wave-eroded bank or a dune face) can be inclined at an angle no greater than

33 degrees. When a cover of woody plants is added to the slope, especially trees, the angle can be as much as 45 to 50 degrees because the roots and stems lock the sand into a stable slope form. Such oversteepening of wooded slopes is a common occurrence in coastal environments where sand is added to an existing slope by wind or runoff. Alteration or removal of vegetation for roads, trails, structures, or lumbering will initiate slope failure, erosion, and a host of related problems (Fig. 3.4).

3.5 PERSPECTIVES ON SITE

Site as real estate

Invariably, projects and problems in environmental planning involve a parcel of space in the landscape called a site or a project area. It may range in size from less than 1 acre to thousands of acres. Its shape is usually some sort of rectilineal form, a product of mapping systems and the surveyor's coordinant lines. As a physical entity, the site has meaning mainly as a piece of real estate whose value is governed principally by its size and location. In land planning it is the envelope of space for which a use is sought or to which some land use has been assigned and within which a plan will be built.

Site as environment

From the standpoint of the environment and its functions, however, the site as conventionally defined has limited meaning and generally cannot be used to define the scope of environmental analysis for planning and design purposes. The reason why is that the spatial confines of site space usually have little to do with the workings of the environment, that is, with the processes and systems that shape and characterize the landscape of which the site is a part. Air, water, and organisms, for example, move in spaces and patterns that typically show little or no relationship to the space defined by a site. Therefore, as we pursue planning problems involving sites, we must deal with many different envelopes of environmental space as they ultimately relate to a prescribed piece of real estate.

Site in three dimensions

Although we commonly view the site as a two-dimensional plane defined by the surface of the ground and contiguous water features, in reality it is distinctly three dimensional. The third dimension, height and depth, extends the site upward into the atmosphere and downward into the ground. The relevance of atmospheric and sub-

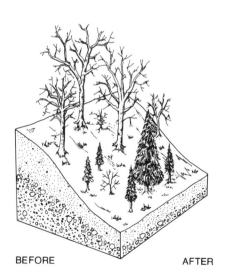

BEFORE   AFTER

Fig. 3.4 Slope failure following clear cutting of forested terrain in the American Northwest. These are not sand dune slopes, but they exhibit the same tendency toward instability once they are deforested. For scale, notice the figure in the failure scar on the right.

terranean phenomena to planning problems is generally secondary compared to surface phenomena. However, concern for groundwater contamination, air quality, and climatic change increasingly calls for serious consideration of these phenomena.

In addition, it is important to appreciate that the atmosphere and the subsurface are sources of forces that drive many of the surface processes. For example, groundwater is the principal source of stream discharge, and solar radiation is the primary source of surface heat. Alteration of these driving forces directly or indirectly affects terrestrial processes such as runoff, erosion, evaporation, and photosynthesis, which may in turn change the fundamental balance of the surface environment including slope stability, wetland trends, streamflow regimes, and the conditions of facilities.

3.6 SPATIAL DIMENSIONS OF THE SITE

Site in dynamic space

Sites are traditionally described according to their forms and features and the spatial relations among them. However, sites can also be described according to their **dynamics,** that is, according to processes that shape their forms and features. In addition to running water, rainfall, wind, and animal movements, these processes are the various land use activities and their byproducts such as noise and air pollution. Each landscape process is part of a flow system and can usually be described in terms of direction, velocity, mass, and force.

If we stand on a site, no matter where it is located, you can imagine that you are at the intersection of several flow systems that occupy different levels or strata of space at, above, and below the surface. Each flow system originates somewhere, usually offsite, and goes somewhere else after it has crossed the site. As it moves through the site, the flow is inevitably changed in some way as it interacts with the various forms and features of the site (Fig. 3.5).

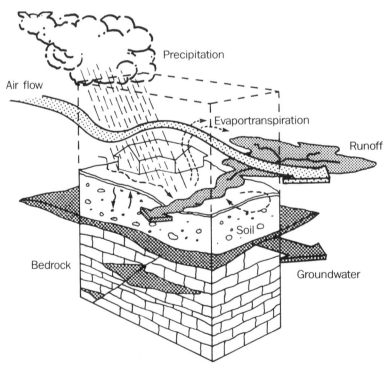

Fig. 3.5   The systems associated with a planning site and the associated patterns of flow.

The upper tier

Air occupies the **upper level or tier** of the site. Airflow usually originates far beyond the site because most winds are driven by regional scale forces, namely, pressure differences among air masses. The movement of air over the surface can be described as a fluid layer called the atmospheric boundary layer. This layer, which measures about 1000 feet deep, is dragged over the earth's surface by the general motion of the larger atmosphere. As it slides over the surface, **airflow** in the lower levels is slowed substantially because of the frictional resistance imposed by the landscape. As a result, wind velocities at ground level are usually a small fraction of those just 25 to 50 feet above the surface.

Airflow

The change in wind velocity with height above the ground is described by a standard curve called the normal wind velocity profile (see Fig. 15.5). This curve reveals that the greatest change in velocity can be expected in the lower 100 feet of the boundary layer where most planning and design activities are focused. The exchange of heat, moisture, and pollutants with the overlying atmosphere takes place across this zone, and the faster the airflow the greater the rate of exchange. This explains the requirement that factory and power plant exhaust stacks be heightened as a means of reducing local pollutant concentrations near the ground.

The middle tier

The **middle tier** of this model is the landscape per se, which extends from the upper limits of the vegetation canopies and tops of structures to the lower limits of root systems, buildings, and utility systems (Fig. 3.5). This is decidedly the most active layer of the landscape, with a host of flows taking on complex motions and exchanges. Although most movement is horizontal, some is decidedly vertical. Water, the dominant agent, is delivered vertically as precipitation then moves laterally as runoff.

Runoff

Runoff assumes a variety of flow forms as it moves over the surface, depending on slope, soil, and vegetation conditions. It may occur in thin sheets that move at velocities as low as 0.1 foot per second to streams that move at velocities up to 6 feet per second.

In site planning, runoff is one of the most serious considerations in terms of both water quantity and quality. In general, land development of any sort results in increased stormflows and decreased water quality. Since every site is part of a flow system, local loading of runoff is always passed on, and the problem tends to become cumulative downhill and downstream. Realization of this fact led to the first guidelines and rules for on-site management of stormwater in site planning to control flooding.

Wetlands

Where drainage is impeded by natural or other means, water may collect locally and initiate **wetland** formation. A dependable and abundant water supply encourages the development of special plant communities with distinctive floristic compositions and strong productivities. The organic matter added to the moist soil from plant remains further improves the water-holding capacity of the wetland, and advances its development and stability. This is one way in which the landscape becomes differentiated into zones of particular hydrologic, soil, and ecological character.

The lower tier

The lower tier of the site is comprised of the soil mantle and underlying bedrock (Fig. 3.6). Once considered relevant to planning only in terms of building foundations and drainage, today the subsurface environment must be given more detailed attention because it contains groundwater. **Groundwater,** the largest reservoir of fresh (liquid) water on the planet, is widely threatened by contamination from surface pollutants and buried waste. Unlike surface water, which is flushed from the land relatively quickly, groundwater moves so slowly that once contaminated it remains polluted for decades and even centuries.

Groundwater

Groundwater moves in huge bodies (called aquifers) at rates of a fraction of a foot per day. Because of their large size, aquifers almost always extend well beyond the scale of individual sites (Fig. 3.5). In site planning, therefore, it is useful to know what part of an aquifer the site lies over. For example, does the site lie over the recharge (water-receiving) zone or over the output (water discharge) zone of the aquifer?

Middle tier

Lower tier

Fig. 3.6   The upper part of the lower tier of the landscape exposed in a deep cut. The floor of the cut has exposed the upper surface of the groundwater.

Bedrock   Below the soil mantle lies the zone of **bedrock** geology. In mountainous regions the bedrock protrudes through the soil mantle to the surface, and we usually view it as a sign of ground stability in land use planning. The bedrock can, however, be decidedly unstable in areas of active faults and cavernous limestone. Faults usually occur in swarms running along fault zones. Earthquakes can occur anywhere in the fault zone, and their destructiveness is governed by the magnitude of the energy release as well as the nearness of the earthquake to the surface and its proximity to urban type development. In the case of cavernous limestone, the concern is with surface collapses and associated groundwater flows. Not all limestone is cavernous, but where it is, such as in central Florida, collapse features and caverns should be located and taken into account in land use planning.

3.7 SOURCES OF ENVIRONMENTAL DATA FOR SITE PLANNING

Field investigation   Despite the technological advances in the acquisition and processing of environmental data, the analysis and evaluation of the landscape still rely heavily on **field investigations.** This is especially so for problems involving small to medium-sized sites (several acres to several hundred acres) for which the resolution of secondary data sources, such as satellite imagery, soils maps, and standard topographic maps, is not well suited. Although these sources are helpful in understanding the regional context, the internal character of the typical site falls between the cracks, as it were.

Secondary sources   For large problem areas we must, of course, rely mainly on **secondary sources** to gain a sense of the character of the landscape and its environmental setting. Inevitably, however, field observation is also necessary, but it must usually follow the examination of secondary sources and serve as a ground truth exercise to test the validity of our initial ideas about the makeup and operation of the environment. Among the secondary sources, topographic contour maps are probably the most valuable.

Topographic contour maps

Topographic contour maps are published by the U.S. Geological Survey and in Canada by the Department of Energy, Mines and Resources. The maps are published at a variety of scales and are available from both the government and private outlets. In the United States, coverage ranges from the entire coterminous United States on one sheet to coverage of a local area of about 55 square miles. The latter sheets, called 7.5-minute quadrangles (because they cover about 7.5 minutes of latitude) are the most useful for planning purposes. The comparable sheets in Canada are the 1 : 10,000 (1 cm to 100 meters) topographic base maps.

The 7.5-minute quadrangles and their correlatives in Canada are an excellent sources of information on drainage systems, topographic relief, and slopes and are helpful in locating land use features, water features, and wooded areas. The 7.5-minute maps are printed at a scale of 1 : 24,000 (about 0.4 mile to the inch) with a contour interval of 10 feet. Today most planning projects involving major facilities call for highly detailed topographic maps at much larger scales (often as large as 1 inch to 100 feet or 1 inch to 50 feet), and for these, aerial mapping companies must be specially contracted.

Soil maps

Soil maps in the United States are prepared by the U.S. Soil Conservation Service and published county by county in a booklet called county soil reports. These map reports give the classification and description of soils to a depth of 4 to 5 feet. Most boundary lines between soil types are highly generalized and should be checked in the field for site planning problems. Unfortunately, the scale of the soil maps (usually at 1 : 20,000) is larger than that of the 7.5-minute U.S. Geological Survey topographic maps, prohibiting easy compilation of soil and topographic data on a single map. Chapter 5, "Soil and Land Use Suitability," discusses soil maps in more detail.

Aerial photographs

Aerial photographs are available for virtually all areas of the United States and Canada. In the United States they are regularly produced by various governmental agencies including the U.S. Soil Conservation Service, the U.S. Forest Service, and the U.S. Bureau of Land Management. Standard aerial photographs are available in 9 inch by 9 inch formats in black and white prints that are suitable for stereoscopic (three-dimensional) viewing. Individual photographs can be enlarged for planning purposes to any desired scale, and although they cannot be used as a source of precise locational information (because of inherent photographic distortions), aerial photographs are an excellent source of information on vegetation, land use, and water features.

Special sources

Increasingly, **special sources** of data and information are available, especially for populous regions. Many states and counties contract their own aerial photographic surveys on a regular basis with imagery in black and white, color, and infrared formats. Information on water resources, wetlands, and other resources are available for selected areas as a result of research projects, environmental impact reports, or planning projects.

The U.S. Geological Survey is active in every state. Besides topographic maps, the Survey also publishes a wide range of other maps, as well as data and reports for various local and regional problems and resources. These include earthquake hazard maps, stream discharge records, and maps of geological formations. The same holds for the U.S. Environmental Protection Agency (EPA) and the National Oceanic and Atmospheric Administration (NOAA), each of which produces a variety of maps, reports, and data on different topics for different regions and communities. The body of special information sources is huge and growing rapidly; space prohibits us from describing them here. Indeed, it is probably fair to say that it is impossible for any individual to keep track of this mass. Therefore, in the face of a planning problem in some location it is advisable to move quickly to local clearinghouses such as planning commissions, environmental agencies, and universities to find the special sources.

3.8 SELECTED REFERENCES FOR FURTHER READING

Brunsden, D., and Thornes, J. B. "Landscape Sensitivity to Change." *Transactions of the Institute of British Geographers* 4, 1979, pp. 463–484.

Forman, R. T. T., and Godron, M. *Landscape Ecology.* New York: Wiley, 1986, 619 pp.

Marsh, W. M. *Earthscape: A Physical Geography.* New York: Wiley, 1987, 510 pp.

Marsh, W. M., and Dozier, J. "Magnitude and Frequency Applied to the Landscape." In *Landscape: An Introduction to Physical Geography.* New York: Wiley, 1981.

Raup, H. M. "Vegetational Adjustment to the Instability of the Site." *Proceedings and Papers of the Sixth Technical Meeting.* Edinburgh: International Union for the Conservation of Nature and Natural Resources, 1959.

Selby, M. J. *Earth's Changing Surface: An Introduction to Geomorphology.* Oxford: Clarendon Press, 1985, 607 pp.

Wendell, Berry. *The Unsettling of America: Culture and Agriculture.* New York: Avon, 1978, 228 pp.

Wolman, M. G., and Gerson, R. "Relative Time Scales and Effectiveness of Climate in Watershed Geomorphology." *Earth Surface Processes* 3, 1978, pp. 189–208.

Wolman, M. G., and Miller, J. P. "Magnitude and Frequency of Forces in Geomorphic Processes." *Journal of Geology* 58, 1960, pp. 54–74.

4

TOPOGRAPHY, SLOPES, AND LAND USE PLANNING

4.1 INTRODUCTION

Given the choice of a place to live, most of us will choose hilly ground over flat ground. This is not surprising, for to most people, hilly terrain is more attractive because it has greater variations in vegetation, ground conditions, and water features, to say nothing of the opportunities it affords for vistas and privacy in siting houses. Our success with establishing and nurturing land uses on hillslopes, however, is not equal to our love for them. In fact for many land uses, slopes are decidedly inferior places to build.

Land use–slope relations   Level or gently sloping sites are usually necessary for industrial and commercial buildings. Cropland is generally limited to slopes of less than 10 degrees (18 percent), because of the performance and safety restrictions posed by the operation of tractors and field machinery. In the era of horse and oxen power, slopes of 15 degrees (26 percent) or steeper could be used for cultivated crops. The influence of slopes and topography on the alignments of modern roads depends on the class of the road; the higher the class, the lower the maximum grades allowable. Interstate class expressways (divided, limited access, four or six lanes) are designed for high-speed, uninterrupted movement and are limited to grades of 4 percent, that is, 4 feet of rise per 100 feet of distance. On city streets, where speed limits are 20 to 30 mph, grades may be as steep as 10 percent, whereas driveways may be as steep as 15 percent.

Slope and environment   Besides influencing land use, slopes also influence various environmental components of the landscapes. High on the list is the influence on stormwater runoff. Runoff rates are higher on steep slopes, and in developed areas, stormwater quality tends to decline with higher runoff rates. The performance of septic drainfields for residential sewage disposal also declines with steeper slopes. On balance, slopes influence so many important aspects of the landscape and land use that they have become one of the top two or three environmental criteria in regulating development at the community level. Not surprisingly, the slope map is probably the most widely used tool for evaluating the environmental suitability of development proposals by planning agencies.

4.2 SLOPE PROBLEMS

Misuse of slopes   The need to consider topography in planning is an outgrowth of the widespread realization not only that land uses have slope limitations but also that slopes have been misused in modern land development. The misuse arises from two types of practices: (1) the placement of structures and facilities on slopes that are already unstable or potentially unstable; and (2) the disturbance of stable slopes resulting in failure, accelerated erosion, and/or ecological deterioration of the slope environment.

The first type can result from inadequate survey and analysis of slopes in terrain that has a history of slope instability. More infrequently, however, it probably results from inadequate planning controls (for example, zoning and environmental ordinances) on development. In some instances, admittedly, surveys reveal no evidence of instability, and failure of a slope catches inhabitants completely unawares.

Disturbance of slope environments is unquestionably the most common source of slope problems in North America. Three types of disturbances stand out:

Causes of disturbance   ■ *Mechanical cut and fill* in which slopes are reshaped by heavy equipment. This often involves steepening and straightening, resulting in a loss of the equilibrium associated with natural conditions; in Canada and the United States this is best exhibited in mining areas and along major highways.

■ *Deforestation* in a hilly terrain by lumbering operations, agriculture, and urbanization. This not only results in a weakened slope because of the reduced stabiliz-

Fig. 4.1 Slope erosion resulting from alteration of drainage, vegetation, and soil in residential development.

ing effect of vegetation, but also increases stress from runoff and groundwater because discharge rates are increased (see Fig. 3.4).

■ *Improper siting and construction* of buildings and related facilities, leading to an upset in the slope equilibrium because of the alteration of vegetation, slope materials, and drainage (Fig. 4.1).

4.3 MEASUREMENT OF SLOPES AND TOPOGRAPHY

Years ago the configuration of the terrain could be measured only by field surveying. In its simplest form, this involved projecting a level line into the terrain from a point of known elevation and then measuring the distances above and below the line to various points in the terrain. Once elevation points were known, a contour map could be constructed.

Topographic contour map **Contour maps** are comprised of lines, called *contours,* connecting points of equal elevation. In modern mapping programs, such as the one practiced by the U.S. Geological Survey, the contours are drawn from specially prepared sets of aerial photographs. These photographs and the optical apparatus used to view them enable the mapper to see an enlarged, three-dimensional image of the terrain. Based on this image, the mapper is able to trace a line, the contour, onto the terrain at a prescribed elevation. The contour elevation is calibrated on the basis of survey markers, called *bench marks,* placed on the land by field survey crews.

Calculating percent slope To determine the inclination of a slope from a topographic contour map, we must know the scale of the map and the elevation change from one contour to the next, called the *contour interval.* With these, the change in elevation over distance can be measured, and in turn a percentage can be calculated:

$$\text{percent slope} = \frac{\text{change in elevation}}{\text{distance}} \times 100$$

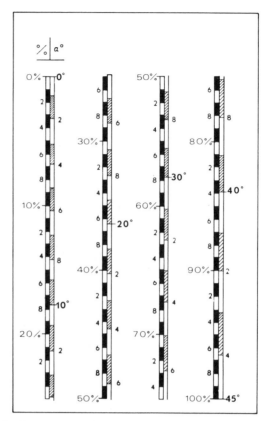

Fig. 4.2 Degree equivalence of percent slope up to 100 percent.

This is one of the two conventional expressions for slope, the other being degrees. Conversions can be made for degrees or percentages with the aid of the diagram in Fig. 4.2.

4.4 SLOPE MAPPING FOR LAND USE PLANNING

To avoid costly damage to the environment or to structures and utilities, it is necessary to make the proper match between land uses and slopes. In most instances this is simply a matter of assigning to the terrain uses that would (1) not require modification of slopes to achieve satisfactory performance, and (2) not themselves be endangered by the slope environment and its processes. Generally speaking, topographic contour maps alone do not provide information in a form suitable for most planning problems. The contour map must instead be translated into a map made up of slope classes tailored to planning problems. The utility of such slope maps is a function of (1) the criteria used to establish the slope classes, and (2) the scale at which the mapping is undertaken.

Mapping scale   The scale of mapping and the level of detail that are obtainable are strictly limited by the scale and contour interval of the base map. In areas where maps of two or three different scales are available, the scale chosen should be the one that best suits the scale of the problem for which it is intended, such as site plan review, master planning, or highway planning.

Setting slope classes   The criteria used to set the slope classes are dependent foremost on the problems and questions for which the map will be employed (Fig. 4.3). For areas under the pressure of suburban development, the maximum and minimum slope limits of the various community activities would be one set of criteria. Another would be the natural limitations and conditions of the slopes themselves, which are taken up in the next section. With respect to land use activities, we would want to know the optimum slopes for parking lots, house sites, residential streets, playgrounds and lawns, and so on (Table 4.1).

Besides In addition to the selection of slope classes and the appropriate base map, the preparation of a slope map also involves:

Building the slope map   **1.** *Definition of the minimum size mapping unit.* This is the smallest area of land that will be mapped, and it is usually fixed according to the base map scale, the contour interval, and the scale of the land uses involved. For 7.5-minute U.S. Geological Survey quadrangles (1 : 24,000), units should not be set much smaller than 10 acres, or 660 feet square.

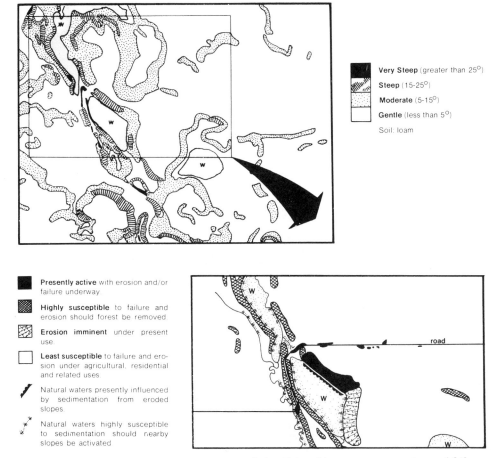

Fig. 4.3 Slope classification for the purpose of identifying slopes prone to erosion and failure. The area around the water features is abandoned farmland.

Table 4.1   Slope Requirements for Various Land Uses

Land Use	Maximum	Minimum	Optimum
House sites	20–25%	0%	2%
Playgrounds	2–3%	0.05%	1%
Public stairs	50%	—	25%
Lawns (mowed)	25%	—	2–3%
Septic drainfields	15% *	0%	0.05%
Paved surfaces			
Parking lots	3%	0.05%	1%
Sidewalks	10%	0%	1%
Streets and roads	15–17%	—	1%
20 mph	12%		
30	10%		
40	8%		
50	7%		
60	5%		
70	4%		
Industrial sites			
Factory sites	3–4%	0%	2%
Lay down storage	3%	0.05%	1%
Parking	3%	0.05%	1%

* Special drainfield designs are required at slopes above 10 to 12 percent.

2. *Construction of a graduated scale* on the edge of a sheet of paper, representing the spacing of the contours for each slope class. For example, on the 7.5-minute quadrangle, where 1 inch represents 2000 feet and the contour interval is 10 feet, a 10 percent slope would be marked by a contour every 1/20 inch.

3. *Next, the scale should be placed on the map* in a position perpendicular to the contours to delineate the areas in the various slope classes (Fig. 4.4).

4. *Finally,* each of the areas delineated should be coded or symbolized according to some cartographic scheme.

4.5 INTERPRETING STEEPNESS AND FORM

Composition and angle of repose

In addition to land use requirements, we must also know what sort of soil and rock material comprises the slope to interpret accurately the meaning of different inclinations. For any earth material, there is maximum angle, called the **angle of repose,** at which it can be safely inclined and beyond which it will fail. The angle of repose varies widely for different materials, from 90 degrees in strong bedrock to less than 10 degrees in some unconsolidated materials. Moreover, in unconsolidated material it may vary substantially with changes in water content, vegetative cover, and the internal structure of the particle mass. This is especially so with clayey material: A poorly compacted mass of saturated clay may give way at angles as low as 5 percent, whereas the same mass of clay with high compaction and lower water content may be able to sustain angles greater than 100 percent. Coarse materials, such as sand, pebbles, cobbles, boulders, and bedrock itself, are less apt to vary with changes in compaction and water content. Therefore, it is possible to define some representative angles of repose for them (Fig. 4.5). Beyond these angles, these materials are susceptible to failure in which the ground ruptures and slides, slumps, or falls.

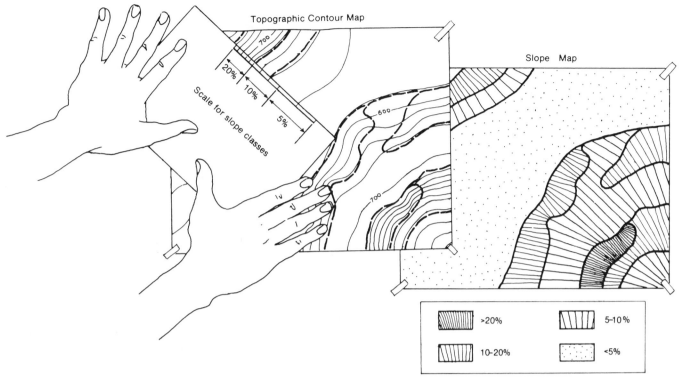

Fig. 4.4 Schematic diagram showing the use of a scale mapping slope. The lower map shows the results.

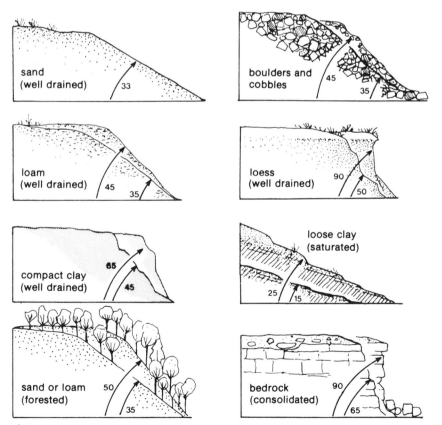

Fig. 4.5 Angles of repose for various types of slope materials. Angles are given in degrees.

Role of vegetation   The **influence of vegetation** on slope is highly variable depending on the type of vegetation, the cover density, and the type of soil. Vegetation with extensive root systems undoubtedly imparts added stability to slopes comprised of soils of clay, silt, sand, and gravel, but for very coarse materials such as cobbles, boulders, and bedrock, the influence of vegetation is probably insignificant. On sandy slopes the presence of woody vegetation can increase the angle of repose by 10 to 15 degrees producing a metastable or conditional situation. Under this arrangement, loss of the cover on such slopes is almost certain to trigger failure.

Slope profile   In addition to the overall angle, shape or form can also be an important factor in slope analysis. Shape is expressed graphically in terms of a **slope profile,** which is basically a silhouette of a slope drawn to known proportions with distance on the horizontal axis and elevation on the vertical axis. The vertical axis is often exaggerated to ease construction and accentuate topographic details (Fig. 4.6).

Slope form   Five basic **slope forms** are detectable on contour maps: straight, S-shape, concave, convex, and complex (Fig. 4.7). Understanding these forms for problems of land use planning and landscape management usually requires understanding local geologic, soil, hydrologic, and vegetative conditions. In areas where slopes are comprised of unconsolidated materials (soils and various types of loose deposits), and bedrock is found at great depths, slope form often varies with the vegetative cover, soil composition, and the recent and past occurrence of events such as undercutting by rivers, excavations by humans, landslides induced by earthquakes, and erosion associated with deforestation.

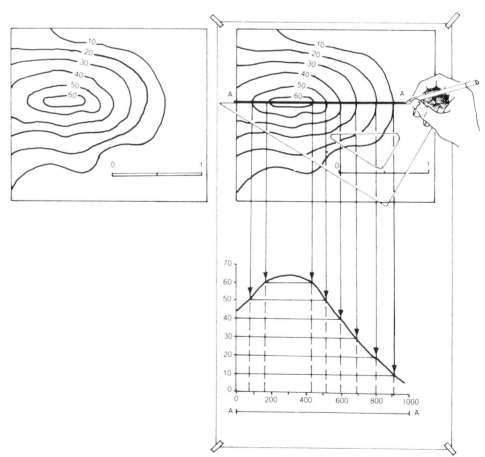

Fig. 4.6   Construction of a slope profile from a topographic contour map.

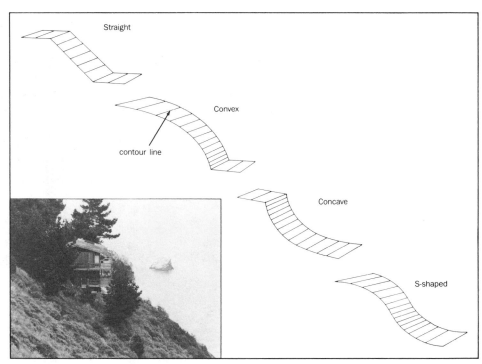

Fig. 4.7 Four basic slope forms: *from top:* straight, convex, concave, and *S*-shaped with corresponding contour spacing as it appears on a topographic map. Inset photograph shows a dangerously steep straight slope.

Smooth *S*-shapes usually indicate long-term slope stability and a state of equilibrium among slope forces. Such slopes rarely exceed 45 degrees inclination and are usually secured against heavy erosion by a substantial plant cover. Concavities in otherwise straight or *S*-shaped slopes are often signs of failures, such as slides or slumps, and may suggest a general susceptibility to failure for slopes of this class and situation. From the air, scars caused by slope failure or severe erosion can often be identified on the basis of breaks in the plant cover. Fresh scars are marked by light tones on aerial photographs, and older scars by less mature vegetation or different plant species (Fig. 4.8).

4.6 ASSESSING SLOPES FOR STABILITY

Indicators of instability

Many criteria should be taken into account in assessing the susceptibility of slopes to failure. At the top of the list are the angle and composition of the slope (both soil and bedrock) and the history of slope activity. Steep slopes with a record of **instability** stand a greater chance of failure when subjected to development because construction activity, loss of vegetation, and changes in drainage typically lower the stability threshold. If a rock formation or sediment layer of known instability (or high erodibility) is situated within the slope, the potential for failure is even greater.

Vegetation and conditional stability

Plant cover is another important criterion inasmuch as devegetated slopes show a much greater tendency to fail than fully vegetated ones. Studies of slopes in western United States show that clear-cut slopes and slopes cut by logging roads fail more frequently under the stress of heavy precipitation than do fully forested, undisturbed ones. Especially significant in this context are conditionally stable slopes, called *metastable slopes,* which are discussed in section 3.4 of the previous chapter. These slopes

Fig. 4.8   Slope failure scars marked by breaks in the vegetative cover in the walls of a large gully.

would be unstable were it not for a particular component such as vegetation which holds them against failure (see Fig. 3.4).

Undercutting, earthquakes, and drainage
    Slope **undercutting** and **earthquake** activity are also significant. Active erosion at the foot of a slope by waves, rivers, or human excavation produces steeper inclinations and less confining pressure on the lower slope, thereby increasing the failure potential. When earthquakes jar rock and soil material, interparticle bonds may be weakened and the material's resistance to failure reduced. Some of the worst disasters from slope failure have been triggered by earthquakes.

    Finally, **drainage** must be considered. Though often difficult to evaluate, soil water and groundwater can have a pronounced influence on slope stability: (1) the addition of water to clayey soils can transform them from solid to plastic and liquid states, thereby reducing their resistance to displacement; (2) groundwater seepage can produce undermining of slopes by sapping and piping; and (3) pore-water pressure near seepage zones may weaken the skeletal strength of soil materials within a slope (Fig. 4.9).

Synthesizing slope factors
    Unfortunately, the means to integrate analytically all these variables have not been developed, and for large areas, field and laboratory testing are not economically feasible. Therefore, evaluations of slope stability for purposes of land use planning and environmental management must be based on some sort of systematic review of the previous criteria. Whether all these criteria can be used depends on the availability and reliability of data sources. Generally, topographic contour maps, aerial photographs, geologic maps, siesmic maps, and soil maps are used as data sources, but they require interpretation and adaptation because of differences in scale, resolution, and units of

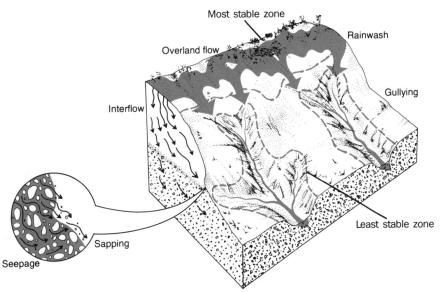

Fig. 4.9 Schematic diagram showing the influence of drainage on slope stability. The slope is least stable where groundwater seeps from the ground.

measurement. When the desired criteria can be employed, the map overlay technique has been used to delineate areas of different levels of slope stability.

4.7 APPLICATIONS TO COMMUNITY PLANNING

Slopes and community development

In the absence of effective planning controls on development and the base information necessary to help guide decision making, many American and Canadian communities have in the past several decades seen development creep over the terrain, enveloping sloping and flat ground alike. Unlike development of an earlier era when the decision maker, developer, and resident were one and the same, in modern development these roles are often played by different and separate parties. As a result, in the modern, large-scale development project, poor decisions on siting by the developer are upon sale of the property inherited by the buyer, and when a problem eventually arises, it becomes the reponsibility of the owner resident. Complicating matters further, the property may have a second or third owner by the time the problem actually surfaces. The social and financial costs for remedial action are typically high and must be borne by the current property owner, by the community, by some higher level of government, or by all three parties. This harsh lesson has taught communities that the tendency to push development beyond the terrain's capacity must be curbed by land use regulations.

As a result, environmental ordinances based on slope have been enacted in communities throughout Canada and the United States. The rationale behind local slope ordinances varies. In some communities, they are designed for growth control, in others for environmental protection, and in still others for hazard management. In any case, the implementation of slope-based environmental ordinances necessitates (1) building a slope map showing suitable and unsuitable terrain, and (2) establishing a procedure to review and evaluate development proposals and site plans.

Slope-based ordinances

Communities use several different approaches in designing **slope-related ordinances.** One approach is based on development density and average slope inclination within specified land areas or units. Terrain units (such as valley floors or foothills)

Table 4.2 Undisturbed Area Requirements for Sloping Ground in Three California Communities

Percent Slope (avg.)	Chula Vista	Pacifica	Thousand Oaks
10	14%	32%	32.5%
15	31%	36%	40%
20	44%	45%	55%
25	62.5%	57%	70%
30	90%	72%	85%
35	90%	90%	100%
40	90%	100%	100%

comprising many individual but similar slopes are assigned a maximum allowable density of development according to the average slope inclination (Fig. 4.10). The percentage of ground to be left undisturbed as required by three California communities is shown in Table 4.2. In Chula Vista, for example, terrain with slopes averaging above 30 percent requires that for each acre of development 9 acres be left in an undisturbed state.

A second approach is based strictly on the inclination of individual slopes. Each slope over a specified area, usually a proposed development site, is mapped according to the procedure described earlier in the chapter. Four or five classes are usually used, and for each there is a maximum allowable density set by ordinance. In Austin, Texas, for example, residential density of the cluster variety is limited to one unit per acre for

Fig. 4.10 An example of terrain units in an area of mountainous topography. Highest densities would be allowed in class I where slopes average 10 percent or less.

slopes in the 0 to 15 percent class. For slopes in steeper classes, 15 to 25 percent and 25 to 35 percent, development is allowable only on approval of a formal request.

The third approach employs several slope characteristics in addition to inclination. For example, slopes comprised of unstable soils, conditionally stable forested slopes, and scenically valued slopes are mapped in combination with slope inclination. Development plans are compared directly to the distribution of each factor. This approach is commonly employed in areas of complex terrain where regulations based on inclination alone would prove inadequate.

4.8 CASE STUDY

Slope as a Growth Control Tool in Established Communities

W. M. Marsh

Years ago, when rural communities in the United States and Canada were setting up their systems of government, large areas of undeveloped land were often declared part of the community by virtue of the exaggerated alignment chosen for the town or village limits at the time of incorporation. These areas were often drawn into maps of the community with little or no attention to the nature of the terrain, and, in most cases, no realistic expectation on the part of the town fathers that the community itself would ever expand into them. Some communities even went so far as to plat these areas, that is, subdivide them on paper into residential lots, city blocks, streets, and neighborhoods.

In recent decades, many of these communities have expanded at unprecedented rates, rapidly filling in empty areas. Where these areas are already platted, the communities often find that they have little control over where development takes place. Their only resource is to formulate planning ordinances to help manage new development and keep the community in balance with its resource base.

Planning ordinances aimed at regulating new development can take various forms. One form is a growth-control ordinance that simply sets limits on the amount, type, and rate of development. This can be accomplished, for example, by setting limits on land use density or by setting quotas on the approval of building permits. Another form is the environmental ordinance that sets environmental restrictions on development. Some California communities use water supply as the restricting factor. More commonly, communities use one or more landscape features such as slope, soil, wetland, and threatened species to regulate development.

For the northern Michigan community shown in the accompanying map, platting was carried out long ago when development on steep slopes was not a great concern. Today, however, it is a concern because the vistas over Lake Superior are highly attractive to prospective home builders and the high slopes are accessible to modern vehicles. To protect this valuable part of the community environment, a slope ordinance is clearly needed.

To be most effective, the ordinance should be based on rational criteria that justify the controls imposed on land users. In other words, the reasons for not building on slopes should appeal to the citizen's logic from both a personal and community standpoint. In this case, the slopes are composed on sandy soil held in place by hardwood forests, and changes in the balance among the forces acting on the slope face could easily lead to instability and extensive damage downslope. This can be demonstrated by documentation from scientific and planning literature reporting on problems in similar settings. In addi-

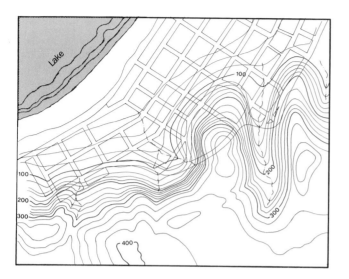

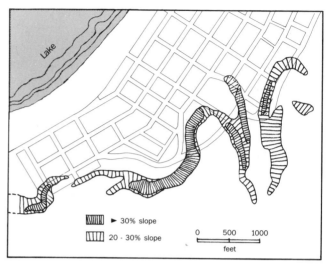

▶ 30% slope

20 - 30% slope

0   500   1000
feet

tion, residential development on these slopes would not be served by the city sewer systems and therefore would require on-site sewage disposal. Evidence is abundant and compelling on the severe limitation that steep slopes pose to on-site (septic) sewage systems. Based on these and other reasons, there is ample justification in this community for invoking slope as a growth-limiting factor for residential and other types of development. ■

4.9 SELECTED REFERENCES FOR FURTHER READING

Bailey, Robert G. *Land Capability Classification of the Lake Tahoe Basin, California-Nevada.* Washington, D.C.: Forest Service, U.S. Department of Agriculture, 1974, 32 pp.

Briggs, Reginald P., et al. "Landsliding in Allegheny County, Pennsylvania." *Geological Survey Circular 728,* 1975, 18 pp.

Carson, M. A., and Kirkby, M. J. *Hillslope Form and Process.* Cambridge, United Kingdom: Cambridge University Press, 1972, 475 pp.

City of Austin. *Comprehensive Watersheds Ordinance.* Austin, Tex.: 1986.

Gordon, Steven I., and Klousner, Robert D., Jr. "Using Landslide Hazard Information in Planning: An Evaluation of Methods." *Journal of the American Planning Association,* 1986, 52:4, pp. 431–442.

Milne, R. J., and Moss, M. R. "Forest Dynamics and Geomorphic Processes on the Niagara Escarpment, Collingwood, Ontario," In *Landscape Ecology and Management*, Montreal: Polyscience Publications, 1988.

Schuster, Robert L., and Krizek, Raymond J. *Landslides: Analysis and Control.* Washington, D.C.: National Academy of Sciences, 1978, 234 pp.

Utgard, R. O., et al. *Geology in the Urban Environment.* Minneapolis: Burgess, 1978, 355 pp.

Vitek, John D., and Marsh, William M. "Landslide Hazard Mapping for Local Land Use Planning." In *Environmental Analysis for Land Use and Site Planning.* New York: McGraw-Hill, 1978, 292 pp.

Way, Douglas S. *Terrain Analysis: A Guide to Site Selection Using Aerial Photographic Interpretation.* Stroudsburg, Penn.: Dowden, Hutchinson and Ross, 1973, 392 pp.

5

SOIL AND LAND USE SUITABILITY

5.1 INTRODUCTION

The relationship between soil composition and agriculture is apparent at practically any scale of observation, especially in areas of more traditional agriculture. The relationship between soil composition and other types of land uses, however, is often not so apparent. At least part of the reason for this in North America is that developers have given precious little attention to soils, especially in the last several decades. Among the factors contributing to this state of affairs is a sense of complacency about soils created by a popular impression that modern engineering technology can overcome problems of the soil. Granted, the technology does exist to build practically any sort of structure in or on any environment. However, the costs involved in terms of both dollars and environmental damage are often prohibitive. Increasingly, decision makers are turning to soil surveys as a guide in site selection for residential, industrial, and other forms of development that involve surface and subsurface structures.

An additional consideration is the heightened concern over solid and hazardous waste disposal in the soil. Finding new disposal sites is a perennial problem requiring, among other things, careful evaluation of soil, topography, and drainage. It has also come to light that most urban areas contain scores of hidden disposal sites and waste dumps that pose not only an environmental threat but also a serious liability to development. If buried waste is encountered in constructing facilities, such as roads, buildings, and utilities, the site may have to be abandoned and/or the waste excavated and properly disposed somewhere else.

5.2 SOIL COMPOSITION

Several features, or *properties,* are used to describe soil for problems involving land development. Of these, texture and composition are generally the most meaningful; from them we can make inferences about bearing capacity, internal drainage, erodibility, and slope stability.

Composition refers to the materials that make up a soil. Basically, there are just four compositional constituents: mineral particles, organic matter, water, and air. *Mineral particles* **Mineral particles** comprise 50 to 80 percent of the volume of most soils and form the all-important skeletal structure of the soil. This structure, built of particles lodged against each other, enables the soil to support its own mass as well as that of internal matter such as water and the overlying landscape, including buildings. Sand and gravel particles generally provide for the greatest stability and, if packed solidly against one *Bearing capacity* another, will usually yield a relatively high bearing capacity. **Bearing capacity** refers to a soil's resistance to penetration from a weighted object such as a building foundation. Clays tend to be more variable in stability with loosely packed, wet particle masses having a tendency to compress and slip laterally under weight (stress) (Table 5.1).

Organic matter The quantity of **organic matter** varies radically in soils, but it is extremely important for both negative and positive reasons. Organic particles usually provide weak skeletal structure with very poor bearing capacities. Organic matter tends to compress and settle differentially under roadbeds and foundations, and when dewatered, it may suffer substantial volume losses, decomposition, and wind erosion. Deep organic soils, which may reach thicknesses of 20 feet or more, of course pose the most serious limitations to facility development and land use in general.

On the positive side, organic matter is vital to the fertility and moisture content of topsoil. Indeed, the loss of topsoil from agricultural lands by runoff and wind erosion is viewed as one of the most serious environmental issues of our time. The role of organic matter in the terrestrial water balance is underscored by the water storage function of

Table 5.1 Bearing Capacity Values for Rock and Soil Materials

Class		Material	Allowable Bearing Value, tons per square foot
1		Massive crystalline bedrock, e.g., granite, gneiss	100
2	rock	Metamorphosed rock, e.g., schist, slate	40
3		Sedimentary rocks, e.g., shale, sandstone	15
4		Well-compacted gravels and sands	10
5		Compact gravel, sand/gravel mixtures	6
6		Loose gravel, compact coarse sand	4
7		Loose coarse sand; loose sand/gravel mixtures, compact fine sand, wet coarse sand	3
8	soil materials	Loose fine sand, wet fine sand	2
9		Stiff clay (dry)	4
10		Medium-stiff clay	2
11		Soft clay	1
12		Fill, organic material, or silt	(fixed by field tests)

Source: Code Manual, New York State Building Code Commission.

topsoil and organic deposits in wetlands. Topsoil takes up significant amounts of precipitation and therefore helps reduce runoff rates. Organic deposits often serve as moisture reservoirs for wetland vegetation as well as points of entry for groundwater recharge.

5.3 SOIL TEXTURE

Definition   The mineral particles found in soil range enormously in size from microscopic clay particles to large boulders. The most abundant particles, however, are sand, silt, and clay, and they are the focus of examination in studies of soil texture (Fig. 5.1). *Texture* is the term used to describe the composite sizes of particles in a soil sample, say, several representative handfuls. To measure soil texture, the sand, silt, and clay particles are sorted out and weighed. The weights of each size class are then expressed as a percentage of the sample weight.

Since it is unlikely that all the particles in a soil will be clay or sand or silt, additional terms are needed for describing various mixtures. Soil scientists use 12 basic terms for texture, at the center of which is the class *loam,* an intermediate mixture of

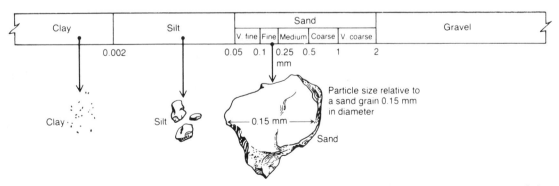

Fig. 5.1   A standard scale of soil particle sizes; the illustrations give a visual comparison of clay and silt with a sand particle 0.15 mm in diameter.

sand, silt, and clay. According to the United States Soil Conservation Service (SCS), the loam class is comprised of 40 percent sand, 40 percent silt, and 20 percent clay. Given a slightly heavier concentration of sand, say 50 percent, with 10 percent clay and 40 percent silt, the soil is called *sandy loam.* In agronomy, the textural names and related percentages are given in the form of a triangular graph (Fig. 5.2). If we know the percentage by weight of the particle sizes in a sample, we can use this graph to determine the appropriate soil name.

Field hand test
    In the field, **soil texture** can be estimated by extracting a handful of soil and squeezing it into three basic shapes: (1) *cast,* a lump formed by squeezing a sample in a clenched fist: (2) *thread,* a pencil shape formed by rolling soil between the palms; and (3) *ribbon,* a flattish shape formed by squeezing a small sample between the thumb and index finger (Fig. 5.3). The behavioral characteristics of the soil when molded into each of these shapes, if they can be formed at all, provides the basis for a general textural classification. The sample should be damp to perform the test properly.

    Behavior of the soil in the hand test is determined by the amount of clay in the sample. Clay particles are highly cohesive, and, when dampened, they will behave as a plastic. Therefore, the higher the clay content in a sample, the more refined and durable the shapes into which it can be molded. Table 5.2 gives the behavioral traits of five common soil textures.

Sieving
    Another method of determining soil texture involves the use of devices called **sediment sieves,** screens that have been built with a specified mesh size. When the soil is filtered through a group of sieves, each with a different mesh size, the particles become sorted in corresponding size categories. Each category can be weighed and the weight expressed as a percentage of the total sample weight, in order to make a textural determination.

    Although sieves work well for silt, sand, and larger particles, they are not appropriate for clay particles. Clay is too small to sieve accurately; therefore, in clayey soils

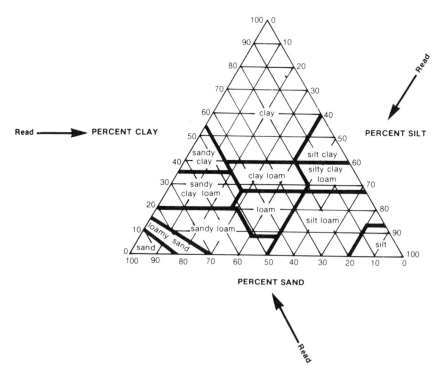

Fig. 5.2   Soil textural triangle, including the major subdivisions, used by the U.S. Department of Agriculture.

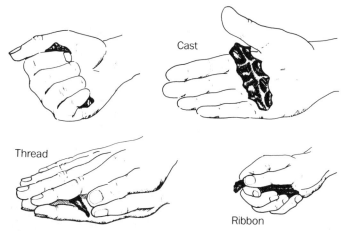

Fig. 5.3 The basic shapes used in the field hand test. See Table 5.2 for evaluation criteria in determining soil textural type.

the fine particles are measured on the basis of their settling velocity when suspended in water. Since clays settle so slowly, they are easily segregated from sand and silt. The water containing the clay can be drawn off and evaporated, leaving a residue of clay, which can be weighed.

5.4 SOIL MOISTURE AND DRAINAGE

Forms of soil water
The water content of soil varies with particle sizes, local drainage and topography, and climate. Most water in the soil occupies the spaces between the particles; only in organic soils and certain clays do the particles themselves actually absorb measurable amounts of water. Two principal **forms of water** occur in both mineral and organic soils: capillary and gravity. Capillary water is a form of molecular water, so-called

Table 5.2   Behavioral Characteristics of the Basic Shapes Used in the Field Hand Test and the Soil Type Represented by Each

Field Test (Shape)	Soil Type				
	Sandy Loam	*Silty Loam*	*Loam*	*Clay Loam*	*Clay*
Soil cast	Cast bears careful handling without breaking	Cohesionless silty loam bears careful handling without breaking; better-graded silty loam casts may be handled freely without breaking	Cast may be handled freely without breaking	Cast bears much handling without breaking	Cast can be molded to various shapes without breaking
Soil thread	Thick, crumbly, easily broken	Thick, soft, easily broken	Can be pointed as fine as pencil lead that is easily broken	Strong thread can be rolled to a pinpoint	Strong, plastic thread that can be rolled to a pinpoint
Soil ribbon	Will not form ribbon	Will not form ribbon	Forms short, thick ribbon that breaks under its own weight	Forms thin ribbon that breaks under its own weight	Long, thin flexible ribbon that does not break under its own weight

because it is held in the soil by the force of cohesion among water molecules. Under this force, water molecules are mobile and can move from moist spots to dry spots in the soil. In the summer, most capillary water transfer is upward toward the soil surface as water is lost in evaporation and transpiration.

Gravity water is liquid water that moves in response to the gravitational force. Its movement in the soil is preponderantly downward, and it tends to accumulate in the subsoil and underlying bedrock to form groundwater. Groundwater completely fills the interparticle spaces: thus below the watertable the soil is largely devoid of air.

Drainage processes   References to **"drainage"** in soil reports usually refer to gravity water and a soil's ability to transfer this water downward. Three terms are used to describe this process: (1) *infiltration capacity,* which is the rate at which water penetrates the soil surface (usually measured in cm or inches per hour); (2) *permeability,* which is the rate at which water within the soil moves through a given volume of material (also measured in cm or inches per hour); and (3) *percolation,* which is the rate at which water in a soil pit or pipe within the soil is taken up by the soil (used mainly in wastewater absorption tests and measured in inches per hour). Reference to poor drainage, for example, means that the soil is frequently or permanently saturated and may often have *Meaning of "well drained"*   water standing on it. Terms such as "good drainage" and **"well drained"** mean that gravity water is readily transmitted by the soil and that the soil is not conducive to prolonged periods of saturation. Soil saturation may be caused by the local accumulation of surface water (because of river flooding or runoff into a low spot, for example), or by a rise in the level of groundwater within the soil column (because of the raising of a reservoir or excessive application of irrigation water, for example), or because the particles in the soil are too small to transmit infiltration water (because of impervious layers within the soil or clayey soil composition).

5.5 SOIL, LANDFORMS, AND TOPOGRAPHY

Nearly all soils are formed in deposits laid down by geomorphic processes of some sort; for example, wind, glacial meltwater, ocean waves, river floods, and landslides (Fig. 5.4). Once in place, the surface layer of these deposits is subject to alteration by processes associated with climate, vegetation, surface drainage, and land use. Depend-*Soil formation*   ing on the type of deposit (e.g., sand, rock rubble, marine clay, or wind-blown silt), bioclimatic conditions, and local drainage, these processes in time produce a complex medium, usually 1 to 2 m deep, known as soil or the "solum." This is what soil scientists measure and map in conducting county soil surveys. Below the solum, the bulk of most deposits, however, retains the basic properties imparted to them during their formation. This fact is especially significant in land development problems, because building footings, basements, roadbeds, slope cuts, and the like are built in these materials.

Landform–soil relations   Geomorphologists have developed a basic taxonomy of the landforms associated with various types of deposits, making it possible to infer certain things about soil materials based on a knowledge of landforms. Any attempt to correlate landforms and soils, however, must recognize the limitations of geographic scale. Generally, the extremes of scale provide the least satisfactory results. At the scale of individual landform features, such as floodplains, sand dunes, or outwash plains, the correlation can be quite good for planning purposes (Fig. 5.5). Table 5.3 lists a number of landform features and the soil composition and drainage associated with each.

Toposequence   Within many depositional features there are also predictable trends in soil makeup related to topographic gradients. Such trends are called **toposequences,** and identification of them can lead to valuable information for site planning. In the case of an alluvial fan, for example, texture tends to grade coarse to fine from the top to the toe. In addition, alluvial fans are structurally complex, being comprised of many layers of

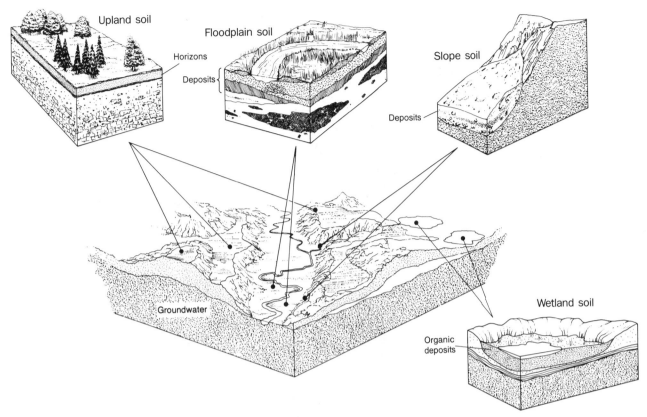

Fig. 5.4 Common sources and settings of deposits in which soils form: wetland, slope, floodplain, and upland wind deposits.

sediment, some of which may be saturated and unstable for building. Another type of deposit, talus slopes, is comprised of rock fragments that have fallen into place from an upper slope. In contrast to alluvial fans, particle size tends to increase downslope, and drainage is good at all levels. On vegetated hillslopes, toposequences are usually more subtle and limited largely to the surface layer. Topsoil, in particular, will vary with slope steepness, with the weakest development near midslope where the inclination is greatest and runoff removes most organic litter. Near the toe of the slope, topsoil thickens as runoff slows down and organic matter is deposited (Fig. 5.6).

5.6 APPLICATIONS TO LAND PLANNING

Published soil surveys

In both the United States and Canada, governmental agencies have conducted extensive surveys to map and classify soils. **Soil surveys** were originally designed to serve agriculture, but since 1960 or so they have been expanded to serve community land use and environmental interests as well. As we noted in Chapter 3, the Soil Conservation Service (SCS), an agency of the U.S. Department of Agriculture, is responsible for soil surveys in the United States. Surveys are organized by county, and the results are published in a volume called a county soil survey which contains soil descriptions, various data and guidelines on soil uses and limitations, and maps of soil distributions. At the most fundamental level, the soil surveys provide data and information in three key areas: soil drainage, soil texture, and soil composition. They are limited in three respects: major metropolitan areas are omitted; the map scale and accuracy are mar-

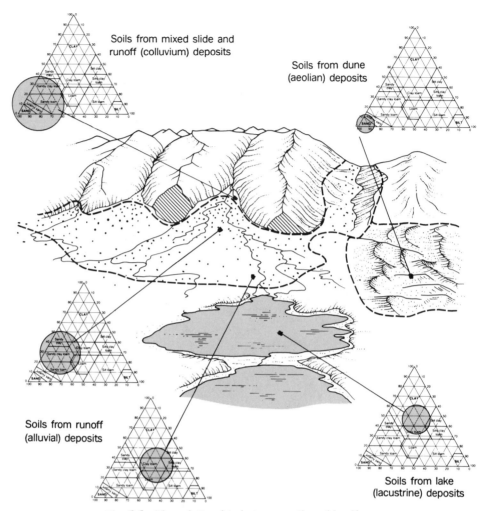

Fig. 5.5 The relationship between soils and landforms.

ginal for sites of less than 100 acres; and the depth of analysis is limited to the upper 4 to 5 feet of soil.

In planning problems dealing with community development, including residential, industrial, commercial, and related land uses, soil composition is one of the first considerations. **Organic soils** are at the top of the list because they are highly compressible under the weight of structures, and they tend to decompose when drained. Where the organic mass is shallow, it is possible to excavate and replace the soil with a better material, but this is often financially expensive and ecologically harmful. Excavation and fill costs generally range from $3 and $6 per cubic yard. From the ecological standpoint, we must recognize that organic soils are often indicative of the presence of wetlands that may support valued communities of plants and animals. On balance, then, organic soils should generally be avoided as development sites.

Organic soil limitations

For **mineral soils,** texture and drainage are the important considerations. Coarse-textured soils, such as sand and sandy loam, are preferred for most types of development because bearing capacity and drainage are usually excellent (see Table 5.1). As a result, foundations are structurally stable and usually free of nuisance water. Clayey soils, on the other hand, often provide poor foundation drainage, whereas bearing capacity may or may not be suitable for buildings. In addition, certain types of clays are prone to shrinking and swelling with changes in soil moisture, creating stress on

Mineral soil suitability

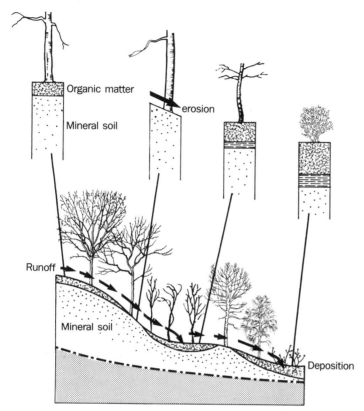

Fig. 5.6 A typical example of soil variation associated with a toposequence across a hillslope. Organic matter increases markedly on the gentler parts of the slope where runoff is slower.

foundations and underground utility lines (Fig. 5.7). Therefore, development in clayey soils may be more expensive because special footings and foundation drainage may be necessary. Accordingly, site analysis often requires detailed field mapping followed by engineering tests to determine whether clayey soils may pose bearing capacity, drainage, and other problems.

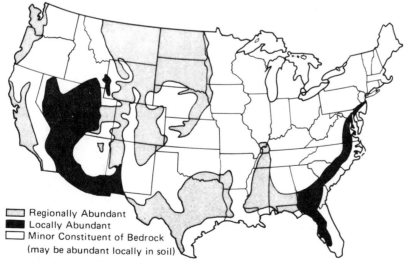

Fig. 5.7 The distribution of near-surface rock containing clay prone to swelling and shrinking. In soil, this clay (montmorillonite) is responsible for stress and cracking of foundations and utility lines.

Table 5.3   Landforms and Soil Materials

Feature	Composition	Drainage
Alluvial fan	Complex: sand, silt, clay with fraction pebbles and cobbles, markedly stratified and highly heterogeneous	Variable: upper portions may be well drained, lower portions may be very poor owing to groundwater seepage
Arroyo (also gulch or wash)	Complex: silt, sand, and pebbles in bed and valley of stream in arid setting	Poor; subject to seasonal and flash flooding
Barrier beach	Sand and pebbles	Good, but watertable often within several feet of surface
Beach	Variable; typically sand and pebbles but may also be clayey and silty or bedrock and rock rubble	Good if sandy, but watertable usually within several feet of surface
Beach ridge	Mainly sand, but pebbles common in lower portion	Excellent, especially in those with high elevation
Bog	Organic (muck, peat) with fraction mineral clay	Very poor
Cuesta	Bedrock often with partial coverage of thin soil and talus footslope	Good, but groundwater seepage common along footslope
Cusp or cuspate foreland	Sand and pebbles	Good, but watertable often within several feet of surface
Delta	Complex: usually clay, silt, and sand with local concentrations of organic material in stratified mass	Very poor to poor; high watertable; subject to frequent flooding
Drumlin	Clayey with admixture of coarser fractions as large as boulders	Good to poor
Escarpment (*see* Cuesta)		
Esker	Stratified sand and pebble mixture (gravelly) in the form of a sinuous ridge	Excellent
Floodplain	Complex: all varieties of soil possible including organic; assortment of stratified channel deposits with fraction flood and colluvial deposits	Poor to very poor; subject to high watertables and flooding
Ground moraine	Often sand, silt, clay admixture, but may be highly variable ranging from compacted clays to sand, pebbles, cobbles, boulders; usually gently rolling	Good to poor
Kame	Mainly stratified sand and gravel in the form of a conical-shaped hill	Excellent
Lake plain	Clayey with local concentrations of beach and dune sand	Poor to fair
Lake terrace	Usually sand and pebbles but may be bedrock or clay and silt	Excellent to good
Levee	Sand, silt, and clay deposits resting on floodplain (channel) sediments	Poor; slightly better than adjacent floodplain
Marsh	Organic (muck, peat) with fraction mineral clay	Very poor
Moraine	Often sand, silt, clay mixture, but may be highly variable ranging from compacted clays to sand, pebbles, cobbles, boulders; usually in form of irregular hilly terrain	Good to poor
Outwash plain	Sandy	Usually excellent, but high watertable in some locales

Table 5.3 *(Continued)*

Feature	Composition	Drainage
Pediment	Thin layer of sand and gravel over bedrock	Good, but infiltration capacity may be poor
River terrace	Variable; stratified clays, silts, sand	Excellent to fair
Sand dune (barchans, seifs, parabolic, hairpin, transverse, or coastal)	Pure sand	Excellent
Scarp (*see* Cuesta)		
Scree slope	Cobbles and pebbles (30°–40° slope)	Excellent
Spit	Sand and pebbles	Good, but watertable often within several feet of surface
Swamp	Organic (muck, peat) with fraction mineral clay	Very poor
Talus slope	Boulders in slabs, sheets or blocks (30°–40° slope)	Excellent
Tidal flat	Sand, silt, or clay with local concentrations of organic material	Very poor
Till plain	Often sand, silt, clay admixture, but may be highly variable ranging from compacted clays to sand, pebbles, cobbles, boulders (usually gently rolling)	Good to poor

Source: Adapted from William M. Marsh, *Environmental Analysis for Land Use and Site Planning* (New York: McGraw-Hill, 1978).

Scale considerations

In preparing soil maps, the **scale of analysis** is often as important as the types of analysis. For regional-scale problems, SCS maps are generally suitable and indeed are widely used along with topographic maps and other published sources of data to identify suitable locations for various land uses. At the site scale, however, SCS reports and maps are usually too general for most projects. In these cases, a finer grain of spatial detail is called for, which can be provided in part by refining the SCS soil boundaries with the aid of a large, site-scale topographic map. This is based on the fact that many borders of soil types on SCS maps follow topography, and at a site scale of detail, topographic trends and details are much more apparent than the soil scientist could detect in building the original map. Therefore, where adjacent soils are clearly terrain-specific, the configuration of the border can be articulated much more accurately on large-scale site maps (Fig. 5.8).

Soil analysis for site planning

Beyond SCS considerations, or in areas not covered by SCS maps, **soil analysis for site planning** should begin with two basic considerations. The first is the recent geomorphic history of the area so that we will have some idea of what types of materials to expect. This information can be obtained through a telephone call to a local university (geography, geology, or soil science department), the state geologist's office, or the county SCS office. In any case, we need to know at the outset whether we are in an area of marine clay, sand dune deposits, glacial outwash, or whatever. The second consideration is local topography and drainage. Using topographic maps and field inspection, drainageways (stream valleys, swales, and floodplains) and areas of impeded drainage (wetlands, ponds, and related features) should be mapped. These are the zones where poorly drained and organic soils will most likely be found. The remaining area can be defined as slopes and upland surfaces, and, although soil texture may vary within these zones, drainage should be better and organic deposits less likely.

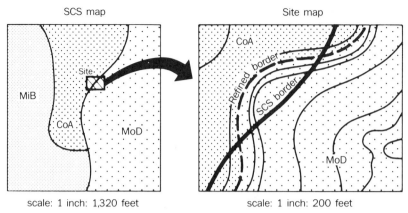

SCS map   Site map

scale: 1 inch: 1,320 feet   scale: 1 inch: 200 feet

Fig. 5.8   Refinement of SCS soils map at the site scale using a detailed topographic map.

Field testing   Within this framework, a limited testing program can be carried out by digging holes at selected points along swales, floodplains, hillslopes, and ridgetops. This is best accomplished with a backhoe, which can quickly excavate to a depth of 2 m or more, but a shovel or soil auger will suffice for shallower depths. Once a test pit is excavated, the following questions can be answered:

■   Is the material below the surface mainly organic?

■   Does water rapidly seep into and eventually fill most of the pit?

■   Is buried debris (organic matter, landfill material, or rubble of any sort) present?

If the answer to any of these questions is yes, the soil should generally be classed as unsuitable for development. Further analysis may be required for engineering purposes, but for site planning this level of investigation is adequate for laying out use zones, circulation systems, and defining building sites (Fig. 5.9).

Soil borings are test holes used to measure the strata and composition of soil materials at depths greater than 3 meters (10 feet). In most instances borings are necessary only where facilities are to be built or where there is a suspected problem concerning groundwater or bedrock. The depth to which a boring is made depends on the building program requirements (for example, heavy buildings or light buildings), the types of materials encountered underground, and the depth to bedrock. If the soil mantle is relatively thin, say, less than 10 meters, and the bedrock stable, the footings for large buildings will usually be placed directly on the bedrock. In areas of unstable soils, such as poorly consolidated wet clays, or weak bedrock, such as cavernous limestone, special footings are usually required to provide the necessary stability.

5.7 PLANNING CONSIDERATIONS IN SOLID WASTE DISPOSAL

The problem   One of the most pressing land use problems in urbanized and industrial areas today is the disposal of solid waste: municipal garbage, chemical residues from industry, rubble from mining and urban development, various forms of industrial and agricultural debris, and, most recently, nuclear residue from power plants and military manufacturing and development installations. Because of the large volumes involved and/or the composition or form of this material, it is neither economically nor technically feasible to dispose of this waste in conventional sanitary sewer systems; that is, those involving diffusion in water and transport through underground pipes to a treatment plant. Of

Fig. 5.9 A backhoe excavating soil test pits and a photograph of a test pit revealing buried organic matter at a depth of 1.5 m (5 ft).

Sanitary landfill   the alternatives remaining, the practice of burial in the ground, called **sanitary land-filling,** is the preferred disposal method (Fig. 5.10). Most other disposal methods are either environmentally unacceptable or too expensive for most waste. These include burning, open dumping, ocean dumping, and deep earth injection. Increasingly, however, with revelations that landfills are resulting in contamination of soil and groundwater, it has become more apparent that both solid and hazardous wastes will have to be disposed of in more elaborate and expensive ways.

Solid waste can be divided into four major types: mining debris, industrial refuse, agricultural waste, and urban garbage. Mining debris and agricultural waste account for 90 percent of the solid waste produced in the United States each year. Urban and industrial waste, though comparatively low in total output, present the most widespread and serious solid waste disposal problem for planners, however. Several factors account for this, including the issue of groundwater contamination and public health, the growing concern over hazardous waste, the conflict over aesthetic and real estate values, the limited availability of land around cities for disposal sites, and the high cost of garbage collection and hauling in urban areas. In addition, the production of urban and industrial waste has been rising steadily in most parts of the United States.

Site selection criteria   The **selection of a disposal site** for urban and industrial solid waste is one of the most critical planning processes faced in suburban and rural areas today. Properly approached, it should be guided by three considerations: (1) *cost,* which is closely tied to land values and hauling distances; (2) *land use* in the vicinity of the site and along hauling routes; and (3) *site conditions,* which are largely a function of soil and drainage. In both urban and industrial landfills, the chief site problem is containment of the liquids that emanate from the decomposing waste.

These fluids are collectively called *leachate* and are composed of heavy concentrations of dissolved compounds that can contaminate local water supplies. Leachates are often chemically complex and vary in makeup with the composition of the refuse. Moreover, the behavior of leachates in the hydrologic system, especially in ground-

Fig. 5.10 A sanitary landfill operation. The mass of garbage (above) is mounded up and interlaid with clayey soil. The final mass (below) is covered with a soil sheet several feet thick and then vegetated.

water, is poorly understood. Therefore, the general rule in landfill planning and management is to restrict leachate from contact with either surface or subsurface water. Instances of groundwater contamination by leachates typically result in the loss of potable water for many decades.

   Leachate containment may be accomplished in some cases by merely selecting the right site. An ideal fill site should be excavated in soil that is effectively impervious,

Preferred site conditions

neither receives nor releases groundwater, and is not subject to contact with surface waters such as streams or wetlands. Dense (compact) clay soils and relatively high-level ground are the preferred site characteristics. In addition, the clay should not be interlayered with sand or gravel, not subject to cracking upon drying, and stable against mass movements such as landslides.

Where these conditions cannot be met, the site must be modified to achieve the satisfactory performance. If the soils are sandy and permeable, for example, a liner of clay or a synthetic substance such as vinyl must be installed to gain the necessary imperviousness. The same measure must be taken in stratified soils, wet soils, sloping sites, and sites near water features and wells. In many areas of the United States and Canada, however, the decision to modify a site is not left up to the landfill developer or operator because strict regulations often govern which sites can even be considered for landfills. Thus inherently poor sites are often eliminated from consideration by virtue of planning policy.

Management planning

In addition to a formal site selection and preparation plan, a growing number of local and state/provincial governments are requiring the preparation of a **management plan** for the design and operation of landfills. In the case of sanitary landfills for municipal garbage, the planner is asked to address the following:

1. Compartmentalization of the filling into cells or self-contained units of some sort.
2. Phasing of the operation; for example, excavation and filling of a limited portion of area at any one time.
3. Landscaping, pest control, and protection of the site during operations.
4. Limiting the total thickness of refuse by interspersing layers of soil within the garbage.
5. Backfilling over the completed fill with a layer of soil with a provision for vent pipes to release gases, if necessary (Fig. 5.10).
6. Preparation of a plan for grading, landscaping, and for future use of the site.

5.8 CASE STUDY

Mapping Soil at the Site Scale for Private Development

W. M. Marsh

The aim in mapping soils for planning and architectural projects is clearly different than it is for agricultural purposes. Where the main question is the suitability of soil for facilities such as roads and buildings, rather than the suitability for crops, the scope of the study and parameters investigated must be defined accordingly. This requires a clear understanding of the development program: that is, what is to be built, how much floor space is called for, what ancillary facilities will be needed (parking and the like), what utility systems are necessary, and so on. These elements of the program must be known to determine (1) the scales at which mapping must be conducted; (2) the soil features (parameters) that should be recorded; and (3) the depth to which soil must be examined.

The results of the soil survey, along with the results of related studies such as drainage, slope, and traffic, are used to formulate alternative plans for development of the site. In this particular project, which called for a large research/office facility in a campuslike setting, it was important to determine not only certain standard parameters such as texture and drainage, but also the soil environment in terms of the processes and factors that shape soil formation. The resultant soil map was instrumental in defining buildable land units, which in turn served as a framework for the formulation of alternative develop-

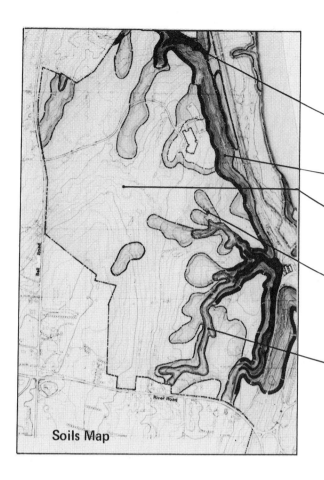

Soils Map

Valley Soil: diverse with heavy concentrations of large boulders; channel and slope deposits; prone to flooding and high watertable

Slope Soil: loamy with dry surface; rapid runoff; prone to failure and erosion if disturbed and/or deforested

Upland Soil: silty loam; well drained in most months but may be moist at depths of 1-2 feet; bearing capacity generally good, but foundation drainage may be needed

Transition Soil: silty loam; seasonally very wet; runoff collection zones; drainage somewhat better where once cultivated and tiled; piping active near channels; good potential for stormwater control areas; limited potential for structures

Wetland Soil: silty clay loam with appreciable organic fraction; serious drainage problems in most months; unsuitable for building

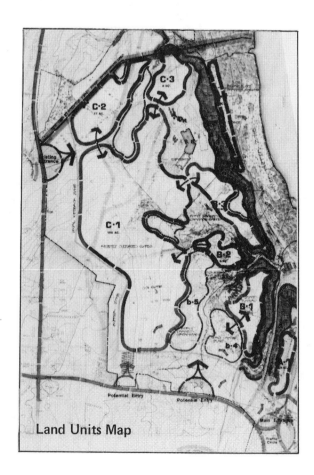

Land Units Map

ment plans. Following the selection of an alternative, engineers conducted more detailed soil analyses according to specific locations designated for buildings and facilities in the plan.

Understanding some of the physical dynamics of the soil environment is important not only in the placement of facilities, but also in designing the management programs that should accompany their operations. These include stormwater management, design landscaping, habitat conservation, and site security.

5.9 SELECTED REFERENCES FOR FURTHER READING

Briggs, David. *Soils.* Boston: Butterworths, 1977, 192 pp.

Colonna, Robert A., and McLaren, Cynthia. *Decision-Makers Guide to Solid Waste Management.* Washington, D.C.: Government Printing Office, U.S. Environmental Protection Agency, 1974, 157 pp.

Davidson, Donald A. *Soils and Land Use Planning.* New York: Longman, 1980, 129 pp.

Eckholm, Erik P. *Losing Ground.* New York: W. W. Norton, 1976, 223 pp.

Gordon, S. I., and Gordon, G. E. "The Accuracy of Soil Survey Information for Urban Land Use Planning." *Journal of the American Planning Association,* 47: 3, 1981, pp. 301–312.

Hills, Angus G., et al. *Developing a Better Environment: Ecological Land Use Planning in Ontario, A Study Methodology in the Development of Regional Plans.* Toronto: Ontario Economic Council, 1970, 182 pp.

Hopkins, Lewis D. "Methods of Generating Land Suitability Maps: A Comparative Evaluation." *Journal of the American Institute of Planners,* October 1977, pp. 388–400.

Metropolitan Area Planning Commission. *Halifax-Dartmouth Metro Area, Natural Land Capability.* Halifax, Nova Scotia: Nova Scotia Department of Development, 1973, 71 pp.

Pettry, D. E., and Coleman, C. S. "Two Decades of Urban Soil Interpretations In Fairfax County, Virginia." *Geoderma* 10, 1973, pp. 27–34.

Soil Society of America. *Soil Surveys and Land Use Planning.* Madison, Wis.: Soil Society of America, 1966.

6

SOILS AND WASTEWATER DISPOSAL

6.1 INTRODUCTION

Historical context

Until this century, soil served as the primary medium for the disposal of most human waste. Raw organic waste was deposited in the soil via pits or spread on the surface by farmers. In either case, natural biochemical processes broke the material down, and water dispersed the remains into the soil, removing most harmful ingredients in the process. But this practice often proved ineffective where large numbers of people were involved, because the soil became saturated with waste, exceeding the capacity of the biochemical processes to reduce the concentration of harmful ingredients to safe levels.

The results were occasionally disastrous to a city or town. Water supplies became contaminated and rats and flies flourished, leading to epidemics of dysentery, cholera, and typhoid fever. In response to these problems, efforts were made in the latter half of the 1800s to dispose of human waste in a safer manner.

In cities, where the problems were most serious, sewer systems were introduced, allowing waste to be transported through underground pipes to a body of water, such as a river or lake, beyond the city. Later this practice gave rise to critical water pollution problems, but it did solve the immediate problem of human health. Outside the cities, people continued to use pit-style privies until well into the twentieth century. But with the growth of suburban neighborhoods after 1930, the outdoor toilet proved unacceptable. In its place came the septic tank and drainfield for individual homes. Within the cities, large-scale treatment systems were introduced to help manage the water pollution problem created by sewer discharges.

6.2 THE SOIL-ABSORPTION SYSTEM

Purpose

The septic drainfield method of waste disposal is one version of a soil-absorption system (SAS), so-called because it relies on the soil to absorb and disperse wastewater. The system is designed to keep contaminated water out of contact with the surface environment and to filter chemical and biological contaminants from the water before they reach groundwater, streams, or lakes. The contaminants of greatest concern are nitrogen and phosphorus, which are nutrients for algae growth in aquatic systems, and certain forms of bacteria, which are hazardous to human health.

Most SAS systems are comprised of two components: (1) a holding or septic tank where solids settle out; and (2) a drainfield through which "gray" water is dispersed into the soil. The drainfield is made up of a network of perforated pipes or jointed tiles from which the fluid seeps into the soil (Fig. 6.1). Several different layout configurations are commonly employed.

Soil permeability

Critical to the operation of a soil-absorption system is the rate at which the soil can receive water. Soils with high permeabilities are clearly preferred over those with low permeabilities. **Permeability** is a measure of the amount of water that will pass through a soil sample per minute or hour. In the health sciences, permeability is measured by the percolation rate, the rate at which water is absorbed by soil through the sides of a test pit such as the one shown in Fig. 6.2. The "perc" test is usually conducted *in situ,* meaning that it is conducted in the field rather than in the labora-

Percolation controls

tory. The **percolation** rate of a soil is controlled by three factors: *soil texture, water content,* and *slope.* Fine-textured soils generally transmit water more slowly than coarse-textured soils do, and thus have lower capacities for wastewater absorption. On the other hand, fine-textured soils are more effective in filtering chemical and bacterial contaminants from wastewater. The ideal soil, then, is a textural mix of coarse particles (to transmit water) and fine particles (to act as an effective biochemical filter).

Soil moisture tends to reduce permeability in any soil; therefore, soils with high

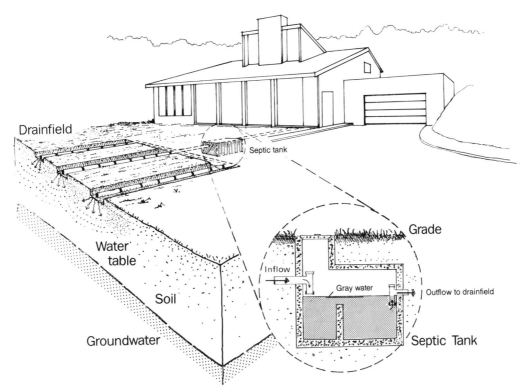

Fig. 6.1 A standard design for a septic tank and drainfield. Solid waste accumulates in the septic tank while the gray water flows into the drainfield where it seeps into the soil.

watertables are limited for wastewater disposal. Slope influences percolation inasmuch as it affects the inclination of the drainfield. If the slope of the ground exceeds 3 to 4 feet per 100 feet, it is difficult to arrange the drainfield at an inclination gentle enough (2 to 4 inches per 100 feet is recommended) to prohibit gray water from flowing rapidly down the drain pipes and concentrating at the lower end of the drainfield. In addition, the soil layer must be deep enough so that bedrock does not retard the entry of percolating water into the subsoil (Fig. 6.3).

6.3 ENVIRONMENTAL IMPACT AND SYSTEM DESIGN

Soil-absorption systems are a standard means of sewage disposal throughout the world. In the United States, as much as 25 percent of the population relies on these systems; in developing countries such as Mexico, fully 80 to 90 percent of the population uses some form of soil absorption for waste disposal, including pit-style privies. Not surprisingly, a high percentage of these systems do not function properly, often resulting in serious health problems and environmental damage.

SAS failure   The causes of **system failure** are usually tied to one or more of the following: improper siting and design of the drainfield, overloading (that is, overuse), inadequate maintenance of septic tank and tile system, and loss of soil percolation capacity due to clogging of interparticle spaces or groundwater saturation of the drainfield bed. Failure often results in the seepage of wastewater into the surface layer of the soil and onto the ground. Here humans are apt to come into contact with it, it may enter groundwater and contaminate wells, and it may enter lakes and streams, contaminating water supplies and fostering the growth of algae and related organisms.

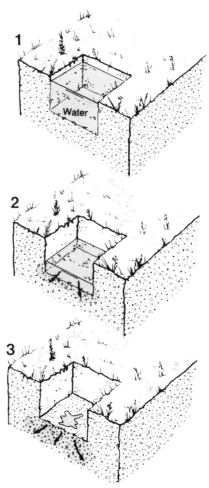

Fig. 6.2 The basic idea of the percolation test. A small pit is excavated, filled with water, allowed to drain, then refilled with water and allowed to drain again. The rate of fall in the water surface is the "perc" rate.

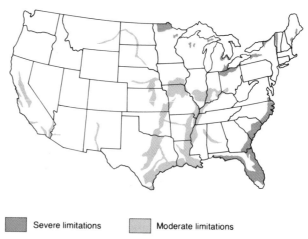

Severe limitations   Moderate limitations

Fig. 6.3 The general distribution of soils with limitations to soil absorptions systems in the coterminous United States. Locally, areas with limitations may be found just about anywhere in the U.S. and Canada.

Fig. 6.4 An algae bloom resulting in part from seepage of nutrients into the lake from drainfields.

Water pollution

Enrichment of lakes, ponds, and reservoirs with wastewater seepage is a leading cause of the deterioration of recreation waters in the United States and Canada. Where nitrogen and phosphorus, the nutrients of greatest concern, enter a lake, for example, the productivity of algae and other aquatic plants usually rises substantially, resulting in greater organic mass. This mass not only fills in the lake bottom, but as it decays, the consuming bacteria use up available oxygen in the water. In time, the water's oxygen content declines, fish species change to less desirable species and the lake develops an overgrown (i.e., overfed) character which is often unsightly and smelly (Fig. 6.4).

SAS design criteria

Avoidance of public health and water pollution problems from soil-absorption systems begins with site analysis and soil evaluation. Soils with percolation rates of less than 1 inch per hour are considered unsuitable for standard soil-absorption systems. For soils with acceptable percolation rates, additional criteria must be applied: slope, soil thickness (depth to bedrock), and seasonal high watertable. Given that these criteria are satisfied, the system can now be designed. The chief design element is drainfield size, and it is based on two factors: (1) the actual soil percolation rate, and (2) the rate at which wastewater will be released to the soil, that is, the loading rate. For residential structures, the loading rate is based on the number of bedrooms; each bedroom is proportional to two persons. The higher the loading rate and the lower the percolation rate, the larger the drainfield required (Fig. 6.5).

Maintenance and life cycle

Successful operation of the system necessitates regular maintenance, especially the removal of sludge from the septic tank, avoidance of overloading, and the lack of interference from high groundwater. The last-named may occur during unusually wet years or because of the raising of a nearby reservoir, for example. On the average, the lifetime of a drainfield is 15 to 25 years, depending on local conditions. At this time the soil may be too wet to drain properly, because the watertable has been raised after years of recharge from drainfield water, and/or the soil may have become clogged with minute particles. In addition, the buildup of chemicals such as phosphorus may become excessive, thereby reducing the filtering capacity of the soil. In any event, old drainfields should be abandoned and a new one constructed in a different location.

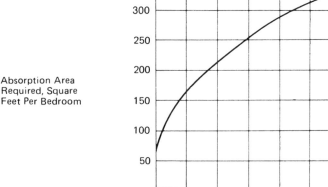

Fig. 6.5 Absorption area requirements based on soil-percolation rates.

6.4 ASSESSING SOIL SUITABILITY FOR ON-SITE DISPOSAL

Data sources

The suitability of an individual site for wastewater disposal is best determined by field inspection and percolation tests. For planning problems involving large areas, however, this is not always possible to carry out in detail, and it is necessary to resort to less expensive methods for an assessment of soil suitability. In most cases, the investigator must rely on existing maps and **data,** as is illustrated by the Nova Scotia case study at the end of the chapter. The best **sources** in the United States are the county soil reports produced by the Soil Conservation Service; in Canada, they are soil maps produced by the provinces or regional environmental agencies. Where SCS studies are not available, the investigator must turn to other sources and synthesize existing maps and data into information meaningful to wastewater disposal problems.

The maps in Fig. 6.6 are part of a set of maps produced by the United States Geological Survey for a land use capability study in Connecticut. Three of these maps (slope, seasonal high watertable, and depth to bedrock) are directly applicable to wastewater disposal problems. However, the fourth map, called "unconsolidated materials," must be used in place of soil type or soil texture. The six classes of materials must be translated into their soil counterparts, and the soils, in turn, into their potential for wastewater disposal. For example:

Unconsolidated Material on USGS Map	Approximate Soil Equivalent	Potential for Wastewater Disposal
Till	Loam	Good
Compacted till	Loam, perhaps clayey, that drains poorly	Fair/poor
Clay deposit	Clay; clayey loam	Poor
Sliderock deposit	Rock rubble	Poor
Swamp	Organic: muck, peat	Poor
Sand or sand and gravel deposits	Sand; sandy loam; gravel	Fair

Map synthesis

With this in hand, we can proceed to combine the four maps and produce a suitability map for wastewater disposal. One procedure for this sort of task involves assigning a value or rank to each trait according to its relative importance in wastewater absorption. In this case, three ranks are possible for each of the four traits, and each can be assigned a numerical value (Table 6.1): good (3), fair (2), and poor (1) according to the translation above. For any area or site, the relative suitability for wastewater disposal can be determined by simply summing the four values. The final step is to establish a numerical scale defining the limits of the various suitability classes. The classes should be expressed in qualitative terms, for example, as high, medium, or low, because as numerical values they are meaningless and often misleading in terms of their relative significance.

SCS Maps

Modern soil surveys by the Soil Conservation Service present a somewhat different arrangement. First, all data and information are organized and presented according to soil type. Second, in many areas the SCS provides information on soil suitability for wastewater disposal by SAS. In that case, all one need do is to map the various SCS classes and record the criteria and rationale for each. However, the criteria and rationale used are not always clear, or one may wish to add or delete certain criteria depending on the land use problem and/or local conditions. In such instances, the procedure would be largely the same as that outlined previously, except that the mapping unit is already established (Fig. 6.7) and the data base may be different. County soil reports often include data on permeability, seasonal high watertable, and

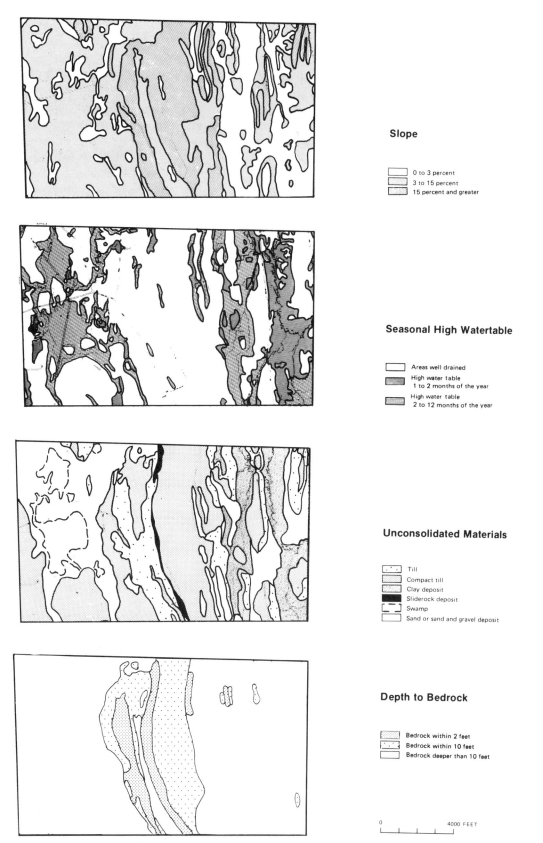

Slope

0 to 3 percent
3 to 15 percent
15 percent and greater

Seasonal High Watertable

Areas well drained
High water table
1 to 2 months of the year
High water table
2 to 12 months of the year

Unconsolidated Materials

Till
Compact till
Clay deposit
Sliderock deposit
Swamp
Sand or sand and gravel deposit

Depth to Bedrock

Bedrock within 2 feet
Bedrock within 10 feet
Bedrock deeper than 10 feet

0   4000 FEET

Fig. 6.6 A series of maps compiled as part of a land capability study that can be used to assess on-site wastewater disposal suitability. (From the U.S. Geological Survey.)

Table 6.1 Criteria and Numerical Values for SAS Suitability for Maps in Figure 6.6

	Trait ⟶ *Material*	*Depth to Bedrock*	*Seasonal Watertable*	*Slope*
3 (good)	Till	>10 ft.	Well drained	0–3%
2 (fair)	Sand, sand and gravel, compacted till	2–10 ft.	1–2 mos. high watertable	3–15%
1 (poor)	Clay, sliderock, swamp	<2 ft.	2–12 mos. high watertable	>15%

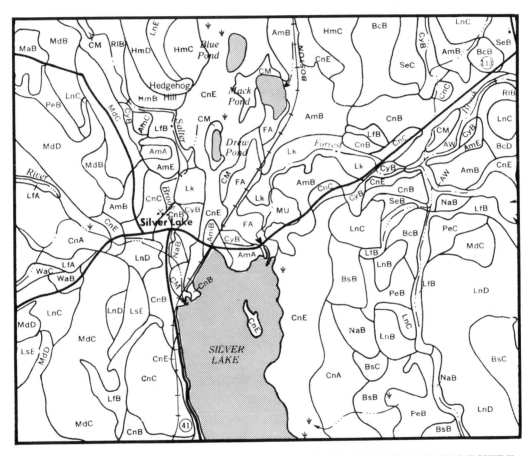

SOIL MAP   CARROLL COUNTY, NEW HAMPSHIRE

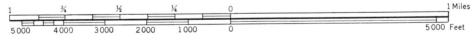

U. S. DEPARTMENT OF AGRICULTURE
SOIL CONSERVATION SERVICE
FOREST SERVICE

Fig. 6.7 An excerpt from a standard U.S. Soil Conversation Service map. The letters denote different soil types.

Table 6.2   Procedure for Soil Suitability Classification for SAS

Step 1. Select the traits for evaluation and build a matrix listing each soil type and each trait. For example:

Soil	Texture	Depth to Bedrock	TRAIT Depth to Seasonal Watertable	Permeability	Slope
Becket:					
Berkshire:					
Chocorua:					

Step 2. Set up a ranking system such as that in Table 6.1 and complete the matrix by assigning a numerical value to each soil trait.
Step 3. Total the ranking values for each soil type or series.
Step 4. Based on these totals, classify the soils as high, medium, or low.
Step 5: Go to the soils map and color the areas that correspond to each suitability class. For this you will need to devise a three-part color scheme and map legend.

depth to bedrock as well as texture and slope. Where data are available for these criteria, the steps listed in Table 6.2 can be used to build a soil suitability map for wastewater disposal.

6.5 ALTERNATIVES TO STANDARD SAS

Finally, it is necessary to mention the various **alternatives** to the standard soil-absorption system. These are treatment systems designed to overcome various soil and topographic limitations at the site scale. The actual use of alternative systems varies from place to place, depending on local health and planning regulations. The simplest alternative is the waterless toilet, which eliminates the need for all or part of the *Waterless system* drainfield in the standard residence. The **waterless system** is designed to concentrate solid waste and dispose of it in an environmentally safe manner; for example, as soil compost after it is free of disease agents. This system is viewed very favorably by many communities because (1) it eliminates the need to handle and process large amounts of contaminated water, and (2) it greatly reduces domestic water use. Another system that reduces the need for a large drainfield involves separating toilet water from wastewater from sinks, washers, bathtubs, etc. The toilet water is directed to the drainfield, whereas the other water, which is not laden with pathogens, can be reused to irrigate lawns and gardens.

Where soils are the limitation, several other alternatives are possible. One involves replacing the upper 2 feet of soil with a fill medium of the desired percolation and *Earth mound system* absorption values. A related system, called **earth mound,** involves building a drainfield above ground level in a pile of soil medium that contains the release pipes. A pump is used to force the gray water into the drainfield.

In areas where slopes are the chief limitation, drainfields can sometimes be laid out in several terraces. The drainfield is compartmentalized, and gray water is distributed according to the size and capacity of each terrace compartment. Another method utilizes a pipe system to transfer wastewater to a suitable disposal site. This system *Grinder/pump system* usually incorporates a **grinder** to break up the solids, a storage tank, and a **pump** to force the water to the disposal site. The grinder/pump system can be used to tie a number of houses into a single disposal system.

With the exception of the waterless toilet, construction and maintenance costs are usually greater for alternative systems than they are for the standard soil-absorption system. In addition, they require more attention in their design, and permitting by local regulatory agencies may be more difficult in many parts of the United States and Canada. In many places the waterless toilet, in particular, is not accepted for standard residential units. However, where water supply is an issue or where there is a concern about the contamination of groundwater and streams, the waterless toilet is gaining serious attention.

6.6 CASE STUDY

■ Planning for Wastewater Disposal Using Soil Maps, Nova Scotia

Michael D. Simmons

Although population growth in Nova Scotia has been slow, recent decades saw a relatively large number of housing starts as a result of the breakup of households, the availability of government housing assistance, and a general trend toward rural and suburban settlement. Many of these new homes were built on unserviced lots within commuting distance of urban centers. To help in planning where homes should and should not be built, the Province of Nova Scotia appointed a task force in 1972 to determine soil suitability for on-site wastewater disposal.

The basic soil units and maps of the Nova Scotia soil survey served as the geographic base. The criteria for wastewater disposal were based on guidelines established by the Nova Scotia Department of Public Health:

■ The percolation rate must be less than 30 minutes per inch; a rate of up to 60 minutes per inch may be acceptable with suitable modifications.

■ Depth to bedrock must be 4 feet or more below the disposal field; that is, about 6 feet below the surface.

■ The groundwater table must also be at least 4 feet below the disposal field, and the drainfield site must not be in a marshy area or an area subject to flooding.

■ Topography, or relative elevations within the lot, must be considered.

In addition to the factors covered by the guidelines, three other limitations were considered:

■ Prolonged or periodic saturation of the surface soil layers associated with a perched watertable or flooding.

■ Excessively rapid percolation, permitting contamination of groundwater supplies.

■ Excessive slope of the land surface

These criteria were compared with the soil survey data base, and six operational criteria were defined: (1) percolation rate too slow, (2) bedrock less than 6 feet from surface, (3) prolonged saturation, (4) seasonal saturation, (5) susceptibility to flooding, and (6) percolation rate too high. In addition to the soil survey, data from public health inspectors, well-drilling logs, as well as additional field tests were used in the mapping program.

In attempting to synthesize the data, inconsistencies were often uncovered between the soil descriptions included in the soil survey and observations based on field inspection. This was attributed to two factors: the scale of mapping and the time or season of field testing. Soil moisture varies seasonally; therefore, in periods of low moisture, soils may appear to perform satisfactorily

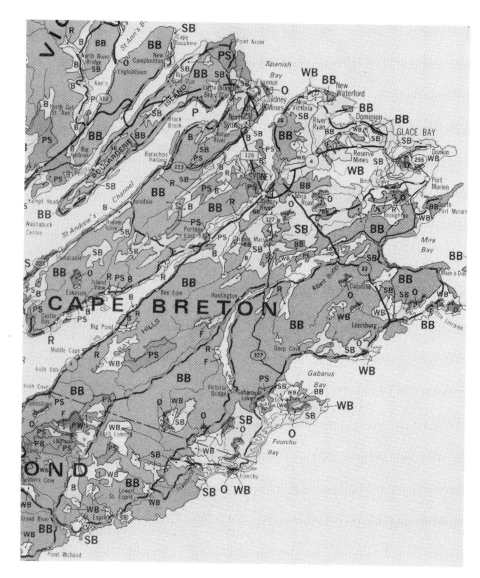

SOILS OF NOVA SCOTIA
LIMITATIONS FOR SEPTIC TANK ABSORPTION FIELDS[1]

Legend

Map Unit Symbol	Primary Limitation	Probability of Occurrence [2]	Secondary Limitation	Probability of Occurrence [2]	Acres ('000)	Hectares ('000)	% of Province
N	NONE TO MODERATE LIMITATIONS	85	NONE	.	709	287	5.5
B	BEDROCK	65	NONE	.	1016	411	7.9
BB	BEDROCK	90	NONE	.	6439	2606	49.4
P	PERCOLATION	90	NONE	.	420	170	3.3
PS	PERCOLATION	90	PERIODIC SATURATION	80	1322	535	10.3
PW	PERCOLATION	90	PROLONGED SATURATION	90	264	107	2.0
PB	PERCOLATION	90	BEDROCK	75	498	201	3.9
SB	PERIODIC SATURATION	90	BEDROCK	80	1073	434	8.3
WB	PROLONGED SATURATION	90	BEDROCK	80	388	157	3.1
R	RAPID PERCOLATION	80	NONE	.	163	66	1.2
WR	PROLONGED SATURATION	90	RAPID PERCOLATION	80	30	12	0.2
F	FLOODING	90	PERCOLATION (RAPID or SLOW)	80	171	69	1.4
▉	OTHER UNSUITABLE AREAS [Swamps, peat bogs, salt marsh, coastal beach, eroded land]	95		.	444	179	3.5

[1]NOTE: Site modifications may be introduced which overcome these limitations. Techniques include the addition of fill, drainage to lower the water table and possibly deep tillage to increase the percolation rate. Detailed investigation of local site conditions are required to determine the feasibility and cost of overcoming the site limitations.

[2]PROBABILITY OF OCCURRENCE

if subjected only to a single percolation test. To identify soils with seasonal limitations, it was found that percolation tests should be performed only in May, early June, and November in most years.

The scale of mapping was a more difficult problem. Because the Province is covered by 14 soils survey reports at small map scales (1 inch to 1 mile, 1 inch to 2 miles, and 1 inch to one-third mile), the detail necessary for site-specific investigations was missing. For this reason, it was necessary to use a mapping technique based on the probability of occurrence of a limitation. This consisted of identifying the one or two major limitations of each soil type and then sampling that soil unit to determine the consistency of occurrence of those limitations. The overall consistency of occurrence ranged from 80 to 90 percent, although in some areas with a bedrock limitation, bedrock was identified in only 50 percent of the sites. A probability of 80 percent indicates that a given limitation could be expected in four out of five development sites selected at random within a given soil mapping unit.

Since mapping was based on the Nova Scotia soil survey, the largest scale maps that could be produced by this project were 1 : 50,000. These maps have been put to a variety of uses: first, as public information vehicles to illustrate the extent and distribution of problem soils; and second, in communities where there has been a reluctance to accept on-site test results, to provide corroborating evidence of problem soils. This has not only strengthened local planning regulatory processes, but has provided guidelines for municipal and regional development plans as well.

Michael D. Simmons is a resource planner with Maritime Resource Management Service, Amherst, Nova Scotia.

6.7 SELECTED REFERENCES FOR FURTHER READING

Clark, John W., et al. "Individual Household Septic-Tank Systems." In *Water Supply and Pollution Control.* 3rd ed. New York: IEP/Dun-Donnelley, 1977, pp. 611–621.

Cotteral, J. A., and Norris, D. P. "Septic-Tank Systems." *Proceedings American Society of Civil Engineers,* Journl of Sanitary Engineering Division 95, no. SA4, 1969, pp. 715–746.

Environmental Protection Agency. "Alternatives for Small Wastewater Treatment Systems." *EPA Technology Transfer Seminar Publication,* EPA–625/4–77–011, 1977.

Huddleston, J. H., and Olson, G. W. "Soil Survey Interpretation for Subsurface Sewage Disposal." *Soil Science* 104, 1967, pp. 401–409.

Last, J. M. *Public Health and Human Ecology.* East Norwalk, Connecticut: Appleton and Lange, 1987.

Public Health Service. "Manual of Septic Tank Practice." United States Public Health Service Publication No. 526, Washington, D.C.: Government Printing Office, 1957.

World Health Organization. *The International Drinking Water Supply and Sanitation Decade Review of Regional and Global Data.* Geneva: WHO Offset Publication No. 92, 1986.

7

GROUNDWATER, LAND USE, AND WASTE RESIDUALS

7.1 INTRODUCTION

Not many years ago, the only consideration given to groundwater in land use planning was as water supply. Groundwater is still an important source of water for residential, industrial, and agricultural land uses, and locating dependable supplies of usable water is still important in planning. Today, however, there is another problem to contend with: groundwater pollution. Groundwater contamination is one of the most alarming of today's environmental problems, especially when we consider that groundwater is the single largest reservoir of fresh, liquid water on the planet.

Role of planning

Although groundwater is often pictured as a remote and complex part of the environment and traditionally is not the domain of planners, it is necessary to remind ourselves that virtually all groundwater begins and ends in the landscape. Therefore, changes in the surface environment, especially those involving land use activity can, and usually do, affect groundwater in some way. For land use and environmental planners the problem is not only knowing what the polluting activities are, but also finding the proper location for them relative to the local groundwater system. Indeed, the first line of defense in groundwater protection is judicious site selection for land uses with high impact potentiality.

Hidden waste sites

The responsibility of the planner today goes even further, for it is also necessary to contend with hidden sources of soil and groundwater contamination. The U.S. Environmental Protection Agency estimates that there may be as many as 50,000 landfills containing hazardous waste in the United States. Most of these lie in and around metropolitan regions, and for a surprisingly large number of them, the locations are unknown. Increasingly, new landowners are uncovering these landfills and are being forced to realize the expense and liability connected with cleanup and restoration. Thus, to the list of considerations in environmental assessment site selection and site planning we must add that of unrecorded landfills.

7.2 GROUNDWATER SOURCES AND FEATURES

Gravity water

Groundwater begins with surface water seeping into the ground. Below the surface, the water moves along two paths: (1) some is taken up by the soil, and (2) some is drawn by gravity to greater depths. The latter, called **gravity water,** eventually reaches a zone where all the open spaces (interparticle voids and the cracks in bedrock) are filled with water. This zone is called the *zone of saturation* or the *groundwater zone.*

The upper surface of the groundwater zone is the *water table* (Fig. 7.1). In some materials the water table is a visible boundary line, but often it is little more than a transition zone. Below the water table the groundwater zone may extend several thousand meters into the earth. The actual water content, however, varies with different materials at various depths.

Porosity

The total amount of groundwater that can be held in any material is controlled by the material's porosity. **Porosity** is the total volume of void space in a material. It commonly varies from 10 to 30 percent in soils and near-surface bedrock (Fig. 7.2). In general, porosity decreases with depth, and at depths of several thousand meters, where the enormous pressure of the rock overburden closes out void spaces, it is typically less than 1 percent.

Aquifers

In most areas the materials underground are arranged in layers, formations, or zones with different groundwater capacities. Those materials with especially large concentrations of usable groundwater are widely known as **aquifers.** Many different types of materials may form aquifers, but porous material with good permeability, such as beds of sand and fractured rock formations, are usually the best. An aquifer is evaluated or ranked according to how much water can be pumped from it (without

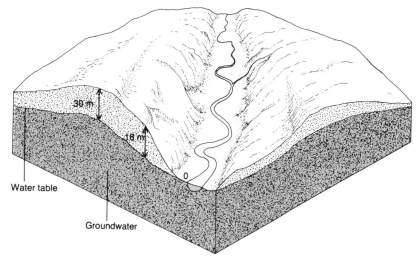

Fig. 7.1 The general relationship between the configuration of the watertable and that of the overlying terrain. The variation in the elevation of the watertable is usually less than that of the land surface, resulting in many intersections between groundwater and the surface of the land.

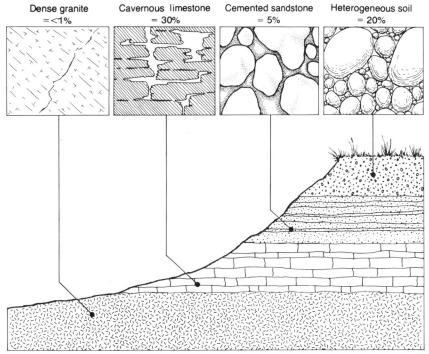

Fig. 7.2 Porosities of four materials near the surface. In all materials, porosity decreases with depth because the great pressure exerted by the soil and rock overburden tends to close the voids. Porosity can be as high as 45 percent in some near-surface bedrock, but it is rarely higher than 2 to 3 percent at depths exceeding 2000 m.

causing an unacceptable decline in its overall water level) and on the quality of its water. With respect to water quality, highly mineralized water, such as saltwater, is not generally usable for agriculture and municipal purposes, and aquifers containing such water are usually not counted among an area's groundwater resources.

Aquifer materials   Aquifers form in two types of materials: *consolidated* (mainly bedrock) and *unconsolidated* (mainly surface deposits) (Fig. 7.3). In the central part of North America, where glacial deposits lie over sedimentary bedrock, aquifers are found in both the bedrock and the surface deposits. Owing, however, to the extreme diversity of glacial deposits in many areas, aquifers in this class tend to vary greatly in size, depth, and water supply. Bedrock aquifers tend to be more extensive, often covering hundreds of square miles in area.

In large river lowlands, such as the Mississippi and Missouri valleys, extensive shallow aquifers (at depths less than 100 meters) are formed in the river deposits. These aquifers are recharged (i.e., replenished) by river water, and their supplies fluctuate with the seasonal changes in riverflow. In addition, they are distinctive for their geographical distributions as they tend to form ribbons following the floors of river valleys.

In the American West, aquifers are found in both deposits and bedrock, but large areas are without aquifers that will yield more than small flows, say, less than 50 gallons

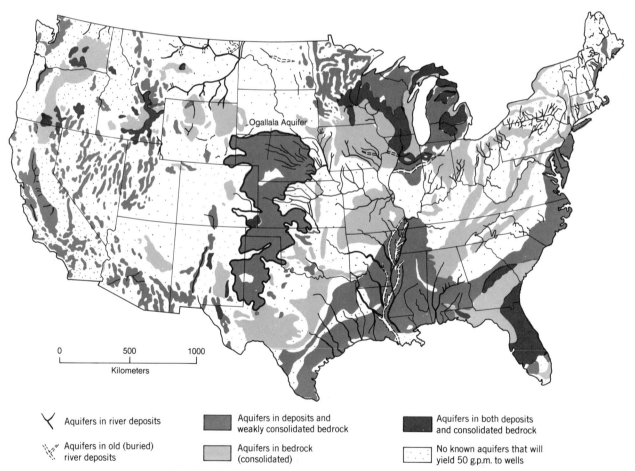

Y Aquifers in river deposits

Aquifers in old (buried) river deposits

Aquifers in deposits and weakly consolidated bedrock

Aquifers in bedrock (consolidated)

Aquifers in both deposits and consolidated bedrock

No known aquifers that will yield 50 g.p.m. to wells

Fig. 7.3 Distribution of major aquifers in the coterminous United States. A major aquifer is defined as one composed of material capable of yielding 50 gallons per minute or more to an individual well and having water quality generally not containing more than 2000 parts per million of dissolved solids.

of water per minute. In addition, many aquifers in the diverse mountainous terrain of western North America are localized in scale because they are formed in deposits associated with individual mountain slopes and intervening basins (Fig. 7.3).

Groundwater basin   A group of aquifers linked together in a large flow system is called a **groundwater basin.** Groundwater basins are typically complex three-dimensional systems characterized by vertical and horizontal flows among the various groundwater bodies—both those that would qualify as aquifers and those that would not—and between groundwater bodies and the surface (Fig. 7.4).

The spatial configuration of a groundwater basin is determined largely by regional geology, that is, by the extent and structure of the deposits and rock formations that house the groundwater bodies. Because these deposits and formations usually differ vastly in their size, composition, and shape, exactly how the various bodies of groundwater in a basin are linked together at different depths is seldom clear. This uncertainty is significant not only in planning for water supplies, but also in understanding the spread of contaminants from among aquifers.

7.3 THE GROUNDWATER FLOW SYSTEM

If we were to map the elevations of aquifers, we would find that essentially all bodies of groundwater are inclined (tilted) to some degree. This can be verified for most shallow aquifers by tracing the elevation of the water table across the landscape: the water table rises and falls with surface topography. In deeper aquifers groundwater commonly slopes with the dip of rock formations. The rate of change in elevation across an aquifer *Hydraulic gradient*   or segment of the water table is termed the **hydraulic gradient**, and it is calculated in the same fashion as topographic slope.

The flow of groundwater is driven by gravity along the hydraulic gradient. For a given material, the steeper the hydraulic gradient, the faster the rate of flow. To determine the flow velocity of groundwater, it is necessary to know not only the hydraulic gradient, but also the resistance imposed on the water by the material it is moving through. *Resistance* is a function of permeability which is determined by the

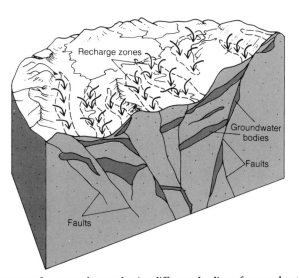

Fig. 7.4 The concept of a groundwater basin: different bodies of groundwater fed by one or more recharge areas within a common geological setting.

Velocity

size and interconnectedness of void spaces. For clays permeability is low; for sands and gravels, it is high. The basic formula for groundwater **velocity,** known as Darcy's Law, is

$$V = I \cdot k$$

where V is velocity, I is hydraulic gradient, and k is permeability.

Compared to the flow velocities of surface water, groundwater is extremely slow. Typical velocities for large aquifers are only 15 to 20 meters (50 feet to 65 feet) per year. The time it takes water to pass through an aquifer, which is called *residence time* or *exchange time,* measures in decades and centuries. In the case of a typical aquifer 5 kilometers or so in diameter, for example, residence time could be between 250 and 350 years. This has serious implications for groundwater management because the time required for nature to flush contaminants from polluted aquifers is inconveniently long by human standards.

Recharge

Recharge is the term given to gravity water supplied to a body of groundwater from surface sources, such as soil, wetlands, and lakes. Although some aquifers, especially shallow ones, receive recharge water from a broad (nonspecific) surface area, many aquifers are recharged from specific areas, called *recharge zones.* These zones may be places where (1) surface water accumulates such as in a wetland or a topographic depression, (2) where there is highly permeable soil or rock formation at the surface, or (3) where an aquifer is exposed at or near the surface (Fig. 7.5). In all cases, recharge zones are critical to aquifer management because they are the points of most ready access for contaminants from land use activity.

When recharge water enters the aquifer, its continued movement depends on the permeability of the material it encounters and the aquifer's hydraulic gradient. If an aquifer receives rapid recharge, but the material is of low permeability (i.e., high

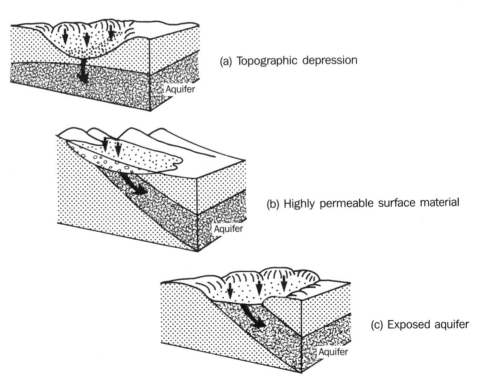

Fig. 7.5 Three types of recharge areas: (1) a topographic depression such as a wetland; (2) a highly permeable surface material such as an alluvial fan or talus slope; and (3) an exposed area of aquifer such as near an escarpment.

resistance), the new groundwater tends to build up. As a result, the hydraulic gradient steepens, but as it does, so does flow velocity, according to Darcy's Law. Under such conditions the hydraulic gradient will continue to rise until the rate of lateral flow, or *transmission,* is equal to the rate of recharge. Where recharge is low and permeability is high, on the other hand, the hydraulic gradient will fall until the rates of transmission and recharge are equal.

Recharge rates   In general, shallow aquifers have a capacity to recharge much faster than deeper ones. Although average **recharge rates** decrease more or less progressively with depth, as a whole aquifers within 1000 meters of the surface require several hundred years (300-year average) to be completely renewed, whereas those at depths greater than 1000 meters require several thousand years (4600-year average) for complete renewal. This difference is related not only to the distance recharge water must travel, but also to the fact that percolating water moves slower in the smaller spaces found at great depths.

Although large quantities of groundwater remain in some aquifers for thousands of years, most water remains underground for periods ranging from several years to several centuries. Aside from pumping, groundwater is released to the surface mainly through (1) *capillary rise* into the soil from which it is evaporated or taken up by plants; and (2) *seepage* to streams, lakes, and wetlands from which it runs off and/or evaporates.

Many different geologic and topographic conditions can produce seepage. In mountainous areas, for example, it can be traced to fault lines and outcrops of tilted formations (Fig. 7.6). In areas where bedrock is buried under deep deposits of soil, *Groundwater seepage*   **groundwater seepage** is usually found along the lower parts of slopes. Steep slopes represent "breaks" in elevation that may be too abrupt to produce a corresponding elevation change in the water table. Under such conditions, the water table may intercept the surface, especially in humid regions where the water table is high. If the resultant seepage is modest, a spring is formed, but if it is strong, a lake, wetland, or stream may be formed. *Seepage zones,* also called *discharge areas,* are ecologically significant in any geographic setting because they provide dependable water supplies and temperate thermal conditions.

Which type of water feature develops from groundwater seepage depends on a host of conditions, including the rate of seepage, the size of the depression, and the rate of water loss to runoff and evaporation. Most of the thousands of inland lakes of *Seepage lakes*   Minnesota, Wisconsin, Michigan, and Ontario, for example, are **"seepage"-type lakes** whose water levels fluctuate with the seasonal changes in the elevation of the water table. Most of these lakes are connected to wetlands or over thousands of years evolve into wetlands as they are filled in with organic debris.

7.4 GROUNDWATER WITHDRAWAL AND AQUIFER IMPACT

Groundwater is used for drinking, agriculture, and industry in every part of North America. In rural areas, it provides more than 95 percent of the drinking water and about 70 percent of the water used in farming. Between 25 and 50 percent of the communities in the United States and Canada depend on groundwater for public water supplies.

Water supply   The best aquifers for **water supply** are those containing vast amounts of pure water that can be easily withdrawn without causing an unacceptable decline in the head (elevation) of the aquifer. Two conditions must exist if an aquifer is to yield a dependable supply of water over many years. First, the rate of withdrawal must not exceed the transmissibility of the aquifer. Otherwise, the water is pumped out faster than it can be supplied to the well, and the safe well yield will soon be exceeded. *Safe*

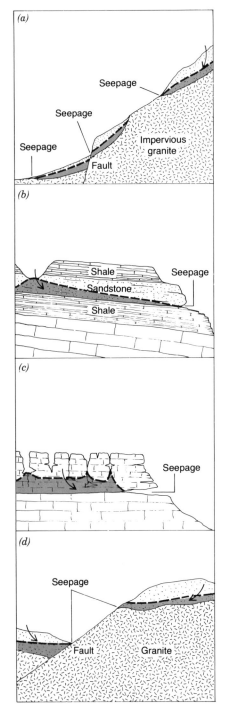

Fig. 7.6 Seepage zones associated with physiographic settings: (a) unconsolidated sediments over impervious bedrock; (b) inclined sandstone over shale; (c) cavernous limestone over unweathered limestone; (d) unconsolidated materials broken by a fault.

well yield is defined as the maximum pumping rate that can be sustained by a well without lowering the water level below the pump intake. Second, the rate of total withdrawal should not outrun the aquifer's recharge rate, or else the water level in the aquifer will fall. When an aquifer declines significantly, the *safe aquifer yield* has usually been exceeded, and if the *overdraft* is sustained for many years, the aquifer will be depleted.

In arid and semiarid regions where groundwater is pumped for irrigation, the safe aquifer yield is typically exceeded and often greatly exceeded. In the American West, many aquifers took on huge quantities of water during and after the Ice Age several thousand years ago; today these reserves are being withdrawn at rates far exceeding present recharge rates. Unless pumping rates are adjusted to recharge rates, the water level will decline, wells will have to be extended deeper and deeper, and these aquifers will eventually be depleted.

Aquifer decline   In parts of Arizona, the water level in some aquifers is declining as much as 6 meters a year because of heavy pumping for agriculture and urban uses. In the Great Plains the Ogallala Aquifer, which stretches from Nebraska to Texas and is one of the largest groundwater reservoirs in the world, is declining at a rate of 0.15 to 1.0 meter per year because of heavy irrigation withdrawals (Fig. 7.3). With the current shifts in the U.S. population to the Southwest, it appears that demands on these dwindling groundwater reserves will be even greater in the next several decades. At the same time, demands may decline somewhat in the water-rich Midwest and Northwest of the United States as portions of these regions lose population.

In and around urbanized areas (or agricultural areas with high concentrations of large wells), the groundwater level in aquifers may not only be greatly depressed by heavy pumping but also develop a very uneven upper surface. This happens where a high rate of pumping from an individual well is maintained for an extended period of time, causing the level of groundwater around the well to be drawn down by many meters or tens of meters. The groundwater surface takes on a funnel shape, as on the *Cone of depression*   water surface above an open drain in a bathtub, and is called a **cone of depression.**

As the cone of depression deepens with pumping, the hydraulic gradient increases, causing faster groundwater flow toward the well. If the rate of pumping is not highly variable, the cone usually stabilizes in time. However, if many wells are clustered together, as is often the case in urbanized areas, they may produce an overall lowering of the water table as the tops of neighboring cones intersect each other as they widen with drawdown. If the wells are of variable depths, this may result in a loss of water to shallow wells as the cones of big, deep wells are drawn beyond the shallower pumping depths.

Drawdown of groundwater over a large area can also lead to loss of volume in the *Ground subsidence*   groundwater-bearing materials. This may result in **subsidence** in the overlying ground, as it has in Houston, Texas, for example, where much of the metropolitan area has subsided a meter or more with groundwater depletion. In addition, cones of depression can accelerate the migration of contaminated water because they increase hydraulic gradients and transmission velocities. In coastal areas, groundwater drawdown may also lead to the intrusion of salt groundwater beneath the mass of fresh groundwater.

7.5 SOURCES OF GROUNDWATER CONTAMINATION

The sources of groundwater contamination are very widespread in the modern landscape. They include all major land uses; industrial, residential, agricultural, and transportational. Planning for groundwater protection, therefore, is not limited to urban and industrial landfills, as is widely thought, but includes agricultural, mining, residential, highway, and railroad activities as well. The level of concern or precaution, however, is not everywhere equal because (1) groundwater susceptibility to contamination varies widely from place to place, (2) the contaminant loading rate varies with land use type and practices (such as in pesticide applications with different farming methods), and (3) the contaminants released to the environment vary in their harmfulness to humans and other organisms.

Major contaminant sources   The following are the six major classes of groundwater **contamination sources:**

■ *Landfills:* Buried wastes, both solid and hazardous, which discharge contaminated liquids called *leachate* (also see Section 5.7). The composition of leachate varies with composition of the landfill. For urban landfills made up of residential garbage, the leachate may be heavy in organic compounds such as methane and benzene; for agricultural wastes, the leachate may be heavy in nutrients such as phosphorus and nitrogen as well as organic compounds; and for industrial wastes it is commonly heavy in trace elements, that is, metals such as lead, chromium, zinc, and iron, as well as a host of other contaminants including organic compounds, petroleum products, and radioactive materials.

■ *Farmlands*: Agricultural fertilizers and pesticides which are carried by soil water and gravity water to aquifers. Fertilizers are composed principally of nitrogen and phosphorus. Nitrogen, which is the most mobile of the two in soil and groundwater, commonly shows up in aquifers and poses a serious health problem in water supplies. Pesticides are heavy in organic compounds, mostly synthetic compounds such as diazinon, fluorene, benzene, and chloroform.

■ *Urban stormwater*: Runoff from developed areas, especially streets, parking lots, industrial and residential surfaces, is normally rich in a wide variety of contaminants. Most stormwater is discharged into streams, but a significant share of it goes directly into the soil (Fig. 7.7). Although concentrations of most contaminants are reduced by soil filtration, an appreciable load may also be transported through to the groundwater zone. This includes metals (e.g., lead, zinc, and iron), organic compounds (mainly insecticides such as diazinon and malathion), petroleum residues, nitrates, and road salt.

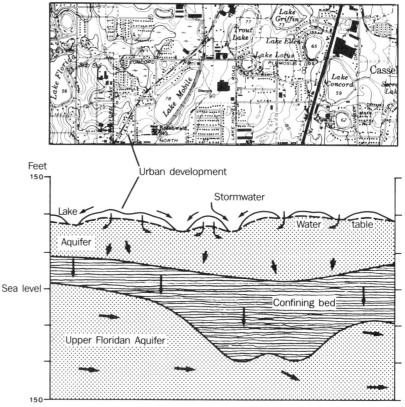

Fig. 7.7 The relationship of the water table aquifer to surface drainage in the urbanized area around Orlando, Florida.

■ *Drainfields*: Release of sewage effluent water into the soil through seepage beds. The sewage is produced by household drainfields or community drainfields and when fed to the ground, large amounts of nitrogen, sodium, and chlorinated organic compounds may be discharged into groundwater.

■ *Mining*: Mineral extraction and related operations, such as refinement, storage, and waste disposal, yield a variety of contaminants to surface and groundwater. Some operations are especially harmful, such as certain gold mining operations which employ a leaching technique based on the application of cyanide to crushed rock. In most operations, such as coal, iron ore, and phosphate, contaminants are discharged in leachate from decomposing waste rock.

■ *Spills and Leakage*: Here the possibilities seem endless. Spills made up of petroleum products, various organic compounds, fertilizers, metals, and acids are most common along highways, railroads, and in and around industrial complexes. Leakage from underground storage tanks (of which there are more than 10 million in the United States and Canada), pipelines, and chemical stock piles are also widespread. Residential land uses also contribute: paint, cleaning compounds, car oil, and gasoline, for example. Spills are typically point sources, and where they are associated with a known accident, remedial measures can be applied. However, underground leakages are usually hidden and may go undetected for years.

7.6 APPLICATIONS TO LANDSCAPE PLANNING

Unlike surface water which we can see, measure, and map with comparative ease, groundwater is far more elusive as an environmental planning problem. Among other things, it occupies complex three-dimensional space, with different aquifers and processes operating at different levels. Not surprisingly, it is difficult to determine just how a land use at some location will relate to this vast underground environment. Thus we approach landscape planning for groundwater protection more or less as a probability problem, that is, by estimating the *likelihood* of a land use's impact on groundwater given different locations, layouts, densities, and management arrangements.

Contaminant production sources

In the case of proposals for new land uses, planning for groundwater protection begins with an understanding of the potential for contaminant production. Among the land uses of special concern are *industrial facilities,* including manufacturing installations, fuel and chemical storage facilities, railroad yards, and energy plants; *urban complexes,* including highway systems, landfills, utility lines, sewage treatment plants, and automotive repair facilities; *agricultural operations,* including cropland, feedlots, chemical storage facilities, and processing plants. Land uses of less concern are single-family residential, institutions such as schools and churches, commercial facilities (excluding those with large parking lots), and parks and open space.

Site evaluation

Once the potential for contaminant production is established, the next step is to assess proposed sites for groundwater susceptibility to pollution. This entails learning about aquifer depths and linkage to the surface as well as significance as drinking water sources. Information on water use and well location is usually obtainable from local or state health departments. Most states require that a log be registered with the health department for residential wells which identifies the materials penetrated and the finished depth of the well. In some cases the results of a water quality test may also be on record.

A key question in projects involving land uses with high contaminant production potential is the location of recharge zones. Generally, recharge zones are to be avoided, especially those that feed shallow aquifers (Fig. 7.8). Another important question is the

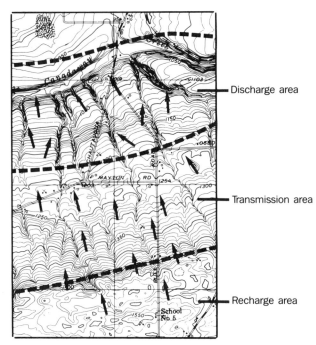

Discharge area

Transmission area

Recharge area

Fig. 7.8   A recharge area upslope from residental wells. Recharge takes place through the small water features at the top of the slope. Such recharge zones are common in glaciated and other landscapes.

permeability of surface materials because permeability controls the rate at which contaminated water and leachate from spills infiltrates the ground.

The shallowest of aquifers is the water table aquifer. It may lie only several meters underground, making it especially prone to contamination. While it is not widely used as a source of drinking water (because health codes usually require wells to be greater than 25 feet deep), the water table aquifer is an important source of water for streams, ponds, and lakes. Pollution plumes can contaminate seepage water discharging into these water features, particularly where they lie within 1000 feet of a pollution source.

Checklist for site evaluation

The planner's **checklist** for assessing the likelihood of groundwater contamination from a proposed land use should include the following (also see Table 7.1):

■   What is the contaminant production potential and the related risks in handling and storing hazardous waste?

■   Does the site lie over an aquifer which (a) presently serves as a source of drinking water; (b) could serve as a future source of drinking water; (c) feeds streams, lakes, and ponds?

■   Is the aquifer of concern a deep or shallow aquifer and is the surface dominated by permeable material such as sand and gravel? Similarly, is the aquifer protected by a confining material, that is, a layer of impervious rock or soil material that limits penetration from sources directly above it?

■   What part of the aquifer system is the site associated with: recharge, transmission, withdrawal, or discharge (seepage)?

■   What is the direction of flow in the aquifer: toward or away from areas of concern? (This is often indicated on groundwater maps by a measure called the potentiometric surface which is an indicator of the overall slope of the aquifer based on readings of well water levels.)

■   Will the proposed facilities fall into direct contact with groundwater because of deep footings, foundation work, underground utilities, and/or tunneling?

Table 7.1 Suggested Criteria in Land Use Planning for Groundwater Protection

Criteria	Desirability	
	Worst	*Best*
Contaminant production	High	None
Handling and storage risk	High (e.g., nonsecured storage areas with open soil)	Low
Aquifer use	Drinking water (many wells within a radius of 1000– 1500 ft)	None
Aquifer depth	Shallow (less than 200 ft)	Deep (greater than 1000 ft.)
Overlying material	Highly permeable (e.g., sands and gravels)	Impermeable (e.g., clayey soil and confining layer)
Aquifer system	Recharge zone	Beyond discharge (seepage) areas
Flow direction	Toward wells	Away from wells

Evaluating existing facilities

For land uses already in place, the problem is to build a management plan to minimize the risk of groundwater contamination. The plan should address the three phases of the system leading to contamination: (1) *production* of contaminants, (2) *removal* from the production and/or disposal site, and (3) *diffusion* into aquifers (Fig. 7.9). Planning for contaminant management and groundwater protection carries the least risk when it is applied early in the system, in the production phase. Basically,

Basic strategies

three **strategies** can be employed to lower risk connected with production: reduce output rates, change technology to less dangerous contaminants, and reduce the risk of accidental spills.

At the removal phase, the objective is to limit the escape of contaminants from the site. The conventional strategy here is safely to contain the contaminants during storage, transportation, and disposal. The U.S. Environmental Protection Agency recommends various methods, including secure landfills of containerized waste. Soil

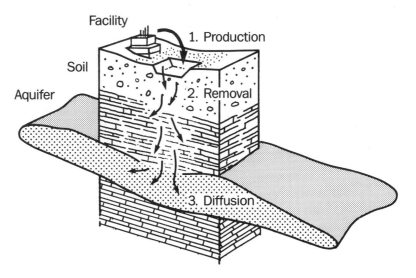

Fig. 7.9 The three-phase system associated with groundwater management: (1) on-site production, (2) removal from the production of disposal site, and (3) diffusion into the aquifer.

conditions are extremely important inasmuch as compact clayey soils retard the advance of leachates because of their low permeabilities, whereas sandy soils allow the advance of leachates because of high permeabilities.

By the time fugitive contaminants have reached the diffusion phase, the likelihood of impact on aquifers and human water supplies has risen dramatically. However, the concentrations and chemical composition of the leachate may attenuate in passage as a result of filtration, adsorption, oxidation, and biological decay. Once the contaminants have invaded an aquifer, preventive measures are no longer feasible and the only options left are (1) corrective pumping (heavy pumping to direct the plume away from wells) or (2) abandonment of vulnerable wells. Again, planning efforts for groundwater protection should be focused early in the system, at the production and site removal phases. Once contaminants escape the site, the environmental risk, technological difficulty of recovery, and recovery expense increase dramatically.

7.7 CASE STUDY

On the Use of Lineaments in Groundwater Planning, Central Texas

Charles Woodruff, Jr.

What sorts of natural features should we look for in the landscape when planning for local groundwater protection? Are there visible indicators in the surface environment that can tell us something about the location and function of the water system underground and how we in turn should begin to arrange land uses to protect this system? To a great extent the answer depends on where you are located. In many places, such as parts of the U.S. Coastal Plain, there is scarcely a clue to provide even the keenest observer and analyst about what may lie undergound. In some places the only clues are variations in slope and soil type by virtue of their general relationship to groundwater recharge and discharge areas. In central Texas, an area of rugged plateaus that have been fractured by faulting, features called lineaments are important surface indicators of the groundwater system.

Lineaments are straight features in the landscape marked by tonal changes in soils, discontinuities in the type or quality of vegetation, breaks in slope, and straight segments of stream channels. They are the surface expressions of undergound fractures in the bedrock, which link the landscape to the groundwater system below. In particular, fractures are a key determinant of the porosity and permeability of bedrock, and as such they exercise a profound influence on the storage and movement of groundwater.

Because of these correlations, lineaments can be helpful in planning and managing the landscape for groundwater protection, inasmuch as they offer a way of ascertaining, among other things, where surface water enters the groundwater system. In addition, they provide a means for understanding groundwater flow patterns. Lineament surveys are especially useful in limestone terrains, owing to the solubility of limestone in water. As water circulates through the fractures in the limestone strata, it enlarges the fractures into sizable conduits. The enlarged conduits channel yet more water, which in turn, dissolves more of the limestone, further enlarging and extending the fracture system.

Lineaments may be used in several ways to assess groundwater regimes in areas such as central Texas. A map showing lineament density can be used to evaluate the geographic variations in the fracture porosity of bedrock. A complementary map is one showing the density of lineament intersections. Both maps can be translated into a statistical surface defining an aggregate population of lineaments within an imposed grid. From the statistical surface, an isometric (contour) map showing relative lineament/intersection density can be constructed which may be used to define relative recharge potential over a prescribed area.

Entry Points for
Surface Water

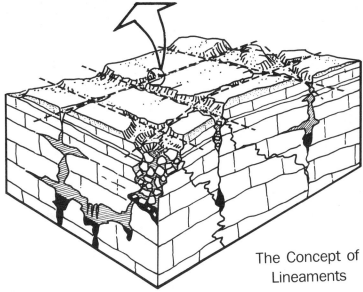

The Concept of
Lineaments

Areas of high fracture porosity pose problems with locating waste disposal facilities or stormwater detention ponds. Because of the potential ease of entry of contaminated water and leachate into rock of high fracture porosity, areas with high lineament density should be avoided in land use planning and site management. Conversely, zones of high lineament density might be used to locate areas suitable for induced recharge. A proposed development might, for example, filter its stormwater and then route the clarified water to a secondary pond located over an area of high lineament density. In addition to the obvious benefit of groundwater recharge, stormwater loading of local streams would be reduced. In some circumstances in central Texas, this induced recharge can be directed to a disjunct part of an aquifer with a limited groundwater reserve to feed springs and streams. In this way, the recharged water could perform an ecological function by supplying headwater seeps and springs in nearby stream valleys that would otherwise dry up in the summer.

Another statistical attribute that lends information to land use planning for groundwater protection is the directional orientation of lineaments. Expressed in the form of a histogram showing the frequency of compass bearings, the overall directional trends of lineament complexes can be defined. This in turn helps identify the directions of local groundwater flow, thereby revealing the spatial associations between different parts of the landscape. This is meaning-

Lineament patterns
(in white)

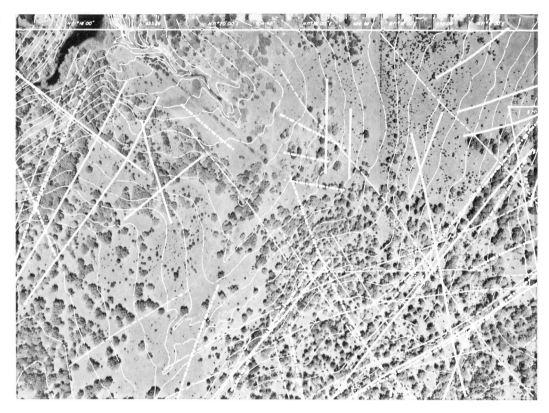

ful in evaluating the potential impact of groundwater withdrawal or contamination on users lower in the flow system.

In mapping lineaments, we must be cognizant of the scale limitations of various maps and imagery. Curiously, the patterns of lineaments change—and often drastically—at different scales of observation. Nonetheless, all scales appear to provide useful information for planning problems at the corresponding scale. At the regional scale, satellite and high-altitude aerial imagery reveal lineament patterns corresponding to gross structural (geologic) trends meaningful to deep groundwater aquifers. At intermediate scales, aerial photographs and standard topographic maps provide areawide data on lineaments and groundwater supplies related to local structural and geomorphic controls. Large-scale aerial photography and topographic maps provide the most detailed picture of lineaments, revealing the site-specific grain of the shallow groundwater system.

Charles Woodruff, Jr., is a consulting geologist in Austin, Texas, who specializes in hydrogeologic problems. ■

7.8 SELECTED REFERENCES FOR FURTHER READING

Butler, Kent S. "Managing Growth and Groundwater Quality in the Edwards Aquifer Area, Austin, Texas." *Public Affairs Comment* 29:2, 1983, 10 pp.

DiNovo, Frank, and Jaffe, Martin. *Local Groundwater Protection: Midwest Region.* Washington, D.C.: American Planning Association, 1984, 327 pp.

Josephson, Julian. "Groundwater Strategies." *Environmental Science and Technology* 14:9, 1980, pp. 1030–1035.

National Research Council. *Groundwater Contamination: Studies in Geophysics.* Washington, D.C.: National Academy Press, 1984, 189 pp.

Page, G. W. *Planning for Groundwater Protection.* New York: Academic Press, 1987, 387 pp.

Pye, V. I., Patrick, Ruth, and Quarles, John. *Groundwater Contamination in the United States.* Philadelphia: University of Pennsylvania Press, 1983, 314 pp.

Rutledge, A. T. "Effects of Land Use on Ground-water Quality in Central Florida—Preliminary Results: U.S. Geological Survey Toxic Waste—Ground-Water Contamination Program." *Water-Resources Investigations Report 86–4163,* Washington, D.C., U.S. Government Printing Office, 1987, 49 pp.

Tripp, J. T. B., and Jaffe, A. B. "Preventing Groundwater Pollution: Towards a Coordinated Strategy to Protect Critical Recharge Zones." *Harvard Environmental Law Review* 3:1, 1979, pp. 1–47.

U.S. Council on Environmental Quality. *Contamination of Groundwater by Toxic Organic Chemicals.* Washington, D.C.: U.S. Government Printing Office, 1981, 84 pp.

8

STORMWATER DISCHARGE AND LANDSCAPE CHANGE

8.1 INTRODUCTION

One of the most serious problems associated with land development is the change in the rate and amount of runoff reaching streams and rivers. Both urbanization and agricultural development effect an increase in overland flow, resulting in greater magnitudes and frequencies of peak flows on streams. The impacts of this change are serious, both financially and environmentally: property damage from flooding is increased, water quality is reduced, channel erosion is accelerated, and habitat is degraded.

Responsible planning and management of the landscape depend on accurate assessment of the changes in runoff brought on by land development. In the United States and parts of Canada this problem has reached epidemic proportions, and in most communities developers are now required to provide analytical forecasts of the changes in overland flow and stream discharge resulting from a proposed development. Such forecasts are used not only as the basis for recommending alternatives to traditional stormwater systems in order to reduce environmental impact, but also for evaluating the performance of an entire watershed that is subject to many development proposals.

8.2 OVERLAND FLOW

Disposition of rainfall   Most precipitation reaching the ground is disposed of in three ways. Some is absorbed directly by the soil in a process known as *infiltration*. Some, called *depression storage*, collects on the ground in small hollows and pockets (Fig. 8.1a). The remainder, called *overland flow*, runs off the surface, eventually joining streams and rivers. The percentage of precipitation going to overland flow varies drastically in the modern landscape. In heavily vegetated terrain, infiltration appears to be so high that overland flow is practically negligible; instead, streams gain their discharge from groundwater, interflow, and channel precipitation. In dry areas and areas where forest and groundcover have been cleared and replaced by agriculture, settlements, and related land uses, overland flow is, by contrast, substantial (Fig. 8.1b).

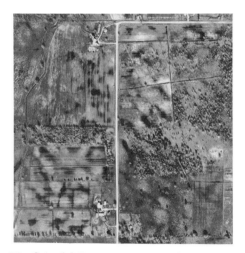

Fig. 8.1   (a) Depression storage (dark spots) in a rural landscape. This water is withheld from overland flow. (b) The corresponding scene after development. Not only has depression storage been obliterated, but much of the ground is covered with hard surface materials.

Influences on overland flow

If we examine the ground to determine what factors control overland flow, we will find that land cover (vegetation and land use), soil type, and surface inclination (slope) are the chief controls. Figure 8.2 illustrates the relationship among overland flow, soil, and vegetative cover on a hillslope. As a general rule, overland flow increases with slope, decreases with soil organic content and particle size, increases with ground coverage by hard surface material such as concrete and asphalt, and decreases with vegetative cover.

Coefficient of runoff

For a particular combination of these factors, a **coefficient of runoff** can be assigned to a surface. This is a dimensionless number between 0 and 1.0 that represents the proportion of a rainfall available for overland flow after infiltration has occurred. A coefficient of 0.60, for example, means that 60 percent of rainfall (or snowmelt) is

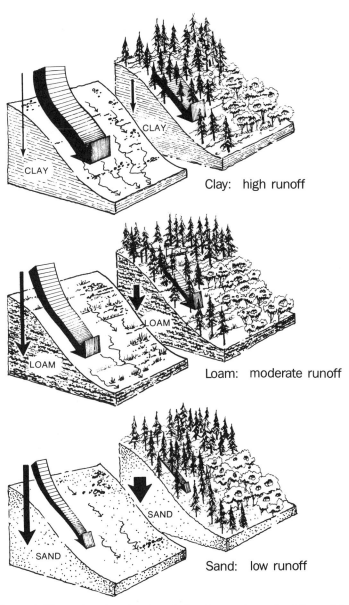

Clay: high runoff

Loam: moderate runoff

Sand: low runoff

Fig. 8.2 Schematic illustration showing the relative changes in overland flow with soil type and vegetation.

Table 8.1   Coefficients of Runoff for Rural Areas

Topography and Vegetation	Open Sandy Loam	Clay and Silt Loam	Tight Clay
Woodland			
Flat (0–5% slope)	0.10	0.30	0.40
Rolling (5–10% slope)	0.25	0.35	0.50
Hilly (10–30% slope)	0.30	0.50	0.60
Pasture			
Flat	0.10	0.30	0.40
Rolling	0.16	0.36	0.55
Hilly	0.22	0.42	0.60
Cultivated			
Flat	0.30	0.50	0.60
Rolling	0.40	0.60	0.70
Hilly	0.52	0.72	0.82

available for overland flow, whereas 40 percent was lost to infiltration.[1] Table 8.1 lists some standard coefficients of runoff for rural areas based on slope, vegetation, and soil texture. For urban areas, coefficients are mainly a function of the hard surface cover, and a number of values are given in Table 8.2.

8.3 COMPUTING RUNOFF FROM A SMALL WATERSHED

Rational method

The runoff generated from a small watershed (usually less than 1000 acres in area) can be computed by means of a simple manipulation called the **rational method.** This method is based on a formula that combines the coefficient of runoff with the intensity

Table 8.2   Coefficients of Runoff for Selected Urban Areas

Commercial:	
Downtown	0.70–0.95
Shopping centers	0.70–0.95
Residential:	
Single family (5–7 houses/ac)	0.35–0.50
Attached, multifamily	0.60–0.75
Suburban (1–4 houses/ac)	0.20–0.40
Industrial:	
Light	0.50–0.80
Heavy	0.60–0.90
Railroad yard	0.20–0.80
Parks, Cemetery	0.10–0.25
Playgrounds	0.20–0.40

[1] Actually, several factors contribute to the uptake of rain by the landscape, including interception by vegetation, depression storage, detention by surface objects, and evaporation. On rough surfaces, depression storage can take up 0.25 inches or more of a rainfall.

of rainfall and the area of the watershed. The outcome gives the peak streamflow (discharge) for one rainstorm at the mouth of the watershed:

$$Q = A \cdot C \cdot I$$

Where

Q = discharge in cubic feet per second
A = area in acres
C = coefficient of runoff
I = intensity of rainfall in feet/hour

Design storm

To use the rational method, it is necessary to generate some essential data. Besides the obvious need to measure the area of the watershed and determine the correct coefficient of runoff, we must select an appropriate rainfall intensity value. Obviously, a wide variety of rainstorms deliver water to the watershed, and one storm which is likely to produce significant runoff, called the **design storm,** has to be selected in order to perform the computation. The design storm is defined according to local rainfall records for intensive storms of short duration (usually 1 hour), which occur, for example, on the average of once every 10 years, 25 years, or 100 years. These storms are called, respectively, the 10-year, 25-year, and 100-year storms of 1-hour duration. Which storm should be used usually depends on the recommendation of the local agency responsible for stormwater management. Figure 8.3 gives the values over the coterminous United States and the southern fringe of Canada for the 10-year, 1-hour storm. For more accurate values based on local records, local agencies should be consulted.

Once the desired storm has been selected, a second step must be taken to arrive at the actual value to be used in making the discharge computation. This step is based on two facts: (1) within the period of a rainstorm, say, 60 minutes, the actual intensity of

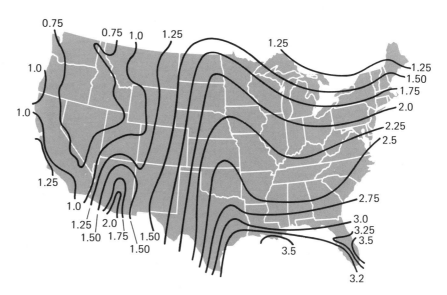

Fig. 8.3 The amount of rainfall that can be expected in the 10-year storm of 1 hour duration.

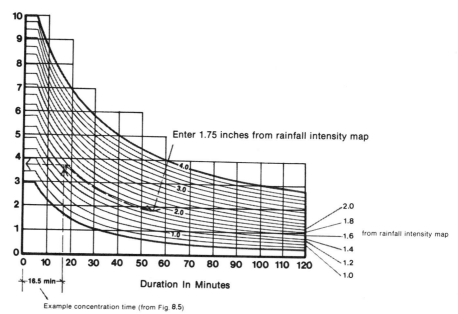

Rainfall Intensity
In Inches Per Hour

Enter 1.75 inches from rainfall intensity map

from rainfall intensity map

Duration In Minutes

16.5 min

Example concentration time (from Fig. 8.5)

Fig. 8.4 Rainfall intensity curves. To use the graph, first find the desired rainfall value among the curves, then find the appropriate concentration time on the base of the graph. The rainfall intensity value is read from the intersection of the two on the left vertical scale as shown in the example.

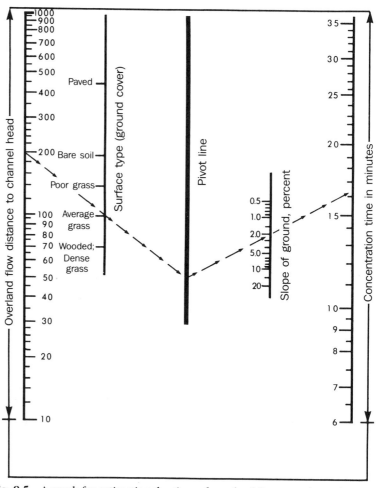

Fig. 8.5 A graph for estimating the time of overland flow to a channel or inlet.

Table 8.3 Overland Flow Velocities

Distance to Channel Head	Pavement	Turf	Barren	Residential
Around 100 ft.	0.33 ft/sec	0.20 ft/sec	0.26 ft/sec	0.25–0.33 ft/sec
Around 500 ft.	0.82 ft/sec	0.25 ft/sec	0.54 ft/sec	0.50–0.65 ft/sec

Concentration time

rainfall initially rises, hits a peak, and then tapers off; and (2) the time taken for runoff to move from the perimeter to the mouth of the watershed, called the **concentration time,** varies with the size and conditions of the watershed. Combining these two facts, we can see that in a small watershed the concentration time may be less than the duration of the storm. Therefore, in order to accurately compute the peak discharge for the storm in question, we must use the value of rainfall intensity that corresponds to the time of concentration. The graph in Fig. 8.4 gives representative curves for various storms and shows how to use the graph based on an example storm intensity of 1.75 inches per hour and a concentration time of 16.5 minutes.

Reliable estimates of the concentration time are clearly important in computing the discharges from small watersheds. The approach to this problem generally involves making separate estimates for (1) the time of overland flow; and (2) the time of channel flow, and then summing the two. The graph in Fig. 8.5 can be used to estimate the time of overland flow if three things are known: (1) the length of the path (slope) from the outer edge of the watershed to the head of channel flow; (2) the predominant groundcover; and (3) the average slope of the ground to the head of channel flow. If these are not known, we must resort to an approximation based on representative overland flow velocities (Table 8.3).

The velocity of channel flow is generally much greater than that of overland flow, and if the slope, roughness, and geometry of the channel are known, velocity can be computed using the Manning formula:

$$v = 1.49 \frac{R^{2/3}s^{1/2}}{n}$$

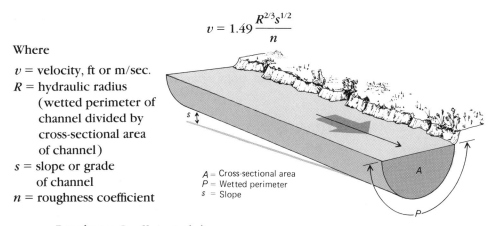

Where

v = velocity, ft or m/sec.
R = hydraulic radius (wetted perimeter of channel divided by cross-sectional area of channel)
s = slope or grade of channel
n = roughness coefficient

A = Cross-sectional area
P = Wetted perimeter
s = Slope

Roughness Coefficients (n)

Natural stream channel	
Gravel bottom with cobbles and boulders	0.040–0.050
Cobble bottom with boulders	0.050–0.070
Unlined open channel, soil bottom	0.020–0.025
Grassy swale, 12-inch grass	0.090–0.180
Overland flow surface	
Compact clay	0.030
Dense sod or shrubs	0.035–0.040

8.4 USING THE RATIONAL METHOD

As a forecasting device, the rational method is suited best not only to watersheds that are small, but also to those that are partially or fully developed. Beyond that, the reliability of the method depends on the accuracy of the values used for the coefficient of runoff, the concentration time, the drainage area, and the rainstorm intensity. With the exception of the latter, the necessary data may be generated through field observations and surveys or from secondary sources, in particular, topographic maps, soils maps, and aerial photographs.

Computational procedure

Given that the pertinent data are in hand, the following **procedure** may be used to compute the discharge resulting from a specified rainstorm. Steps 1 through 7 apply to peak discharge and step 8 to total discharge.

1. Define the perimeter of the watershed and measure the watershed area.

2. Subdivide the watershed according to cover types, soils, and slopes. Assign a coefficient of runoff to each, and measure each subarea.

3. Determine the percentage of the watershed represented by each subarea and multiply this figure by the coefficient of runoff of each. This will give you a coefficient adjusted according to the size of the subarea.

4. Sum the adjusted coefficients to determine a coefficient of runoff for the watershed as a whole.

5. Determine the concentration time using the graph in Fig. 8.5 and the Manning formula.

6. Select a rainfall value for the location and rainstorm desired. Using this value and the concentration time, identify the appropriate rainfall intensity from the curves in Fig. 8.4.

7. Multiply the watershed area times the coefficient of runoff times the rainfall intensity value to obtain peak discharge in cubic feet per second. (Actually, the answer is in acre inches per hour; however, these units are so close to cubic feet per second that the two are interchangeable.)

8. The total amount of discharge produced as a result of a storm can also be computed with the rational formula except in this case the one-hour rainfall value is used, and we would solve for acre feet or cubic feet per hour.

8.5 TRENDS IN STORMWATER DISCHARGE

The clearing of land and the establishment of farms and settlements has been the dominant geographic change in the North American landscape in the past 200 years.

Flow magnitude and frequency

Almost invariably, this has led to an increase in both the amount and rate of overland flow, producing larger and more frequent peak flows in streams. With the massive urbanization of the twentieth century, this trend has become even stronger and has led to increased flooding and flood hazard, to say nothing of the damage to aquatic environments.

Sources of change

From a hydrologic standpoint, the source of the problem can be narrowed down to changes in two parameters: (1) the drastic increase in the coefficient of runoff in response to land clearing, deforestation, and the addition of impervious materials to the landscape (Fig. 8.6); and (2) the corresponding decrease in the concentration time (Fig. 8.7, upper diagram). In agricultural areas, this decrease is brought about by the construction of field drains and ditches as well as the straightening and deepening of stream channels. With urbanization, ditches are replaced with stormsewers, small

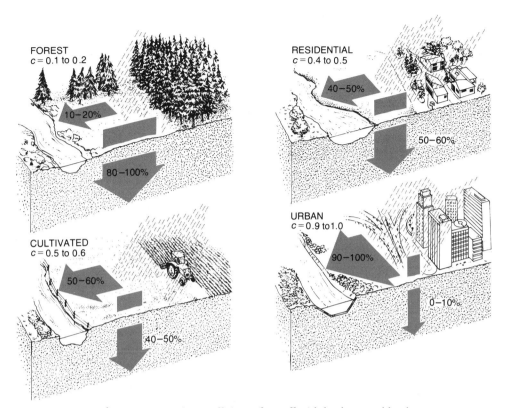

Fig. 8.6 Changes in the coefficient of runoff with land use and land cover.

streams are piped underground, and gutters are added to streets, all of which may reduce concentration times by more than tenfold. Together these changes produce a significant increase in the magnitude and frequency of peak discharges in receiving streams (Fig. 8.7, lower diagram). Changes in a third parameter, rainstorm intensity, may also contribute to discharge increases; storm magnitudes appear to be on the rise in metropolitan areas in the United States. At the present, however, it is difficult to generalize about this trend because it is apparent only in certain metropolitan areas, but most large urban areas appear to be affected.

8.6 STORMWATER MITIGATION

Community ordinances increasingly place stringent performance standards on developers, often calling for a zero net increase in stormwater discharge from a site as a result of development. This means that the rate of release across the border of a site can be no greater after development than before. A basic dilemma thus arises because most forms of development effect an increase in runoff, but at the same time themselves require relief from stormwater.

Mitigation strategies   Three **strategies** may be used to achieve management of stormwater: (1) store the excess water on or near the site, releasing it slowly over a long time; (2) return the excess water to the ground, where it would have gone before development; (3) plan the development such that runoff is not significantly increased. The first is the most common strategy. Its main objective is to reduce the rate of stormwater delivery to

Detention basins   streams, and it usually involves the construction of **detention basins** (Fig. 8.8a). These are ponds sized to store the design storm and then allow it to discharge at a

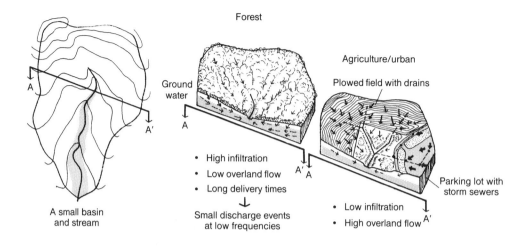

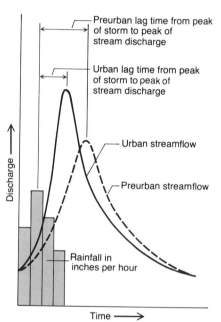

Fig. 8.7 Above, changes in the hydrology of a small watershed as a result of development. Below, the resultant change in stream discharge shown by a larger and quicker hydrograph after urbanization.

specified rate. For instance, if a design storm generates a total runoff of 4.2 acre feet (182,952 cubic feet) in one hour, and the allowable release rate is 12 cubic feet per second (43,200 cubic feet per hour), then about 3.2 acre feet of gross storage are needed. Basins that store water on a long-term basis are called *retention basins,* and they are generally used in areawide stormwater management.

The second strategy utilizes soil infiltration and is usually accomplished on-site. *On-site disposal* Stormwater is directed into vegetated areas, shallow depressions, troughs, or pits, from which it percolates into the ground (Fig. 8.8b). Since infiltration rates are slow relative to the rates of rainfall, this strategy is usually most effective for small storms or the water produced by the first part of large rainstorms. The lower diagram in Fig. 8.8 illustrates a concept based on depression storage in residential development. For a

0.25 acre lot (11,000 square feet), the entire volume of a 0.5 inch rainfall can be held in an area of 1400 square feet at a depth of 4 inches. In dry regions this method may prove to be an effective means of recharging local soil moisture supplies.

Cluster development

The third strategy reduces the need for corrective measures and relies on prudent site planning to resolve the stormwater problem. Strict attention is paid to surface materials, avoiding impervious materials wherever possible, and to density ratios, that is, the balance between developed land and open space. Planned unit developments (PUD) are one means of reducing impervious areas by clustering buildings and related facilities (Fig. 8.8c). Clustering improves the ratio of dwelling units to soft surface areas. Although it is possible to achieve zero net increase in runoff solely through careful site planning, especially when former farmland is involved, most successful stormwater management requires a combination of strategies.

Selecting mitigation measures

Which strategies and mitigation measures should be used depends on many factors, including local topographic and soil conditions and the character of the development program and its layout. In some areas there is no choice in the matter because local ordinances dictate what is to be used. Where there is a choice, however, several criteria can be used to guide the **selection of stormwater mitigation measures.** The first is discharge magnitude. The question is where within the flow system to focus mitigation: (a) on small flows in and around sites, or (b) on large flows downstream. This is significant because the force of running water, that is, the stress it exerts on the channel environment, increases substantially with discharge. As a rule,

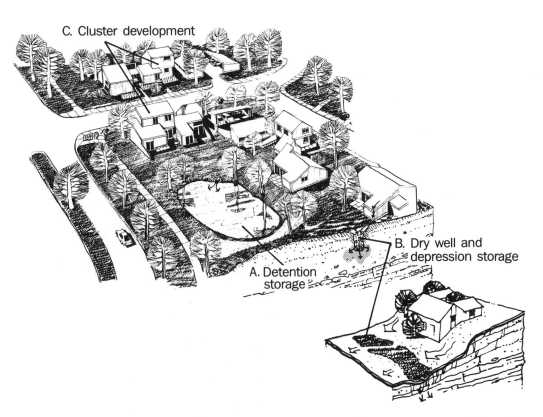

Fig. 8.8 Examples of stormwater mitigation measures: (a) detention storage, (b) on-site infiltration, and (c) cluster development. The lower drawing illustrates a version of (b) based on depression storage.

therefore, large flows are inherently more difficult to contain and regulate than small ones. It follows that large flows usually require substantial engineering treatments, whereas small flows can usually be handled as a part of landscape design treatments.

The second criterion is environmental compatibility. This addresses the questions of (1) environmental sacrifices and tradeoffs such as wetland impacts and habitat loss and (2) compatibility with the landscape design scheme as an aesthetic and land use issue (Fig. 8.9). The second question includes the potential for multiple uses, such as recreation and habitat enhancement. The third criterion is cost, both construction and maintenance, and the fourth criterion is liability. The risks of children around stormwater ponds and the hazards associated with downstream flooding are the principal liability concerns.

8.7 THE CONCEPT OF PERFORMANCE

Any effort to plan and manage the environment rests on a concept about how the environment should perform. When plans are formulated, the objective is either to guide and structure future change in order to avoid undesirable performance and/or to improve performance in an environment, setting, or system whose existing performance is judged to be inadequate. The phrase *judged to be inadequate* is important because any judgment on performance is based on human values. "That stream floods too often and it poses a danger to local inhabitants," is a value judgment by someone about environmental performance. Similarly, an ordinance restricting development from wetlands reflects a societal value about either the performance of wetlands, the performance of land use, or both.

Performance goals   In watershed planning and management, **performance goals** must be set early in the program to determine the *best management practices* (BMPs) to be used in the

Fig. 8.9 Retention ponds in Iowa farm country built for flood control. While compatible with agricultural purpose, such measures may conflict with other perspectives such as habitat conservation and downstream water supply.

planning process. Generally, the larger the watershed, the more difficult the task is because large watersheds usually involve many communities and interest groups with different views and policies on the matter. The task is usually less complex for a small watershed, not only because fewer players are involved, but also because the watershed itself is less complex.

The process of formulating performance goals and BMPs usually begins with the definition of local (watershed land users) values, attitudes, and policies. Next, regional factors are considered, in particular, policies pertaining to development intensity, stormwater retention, wetlands, open space, and the like. In addition, the values and needs, both articulated and apparent, of downstream riparians must be given serious consideration. Where, for instance, upstream users depend on a watershed and its streams to remove stormwater, and downstream riparians have set a goal around the maintenance of habitat and quality residential land near water courses, the two goals are in conflict, and, unless modified, the downstream group stands little chance of success.

A third consideration in setting performance goals is the carrying capacity of the watershed based on its biophysical character. The watershed must be evaluated as an environmental entity and weighed against the proposed goals based on local and regional values and policies. A watershed and streams that could not support a trout population under predevelopment conditions certainly cannot support one after development; therefore, a performance goal of habitat quality suitable to sustain trout would be physically unrealistic. It is usually the role of the environmental specialist in hydrology, soils, ecology, or forestry, for example, to examine the watershed, determine its condition and potentialities, and recommend appropriate modifications in proposed performance goals.

Performance standards   Once performance goals have been formulated, **performance standards** and controls have to be defined. Performance standards are the specific levels of performance that must be met if goals are to be achieved. For example, a stormwater discharge might call for zero net increase in peak discharges on first-order streams after a particular date or development density has been reached. This means that in planning new development it is necessary to take into account all changes in land use activities in the watershed at this time and determine from the balance of both positive and negative changes whether special measures or strategies are needed. If, for instance, cropland is being converted to woodland at the same time woodland is being cleared for new residential development, analysis may show that one change offsets the other, thereby maintaining the performance standard of zero net change in stormwater discharge.

Performance controls   **Performance controls** are the rules and regulations used to enforce the standards and goals. These may be specific ordinances limiting the percentage of impervious surface, requirements for site plan review and approval, or incentives such as tax breaks for restoring open space. Controls are necessary because without them the plan has no real "teeth" and thus no regulatory strength.

8.8 CASE STUDY

▪ Increased Flooding in an Urban Water Course, Metro Toronto

J. C. Mather

Highland Creek drains an area of 42.6 square miles in the borough of Scarborough, part of the Toronto metropolitan region. On August 27 and 28, 1976, two severe thunderstorms, producing 1.69 inches and 2.24 inches of rain, respectively, caused significant flooding on the creek with damage reaching nearly $2 million. The August 27 storm had an estimated return period of 20 years, yet produced a flood equivalent to that of a 1-in-37-year event. The storm of the following day, though more severe in terms of rainfall, resulted in less

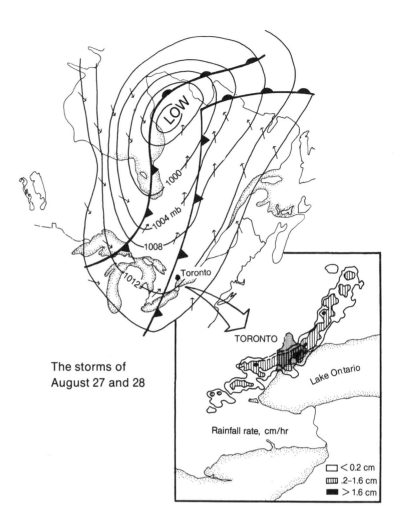

The storms of
August 27 and 28

TORONTO

Lake Ontario

Rainfall rate, cm/hr

☐ < 0.2 cm
▥ .2–1.6 cm
■ > 1.6 cm

damage, partially because its peak flow was routed through a number of pools and small reservoirs cleared by the earlier stormflow.

The source of the storms was two cold fronts associated with a pair of midlatitude cyclones, which passed through southern Canada in quick succession. Strong squall lines developed along the fronts, and weather analysis showed that the heaviest rainfall was actually generated by a number of thunderstorm centers in the squall lines. During the periods of peak rainfall, it appears that most of the watershed was covered by the storms.

A comparison of hydrographs for Highland Creek based on 1954 and 1976 conditions reveals that for the same storm the 1976 peak discharge was more than six times greater than its 1954 counterpart. This dramatic increase is attributed to urbanization of the watershed, channeling of tributaries, massive loadings from stormsewer discharge, and the removal of forest from the floodplain. These factors have combined to produce larger amounts and higher rates of runoff, thereby increasing both the magnitude and frequency of flood flows on Highland Creek.

The policy of the Metro Toronto and Region Conservation Authority to restrict the encroachment of private development on floodplains helped minimize the severity of damage to land use by the two floods. The creek valley now serves two main functions: as open space and as a stormwater collection area. Continued performance in these capacities is possible, provided that action is taken to keep the two functions compatible. This will mean restricting structures from the floodplain and stream channel, locating open space facilities

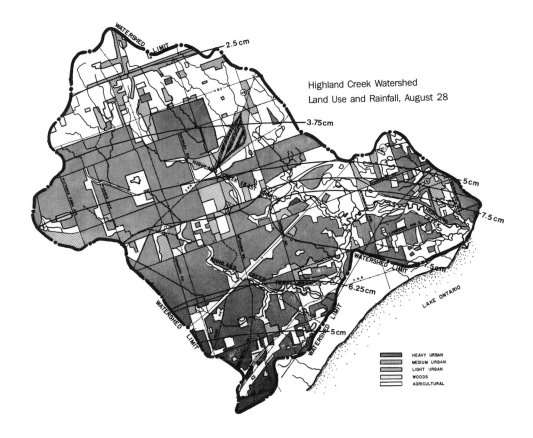

Highland Creek Watershed
Land Use and Rainfall, August 28

HEAVY URBAN
MEDIUM URBAN
LIGHT URBAN
WOODS
AGRICULTURAL

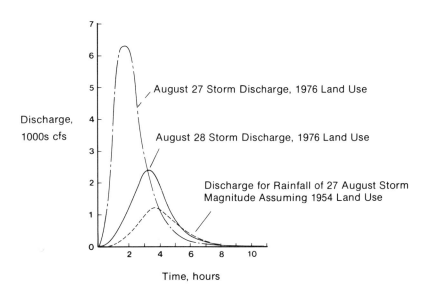

Discharge,
1000s cfs

August 27 Storm Discharge, 1976 Land Use

August 28 Storm Discharge, 1976 Land Use

Discharge for Rainfall of 27 August Storm
Magnitude Assuming 1954 Land Use

Time, hours

away from high flow zones, protecting banks from erosion, and investigating
alternative approaches to stormwater management that do not rely exclusively
on stormsewers and stream channeling.

*J. C. Mather is head of the Flood Control Section, Water Resource Division,
Metropolitan Toronto and Region Conservation Authority.*

8.9 SELECTED REFERENCES FOR FURTHER READING

Dunne, Thomas, and Black, R. D. "Partial-Area Contributions to Storm Runoff in a New England Watershed." *Water Resources Research,* 1970, pp. 1296–1311.

Ferguson, Bruce K. *Controlling Stormwater Impact.* American Society of Landscape Architects, Landscape Architecture Technical Information Services, 1981, 31 pp.

Hewlett, J. D., and Hibbert, A. R. "Factors Affecting the Response of Small Watersheds to Precipitation in Humid Regions." In *Forest Hydrology.* Oxford: Pergamon Press, 1967, pp. 275–290.

Horton, Robert E. "The Role of Infiltration in the Hydrologic Cycle." *American Geophysical Union Transactions* 14, 1933, pp. 446–460.

Marsh, William M., and Dozier, Jeff. "Runoff and Streamflow." In *Landscape: An Introduction to Physical Geography.* Reading, Mass.: Addison-Wesley, 1981, pp. 177–199.

Poertner, Herbert G. *Practices in Detention of Urban Stormwater Runoff.* Chicago: American Public Works Association, 1974, 231 pp.

Seaburn, G. E. "Effects of Urban Development on Direct Runoff to East Meadow Brook, Nassau County, Long Island, New York." *U.S. Geological Survey Professional Paper 627–B,* 1969.

U.S. Soil Conservation Service. *Urban Hydrology For Small Watersheds.* Technical Release No. 55, Washington, D.C., Department of Agriculture, 1975.

Whipple, W., et al. *Stormwater Management in Urbanizing Areas.* Englewood Cliffs, N.J.: Prentice-Hall, 1983.

9

WATERSHEDS, DRAINAGE NETS, AND LAND USE

9.1 INTRODUCTION

Land use and drainage networks

Overland flow moves only a short distance over the ground before it gathers into minute threads of water. These threads merge with one another, forming rivulets capable of eroding soil and shaping a small channel. The rivulets in turn join to form streams and the streams join to form rivers, and so on. This system of channels, characterized by streams linked together like the branches of a tree, is called a **drainage network,** and it represents nature's most effective means of getting liquid water off the land. The area feeding water to the drainage network is the drainage basin, or watershed, and for a given set of geographic conditions, the size of the main channel and its flows increase with the size of the drainage basin.

Early in the history of civilization, humans learned about the advantages of channel networks, for both distributing water and removing it from the land. The earliest sewers were actually designed to carry stormwater, and they were constructed in networks similar to those of natural streams. Whether or not they knew it, the ancients followed the *principle of stream orders* in the construction of both stormsewer and field irrigation systems. This principle describes the relative position, called the *order,* of a stream in a drainage network and helps us to understand the relationships among streams in a complex flow system.

Modern land development often alters drainage networks by obliterating natural channels, adding artificial channels, or changing the size of drainage basins. Such alterations can have serious environmental consequences, including increased flooding, loss of aquatic habitats, reduced water supplies during low flow periods, and lowered water quality. In land use planning generally little attention is paid to drainage networks as geographic entities; however, they are taken seriously by civil engineers who seek to maintain or improve their performance in stormwater removal when basins are developed.

9.2 THE ORGANIZATION OF NETWORKS AND BASINS

Stream orders

The principle of **stream orders** is built on a classification system based on the rank of streams within the drainage network. First-order streams are channelized flows with no tributaries. Second-order streams are those with at least two first-order tributaries. Third-order streams are formed when at least two second-order streams join together, and so on (Fig. 9.1).

Bifurcation ratio

The number of streams of a given order that combine to form the next higher order generally averages around 3.0 and is called the **bifurcation ratio.** From a

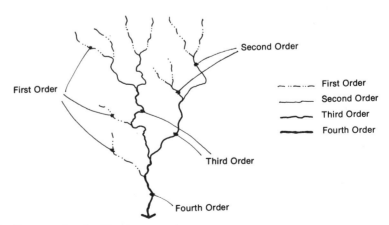

Fig. 9.1   Stream order classification according to rank in the drainage network. This follows the scheme originally defined by Robert Horton.

Table 9.1   Factors Important to the Analysis of Drainage Networks

■ *Number of Streams*—the sum total of streams in each order.
■ *Bifurcation Ratio*—(branching ratio) Ratio of the number of streams in one order to the number in the next higher order.

$$BR = \frac{N}{N_u}$$

Where

BR = bifurcation ratio
N = the number of streams of a given order
N_u = the number of streams in the next highest order

■ *Drainage Basin Order*—Designated by highest order (trunk) stream draining a basin.
■ *Drainage Area*—Total number of square miles or square kilometers within the perimeter (divide) of a basin.
■ *Drainage Density*—Total length of streams per square mile or square kilometer of drainage area.

$$Density = \frac{\text{sum total length of streams (mi. or km)}}{\text{drainage area (mi}^2 \text{ or km}^2)}$$

functional standpoint, this ratio tells us that the size of the receiving channel must be at least three times the average size of the tributaries. For drainage nets in general, a comparison of the total number of streams in each order to the order itself reveals a remarkably consistent relationship, which defines the *principle of stream orders,* in which stream numbers decline with increasing order. Therefore, first-order streams are the most abundant streams in every drainage network.

Given a classification by order of the streams in a drainage net, we can examine the relationship between orders and other hydrologic characteristics of the river system such as drainage area, stream discharge, and stream lengths. This provides a basis for comparing drainage nets under different climatic, geologic, and land use conditions; for analyzing selected aspects of riverflow, such as changes due to urbanization; and for defining zones with different land use potentials. Table 9.1 lists and defines several factors involved in drainage network and basin analysis.

Basin order   Drainage basins or areas can also be ranked according to the stream order principle. First-order drainage basins are those emptied via first-order streams; second-order basins are those in which the main channel is of the second order; a fifth-order basin would be one in which the trunk stream is of the fifth order. Just as all high-order streams are products of a complete series of lower streams, high-order (large) basins are comprised of a complete series of lower-order basins, each set inside the other. This is sometimes referred to as a *nested hierarchy,* as is illustrated in Fig. 9.2.

In accounting for the combined areas of the basins that make up a larger basin, however, not all the land area is taken up by the lower-order basins. Invariably a small percentage of the land drains directly into higher-order streams without passing through the numerical progression of lower-order basins (Fig. 9.3). This is called the *nonbasin drainage area,* and it generally constitutes 15 to 20 percent of the total drainage area in basins of second order or larger.

9.3   MAPPING THE DRAINAGE BASIN

Locating drainage divides   The process of mapping the individual drainage basins within a large drainage net requires finding the **drainage divides** between channels of a particular order. This is best accomplished with the use of a topographic contour map; however, field inspec-

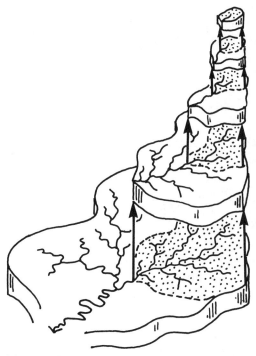

Fig. 9.2 Illustration of the nested hierarchy of lower-order basins within a large drainage basin.

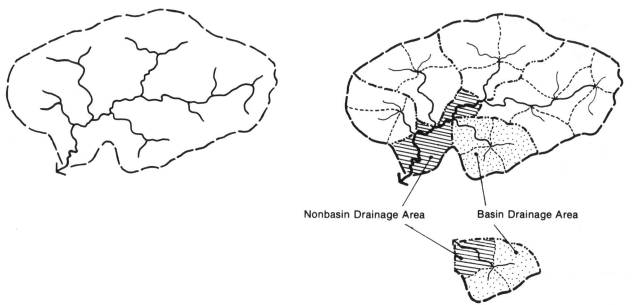

Nonbasin Drainage Area   Basin Drainage Area

Fig. 9.3 Two types of drainage areas can be defined in basins larger than the first order: basin and nonbasin areas. Nonbasin area borders the trunk stream(s) and releases its water directly to the main channel.

tion may be needed in developed areas in order to find culverts, diversions, and other drainage alterations. As a first step, channels should be traced and ranked, taking care to note the scale and the level of hydrographic detail provided by the base map. This is important because maps of large scales will show more first-order streams, owing to the fact that they are usually drawn at a finer level of resolution than smaller scale maps.

In areas of complex terrain, the task of locating basin perimeters can be tedious, but it can be streamlined somewhat if the pattern of surface runoff (overland flow) is first demarcated. This can be done by mapping the direction of runoff using short *Runoff patterns* arrows drawn perpendicular to the contours over the entire drainage area. Two basic **runoff patterns** will appear: divergent and convergent. Where the pattern is divergent, a drainage divide (basin perimeter) is located (Fig. 9.4). These patterns are also illustrated schematically in Figure 9.10.

By connecting all the drainage divides between first-order streams, a watershed can be partitioned into first-order basins. This will account for 80 to 85 percent of the total drainage area, the remainder being nonbasin drainage. From this pattern, second-order basins can be traced, and they are comprised of two or more first-order basins plus a fraction of nonbasin area.

Since perennial streams are fed by both surface water and groundwater, it is also important to be aware that the drainage basins for these two sources may be different. In most instances, however, it is impossible to identify such an arrangement without the aid of an areawide groundwater study. A clue to the existence of a significant difference in the two can sometimes be found in first- or second-order streams that have exceptionally large or small baseflows for their surface drainage area relative to similar streams in the same region.

9.4 TRENDS IN THE DEVELOPMENT OF SMALL DRAINAGE BASINS

Clearing and development of land often have a pronounced influence on drainage networks and basins. Deforestation and agriculture may initiate soil erosion and gully formation. As gullies advance, they expand the drainage network, thereby increasing

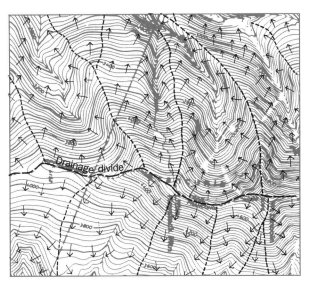

← Runoff direction

Fig. 9.4 Mapping and partitioning the watershed using vectors of overland flow.

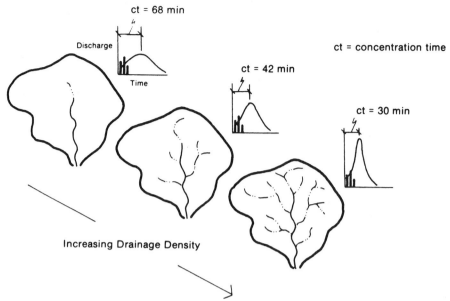

Fig. 9.5 Hydrographs showing the changes brought about by increased drainage density: concentration time is reduced, causing greater peak discharges for a given rainstorm.

the number of first-order streams and the drainage density. The main hydrologic consequence of this is shortened concentration times because the distance that water must travel as overland flow or interflow is reduced (Fig. 9.5). Discharges are in turn larger, large flows occur with higher frequencies, erosion is greater, and water quality can be expected to decline.

Urbanization

Urbanization also leads to considerable change in the shape and density of a drainage network. One of the first changes that takes place is a "pruning" of natural channels, that is, removal of parts of the network. These channels are often replaced by ditches and underground channels in the form of storm and sanitary sewers. Although the *natural network* may be pruned, the *net effect* of urbanization is usually an increase in total channels and in turn an increase in the overall drainage density (Fig. 9.6). Coupled with the lower infiltration rates of urbanized areas, this leads to increased amounts of runoff and shorter concentration times for the drainage basin, both of which produce larger peak discharges. As a result, both the magnitude and frequency of peak discharges are increased for receiving streams and rivers (see Fig. 8.7).

Stormsewers

Stormsewers are underground pipes that conduct surface water by gravity flow from streets, buildings, parking lots, and related facilities to streams and rivers. The

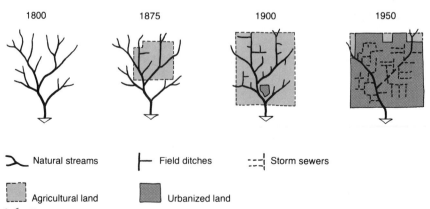

Fig. 9.6 Pruning, grafting, and intensification of a drainage network with land use change.

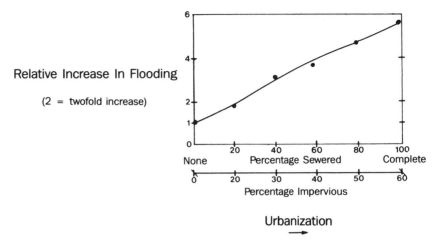

Fig. 9.7 Increased frequency of floodflows related to stormsewering and impervious surface.

pipes are usually made of concrete, sized to the area they serve, and capable of transmitting stormwater at a very rapid rate. Studies show that stormsewers and associated impervious surfaces increase the frequency of floodflows on streams in fully urbanized areas by as much as sixfold (Fig. 9.7).

The graph in Fig. 9.7 assumes that the size of the drainage basin has remained unchanged with sewering. In many instances, however, the size of the basin is also increased as sewering takes place, as is illustrated in the case of the Reeds Lake watershed (Fig. 9.8). The additional drainage area is completely urbanized and laced with stormsewers and produces peak discharges perhaps four to five times larger than drainage areas of comparable size without stormsewers and such heavy development.

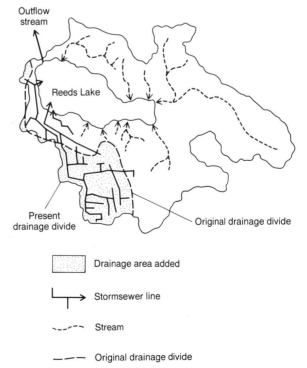

Fig. 9.8 The Reeds Lake watershed showing the drainage added (in tint) through stormsewering.

Agriculture   Modern **agriculture** is also responsible for altering drainage basins and stream networks. In humid regions, farmers often find it necessary to improve field drainage to facilitate early spring plowing and planting. In addition to cutting ditches through and around fields and deepening and straightening small streams, networks of drain tiles

Field drains   are often installed in fields. Drain tiles are small perforated pipes (originally ceramic but now plastic) buried just below the plow layer. They collect water that has infiltrated the soil and conduct it rapidly to an open channel. Although the effects of tile systems on streamflow have not been documented, these systems undoubtedly serve to increase the magnitude and frequency of peak flows locally in much the same way as yard drains and stormsewers do in cities. Another serious hydrologic change associated with agriculture is the draining of wetlands. Wetlands are important in the storage of runoff and floodwater, and where they are eliminated, stream peak flows increase in turn.

Lakes and reservoirs   The watersheds that serve **lakes and reservoirs** (impoundments) follow the same organizational principles as river watersheds, with the impoundment itself representing a segment of some order in the drainage network or a node linking streams of lower orders. On the other hand, the land use patterns are different in one important respect: The heaviest development is usually found in the nonbasin drainage area (see section 11.6 in Chapter 11). This is a discontinuous belt of shoreland that encircles the waterbody and is highly attractive to residential, recreational, and commercial development. As the development takes place, the need for storm drainage usually arises and yard drains, ditches, and stormlines are constructed where, under natural conditions, channels never existed. In addition, the shoreland zone is often expanded inland with stormsewer construction, thereby capturing additional runoff and rerouting it directly to the waterbody.

9.5 PLANNING AND MANAGEMENT CONSIDERATIONS

Since small drainage basins are the building blocks of large drainage systems, it is essential that watershed planning and management programs address the small basin.

Basin components   Most small basins (primarily first, second, and third orders) are comprised of three interrelated parts: (1) an outer, upland zone that generates overland flow and ephemeral channel flows; (2) a low area or collection zone in the upper basin where runoff from the upland zone accumulates; and (3) a central conveyance zone represented by a valley and stream channel through which water is transferred from the collection zone to higher order channels (Fig. 9.9). The hydrologic behavior of each zone is different, and each in turn calls for different planning and management strategies.

Upland and collection zones   The **upland zone** is generally least susceptible to drainage problems. It provides the greatest opportunity for site-scale stormwater management because most sites in this zone have little upslope drainage to contend with and because surface flows are generally small and diffused. By contrast, the **collection zone** in the upper basin is subject to serious drainage problems. Seepage is common along the perimeter, and groundwater saturation can be expected in the lower central areas during much of the year. During periods of runoff, this zone is prone to inflooding, caused by massive stormwater loading from upland surfaces. Inflooding is very common in rural areas of modest local relief; in fact, it is probably the most common source of local flood damage today in much of the Midwest and southern Ontario.

Edge form and function   The edge separating the upland zone and the collection zone is one of the most critical borders in landscape planning. This border is made of two **edge forms:** convex and concave (Fig. 9.10). The convex forms create divergent patterns of runoff and therefore tend to be dry along their axes, indeed very dry in some instances. By contrast, concave forms create convergent patterns of runoff, concentrating flows

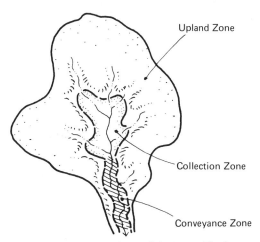

Fig. 9.9 The three main hydrologic zones of a small drainage. The lower two zones are the least suited to development.

downslope, and therefore tend to be wet along their axes. The concave edges are the functional links between the upland surface, where stormflows are generated, and the lowland collection areas where water accumulates and streams head up. As such they are vital management points in the drainage basin, serving as the gateways to the lowland and riparian environments of the collection zone. It follows that the concave edges also represent important habitat corridors between upland and lowland surfaces.

Conveyance zone   The central **conveyance zone** contains the main stream channel and valley, including a small floodplain. The flows in this zone are derived from the upper two zones as well as from groundwater inflow directly to the channel. Groundwater contributions provide the stream baseflow and constitute the vast majority of the stream discharge over the year. Stormwater, on the other hand, is derived mainly from the upper zones, and though small in total, it constitutes the bulk of the largest peak flows in developed or partially developed basins. The central conveyance zone is also

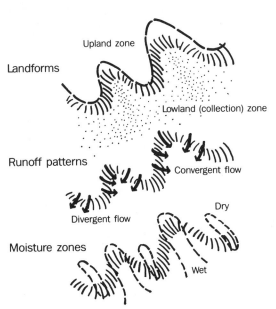

Fig. 9.10 Concave and convex edges and associated runoff patterns.

subject to flooding, but in this case it is outflooding caused by the stream overtopping its banks. Because this zone is prone to comparatively large floods, especially if the upper basin is developed, it is generally least suited to development and most difficult to manage hydrologically. In hilly and mountainous terrain, such as coastal California, where slopes tend to be unstable during wet periods, it is this zone and the upper collection zone that receive the landslide and mudflow debris from slope failures.

Land use implications   Recognition of the constraints and opportunities associated with each of these drainage zones is an important step toward forming development guidelines for small basins. In particular, this provides a rationale for defining the spatial patterns of land units, including buildable land, open space, and special use areas on a basin-by-basin basis. What it does not provide, however, is a rationale for establishing density guidelines. *Density* is a measure of the intensity of development, defined, for example, as percentage impervious surface, total building floor space per acre, or population density. For water and land management, percentage impervious surface is commonly used to define density.

Establishing the appropriate density for a drainage basin should be based on performance goals and standards (see Chapter 8 for a discussion of performance *Basin-carrying capacity*   concepts) and **basin-carrying capacity.** The carrying capacity of a drainage basin is a measure of the amount and type of development it is able to sustain without suffering degradation of water features, water quality, biota, soils, and land use. While this concept is easy to envision, determination of a basin's carrying capacity may be difficult to derive. As a general rule, 30 percent development may be the advisable maximum for most basins, but this can vary with the style of development and the character of the basin.

Basins in hilly or mountainous terrain often have the lowest carrying capacity because of the abundance of steep, unbuildable slopes and the rapid rate of stormwater transfer. In addition, the soil mantle may be thin, which not only minimizes the basin's capacity to filter and retain infiltration water, but often increases the tendency for slope failure during wet periods. For basins with less relief, lower gradients, deep soil mantles, and good soil drainage, the carrying capacity may be considerably higher.

Carrying capacity should take into account factors in addition to the physical character of the basin itself; for example, the nature of the development and drainage conditions downstream, and the character of existing and proposed development within the basin. With respect to the latter, higher land use densities may be allowable where stormwater control such as on-site detention or dry wells can be employed effectively (see Fig. 8.7 in Chapter 8). Where curbs, gutters, and stormsewers are required by community ordinance, stormwater mitigation is a necessity because these drains facilitate pollutant transfer to and increased flooding in receiving streams and waterbodies.

9.6 LAND USE PLANNING IN THE SMALL DRAINAGE BASIN

Step one   The procedure for building land use plans for small drainage basins begins with a definition of the stream system, patterns of runoff, and the three hydrologic zones. Each zone should be analyzed for soils, slopes, vegetation, and existing land use to determine its limitations for development. Steep slopes, runoff collection areas, unstable and poorly drained soils, forested areas in critical runoff zones, and areas prone to flooding and seepage should be designated as nonbuildable. The remaining area is more or less the developable land, and the bulk of it usually lies in the upland zone of the basin separated from the lowlands by the concave and convex edges described earlier (Fig. 9.11a).

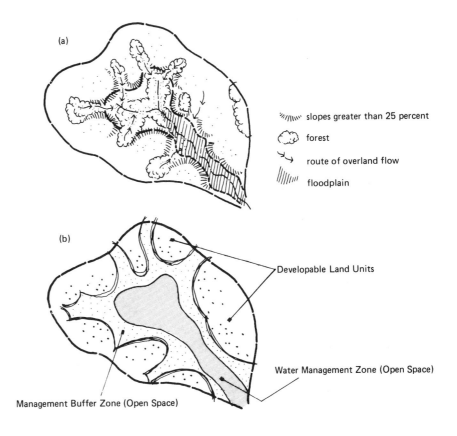

slopes greater than 25 percent

forest

route of overland flow

floodplain

Developable Land Units

Water Management Zone (Open Space)

Management Buffer Zone (Open Space)

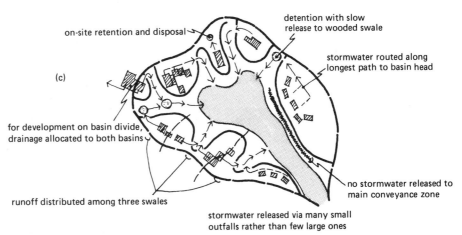

detention with slow
release to wooded swale

on-site retention and disposal

stormwater routed along
longest path to basin head

for development on basin divide,
drainage allocated to both basins

no stormwater released to
main conveyance zone

runoff distributed among three swales

stormwater released via many small
outfalls rather than few large ones

Fig. 9.11 Maps produced as a part of a procedure for land use planning in a small drainage basin: (a) The three hydrologic zones and the significant features of each. (b) The land use units. (c) Some strategies and guidelines in site selection and site planning.

Step two The next step is to define land use units. These are physical entities of land, with the fewest constraints to development in general, that set the spatial scale and general configuration of development (Fig. 9.11b). Within this framework, development schemes may be evaluated and either discarded or assigned to the appropriate land unit. To achieve the desired performance, different options for the siting of different activities should be exercised; for instance, high-impact activities may be assigned to land units that are buffered by forest and permeable soils from steep slopes and runoff collection areas.

Guidelines   In general, the recommended **guidelines** for site selection and site planning in small drainage basins are: (1) maximize the distance of stormwater travel from the site to a collection area or stream; (2) maximize the concentration time by slowing the rate of stormwater runoff; (3) minimize the volume of overland flow per unit area of land; (4) utilize or provide buffers such as forests and wetlands to protect collection areas and streams from development zones; and (5) divert stormwater away from or around critical features such as steep slopes, unstable soils, or valued habitats (Fig. 9.11c).

9.7 CASE STUDY

Watershed Management Planning in an Arid Environment

Richard A. Meganck

Northern Mexico, like the American Southwest, is a region of rapid economic growth with limited water resources. Surface water supplies are scarce, and in most areas development is heavily dependent on groundwater. Locally, groundwater reserves are often linked to basins that are fed by precipitation on surrounding mountain slopes. From the flanks of the basins, water is transmitted through loose deposits into aquifers on the valley floors, and from these aquifers, water is extracted by cities, farms, and industry. Although the mountains receive more precipitation than the valleys and have better moisture balances, the rate of recharge of valley aquifers is generally low. To maintain a water supply over the long run, extraction rates should not exceed recharge rates, and sources of recharge should be well managed.

Saltillo, Mexico, with a population of 300,000, is situated in a desert basin of the Sierra Madre Oriental. Stimulated by a variety of tax incentives, automobile and steel plants have recently been constructed, the population of Saltillo has increased substantially, and the demand for basic services has increased greatly. Most notable among these is the demand for water, 50 percent of which is pumped from a mountain basin just 7 km south of the city, the San Lorenzo Canyon. The canyon's primary land use is agriculture (mostly grazing) with 64 percent of the land held under *ejidos* (government subsidized agricultural villages) and 36 percent under private ownership.

Over the past several decades, poor land use practices have led to such degradation of the canyon that both its hydrologic and agricultural resources

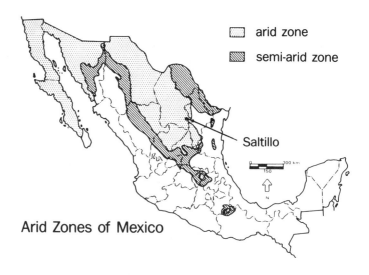

arid zone
semi-arid zone

Saltillo

Arid Zones of Mexico

have declined seriously. Virtually all the original forest cover has been removed; overgrazing has promoted serious soil erosion and stream sedimentation; moreover, large amounts of soil have been mined to supply topsoil for gardens in the villages and cities. Together these activities have reduced the canyon's capacity to capture water and recharge the aquifers that are so essential to Saltillo. At the same time, Saltillo is mining water at increasing rates each year.

Unless remedial measures are taken in the San Lorenzo Canyon (and similar canyons), Saltillo will soon be faced with severe water shortages. Accordingly, the Mexican government and the Regional Development Program of the Organization of American States have agreed to develop a management plan for the San Lorenzo Canyon that could serve as a model for similar areas. Because of the land ownership situation and the long established land use practices of the ejidos, the plan must address both the social and the physical elements of the problem.

An interdisciplinary planning team was formed, management objectives determined, field data collected and analyzed, and a planning framework defined. Finally, a management program was elaborated with the following goals:

- To insure long-term water production and protection of water recharge zones.
- To provide a more diversified and stable economic base for local rural inhabitants (a political reality for acceptance of the plan by local and state officials).
- To stabilize and protect ecosystem processes in the long term.
- To help meet the increasing demand for outdoor recreation and education.
- To resolve potential conflicts with private property owners.

In order to meet these goals and slow the rate of degradation of the canyon, the following actions have been recommended:

1. Enforcement of interim management measures, including an immediate cessation of forestry, grazing, hunting, trapping, and soil mining activities.

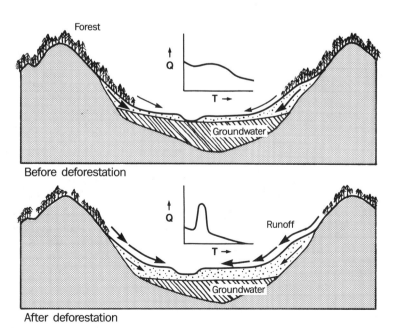

Before deforestation

After deforestation

2. A request for international funds to help underwrite the change for local rural inhabitants from a forestry/grazing economy to one of improving established crop production and diversification to fruit and Christmas-tree operations. (Local private enterprise has already proven the economic success of apple and pine tree production.)

3. Reforestation of approximately 6000 hectares with 6 to 8 million native pines and junipers.

4. The implementation of soil conservation and fire management measures, elimination of undesirable vegetation, protection of vital and endangered habitat, and the eventual reintroduction and management of certain wildlife species.

5. Acquisition of resource development rights on private lands within the proposed multiple use management area through market value purchase, property exchange, life-lease agreements, or other arrangements.

Long-term management of the San Lorenzo Canyon according to this plan should provide a suitable framework to guide ecodevelopment, not only because it addresses the water system as a physical entity, but because it recognizes the complex social and cultural forces at work in the Mexican landscape and the fact that changes in land use practices must be based on sound economic and social incentives.

Richard A. Meganck, a resource planner, is a former project director for the Regional Development Program, Organization of American States. ■

9.8 SELECTED REFERENCES FOR FURTHER READING

Copeland, O. L. "Land Use and Ecological Factors in Relation to Sediment Yield." U.S. Department of Agriculture, *Misc. Publication 970.* Washington, D.C., 1965, pp. 72–84.

Dunne, Thomas, and Leopold, L. B. "Drainage Basins." In *Water in Environmental Planning.* San Francisco: W. H. Freeman, 1978, pp. 493–505.

Dunne, Thomas, Moore, T. R., and Taylor, C. H. "Recognition and Prediction of Runoff-Producing Zones in Humid Regions." *Hydrological Sciences Bulletin,* 20: 3, 1975, pp. 305–327.

Gregory, K. J., and Welling, D. E. *Drainage Basin Form and Process.* New York: Halsted Press, 1973, 456 pp.

Horton, R. E. "Erosional Development of Streams and Their Drainage Basins: Hydrophysical Approach to Quantitative Morphology." *Geological Society of America Bulletin* 56, 1945, pp. 275–370.

Leopold, L. B. "Hydrology for Urban Land Planning—A Guidebook on the Effects of Urban Land Use," *U.S. Geological Survey Circular* 554, 1968, 18 pp.

Leopold, L. B., and Miller, J. P. "Ephemeral Streams: Hydraulic Factors and Their Relation to the Drainage Net." *U.S. Geological Survey Professional Paper 282–A,* 1956.

Meganck, Richard. *Multiple Use Management Plan, San Lorenzo Canyon* (Summary). Organization of American States and Universidad Autonoma Agraria, 1981, 72 pp.

Strahler, A. N. "Quantitative Geomorphology of Drainage Basins and Channel Networks." In *Handbook of Applied Hydrology* (ed. Van te Chow). New York: McGraw-Hill, 1964.

10

STREAMFLOW AND FLOOD HAZARD

10.1 INTRODUCTION

The variability of riverflow has been a serious issue for thousands of years in human settlement and land use. Until the past century or so, relatively little was understood about the sources of streamflow, especially as they relate to runoff. This is not surprising, because runoff is influenced by so many factors. Different combinations of rainfall, snowmelt, groundwater, soil moisture, and infiltration, for example, can produce a wide range in runoff conditions that result in widely different levels of riverflow. In addition, alterations of drainage basins and river channels by humans can have marked influences on flow rates. As land use changes, runoff rates also change, producing corresponding changes in streamflow; accordingly, effective land use planning in river valleys is a source of constant challenge throughout the world.

In the annals of land use studies, river valleys hold a special status because in virtually all agrarian and industrial societies they are among the most attractive and yet hazardous environments for settlement. This, of course, is dramatically illustrated in history by the classical accounts of the great civilizations of the Nile, Indus, and Tigris-Euphrates valleys, which were both nurtured and plagued by their rivers. The dilemma persists in the modern world, and despite efforts to control riverflow, loss of life and property has increased in the past century. In America, river valleys were generally the first geographic settings to receive formal attention in land use planning. This came after 1930 for the most part and has since given rise to local and state ordinances in most areas on the use of floodplains. Nevertheless, the problem grows each year as development slips ahead of floodplain mapping programs and as more or less passive streams are changed to active ones by development in their watersheds.

The quantity of water carried by a stream is termed *discharge*. It is measured in volumetric units of water passing a point on a stream, such as a bridge, over time. The conventional units in English-speaking countries are cubic feet per second, abbreviated "cfs." In recent years, cubic meters have begun to replace cubic feet, but the latter are still widely used in science, engineering, and land planning.

10.2 SOURCES OF STREAMFLOW

Streamflow is derived from four sources: channel precipitation, overland flow, interflow, and groundwater. *Channel precipitation* is the moisture falling directly on the water surface, and in most streams, it adds very little to flow. Groundwater, on the other hand, is a major source of discharge. Groundwater enters the stream bed where the channel intersects the water table and provides a steady supply of water, termed *Baseflow* **baseflow,** during both dry and rainy periods. Owing to the large supply of groundwater available to streams and the slowness of the response of groundwater to precipitation events, baseflow changes only gradually over time.

Interflow is water that infiltrates the soil and then moves laterally to the stream channel in the zone above the water table. Much of this water is transmitted within the soil itself, some of it moving along the soil horizons. Until recently, the role of interflow in streamflow was not understood, but field research has begun to show that next to baseflow, it is the most important source of discharge for streams in forested lands. This research also revealed that overland flow in heavily forested areas makes negligible contributions to streamflow (Fig. 10.1).

Overland flow **Overland flow,** however, is a major source of discharge in dry regions, cultivated lands, and urbanized areas. Overland flow is water that moves directly from the surface of the land into a stream. Since it is not filtered through the soil or the groundwater system, overland flow is released to the stream very rapidly, causing sudden increases in discharge. The quickest response times between rainfall and streamflow occur in

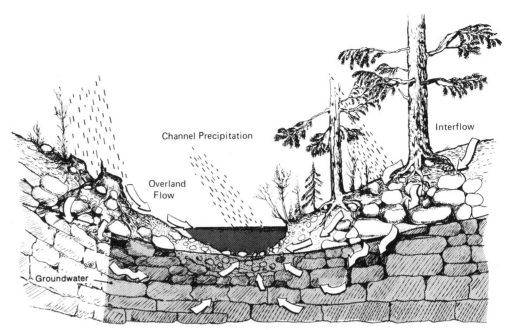

Fig. 10.1 Sources of streamflow: channel precipitation, overland flow, interflow, and groundwater.

urbanized areas where gutter and stormsewer systems are used to route overland flow to streams.

It is important to understand that the relative balance of contributions from these sources changes dramatically with (1) the nature of rainfall and (2) the conditions of the drainage basin. As we illustrated in Chapter 8, land clearing and development tend to reverse the natural balance between overland flow and infiltration. Overland flow increases in volume, and travel time quickens with development, resulting in much greater peak discharges in receiving streams.

Rainfall/runoff relations   The amount and rate of water delivered to streams also varies with rainfall intensity and duration. Light rains rarely produce overland flow but, if extended over days, may supply enough water to the soil and water table to cause an increase in baseflow (Fig. 10.2a). Thus discharge may rise without appreciable contributions from surface runoff. In striking contrast to this situation is the streamflow from a short, heavy rainstorm in which rainfall intensity exceeds soil infiltration capacity. The result is immediate overland flow and a sudden rise in stream discharge. If coupled with a "fast" watershed, that is, one that has been developed and laced with artificial drains, the stormwater load amassed in the stream may be extreme indeed (Fig. 10.2b).

10.3 METHODS OF FORECASTING STREAMFLOW

If the drainage area of a river is relatively small and no discharge records are available, we must make discharge estimates using the rational method (see Chapter 8). However, if chronological records of discharge are available, a short-term forecast of discharge can be made for a given rainstorm using a hydrograph. This method involves plotting the discharge from a watershed over time as the watershed and its streams respond to the rainstorm. The method is called the **unit hydrograph method** *Unit hydrograph method*   because it addresses only the runoff produced in a specified period of time, the time taken for a river to rise, peak, and fall in response to a particular storm. Using rainfall

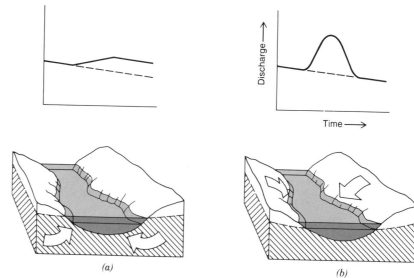

Fig. 10.2 (a) Stream response to a long gentle rainfall that produces groundwater recharge and a rise in baseflow. (b) Stream response to an intensive rainstorm that produces overland flow.

data, then, we can forecast streamflow for selected storms, called standard storms. A *standard rainstorm* is a high-intensity storm of some recurrence (average return) period, for example, 2, 5, or 50 years, that produces a known amount of rise in the river. One method of unit hydrograph analysis involves expressing the hour-by-hour or day-by-day increase in streamflow as a percentage of total runoff. Plotted on a graph, these data form the unit hydrograph for that storm, which represents the runoff added to the prestorm baseflow (Fig. 10.3).

Magnitude and frequency method

To forecast the flows in a large drainage basin using the unit hydrograph method would prove to be difficult because in a large basin conditions may vary significantly from one part of the basin to another. This is especially so with the distribution of rainfall, because the basin is rarely covered evenly by an individual rainstorm. As a result, the basin does not respond as a unit to a given storm, making it difficult to construct a reliable hydrograph. In such cases, we turn to the **magnitude and frequency method** and calculate the probability of the recurrence of large flows based on records of past years' flows. In the United States, these records are maintained by the Hydrological Division of the U.S. Geological Survey for most rivers and large streams. For a basin with an area of 10,000 square kilometers or more, it is not uncommon for the river system to be gauged at five to ten places. The data from each gauging station apply to the part of the basin upstream of that location.

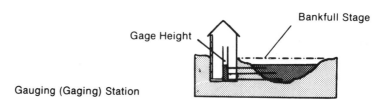

Flow period	Total flow	Storm-flow
0-12 hrs	63 m³/s	6 m³/s
12-24	192	127
24-36	1065	991
36-48	1101	1019
48-60	714	623
60-72	453	354
72-84	275	170
84-96	194	85
96-108	144	28

Peak = 1253; 1175 at hour 36

Flow period	Percentage of total flow
0-12 hrs	0.2%
12-24	3.6
24-36	29.0
36-48	29.8
48-60	18.3
60-72	10.3
72-84	5.0
84-96	2.4
96-100	0.8

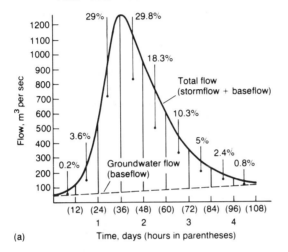

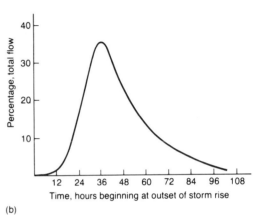

Fig. 10.3 Unit hydrograph for the uppermost part of the Youghiogheny River. Streamflow is expressed as a percentage of total flow.

Discharge data

Since we are concerned mainly with the largest flows, only *peak annual flows* are recorded for most rivers. With the aid of some statistical techniques, we can use these **flow data** to determine the probability of recurrence of a given flow on a river. Key data available for each gauging station include:

▪ *Peak Annual Discharge:* the single largest flow in cubic feet per second (cfs).
▪ *Date of Peak Annual Discharge:* the month and year in which this flow occurred.
▪ *Gauge Height:* the height of water above channel bottom.
▪ *Bankfull Stage:* gauge height when channel is filled to bank level.

Calculation procedure

The following steps outline **a procedure** for calculating the recurrence intervals and probabilities of various peak annual discharges:

▪ First, *rank* the flows in order from highest to lowest; that is, list them in order from biggest to smallest values. For two of the same size, list the oldest first.
▪ Next, determine the *recurrence interval* of each flow:

$$t_r = \frac{n+1}{m}$$

Where

t_r = the recurrence interval in years
n = the total number of flows
m = the rank of flow in question

■ Third, determine the probability (p) of any flow:

■ $$p = \frac{1}{t_r}$$

This will yield a decimal, say 0.5, which can be converted to a percent (50 percent) by multiplying by 100.

■ In addition, it is also useful to know *when* peak flows can be expected; accordingly, the monthly frequency of peak flows can be determined based on the dates of the peak annual discharges. Furthermore, the percentage of peak annual flows that actually produce floods can be determined by comparing the stage (elevation) represented by each discharge with the bankfull elevation of the gauging station, that is, any flow that exceeds bankfull elevation is a flood.

Projecting discharge   Given several decades of peak annual discharges for a river, it is possible to make limited **projections** to estimate the size of some large flow that has not been experienced during the period of record. The technique most commonly used involves projecting the curve (graph line) formed when peak annual discharges are plotted against their respective recurrence intervals. In most cases, however, the curve bends rather strongly, making it difficult to plot a projection accurately (Fig. 10.4). This problem can be overcome by plotting the discharge and/or the recurrence interval data on logarithmic graph paper or logarithmic/probability paper. Once the plot is straightened, a line can be ruled through the points. The process of making a projection can be accomplished by merely extending the line beyond the points and then reading the appropriate discharge for the recurrence interval in question. In Fig. 10.5 the curve was straightened by using a logarithmic scale on the recurrence interval (horizontal) axis. The period of record covers 30 years, but we would like to know the magnitude of the 100-year flow. Assuming that the 100-year (or larger) flow is not represented

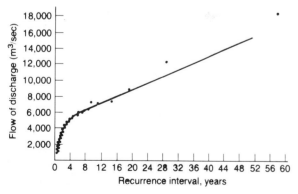

(a)

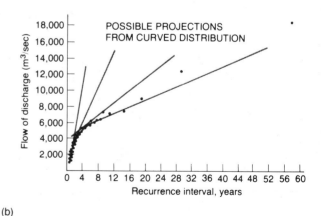

(b)

Fig. 10.4   (a) Graph based on recurrence interval and discharge of peak annual flows, Eel River, California, for the period of 1911–1969. (b) This graph shows why it is impossible to plot one straight graph line from a curved distribution.

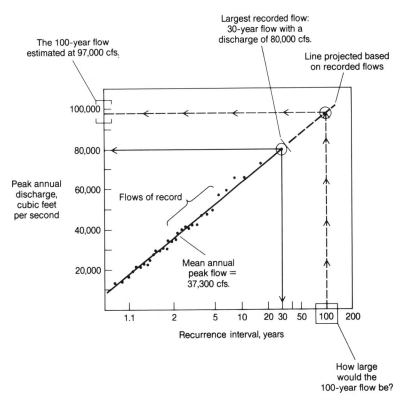

Fig. 10.5 Straightened curve of the distribution of discharges for the Sky Komish River at Gold Bar, Washington. An estimate of the magnitude of flows at intervals beyond 30 years is now possible.

Meaning of flow forecasts

within the 30 years of record, we can project the curve beyond the 30-year event and read the magnitude of the 100-year event, which would be 97,000 cfs, as shown in Fig. 10.5. This figure represents a best approximation of the 100-year flow.

Making **forecasts of riverflows** based on discharge records is extremely helpful in planning land use and in engineering bridges, buildings, and highways in and around river valleys. On the other hand, this sort of forecasting technique has several distinct limitations. First, the period of record is very short compared to total time the river has been flowing; therefore, forecasts are based only on a glimpse of the river's behavior. Second, throughout much of North America, watersheds have undergone such extensive changes because of urban and agricultural development, forestry, and mining that discharge records for many streams today have a different meaning than those several decades ago. Third, climatic change in some areas, for example, near major metropolitan regions, may be great enough over 50 or 100 years to produce measurable changes in runoff. Together, these factors suggest that forecasts based on projections of past flows should be taken as approximations of future flows, and for greatest reliability, they should be limited to events not too far beyond the years of record, say, 50-year, 100-year, and 200-year flows.

10.4 APPLICATIONS TO LAND PLANNING

The principal use of discharge data in land planning is in the assessment of flood hazard. Property damage from floods in the United States and Canada has increased appre-

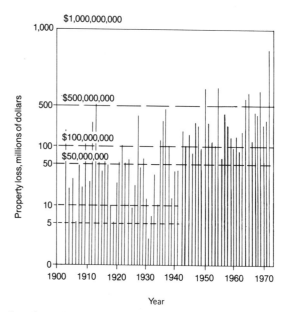

Fig. 10.6   Property loss (in millions of dollars) as a result of floods in the United States over 70 years. (Data from U.S. National Weather Service.)

ciably in this century, and in order to curb this trend, improved understanding, among other things, of the hydrologic behavior of streams and rivers is necessary (Fig. 10.6).

Relating discharge to topography   Detailed analysis of a river's flood potential is a difficult and expensive task. Basically, it involves translating a particular **discharge** into a level (elevation) of flow and then relating that flow level to the **topography** in the river valley. In this manner we can determine what land is inundated and what is not (Fig. 10.7a). This procedure requires accurate discharge and topographic data as well as a knowledge of channel conditions. The latter is necessary in order to compute flow velocity, which is the basis for determining the water elevation in different reaches of the channel, that is, just how high a given discharge will reach.

For planning purposes, however, neither the time nor money is usually available for such detailed analysis. We must, instead, turn to existing topographic maps and existing discharge data and make a best estimate of the extent of various frequencies of flow. The accuracy of such estimates depends not only on the reliability of the data, but also on the shape of the river valley. Where the walls of a river valley rise sharply from the floodplain, the limits of flooding are often easy to define; however, where a river flows through broad lowlands the problem can be very difficult (Fig. 10.7b).

Flood Backwaters and Valley Contours

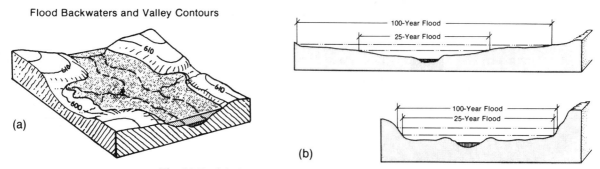

Fig. 10.7   (a) Flood backwaters in relation to valley contours. (b) The influence of valley shape on the extent of the 25-year and 100-year floods.

National Flood Insurance Program

The U.S. **National Flood Insurance Program** is based on a definition of the 100-year "floodplain," and in most areas, the boundaries of this zone are delineated using the method previously described. According to this program, two zones are actually defined: (1) the regulatory *floodway,* the lowest part of the floodplain where the deepest and most frequent floodflows are conducted; and (2) the *floodway fringe,* on the margin of the regulatory floodway, an area that would be lightly inundated by the 100-year flood. Buildings located in the regulatory floodway are not eligible for flood insurance, whereas those in the flood fringe are eligible provided that a certain amount of floodproofing is established (Fig. 10.8).

The flood insurance program is intended to serve as one of the controls to limit development in floodplains. Other controls include zoning restrictions against vulnerable land uses and educational programs to inform prospective settlers of the hazards posed by river valleys.

Reducing flood damage

In the case of river valleys where development is already substantial, the only means of **reducing damage** is to relocate flood-prone land uses or reduce the size of hazardous riverflows. Because of the high costs and the sociological problems associated with relocation, planners often turn to a flow-reduction option. This calls for structural (engineering) changes such as building reservoirs, dredging channels, diverting flows, and/or constructing embankments to confine flow, all of which are expensive and often deleterious to the environment.

10.5 OTHER METHODS FOR DEFINING FLOOD-PRONE AREAS

Many streams are too small to qualify for an official gauging station, yet they merit serious consideration in local land use planning. Communities bordering on such

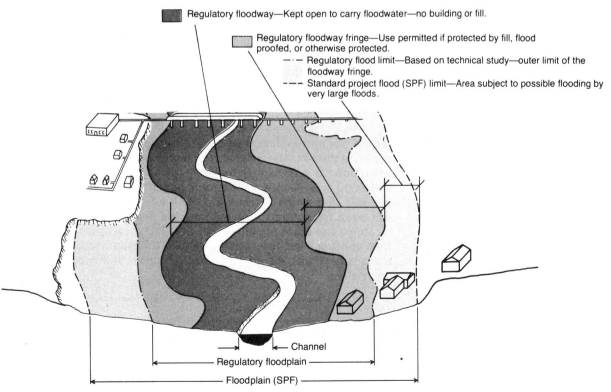

Fig. 10.8 Illustrations defining the regulator floodway and the floodway fringe according to the U.S. National Flood Insurance Program.

streams are often pressed for information not only on flood hazards, but also on many other features of the stream valley that are important to planning decisions. Typical concerns include soil suitability for foundations and basements, siting of sanitary landfills and wastewater disposal facilities, the role of wetlands in the floodplain environment, and the distribution of forests and wildlife habitats. Much of this information can be generated from published sources, in particular, topographic contour maps, aerial photographs, and soil maps.

Floodplain as a landform

Of all the features of the river valley, the **floodplain** is the most important from a planning standpoint. Defined according to geomorphic criteria, the floodplain is the low-lying land along the stream, the outer limits of which may be marked by steep slopes, the valley walls. The floodplain is important for several reasons. First, excluding the stream channel itself, the floodplain is generally the lowest part of the stream valley and thus is most prone to flooding. Second, floodplain soils are often poorly drained because of the nearness of the water table to the surface and saturation by floodwaters. Third, floodplains are formed by incremental erosion and deposition associated with the lateral migration of streams in their valleys. Therefore, the borders of the floodplain can be taken as a good indicator of the extent of alluvial soil. These features are the key indicators for floodplain mapping (Fig. 10.9).

10.6 MAPPING FLOODPLAINS

Contour maps

Floodplains can be delineated in four ways, according to (1) topography, (2) vegetation, (3) soils, and (4) the extent of past flood flows. Topographic **contour maps** can be used to delineate floodplains if the valley walls are high enough to be marked by two or more contour lines. However, those that carry only a single contour, or fall within the contour interval, cannot be delineated, even though they may be topographically distinct to the field observer. In the latter case, aerial photographs can be helpful in mapping this feature. Viewed with a standard stereoscope, topographic features appear exaggerated, thereby making identification of valley features a relatively easy task in many instances.

Aerial photographs

Aerial photographs also enable us to examine vegetation and land use patterns for evidence of floodplains and wet areas. In the prairies and the major farming regions, such as the Great Plains and the Corn Belt, the floodplains of streams and rivers are often demarcated by belts of forest. Similarly, in forested areas the floodplain tree

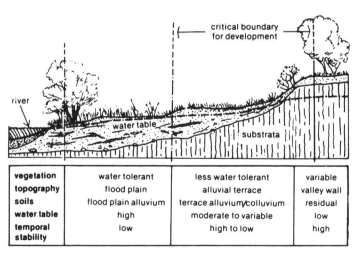

Fig. 10.9   A good illustration of the abrupt change in topography, soils, drainage and vegetation from the floodplain to the valley walls.

covers are sometimes different in composition, and once these differences are known, they can be used to help identify floodplains.

Soil maps   Because river floodplains are built from river deposits, the soils of floodplains often possess characteristics distinctively different from those of the neighboring uplands. They are generally described in the U.S. Soil Conservation Service reports as soils having high water tables, seasonal flooding, and diverse composition. Therefore, **soil maps** prepared by the SCS can also be used in the definition of floodplains. A note of caution is called for in using SCS maps, however, because the SCS bases much of its own decisions for drawing the boundaries of different soil types on topography, vegetation, and land use patterns. Therefore, we must be aware that a good correlation between floodplans based on SCS soil boundaries and floodplains based on observable vegetation, topography, and land use may constitute circular reasoning.

Field surveys   Finally, floodplains may be defined according to the extent of past floodflows. Evidence of past flows may be gained from firsthand observers who are able to pinpoint the position of the water surface in the landscape and from features such as organic debris on fences and deposits on roads that can be tied to the flood. This method usually demands extensive field work, including interviews with local residents.

Synthesizing data   The map overlay technique is most commonly employed in **synthesizing** all these **data.** Although it has been long used by geographers, the application of this technique has been advanced by landscape architects and planners in recent decades for problems involving complex spatial arrangements among multiple sets of data. One overlay scheme involves assigning numerical values to the various classes of each component of the landscape (vegetation, drainage, soils, and the like) according to their land use suitability. The values are then summed and the results used to delineate areas or zones of different development potentials (Fig. 10.10). We should be cautioned against attaching too much meaning to the numerical results, however, because the values are not intrinsic quantities but rather arbitrary numbers assigned to qualitative classes.

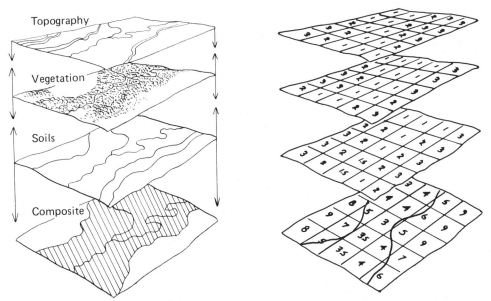

Fig. 10.10 A schematic portrayal of the map overlay technique. *Left,* maps delineating the pertinent features; *right,* these features codified into a numerical scheme based on land use suitability.

10.7 CASE STUDY

Formulating and Evaluating Alternative Solutions to a Flooding Problem, San Pedro, California

Leonard Ortolano

During the early 1970s, the San Francisco office of the U.S. Army Corps of Engineers ("the Corps") was asked to investigate the problem of flooding on San Pedro Creek, a water course in Pacifica, California, just south of San Francisco. Numerous homes and a small shopping center had been built very close to the Creek, and property owners were hopeful that the Corps' study would yield a project that would reduce the flood damages they experienced.

The Corps launched its study in 1973, a time when it was beginning to give increased attention to involving citizens in its planning activities. Because the San Pedro Creek Basin was small (7.2 square miles) and included only about 700 families, it was neither expensive nor difficult to make public involvement activities an integral part of the study. Indeed, one of the first things the Corps did was to organize a citizens' committee to help assure that its planning would be responsive to local concerns. The committee included representatives of homeowners and businesses in the floodplain as well as Pacifica residents from outside the basin who were especially sensitive to questions related to environmental impacts and local taxes and assessments. In addition to organizing a citizens' committee, the Corps also formed a planning team consisting of civil engineers, biologists, and economists on its staff. A "study manager" was assigned to coordinate the team's efforts and tie them in with activities of the citizens' committee.

Based on a reconnaissance investigation, the study manager acquired initial impressions regarding possible ways of reducing flood damages. Early efforts to involve citizens in the study led to some refinements in the study manager's thinking. The following factors were found to be especially important: the maintenance of the San Pedro Creek as a steelhead fishery, the visual character of the Creek, and the costs to Pacifica of any flood-control projects. Preliminary efforts to include other agencies in the study were directed toward the U.S. Fish and Wildlife Service and the California Fish and Game Department. Their views were important since any structural measures proposed to reduce flooding had to be sensitive to the Creek's value as a steelhead fishery. In addition to the issues important to local citizens and other agencies, the Corps of Engineers' planning regulations had to be considered. For example, the Corps' regulations included cost-sharing requirements indicating the funds that had to be provided by nonfederal entities on a Corps flood-control project. All these factors were considered in developing alternative proposals to deal with flooding on the Creek.

The next phase of the study produced a more detailed conception of alternative plans to reduce flood damages and a preliminary analysis of the impact of the different schemes. Although there is no simple way to characterize the activities during this phase, it is instructive to consider how the Corps' recommended solution was reached. Some alternative actions were discussed and then immediately dismissed because the Corps thought they either did not solve the problem or were outside the Corps' authority to study or implement. For example, flood insurance was not viewed as solving the flood problem. As another example, modifications of Pacifica's stormsewer system were viewed as outside the Corps' authority to implement, and thus such modifications were not considered. This dismissal occurred even though the inadequate capacity of the stormdrains contributed to the flooding difficulties.

The Corps examined the following alternative actions: trapezoidal riprap channel, rectangular concrete channel, upstream dam, flood proofing, bypass channel, and a park and floodwall option. Several different appraisals of these alternatives were made, and the citizens' committee judged the options. Pacifica residents who were not on the committee were invited to rank the alternatives by responding to a mail survey. Among the evaluative criteria emphasized by citizens were aesthetics and the use of the creekside area for recreation. The state and federal fish and game agencies evaluated the proposals from the perspective of impact on steelhead. The Corps of Engineers office made its own formal evaluations using benefit-cost analysis and an environmental impact study.

Based on these several appraisals, two proposals emerged as the leading candidates for solving the flood problem. One of these, the park and floodwall alternative, involved creating a 4- to 6-foot high concrete or masonry wall on the right bank of the Creek and modifying the left bank to create a floodway that would accommodate flows in excess of the Creek's capacity (see map). The scheme was designed so that much of the creekside vegetation on the left bank could be retained; the open space in the floodway could serve as a park during nonflood periods. (An earlier scheme, which proposed that the creekside vegetation be removed, had been rejected because the local residents highly prized the vegetation.)

The second proposal that emerged as a contender was the bypass channel alternative. This plan involved use of a 1- to 2-foot right-bank levee combined with an excavated bypass channel in the left-bank open space area (see map).

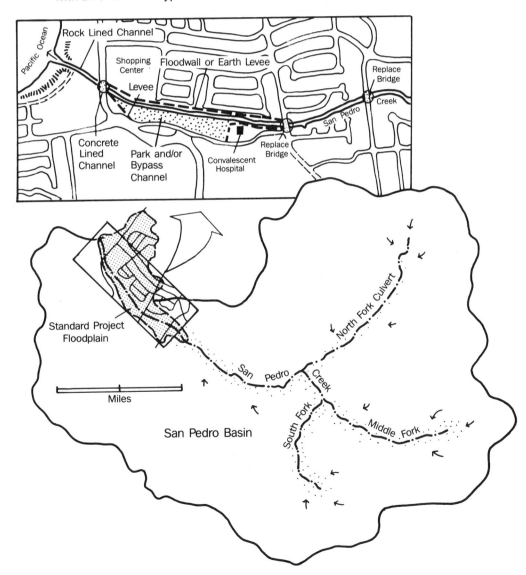

This alternative would preserve almost all of the left bank vegetation, and the open space adjacent to the left bank could be used as a park. Near the final stages of the study, the Corps learned that this proposal would interfere with the California Department of Transportation's plans to relocate and upgrade Highway 1.

The head of the Corps' San Francisco office, the district engineer, was responsible for assimilating all the information that had been generated during the study and for making a recommendation. The district engineer felt the park and floodwall alternative described above was the best option. It had a benefit-cost ratio greater than one, and it was endorsed by the local citizens and all concerned agencies. In addition to treating the flood problem, the recommended alternatives would give local residents a park facility that would enhance their use of the creekside area during nonflood conditions.

Leonard Ortolano is UPS Foundation professor of civil engineering for urban and regional planning at Stanford University.

10.8 SELECTED REFERENCES FOR FURTHER READING

Burby, Raymond J., and French, S. P. "Coping with Floods: The Land Use Management Paradox." *Journal of the American Planning Association* 47: 1981 3, pp. 289–300.

Dunne, Thomas and Leopold, Luna B. "Calculation of Flood Hazard." In *Water in Environmental Planning.* San Francisco: W. A. Freeman, 1978, pp. 279–391.

Erikson, Kai T. *Everything in Its Path: Destruction of Community in the Buffalo Creek Flood.* New York: Simon and Schuster, 1976, 284 pp.

Kochel, R. Craig, and Baker, Victor R. "Paleoflood Hydrology." *Science* 215: 4531, 1982, pp. 353–361.

Ortolano, L. *Environmental Planning and Decision Making.* New York: Wiley, 1984.

Platt, R. H. "Metropolitan Flood Loss Reduction Through Regional Special Districts." *Journal of the American Planning Association,* 52: 4, 1986, p. 467–479.

Rahn, Perry H. "Lessons Learned from the June 9, 1972, Flood in Rapid City, South Dakota." *Bulletin of the Association of Engineering Geologists* 12: 2, 1975, pp. 83–97.

Schneider, William J., and Goddard, J. E. "Extent of Development of Urban Flood Plains." *U.S. Geological Survey Circular 601–J,* 1974, 14 pp.

White, Gilbert F. *Flood Hazard in the United States: A Research Reassessment.* Boulder: University of Colorado, Institute of Behavior Science, 1975.

Wolman, M. Gordon, "Evaluating Alternative Techniques for Floodplain Mapping." *Water Resources Research* 7, 1971, pp. 1383–1392.

11

WATER QUALITY, RUNOFF, AND LAND USE

11.1 INTRODUCTION

The quality of water in lakes and streams has been a national issue in the United States and Canada for a quarter-century or more. Both countries have enacted complex bodies of law calling for nationwide pollution control programs. In the United States, abatement programs have relied overwhelmingly on the modern sewage treatment plant. Treatment plants are mechanical systems that subject wastewater to two or three stages of treatment before it is released to the environment.

Point source pollution

The success of mechanical abatement systems has generally been good for pollution of the point source variety. **Point sources of water pollution** are those characterized by concentrated outfalls from high-intensity land uses. Most examples fall under the general headings of industrial process water and municipal sewage. Surprisingly, the success of the industrial and municipal pollution abatement programs, when weighed against the U.S. national water quality goals, has been substantially less than program proponents originally forecast.

Nonpoint source pollution

The main explanation for this is that in the modern landscape the magnitude of contributions from **nonpoint sources** is much greater than originally estimated. Nonpoint sources are spatially diffused sources that emanate from relatively large areas and enter streams and lakes via stormwater, precipitation, atmospheric fallout, interflow, and groundwater. The prime contributors include urban stormwater, septic system seepage, air pollution, and agricultural runoff (Table 11.1). Because of the size of the source areas, the numerous outfalls involved, and the sporadic nature of the flows, nonpoint pollution does not lend itself to abatement using conventional mechanical systems, that is, treatment plants. Instead, it is generally agreed that nonpoint

Table 11.1   Nonpoint Source Pollution: Sources and Types

Source Environment	*Source Land Use/Process*	*Pollutants*
Landscape	■ Urban stormwater (runoff) ■ Agriculture (runoff) ■ Septic systems (seepage) ■ Spills and leakage: tanks and autos (infiltration) ■ Soil erosion (runoff) ■ Fires (forest, grasslands, wastes)	■ BOD (organic debris) ■ Nutrients (mainly nitrogen and phosphorus) ■ Sediment (sand, silt, and clay) ■ Organic compounds (e.g., diazinon, PCBs, benzene) ■ Heavy metals (e.g., lead, zinc, mercury)
Atmosphere	■ Power plants and industry (exhausts) ■ Residential heating (exhausts) ■ Automobiles (exhausts) ■ Agriculture: wind erosion and sprays ■ Fires (forests, grasslands, and wastes)	■ Petroleum residues (gasoline, grease, oil) ■ Biological (mainly bacteria) ■ Sediment ■ Nutrients ■ BOD ■ Organic compounds
Subsurface	■ Urban stormwater (infiltration) ■ Landfills (leachate) ■ Agriculture (infiltration) ■ Spills and leakage (infiltration and percolation)	■ Heavy metals ■ Acid rain (oxides of sulfur and nitrogen) ■ Nutrients ■ Organic compounds ■ Petroleum residues

source abatement must be approached as an environmental management problem, focusing on the sites, activities, and conditions that produce the pollutants.

Nonpoint sources produce many of the same pollutants as point sources. Chief among these are oxygen-demanding elements, nutrients, organic compounds, and heavy metals. In addition, sediment, acid rain, and petroleum products are significant nonpoint pollutants. Classed according to environment of origin, nonpoint sources fall into three broad classes: atmospheric, landscape, and subsurface (Table 11.1). The landscape is the major contributor, but with rising air pollution and groundwater pollution, atmospheric and subsurface contributions have increased significantly in recent decades. Although it is widely recognized that landscape sources are difficult to abate, atmospheric and groundwater sources are even more difficult, especially atmospheric, because of the need to control complex sources and multijurisdictional arrangements over vast regions. The focus of attention in nonpoint management efforts is land use as it relates to runoff.

11.2 LAND USE–WATER QUALITY RELATIONS

Density relations

The relationship between land use and water quality is a complex one in the modern landscape. As a result, the establishment of scientifically reliable correlations between land use activities and features on the one hand and nonpoint source pollution on the other has not come easily. For urban land uses, however, a fairly reliable correlation has been defined between the annual loading rates for various pollutants and land use based mainly on **density**. The most widely used measure of density is impervious cover, and studies show that pollutant loading of stormwater increases with percentage of impervious cover. Table 11.2 shows the relationship between four pollutants and six land uses representing impervious covers ranging from 12 percent to 95 percent.

Although impervious cover is closely related to pollutant loading, it, of course, is not the direct cause of stormwater pollution. Rather, the amount and types of land use activity associated with impervious cover are the sources of pollution—for example, commercial activity, automobile traffic, air pollution, and garbage production. However, impervious cover cannot be ignored as a contributor to water pollution inasmuch as it promotes pollutant removal from the land by facilitating surface

Table 11.2 Stormwater Pollution for Selected Urban Land Uses

Land Use	Density[a]	Nitrogen[b]	Phosphorus[b]	Lead[b]	Zinc[b]
Residential, large lot (1 acre)	12%	3.0	0.3	0.06	0.20
Residential, small lot (0.25 acre)	25%	8.8	1.1	0.40	0.32
Townhouse apartment	40%	12.1	1.5	0.88	0.50
High rise apartment	60%	10.3	1.2	1.42	0.71
Shopping center	90%	13.2	1.2	2.58	2.06
Central Business District	95%	24.6	2.7	5.42	2.71

[a] Based on percentage of the land covered by impervious (hard surface) material.

[b] Pounds per acre of land per year.

Source: Guidebook for Screening Urban Nonpoint Pollution Management Strategies, Northern Virginia Planning District Commission, 1979.

flushing. Other measures of land use may also be used as indicators of pollution loading—for example, dwelling units per acre and people per acre. As the data in Table 11.3 indicate, pollution loading in residential areas increases with both dwelling units and persons per acre. This is very significant, but equally significant for planning purposes is the rate of pollution loading per person or dwelling units.

Per capita loading   The **per capita loading** rate, that is, the amount of stormwater pollution per person, actually decreases with higher residential densities. By way of example, let us consider residential densities of 0.5, 2.0, and 10 dwelling units per acre. At a density of 0.5 house per acre (2 acre lots), which is equivalent to about 1.25 persons per acre, the per person loading rate for phosphorus is 0.64 pound per year and lead is 0.11 pound per year. At a density of 2 houses per acre (0.5 acre lots), the per person loading rate is 0.18 pound phosphorus and 0.05 pound lead. For townhouse apartments at 10 units per acre, the person loadings are 0.06 pound phosphorus and 0.035 pound lead.

The trend is clear: measured on a per capita basis, large residential lots in the range of 1 to 2 acres tend to be the most damaging to water quality. The reasons are related to the large size of houses, the large numbers of automobiles per household, and the relatively great lengths of roads and drives, among other things. The fact that the per capita loading rate decreases with higher densities suggests that communities should discourage large lot development on the urban fringe and promote cluster development as a means of reducing water pollution.

11.3 WATER QUALITY MITIGATION ON LAND

Slowing response time   Broadly speaking, the first objective in mitigating stormwater quality is to **slow the overall rate of response** of the stormwater flow system (Fig. 11.1). This slowing will induce infiltration and settling of contaminants and reduce rates of surface flushing and erosion. One measure of system response is concentration time. If the concentration times of stormflow, especially those that flush surfaces frequently such as flows from storms in the range of 0.5 to 1.0 inch rainfall, can be extended rather than decreased with development, an important step can be taken toward water quality control.

Strategies   With regard to other mitigation **strategies,** we can approach the problem at three levels: (1) control of pollutant production; (2) control of pollutant removal from the site; and (3) control of pollutant transfer through the delivery system. The first level includes the regulation of land use types, development density, lawn fertilizing, garbage burning, and so on. Considering the per capita pollutant loading rates associated

Table 11.3   Annual Stormwater Pollution Loading for Residential Development

Density	Phosphorus[a]	Nitrogen[a]	Lead[a]	Zinc[a]	Sediment[b]
0.5 unit/ac (1.25 person)	0.8	6.2	0.14	0.17	0.09
1.0 unit/ac (2.5 persons)	0.8	6.7	0.17	0.20	0.11
2.0 units/ac (5 persons)	0.9	7.7	0.25	0.25	0.14
10.0 units/ac (25 persons)	1.5	12.1	0.88	0.50	0.27

[a] Pounds per acre per year.

[b] Tons per acre per year.

Source: Guidebook for Screening Urban Nonpoint Pollution Management Streategies, Northern Virginia Planning District Commission, 1979.

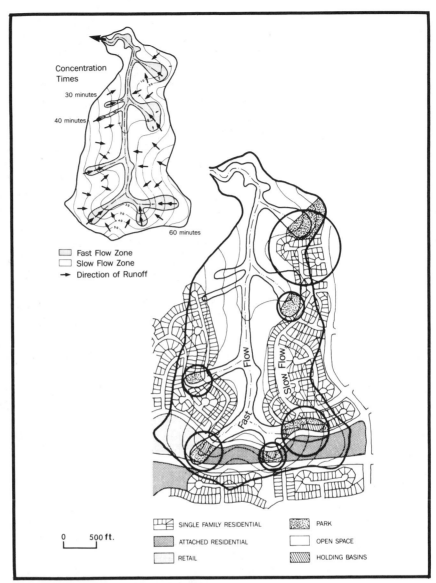

Fig. 11.1 The pattern of runoff travel times in a small basin (inset) and a proposed land use plan designed to minimize acceleration of runoff in fast flow zones by limiting development near channel heads and using stormwater basin and parkland to slow delivery rates to channels.

with large lot residential development, we see that cluster development is clearly an important means of minimizing pollution loading of stormwater in residential areas.

    Measures for controlling transfer of pollutants from the site are aimed largely at regulating the volume of runoff. The most common strategy relies on increasing **soil absorption** through, for example, increasing the ratio of vegetated to impervious groundcover, using porous pavers, and diverting runoff into infiltration beds or dry wells. According to a study conducted in the Washington, D.C., region, soil-absorption measures are the most effective means of removing pollutants from stormwater. This study found that, for soil with average permeability, expected removal capacities are in the range of 35 to 65 percent for total annual phosphorus; 40 to 85 percent for annual biochemical oxygen demand (BOD); and 80 to 90 percent for annual lead, depending on land use type.

Soil absorption

Filter berms

The use of soil as a filter medium has been used experimentally by some communities. Austin, Texas, for example, has favored two such measures in new developments: **filter berms** and filtration basins. Filter berms are elongated earth mounds constructed along the contour of a slope. They are usually constructed of soil containing different grades of sand and a filter fabric and are designed to function in the same fashion as soil infiltration trenches, which have been shown to be highly effective in contaminant removal. With berms and related measures, treatment is limited to small flows, either those from individual lots or small groups of lots. Soil-filtering efficiency is very high according to tests based on the application of treatment plant effluent to soil in various parts of the United States.

Filtration basins

Filtration basins (also called water quality basins or filtering ponds) are concrete structures floored with several grades of sand and a filter fabric through which the stormwater is conducted (Fig. 11.2). Filtration basins are generally used for higher density land uses, such as shopping centers, than would be appropriate for filter berms. They are designed to filter the first 0.5 inch of runoff, the so-called first flush, which is heaviest in contaminants. The performance of filtration basins based on Austin's experience is good for small stormflows (less than 0.5 inch runoff). For first-flush flows the city of Austin reported the following filtering rates: Fecal coliform 76 percent, total suspended solids 70 percent, total nitrogen 21 percent, total Kjeldahl nitrogen 46 percent, nitrate nitrogen 0, total phosphorus 33 percent, BOD 70 percent, total organic carbon 48 percent, iron 45 percent, lead 45 percent, and zinc 45 percent.

Vegetative buffers

Another filtering measure strongly favored by some communities is the **vegetated buffer.** Several experimental studies show that vegetative buffers can be extremely efficient in sediment removal (up to 90 percent or more) if they meet the following design criteria: (1) continuous grass/turf cover, (2) buffer widths generally greater than 50 to 100 feet, (3) gentle gradients, generally less than 10 percent, and (4) shallow runoff depths, generally not exceeding the height of the grass. In hilly terrain, vegetative buffers should, to the greatest extent possible, be located on upland

Fig. 11.2   Filter basin used to reduce contaminant loads in stormwater. Water is filtered through layers of sand which lie between the baffles.

Table 11.4 Representative Removal Efficiencies for Stormwater Holding Basins

Pollutant	Percentage Removal
Suspended sediment	40–75%
Total phosphorus	20–50%
Total nitrogen	15–30%
BOD	30–65%
Lead	40–90%
Zinc	20–30%

Sources: Based on a compilation from various sources by Michael Sullivan Associates, Austin, Texas.

surfaces and integrated with depression storage and soil-filtration measures such as berms and dry wells (see Fig. 8.8).

Holding basins The final class of mitigation measures are those placed in the delivery system. These measures are **holding basins,** usually detention ponds and retention basins. These features are designed to withhold stormwater from the flow system in order to reduce peak discharge. By holding stormwater, water quality can also be improved, especially the early runoff from a storm. Investigators generally point to the importance of sediment settling in stormwater basins and its role in the overall removal of pollutants from the water. Table 11.4 offers representative removal values reported by various studies from retention basins and detention basins. Values tend to be higher for retention basins because they hold water on a permanent basis and have a correspondingly higher potential for sediment settling and biochemical synthesis than detention basins. Retention basins are often larger than detention basins; therefore, retention residence times for stormwater are longer, which also improves their efficiencies.

11.4 EUTROPHICATION OF WATERBODIES

Nutrient loading Among the many problems caused by water pollution, **nutrient loading** is one of the most serious and widespread in North America. Nutrients are dissolved minerals that nurture growth in aquatic plants such as algae and bacteria. Among the many nutrients found in natural waters, nitrogen and phosphorus are usually recognized as the most critical ones, because when both are present in large quantities they can induce accelerated rates of biological activity. Massive growths of aquatic plants in a lake or reservoir will lead to (1) a change in the balance of dissolved oxygen, carbon dioxide, and micro-organisms; and (2) an increase in the production of total organic matter. These changes lead to further alterations in the aquatic environment, most of which are decidedly undesirable from a human use standpoint:

■ Increased rate of basin in-filling by dead organic matter.

■ Decreased water clarity.

■ Shift in fish species to rougher types such as carp.

■ Decline in aesthetic quality; for example, increase in unpleasant odor.

■ Increased cost of water treatment by municipalities and industry.

■ Decline in recreational value.

Eutrophication Together, the processes of nutrient loading, accelerated biological activity, and the buildup of organic deposits are known as **eutrophication.** Often described as the process of aging a waterbody, eutrophication is a natural biochemical process that works hand in hand with geomorphic processes to close out waterbodies. Driven by natural forces alone, an inland lake in the midlatitudes may be consumed by eutrophication within several thousand years, but the rate varies widely with the size, depth, and bioclimatic conditions of the lake. In practically every instance, however, land development accelerates the rate by adding a surcharge of nutrients and sediment to the lake. So pronounced is this increase that scientists refer to two eutrophication rates for waterbodies in developed areas: natural and cultural (Fig. 11.3).

For plants to achieve a high rate of productivity, the environment must supply them with large and dependable quantities of five basic resources: heat, light, carbon dioxide, water, and nutrients. According to the biological principle of limiting factors, plant productivity can be controlled by limiting the supply of any one of these resources. In inland and coastal waters, heat, light, carbon dioxide, and water are abundant on either a year-round or seasonal basis. On the other hand, nutrients often tend to be the most limited resource, not just in terms of quantities but also in terms of types. If both dissolved **nitrogen and phosphorus** are available in ample quantities, productivity is usually high; however, if either one is scarce, productivity may be retarded.

Nitrogen and phosphorus

When introduced to the landscape in the dissolved form, phosphorus and nitrogen show different responses to runoff processes. Nitrogen, which is generally more abundant, tends to be highly mobile, moving with the flow of soil water and groundwater to receiving waterbodies. If introduced to a field as fertilizer, for example, most of it may pass through the soil in the time it takes infiltration water to percolate through the soil column, as little as weeks in humid climates. In contrast, phosphorus tends to be retained in the soil, being released to the groundwater very slowly. As a result, under natural conditions most waters tend to be phosphorus-limited, and when a surcharge of phosphorus is directly introduced to a waterbody, accelerated rates of productivity can be triggered. Accordingly, in water management programs aimed at limiting eutrophication, phosphorus control is often the primary goal. In the study of inland lakes, a classification scheme has been devised based on the total phosphorus (both organic and inorganic forms) content of lake water (Table 11.5).

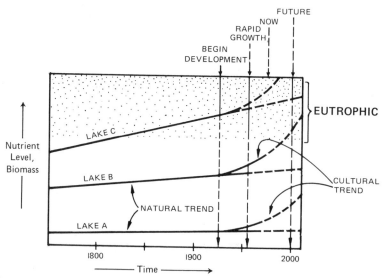

Fig. 11.3 Graph illustrating the concepts of natural and cultural eutrophication. The three sets of curves represent waterbodies at three stages of natural eutrophication as they enter the cultural stage of their development.

Table 11.5 Levels of Eutrophication Based on Dissolved Phosphorus

Level	Total Phosphorus, mg/l	Water Characteristics
Oligotrophic (pre-eutrophic)	Less than 0.025	No algal blooms or nuisance weeds; clear water; abundant dissolved oxygen
Early eutrophic	0.025–0.045	
Middle eutrophic	0.045–0.065	
Eutrophic	0.065–0.085	
Advanced eutrophic	Greater than 0.085	Algal blooms and nuisance aquatic weeds throughout growing season; poor light penetration; limited dissolved oxygen

Representative mean annual values of phosphorus in phosphorus-limited waterbodies.

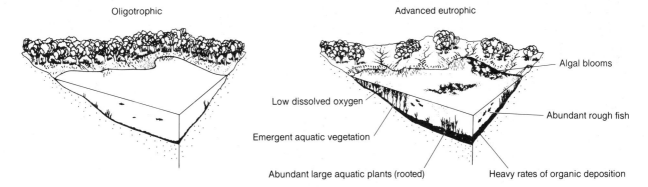

11.5 LAKE NUTRIENT LOADING AND LAND USE

Nutrient budget concept For any body of water it is possible to compute the **nutrient budget** by tabulating inputs, outputs, and storage of phosphorus and nitrogen over some time period. Inputs come from four main sources: point sources, surface runoff (streamflow, stormwater, and the like), subsurface runoff (chiefly groundwater), and the atmosphere. Outputs take mainly three forms: streamflow, seepage into the groundwater system, and burial of organic sediments containing nutrients (Fig. 11.4). Storage of nutrients is represented by plants and animals, both living and dead, which release synthesized nutrients upon decomposition. A formula for the nutrient budget may be written as follows:

$$P + R + O + G + A - Q - S - B = 0$$

where

P = point source contributions

R = surface runoff contributions

O = organic sediment contributions

G = groundwater contributions

A = atmospheric contributions

Q = losses to streamflow

S = losses to groundwater

B = losses to organisms and sediment burial

While the nutrient budget is easy to describe, it has proven very difficult to compute accurately for most waterbodies. The primary reasons for this are: (1) some of the pertinent data, such as nutrient losses to groundwater seepage, are often difficult

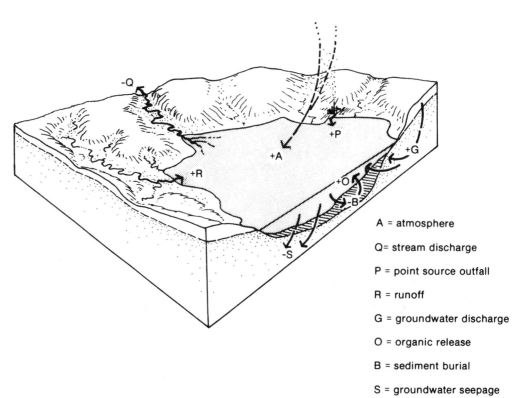

A = atmosphere

Q= stream discharge

P = point source outfall

R = runoff

G = groundwater discharge

O = organic release

B = sediment burial

S = groundwater seepage

Fig. 11.4 Main inputs and outputs of nutrients to a waterbody. Computation of a nutrient budget over some time period tells us the trend of the nutrient concentrations in the water.

to generate; and (2) exchanges of nutrients among water, organisms, and organic sediments are difficult to gauge. As a result, most nutrient budgets are based on a limited set of data, usually those representing streamflow, septic drainfield seepage, point sources, and atmospheric fallout. Recently, however, data have been produced relating land use and surface cover to the nutrient content of runoff.

Nutrient loading of runoff
    In a study of the nitrogen and phosphorus contents of United States streams, the United States Environmental Protection Agency and various state water quality programs made several interesting findings. First, the export of these nutrients from the land by streams tends to vary widely for different runoff events and for different watersheds with similar land uses. Second, although regional variations in nutrient

Table 11.6 Nutrient Loading Rates for Six Land Cover/Use Types

Cover/Use	Nitrogen (kg/km²/yr)	Phosphorus (kg/km²/yr)
Forest	440	8.5
Mostly forest	450	17.5
Mostly urban	788	30.0
Mostly agriculture	631	28.0
Agriculture	982	31.0
Mixed	552	18.5
Golf Course	1500	41.0

Source: J. Omernik, *The Influence of Land Use on Stream Nutrient Levels,* U.S. Environmental Protection Agency, 1977.

export do appear in the United States for small drainage areas, they do not correlate very well with rock and soil type. Instead, nutrient export by small streams tends to correlate best with land use and cover, in particular to the proportion of agricultural and urban land in a watershed. Nitrogen and phosphorus concentrations in streams draining agricultural land, for example, are typically five to ten times higher than those draining forested land.

Based on these findings, it is possible to estimate the nitrogen and phosphorus loading of streams and lakes in most areas. The loading values are applicable to surface runoff, principally channel flow. The values in Table 11.6 are given in kilograms per square kilometer for seven basic land use/cover types. (The definition of each land use/cover type is given in the next section.) Figure 11.5 gives the loading values in milligrams per liter of water (runoff) for agriculture and forest use/cover types for the eastern, middle, and western regions of the coterminous United States. For comparative purposes, examine these values with those representative of the water systems listed in Table 11.7.

Estimating nutrient loading   To determine the **nutrient contributions** to a waterbody, we must first delineate the drainage system and define its drainage areas. This may be a difficult task in developed areas because of the complexity of the land uses and the artificial drainage patterns that are superimposed on the natural drainage system. As a first step, it is instructive to identify the various land uses and major cover types in the area, noting their relationship to the drainage system and water features, what kinds of pollutant

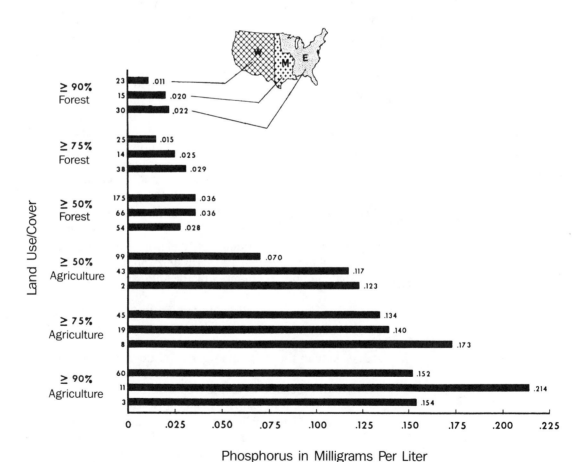

Fig. 11.5 Phosphorus loading values per liter of runoff based on agricultural and forest land use/cover for the coterminous United States.

Table 11.7 Representative Levels of Phosphorus and Nitrogen in Various Waters

Water	*Total P, mg/l*	*Total N, mg/l*
Rainfall	0.01–0.03	0.1–2.0
Lakes without algal problems	Less than 0.025	Less than 0.35
Lakes with serious algal problems	More than 0.10	More than 0.80
Urban stormwater	1.0–2.0	2.0–10
Agricultural runoff	0.05–1.1	5.0–70
Sewage plant effluent (secondary treatment)	5–10	More than 20

Sources include John W. Clark et al., *Water Supply and Pollution Control,* 3rd ed. (New York: IEP/Dun-Donnelley, 1977); and American Water Works Association, "Sources of Nitrogen and Phosphorus in Water Supplies," *Journal of the American Water Works Association* 59, 1967, pp. 344–366.

Remaining steps

they are apt to contribute (both nutrients and other types), and the locations of critical entry points. The **remaining steps** are as follows:

■ Determine the percentage of each drainage area occupied by forest, agriculture, and urban development.

■ Classify each area according to the relative percentages of forest, agriculture, and urban land uses based on the following percentages:

Forest	>75% forested
Mostly forest	50–75% forested
Agriculture	>75% active farmland
Mostly agriculture	50–75% active farmland
Mostly urban	>40% urban development (residential, commercial, industrial, institutional)
Mixed	Does not fall into one of the above classes; for example, 25% urban, 30% agriculture, and 45% forest

■ Using the nutrient-loading values given in Table 11.6, multiply the appropriate value for each area by its total area in square kilometers.

■ To calculate the loading potential from septic drainfield seepage, count the number of homes within 100 yards of the shore or streambank for each drainage area and multiply this number by the following nutrient loading rates:

Phosphorus/Year	*Nitrogen/Year*
0.28 kg/home	10.66 kg/home

■ Combine the two totals for each drainage area for the total input from the watershed. If the *grand* total input from all sources is called for, then atmospheric contributions must also be considered. Atmospheric input need only be considered for water surfaces, since it is already included in the values given for land surfaces. Given a fallout rate for the area in question, this value (in mg/m^2) should be multiplied by the area of the waterbody; this quantity would be added to those from the watershed to obtain the grand total input (less groundwater contributions, if any) to the waterbody.

11.6 PLANNING FOR WATER QUALITY MANAGEMENT IN SMALL WATERSHEDS

Planning for residential and related land uses near water features presents a fundamental dilemma: People are attracted to water, yet the closer to it they build and live, the greater the impact they are apt to have on it. As impacts in the form of water pollution and scenic blight rise, the value of the environment declines, which in turn usually lowers land values (Fig. 11.6). Moreover, the greater the proximity of development to water features, generally the greater the threat to property from floods, erosion, and storms. In spite of these well-known problems, the pressure to develop near water features has not waned in recent years. In fact, it seems to have increased, and in areas where there are few natural water features, developers are often inclined to build artificial ones to attract buyers.

Approaches In planning and management programs aimed at water quality, basically two **approaches** may be employed: preventive and corrective. The corrective approach is used to address an unsatisfactory condition that has already developed—for example, cleaning beaches and surface water after an oil spill. On small bodies of water with weed growth problems, corrective measures may involve treatment with chemicals that inhibit aquatic plants, or basin dredging to remove organic sediments. Such measures are generally used as a last resort for waterbodies with serious nutrient problems and/or advanced states of eutrophication.

Prevention A **preventive approach** is generally preferred for most bodies of water, though it may actually be more difficult to employ successfully. This approach involves limiting or reducing the contributions of nutrients and other pollutants from the watershed by

Fig. 11.6 Environmental damage along a waterbody leading to deterioration of land values.

controlling on-site sources of pollution, limiting the transport of pollutants from the watershed to the lake, or both. Measures to control nutrient sources include improving the performance of septic drainfields for sewage disposal, replacing septic drainfields with community sewage treatment systems, reducing fertilizer applications to cropland and lawns, controlling soil erosion, and eliminating the burning of leaves and garbage. Measures to limit nutrient transport to the lake include filtering water through the soil or a soil medium, on-site retention of stormwater, abolition of stormsewers in site drainage, diversion of low-quality water to sump basins, and the maintenance of wetlands, floodplains, and natural stream channels.

Management planning   The formulation of a water quality **management program** for a waterbody usually begins with an estimate of the nutrient budget. Nutrient contributions are placed in two categories: those that can be managed using available technology and funding, and those that cannot. The latter includes groundwater and atmospheric contribution, whereas the former includes primarily surface and near surface runoff, that is, stormwater, septic drainfield seepage, and the like.

Goals   The second step entails defining management **goals,** such as "to slow the rate of eutrophication," or "to improve on the visual character" of a certain part of the waterbody. This process is important because the goals must be realistic and attainable. Generally speaking, the more ambitious the goals (for example, "to reverse the trend in eutrophication"), the more difficult and expensive they will be to achieve. Once goals are established, a plan (or set of plans) is formulated that identifies the actions and measures that need to be implemented. Some actions, such as a prohibition on the use of phosphorus-rich fertilizers, may apply to the entire watershed, whereas others may apply only to a specific subarea that the nutrient budget data show to be a large contributor. In addition, measures are proposed to limit nutrient production and transport related to future development by defining appropriate development zones, and enacting guidelines on sediment control, stormwater drainage, and sewage disposal.

Finally, after the plan is implemented, the waterbody must be monitored and the results weighed against the original goals, financial costs, and public support. This is a difficult task because it often requires comparing the results with forecasts about what conditions would have been without the plan. Uncertainty often arises relating to the validity of the original forecasts and what the effects of natural perturbations in climatic, hydrologic, or biotic systems may have had in masking or enhancing the efforts of the plan.

Watershed applications   In water quality planning for lakes and ponds, we need to understand the drainage system with which we are dealing. As we noted in Chapter 9, every waterbody is supported by a watershed, which is comprised of many water systems including stream networks, groundwater, and precipitation and evaporation. The runoff system, particularly that on the surface, provides the spatial framework within which land use planning related to water quality management takes place.

The watershed in Fig. 11.7 is typical of that around most impoundments. The bulk of the area is taken up by *subbasins* that drain all but the narrow belt of land along the shore, called *shoreland.* Subbasins are usually emptied via streams, whereas shorelands, being too narrow to develop streams, are drained directly to the waterbody by overland flow and interflow. Land uses in the watersheds of impoundments tend to correlate with these two types of drainage areas. Water-oriented development (recreational activities and residential uses) are concentrated in the shoreland, whereas nonwater-oriented development (agriculture, suburban residential, commercial, and so on) is located in the subbasins.

Management aimed at the shoreland zone usually involves dealing with individual property owners because each site drains directly into the waterbody. In the subbasins, on the other hand, many land uses are integrated by a runoff system that connects

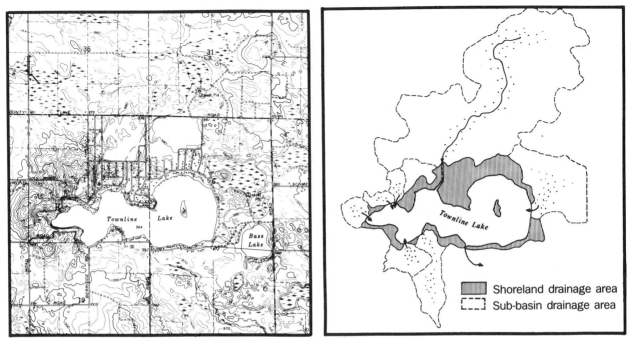

Fig. 11.7 The spatial organization of a small lake watershed showing the two types of drainage subareas: shoreland and subbasin.

to the waterbody at a single point. Management of a subbasin, therefore, is in one respect a more difficult task because many players are often involved and the system is larger and more complex. Subbasins do, however, provide management opportunities that shorelands do not. For example, runoff can be collected at central locations and processed by natural or artificial means to reduce nutrients, sediment, and other impurities.

11.7 CASE STUDY

Drainage Area and Highway Salting Impact of Highway Salting on Water Quality

Robert L. Melvin

The application of salt to highways to reduce ice and snow buildup is a wide-spread practice in the United States and Canada. The amounts of salt applied vary geographically, depending on snowfall, winter temperatures, traffic levels, and state and local highway maintenance policies. In the Midwest and North-eastern United States, annual salt (sodium chloride) applications typically amount to 10 tons per lane mile; that is, 20 tons per mile of a two-lane highway. Salt is highly soluble in a humid environment; therefore such doses can pose a threat to surface and groundwater quality as well as to other components of the environment such as vegetation, soils, and animal habitats. In this century, salt concentrations in the Great Lakes have more than tripled, and 30 to 60 percent of this increase is attributed to road salting.

An initial assessment of the effects of highway salting can be made on the basis of drainage area, highway density, and salt application data. Assuming rain and snow are, over many years, evenly distributed throughout small drainage areas, then differences in the average annual flow of streams can be attributed principally to differences in the size of the drainage area. The larger the drainage area, the greater the dilution of highway salt. Therefore, the ratio

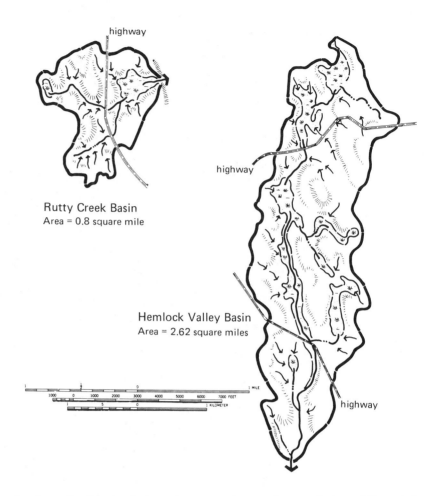

Rutty Creek Basin
Area = 0.8 square mile

Hemlock Valley Basin
Area = 2.62 square miles

of salt application to drainage area can be used as an index of the relative impact of road salt on water quality: the higher the ratio, the lower the relative dilution. The ratio index can also be weighted where necessary for variations in average annual streamflow owing to factors other than drainage area. The following example uses the ratio between salt applied and drainage area to compare the relative effect of the salting of a segment of a two-lane highway in the Rutty Creek drainage basin with the salting of two segments of two similar highways in the Hemlock Valley Brook drainage basin, both in Connecticut. The average annual salt application per lane mile of highway is approximately 8.8 tons.

Rutty Creek Drainage Basin
Area = 0.80 square mile
Lane-miles of highway = 1.66 miles
Ratio of salt application to drainage area

$$= \frac{8.8 \text{ tons} \times 1.66 \text{ lane-miles}}{0.8 \text{ square mile}}$$

$$= 18.3 \text{ tons per square mile}$$

Hemlock Valley Brook Drainage Basin
Area = 2.62 square miles
Lane-miles of highway = 3.5 miles
Ratio of salt application to drainage area

$$= \frac{8.8 \text{ tons} \times 3.5 \text{ lane-miles}}{2.62 \text{ square miles}}$$

$$= 11.8 \text{ tons per square mile}$$

This appraisal indicates significantly less dilution and more environmental impact from highway salting in the Rutty Creek Basin. A more precise evaluation could be made using information on streamflow variability at the sites and salt applications per storm event. Relatively simple evaluations of the type described can identify potential problem areas, leading to detailed field studies and to subsequent alteration of the pattern of deicing agents, the kind of agents used, or the total quantity of agents applied.

Robert L. Melvin is a hydrologist with the U.S. Geological Survey. ■

11.8 SELECTED REFERENCES FOR FURTHER READING

Clark, John W., Viessman, Warren, Jr., and Hammer, Mark J. *Water Supply and Pollution Control.* 3rd ed. New York: IEP/Dun-Donnelley, 1977, 857 pp.

Dillon, P. J., and Vollenweider, R. A. *The Application of the Phosphorus Loading Concept to Eutrophication Research.* Burlington, Ontario: Environment Canada; Center for Inland Waters, 1974, 42 pp.

Marsh, William M., and Hill-Rowley, Richard. "Water Quality, Stormwater Management, and Development Planning on the Urban Fringe." *Journal of Urban and Contemporary Law* 35, 1989, pp. 3–36.

National Academy of Sciences. *Eutrophication: Causes, Consequences, and Correctives.* Washington, D.C.: National Academy of Sciences and the National Research Council, 1969, 463 pp.

Omernik, James M. *Nonpoint Source–Stream Nutrient Level Relationships: A Nationwide Study.* Corvallis, Ore.: U.S. Environmental Protection Agency, 1977, 150 pp.

Smith, R. A., Alexander, R. B., and Wolman, M. G. "Water Quality Trends in the Nation's Rivers." *Science* 235, 1987, pp. 1607–1615.

Soil Conservation Service. *Ponds for Water Supply and Recreation.* Washington, D.C.: U.S. Department of Agriculture, 1971, 55 pp.

Tilton, Donald L., and Kadlec, R. H. "The Utilization of a Fresh-Water Wetland for Nutrient Removal from Secondarily Treated Waste Water Effluent." *Journal of Environmental Quality* 8: 3, 1979, pp. 328–334.

Vallentyne, John R. *The Algal Bowl: Lakes and Man.* Ottawa: Environment Canada; Fisheries and Marine Service, 1974, 186 pp.

Wolman, M. Gordon, and Chamberlin, C. E. "Nonpoint Sources." *Proceedings of the National Water Conference,* Philadelphia Academy of Sciences, 1982, pp. 87–100.

12

SOIL EROSION, LAND USE, AND STREAM SEDIMENTATION

12.1 INTRODUCTION

Soil erosion represents one of the most serious depletions of natural resources in the world today. The Worldwatch Institute estimates that the United States loses 1.5 billion tons of topsoil from cropland each year. This represents more than 7000 pounds (3200 kg) of erosion per acre of land cultivated. While this figure is alarming, the loss rates for China and India are even greater: 27,000 pounds (1200 kg) per acre.[1] In the face of rapidly rising world population, the loss of topsoil to runoff is substantially reducing the food production capability of virtually every agricultural nation (Fig. 12.1). To offset this loss, more land must be opened for farming, and fertilizer application must be increased, both of which add to the overall cost of food production and further soil loss.

Environmental degradation

This is not the only issue associated with soil erosion: the soil material that enters the water systems also causes **environmental degradation.** In particular, the water quality of the receiving streams and lakes is reduced because of added turbidity (muddiness) and chemicals such as nitrogen, phosphorus, and organic compounds, which are washed in with soil particles. Moreover, the heavier sediments glut stream channels and reservoirs, decreasing their capacities to contain large flows. On balance soil erosion damages both upland and lowland landscapes: habitat is lost, productivity declines, carrying capacity is reduced, and the diversity of species is lowered.

12.2 SOIL EROSION AND LAND USE

Agriculture and urbanization

Over the past several thousand years, deforestation, crop **agriculture,** and grazing have promoted the greatest soil erosion. These activities continue to hold that dubious distinction on a worldwide basis today. In the past century or so, however, **urbanization** has become important in the soil erosion issue, especially as it is practiced in North America. The general sequence of land use change that ends in urban development and the corresponding rates of soil erosion are given in Fig. 12.2. A description of the process begins with forest clearing and agricultural development sometime in the 1800s for most areas. Erosion rose sharply with the destruction of natural vegetation and the establishment of cropland and pasture. This trend continued until the first half of the twentieth century when agriculture declined. As abandoned farmland was taken over by weedy vegetation, soil erosion probably declined somewhat as well.

Erosion increased dramatically with urban sprawl in the second half of the twentieth century when farmland, abandoned farmland, and forest were cleared for development. Wholesale exposure of soil during the construction phase of development gave rise to erosion rates as high as 200 tons per acre per year. But this trend is shortlived because the soil is quickly secured under buildings, roads, and landscaped surfaces, as development is completed. Under full urbanization, erosion rates appear to drop to levels less than those associated with twentieth-century agriculture (Fig. 12.3).

12.3 FACTORS INFLUENCING SOIL EROSION

At least four factors must be taken into account in any attempt to forecast soil erosion rates: vegetation, soil type, slope size and inclination, and the frequency and intensity of rainfall. Tests show that intensive rainfalls such as those produced by thunderstorms promote the highest rates of erosion. Accordingly, the incidence of such storms

---

[1] These figures, including those for the United States, represent net loss after contributions from soil formation. Gross soil loss figures would be higher.

Fig. 12.1 Examples of soil erosion from various parts of North America in this century (a) Broken Arrow, Oklahoma (b) Renton, Washington, (c) Avoca, Iowa.

Rainfall erosion index

together with the total annual rainfall can be taken as a reliable measure of the effectiveness of rainfall in promoting soil erosion. The U.S. Soil Conservation Service has translated this into a **rainfall erosion index** that represents the erosive energy delivered to the soil surface annually by rainfall (Fig. 12.4). The index values vary appreciably over the United States, and in some regions, from one side of a state to another. For instance, values decline from 250 to less than 100 from the southeastern to the northwestern corner of Kansas, meaning that on the average erosion on comparable sites should be more than 2.5 times greater in the southeast.

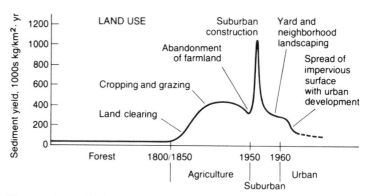

Fig. 12.2 The trend of soil erosion related to land use based on the North American experience.

Vegetation

On most surfaces, **vegetation** appears to be the most important single control on soil erosion. Foliage intercepts raindrops, reducing the force at which they strike the soil surface. Organic litter on the ground further reduces the impact of raindrops, and plant roots bind together aggregates of soil particles, increasing the soil's resistance to the force of running water. The one feature of vegetation that appears to have the greatest influence on erosion is cover density; the heavier the cover, either in the form of groundcover or tree canopy, the lower the soil loss to runoff.

If running water is applied to soils of different textures, sand will usually yield (erode) first. In order to erode clay, the velocity of the runoff would have to be increased to create sufficient stress to overcome cohesive forces that bind the particles together. Similarly, high velocities would also be needed to move pebbles and larger particles because their masses are so much greater than those of sand particles. Thus, in considering the role of soil type in erosion problems, it appears that intermediate textures tend to be most erodible, whereas clay and particles coarser than sand are measurably more resistant (Fig. 12.5). Other soil characteristics, such as compactness

Soil texture and slope

and structure, also influence erodibility, but in general **texture** can be taken as the leading soil parameter in assessing the potential for soil erosion.

The velocity that runoff is able to attain is closely related to the **slope** of the ground over which it flows. Slope also influences the quantity of runoff inasmuch as long slopes collect more rainfall and thus generate a larger volume of runoff, other things being equal. In general, then, slopes that are both steep and long tend to

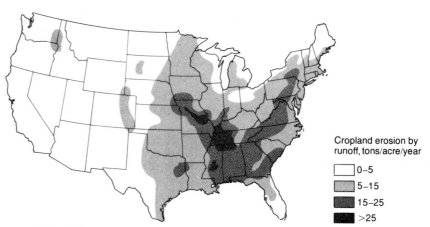

Fig. 12.3 Erosion of cropland by runoff in the United States, 1975.

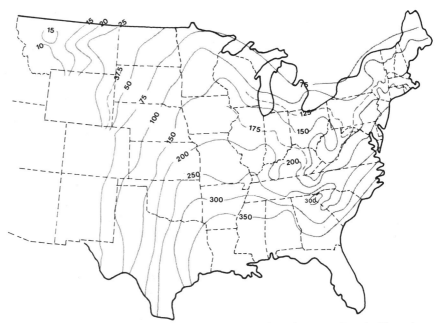

Fig. 12.4 Rainfall erosion index for the United States and southeastern Canada. The values are based on the erosive energy of total annual rainfall times the average annual maximum intensity of the 30-minute rainfall.

produce the greatest erosion because they generate runoff that is high in both velocity and mass. But this is true only for slopes up to about 50 degrees, because at steeper angles, the exposure of the slope face to rainfall grows rapidly smaller, vanishing altogether for vertical cliffs. In land use problems, however, greatest consideration is usually given to slopes less than 50 degrees, particularly insofar as urban development, residential development, and agriculture are concerned. Table 12.1 gives relative values for soil erosion, or the potential for it, based on slope steepness and length for slopes up to 50 percent inclination and 1000 feet length. In using this table, note that the rate of change with slope steepness is not linear, whereas it is with slope length. For example, for a 500-foot slope of 10 percent the value is 3.1, whereas for the same length at 20 percent, the value is 9.3.

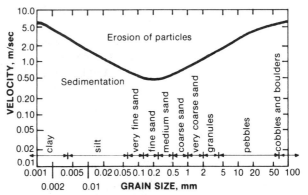

Fig. 12.5 Erosion thresholds of clay-, silt-, sand-, and pebble-sized particles under the force of running water. Sand gives way at the lowest velocities, whereas much higher velocities are required to dislodge clay and very coarse particles.

Table 12.1   Slope Geometry Factor Based on Steepness and Length

Slope Length in Feet	Slope Steepness in Percent														
	4	*6*	*8*	*10*	*12*	*14*	*16*	*18*	*20*	*25*	*30*	*35*	*40*	*45*	*50*
50	0.3	0.5	0.7	1.0	1.3	1.6	2.0	2.4	3.0	4.3	6.0	7.9	10.1	12.6	15.4
100	0.4	0.7	1.0	1.4	1.8	2.3	2.8	3.4	4.2	6.1	8.5	11.2	14.4	17.9	21.7
150	0.5	0.8	1.2	1.6	2.2	2.8	3.5	4.2	5.1	7.5	10.4	13.8	17.6	21.9	26.6
200	0.6	0.9	1.4	1.9	2.6	3.3	4.1	4.8	5.9	8.7	12.0	15.9	20.3	25.2	30.7
250	0.7	1.0	1.6	2.2	2.9	3.7	4.5	5.4	6.6	9.7	13.4	17.8	22.7	28.2	34.4
300	0.7	1.2	1.7	2.4	3.1	4.0	5.0	5.9	7.2	10.7	14.7	19.5	24.9	30.9	37.6
350	0.8	1.2	1.8	2.6	3.4	4.3	5.4	6.4	7.8	11.5	15.9	21.0	26.9	33.4	40.6
400	0.8	1.3	2.0	2.7	3.6	4.6	5.7	6.8	8.3	12.3	17.0	22.5	28.7	35.7	43.5
450	0.9	1.4	2.1	2.9	3.8	4.9	6.1	7.2	8.9	13.1	18.0	23.8	30.5	37.9	46.1
500	0.9	1.5	2.2	3.1	4.0	5.2	6.4	7.6	9.3	13.7	19.0	25.1	32.1	39.9	48.6
550	1.0	1.6	2.3	3.2	4.2	5.4	6.7	8.0	9.8	14.4	19.9	26.4	33.7	41.9	50.9
600	1.0	1.6	2.4	3.3	4.4	5.7	7.0	8.3	10.2	15.1	20.8	27.5	35.2	43.7	53.2
650	1.1	1.7	2.5	3.5	4.6	5.9	7.3	8.7	10.6	15.7	21.7	28.7	36.6	45.5	55.4
700	1.1	1.8	2.6	3.6	4.8	6.1	7.6	9.0	11.1	16.3	22.5	29.7	38.0	47.2	57.5
750	1.1	1.8	2.7	3.7	4.9	6.3	7.9	9.3	11.4	16.8	23.3	30.8	39.3	48.9	59.5
800	1.2	1.9	2.8	3.8	5.1	6.5	8.1	9.6	11.8	17.4	24.1	31.8	40.6	50.5	61.4
900	1.2	2.0	3.0	4.1	5.4	6.9	8.6	10.2	12.5	18.5	25.5	33.7	43.1	53.5	65.2
1000	1.3	2.1	3.1	4.3	5.7	7.3	9.1	10.8	13.2	19.5	26.9	35.5	45.4	56.4	68.7

12.4   COMPUTING SOIL LOSS FROM RUNOFF

Soil loss equation

An estimate of soil loss to runoff can be computed by combining all four of the major factors influencing soil erosion. For this we use a simple formula called the **universal soil loss equation**, which gives us soil erosion in tons per acre per year:

$$A = R \cdot K \cdot S \cdot C$$

Where

A = soil loss, tons per acre per year
R = rainfall erosion index
K = soil erodibility factor
S = slope factor, steepness, and length
C = plant cover factor

In problems involving agricultural land, a fifth factor, cropping management, is also included, but for problems involving nonagricultural land, abandoned farmland, and urban land types, it is not applicable.

Conditions of the equation   In order to interpret the universal soil loss equation reliably, it is necessary to understand two points: (1) the computed quantity of soil erosion represents only the displacement of particles from their original positions; and (2) the soil loss equation is designed for agricultural land, and applications to other situations may or may not be appropriate. Cleared land, former cropland, and construction sites can generally be considered appropriate for application of this method.

What constitutes soil loss depends on the study objectives involved. Strictly speaking, soil erosion takes place when particles are displaced from their place of origin no matter how far they are moved. For planning purposes, however, soil loss is often equated to loss from a study site, depending on the size and configuration of the site and whether the site contains water features that bear protection. For a site such as the one shown in Fig. 12.6, for example, much of the soil lost from the upper slope will be deposited near the foot of the slope. Therefore, in computing the soil loss for the lower surface, we should take into account sediment added from deposition and solve for the net change in the soil mass.

Sources of data   The **data** needed to make a soil loss computation can usually be obtained from topographic sheets, county soil reports, and a few additional maps and tables. Field inspection of the site is recommended to determine plant cover and erosion and deposition patterns. If that is not possible, then ground and aerial photographs may be used instead.

Soil type is expressed in terms of an erodibility factor, or *K factor,* which is a measure of a soil's susceptibility to erosion by runoff. This factor is derived from tests conducted on field plots for each soil series in a state and is given as a dimensionless number between 0 and 1.0. The higher the number, the greater the susceptibility to erosion. In some cases, two numbers are given for a soil, one for disturbed and one for undisturbed ground. Disturbed includes filled and rough graded ground. *K* factors are usually available from county or state offices of the U.S. Soil Conservation Service.

The rainfall erosion values for most states may be read from the map in Fig. 12.4. Those for the western states have not been generated as yet. The slope factor can be read from Table 12.1, and the plant cover factor can be approximated from Table 12.2 based on groundcover and canopy density.

Setup and interpretation   The reliability of soil erosion computations based on the universal soil loss equation depends not only on the accuracy of the data used, but also on the way in which the problem is **set up.** For sites in areas of diverse terrain, the site should be divided into subareas within which soil, slope, and vegetation are reasonably uniform. Soil loss

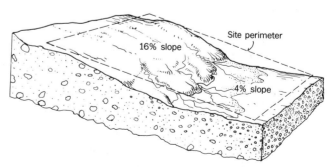

Fig. 12.6 An example of a site comprised of two slope classes, one that yields sediment and the other that accumulates it. Although there may be no net loss of sediment from the site, appreciable erosion occurs on the upper slope. A reliable assessment of erosion on this site must recognize this arrangement.

Table 12.2   Plant Cover Factors

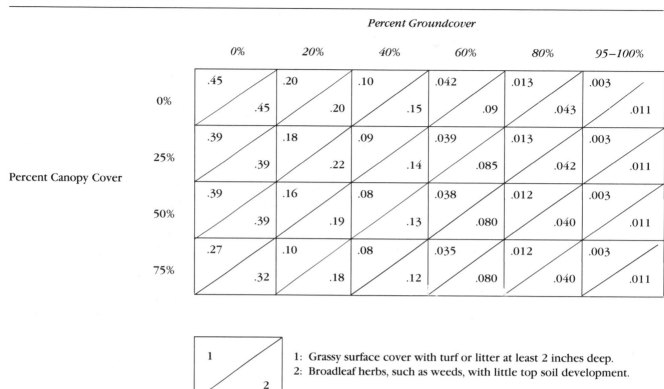

Percent Groundcover

		0%	20%	40%	60%	80%	95–100%
Percent Canopy Cover	0%	.45 / .45	.20 / .20	.10 / .15	.042 / .09	.013 / .043	.003 / .011
	25%	.39 / .39	.18 / .22	.09 / .14	.039 / .085	.013 / .042	.003 / .011
	50%	.39 / .39	.16 / .19	.08 / .13	.038 / .080	.012 / .040	.003 / .011
	75%	.27 / .32	.10 / .18	.08 / .12	.035 / .080	.012 / .040	.003 / .011

1 / 2

1: Grassy surface cover with turf or litter at least 2 inches deep.
2: Broadleaf herbs, such as weeds, with little top soil development.

should be computed for each subarea and then adjusted for any deposition that may be received from adjacent subareas. In making the adjustment for deposition, it is important to consider not only the potential contribution from upslope areas, but also the patterns of gullies, streams, and swales through which runoff and sediment can be funnelled across flat areas and discharged onto low ground or into streams, lakes, and wetlands.

Procedure   To summarize, the **procedure** for computing soil loss from a site may be described in six steps:

1. Define the site (problem area) boundaries on a large-scale base map such as a topographic sheet or soil map.

2. Using aerial photographs, soil maps, topographic maps, and whatever other sources of data are available, divide the site into subareas. If the site is essentially uniform throughout, this is not necessary.

3. For each subarea, assign a *soil erodibility factor* (based on SCS soil series *K*-factor designation), a *slope factor* (read from Table 12.1 based on steepness and length data taken from topographic map), and a *plant cover factor* (read from Table 12.2 based on aerial photographs or field observation).

4. Multiply the appropriate value from the *rainfall erosion* map in Fig. 12.4 times the three factors assigned to the subarea in step 3. The answer is in tons per acre per year.

5. Examine the relations between slopes and drainage patterns in each subarea, identify where sediment would be expected to accumulate, and, if possible, adjust the quantity of soil loss computed in step 4.

6. Determine the total soil loss for the entire site by summing the net amounts of soil loss for each subarea. If this is not possible because of uncertainty over the relationship among various subareas, then the gross soil loss from the subareas should be summed for a gross site total.

12.5 APPLICATIONS TO LAND PLANNING AND ENVIRONMENTAL MANAGEMENT

An important task of most local planning agencies is the review and evaluation of land development proposals for housing, industrial, and commercial projects. Proposals are evaluated according to a host of criteria including soil erosion, or the potential for it. Consideration of soil erosion stems not only from a concern over the loss of top soil and depletion of the soil resource in general, but also from the impact of sedimentation on terrestrial vegetation, wetlands, river channels, and drainage facilities such as stormsewers. To gain the necessary information, developers are often asked to prepare *Critical questions* a site plan and respond to **critical questions** such as these:

▪ What percentage of site lies in slopes of 15 percent or greater, and of this area how much (a) is proposed for development, and (b) if developed, will be affected by construction?

▪ What percentage of this site is forested, grass covered, and shrub covered? How much of each of these covers will be destroyed as a result of development?

▪ What are the minimum distances between the proposed development zone and (a) water features (streams, ponds, reservoirs, and wetlands), and (b) existing drainage facilities (stormsewers, stormwater retention ponds, and ditches)?

▪ What erosion and sedimentation control measures are proposed during (a) the construction phase, and (b) the operational phase of the proposed project?

▪ What is the anticipated length of the construction period, and which months in the year are proposed for (a) land clearing, (b) excavation and grading, (c) construction of building and facilities, and (d) regrading and landscaping (Fig. 12.7)? How does the proposed construction period relate to the seasonal pattern of rainfall, especially the months of heaviest rainstorms?

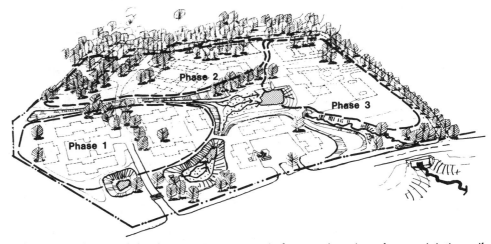

Fig. 12.7 Phasing of development is necessary in large projects in order to minimize soil erosion and sedimentation of local water features. In this project, 25 to 30 percent of the site would be opened at any time.

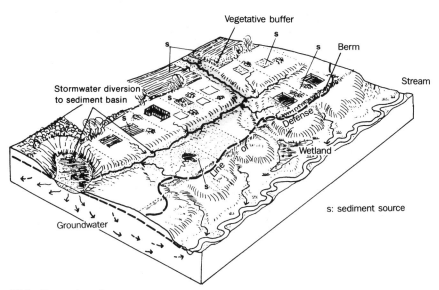

Fig. 12.8   Examples of measures used in construction site management to control erosion and avert sedimentation of water features. Sediment sources are denoted by "s".

Mitigation measures

Control of erosion and sedimentation during the construction phase of development is viewed very seriously in many communities—so much so that many have legislated erosion control ordinances. At the heart of such ordinances are the control measures, or **mitigation measures.** These include a wide variety of techniques and approaches, and there is a very active dialogue among landscape architects, civil engineers, and construction management professionals on this topic. The approaches employed vary widely, depending mainly on local requirements and the level of monitoring and enforcement employed by public agencies. Generally, however, the mitigation measures used are simple and small-scale, aimed at holding an exposed soil in place or at blocking sediment-laden runoff from draining into water features such as streams, ponds, or wetlands. These include the placement of berms around construction zones, the use of fiber nets on slopes, and the use of sedimentation basins to protect drainage features (Fig. 12.8). For further discussion of mitigation, refer to Chapter 11, section 11.3.

12.6 CONSIDERATIONS IN WATERSHED MANAGEMENT

Sediment and the drainage net

The geographer's and planner's perspectives on soil erosion and stream sedimentation must extend beyond the site scale of observation. Every site is part of a larger **drainage** area linked together by a **network** of drainage channels. These channels are collectors for runoff and sediment. In most natural drainage systems, the size of the channel is adjusted to the size of flows it carries, in particular to certain flows of larger than average magnitudes. We reason, therefore, that when two streams join in the network, the size of resultant channel should approximate the sum of the two tributary channels. (Actually it is the *capacity* of the channel, defined by the magnitude of discharge that it can accommodate, that increases with the merger of tributaries.)

Sediment transport capacity also increases with the magnitude of flow. Therefore, in assessing what could happen when sediments are released to streams from an erosion site, it is important to consider the size of the receiving channel and the relative position of the channel in the drainage network. Massive loadings in small streams located in the upper parts of a watershed imply that (1) channels may become

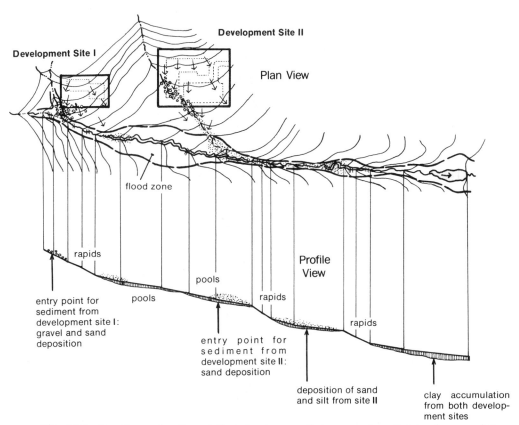

Fig. 12.9 Locations of sedimentation sites in a small stream system. Points of accumulation vary with sediment size, channel shape and gradient, and proximity to sediment source areas.

glutted, thereby reducing their capacities to carry large flows; and (2) sediment in the streambed will remain there for a long time, owing to the limited capacity of the stream to carry it away.

In a watershed where several sites are releasing sediment to a stream network at the same time, the sediment bodies will move through the channel network at uneven rates, making it difficult to assess the impact on the system as a whole. Clays will move through the entire system rapidly, whereas sand and silts will not only move more slowly but also build up at selected points (Fig. 12.9). Often we can estimate where in the drainage system sediment is likely to accumulate based on sediment size and channel shape and gradient. Broad reaches of slow-moving water are the favored deposition sites for sands and silts. Among these, wetlands and impoundments such as reservoirs and lakes are generally considered the most critical from a watershed management standpoint, and it is often necessary to estimate the amount of sediment that would be added to them based on land use practices in the drainage basin.

Basinwide loading   Sediment loading of a drainage **basin** requires a yearly calculation of sediment production on a site-by-site basis for the entire watershed. The locations represented by each of these quantities must be pinpointed in the watershed and the drainage network, taking special care to determine where sediment would actually enter the network. In most cases where a site falls on a drainage divide within the watershed, the site may contribute sediment to two or more channels, as is illustrated by sites 1 and 4 in Fig. 12.10. Once these relationships are known, the receiving waterbodies downstream can be identified and a loading rate can be calculated.

Finally, the sediment loads must be converted to volumetric units to determine

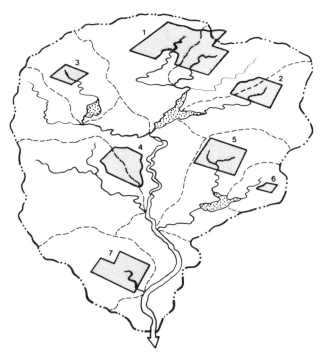

Fig. 12.10 A watershed in which forest has been cleared at seven sites, each of which is related to a different part of the drainage network.

Impoundment sedimentation how much space in the channel or **impoundment** the sediments will actually take up. The following sediment densities are recommended:

■	clay	= 60–80 lbs/ft^3
■	clay/silt/sand mixture	= 80–100 lbs/ft^3
■	sand and gravel	= 95–130 lbs/ft^3

Using an intermediate value of 90 pounds per cubic foot, we find that a reservoir receiving 10,000 tons of sediment per year would lose 222,000 ft^3 (8200 yds^3) of volume each year. Given a reservoir capacity of 2,000,000 ft^3 (one, for example, with dimensions of 200 feet wide, 1000 feet long, and 10 feet deep) the life of the reservoir would be only nine years.

For impoundments that have low residence times, that is, those that exchange water in only a matter of hours or several days rather than months or years, most of the clays will not settle out. Owing to their small sizes, clay particles settle exceedingly slowly, allowing most to pass through small impoundments. Impoundments with long residence times, which may be as great as 10 to 12 years in some lakes, retain fine sediments and deposit them over the lake floor, burying or coating bottom organisms.

12.7 CASE STUDY

Erosion and Sediment Control Planning for a Strip Mining Operation, Western Maryland

Phil Shumaker

This project called for the formation of an erosion and sediment control plan in connection with a small strip mining operation. The program involved the mining of two shallow coal seams on a 60-acre site in the Allegheny Plateau

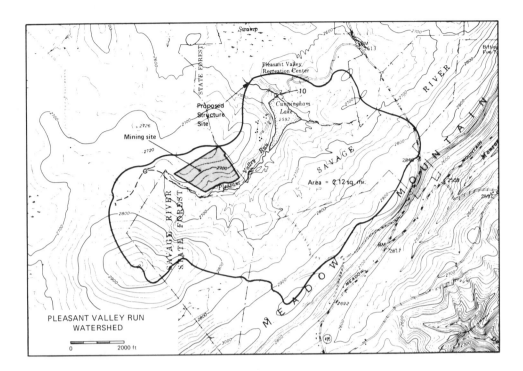

PLEASANT VALLEY RUN
WATERSHED

area of western Maryland. Of critical importance was the location of the site near a stream and lake within a small watershed, called the Pleasant Valley Run. The mining site is situated on a side slope of the stream valley about 1500 feet upstream of the lake. The objective of the control plan was to insure protection of the stream, lake, and related habitat from runoff, sediments, and contaminants emanating from the mining operation.

Both coal seams outcrop along the northern side of the Pleasant Run Valley and dip northwestward at angles of 4 to 5°. Core samples indicated that the overburden resting on the lower seam is primarily composed of a soft yellow clay with a thin bed of dark-gray shale between the clay and the coal seam. The strata overlying the upper seams consist of thinly bedded shale and sandstone. The analysis of overburden material indicated that the shale near the coal seam has a high pyrite content and, therefore, a high acid-forming potential. This required treatment of all water pumped from the pit as well as burial of all acid shale away from the mine perimeter and floor.

Preliminary soil analysis indicated that topsoil material (defined in this case as that portion of the soil that is capable of supporting vegetation with little or no special preparation) is extremely thin in the mining area. On the whole, the soils, even before the mining, had a high runoff potential; therefore, they were graded in order to ensure maximum infiltration. Topsoil material was placed on the surface whenever possible and further supplemented by the high alkaline, potassium, and phosphorus-rich yellow clay.

In designing erosion and sediment control structures and in scheduling the planting program, climate data on rainfall intensity and freezing were carefully analyzed. The data indicated that the intensity of 10-year, 1-hour rainfall is 2.25 inches. Accordingly, each structure was designed to handle runoff from such a storm with provisions for an emergency spillway to handle a 25-year storm. Freeze data defined the growing season as averaging only 122 days between late spring and early fall. Planting of all vegetative species was conducted during this period to ensure maximum survival and early growth.

The drainage area of Pleasant Valley Run is 2.12 square miles, and of this area, 63.6 acres (7.1 percent) were disturbed by mining and associated operations. The desire to protect Cunningham Lake and reduce the amount of runoff

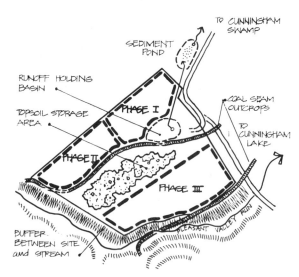

and sediment pollution directly entering Pleasant Valley Run required directing runoff away from the valley and lake. Owing to the dip of the underlying strata, it was feasible to direct the runoff from the mined area into the pit and then pump it into a sediment pond from which it was discharged into Cunningham Swamp downstream from the lake. Cunningham Swamp served as a natural filter area for the runoff from the mined area and the haulage road. Observation indicated that vegetated strips between the mined area and adjacent streams as well as the area along the haulage road and below the outlet of the sediment pond possessed good stands of erosion-resisting plant species, which acted as effective filters for sediment.

The mining operation consisted of three separate phases. All three phases used the same haulage road and sediment pond. In all three phases, the mined surface was backfilled to original contour and secured in such a manner as to encourage absorption of precipitation and prevent ponded water. The backfill also was graded to direct runoff into marginal areas at gradual velocities and in small quantities, thereby limiting sediment transport.

The planting program began with a temporary cover of quick-growing grasses (oats and rye) to guard against erosion in the short term. This was followed by seeding of the entire site in permanent grasses. After one year, selected tree species were introduced with the goal of eventually reforesting the site in a manner compatible with the tree cover of nearby Savage State Forest.

Phil Shumaker is an engineer with Delta Mining, Inc., Grantsville, Maryland. ■

12.8 SELECTED REFERENCES FOR FURTHER READING

Dissmeyer, G. E. "Erosion and Sediment from Forest Land Uses, Management Practices and Disturbances in the Southeastern United States." In *Proceedings of the Third Federal Inter-Agency Sedimentation Conference,* Water Resources Council, 1976, pp. 1-140–1-148.

Environmental Protection Agency. *Erosion and Sediment Control: Surface Mining in the Eastern United States.* U.S. EPA Technology Transfer Seminar Publication, 1976.

Ferguson, Bruce K. "Erosion and Sedimentation in Regional and Site Planning." *Journal of Soil and Water Conservation,* 36: 4, 1981, pp. 199–204.

Heede, B. H. "Designing Gully Control Systems for Eroding Watersheds." *Environmental Management* 2: 6, 1978, pp. 509–522.

Hjulström, F. "Transport of Detritus by Moving Water." In *Recent Marine Sediments: A Symposium* (ed. P. Trask). Tulsa, Okla.: American Association of Petroleum Geologists, 1939.

Soil Conservation Service. "Procedure for Computing Sheet and Rill Erosion on Project Areas." *Technical Release No. 51.* Washington, D.C.: Department of Agriculture, 1975, 15 pp.

Soil Conservation Service. *Standards and Specifications for Erosion and Sediment Control in Developing Areas.* College Park, Md.: U.S. Department of Agriculture, 1975.

Wolman, M. G. "A Cycle of Sedimentation and Erosion in Urban River Channels." *Géografiska Annaler* 49A, 1967, pp. 385–395.

13

SHORELINE PROCESSES, SAND DUNES, AND COASTAL ZONE MANAGEMENT

13.1 INTRODUCTION

One of the nagging and costly problems in coastal zones is shore erosion flooding and property damage. In the United States and Canada, which together account for more than 200,000 miles of coastline, this problem has grown significantly in the past two decades, not because the oceans and lakes are behaving differently than they did years ago, but because of increased development and use of the coast. This problem has given rise to heavy financial and emotional investment and, for many of the 100 million or more North Americans who live on or near a coast, has led to a bittersweet relationship with the sea. The costs to individuals and society are rising. In response, efforts to manage and protect coastal lands have reached critical levels at community, state/provincial, and national levels. And with the prospects for rising sea levels and increasing population in the next 50 years, the problem is sure to become exceedingly acute.

In 1972, the U.S. federal government passed the Coastal Zone Management Act, which provides for the formulation of coastal planning and management programs at the state level. Among the responsibilities of the state programs is the classification of coastlines according to their relative stability, including the potential for erosion. To make such a determination, it is necessary to understand not only the physical makeup of the coast, but also the nature of the forces acting on it. The principal force in the coastal zone is wind waves. They are the source of most shore erosion and sediment transport which together shape the shorelines, beaches, and related features.

13.2 WAVE ACTION CURRENTS AND NEARSHORE CIRCULATION

Waves in shallow water

In deep water, waves cannot cause erosion because the motion of the wave does not reach bottom. In **shallow water,** waves not only touch bottom, but they can also exert considerable force against it. Initially, this force is not very great, but as the wave nears shore, it increases rapidly. Where the shear stress of this force exceeds the resisting strength of the bottom material, displacement of particles occurs. Along coasts comprised of loose sediments, such as sand and silts, large quantities of particles are churned up, especially as the waves break near shore.

Wave base

The water depth at which waves begin to move bottom particles is called **wave base** (Fig. 13.1). Wave base depth increases with wave size and is roughly proportional to 1.0 to 2.0 times the wave height. Relative to wavelength, wave base falls at a depth between 0.04 and 0.5 wavelength. The shallow-water zone along a coastline begins at this depth, and since the wave base changes with wave size, the shallow zone actually fluctuates in width with different wave events. In the oceans, however, wave base for large waves is generally considered to average around 10 meters; in the Great Lakes it averages around 3 meters.

Wave size

The ability of waves to erode and transport sediment is a function of the **wave size** and the size and availability of sediment. In deep water, wave size is product of wind velocity, wind duration, and fetch. *Fetch* is the distance of open water over which a wind from a particular direction can blow across a waterbody. The greater the velocity, duration, and fetch, the larger the wave. Forecasts of the size of *deep* water waves can be made using the graph in Fig. 13.2 In *shallow* water, both wave size and velocity decline with bottom friction, turbulence, and erosion.

The direction at which waves approach the shore is also important. Not only does wave size decline in shallow water, but the direction of movement toward shore also changes. Consider a wave approaching shore at an angle with part of the wave in deep water and part in shallow water. The shallow-water segment decelerates, while the

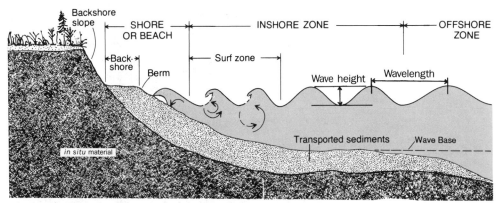

Fig. 13.1 The principal dimensional properties of a wave (right side). When the wave moves into shallow water (see wave base), wavelength shortens and height increases until the wave becomes unstable and breaks. The left side of the diagram identifies the principal feature of the shore cones.

Wave-Size Forecasting Chart

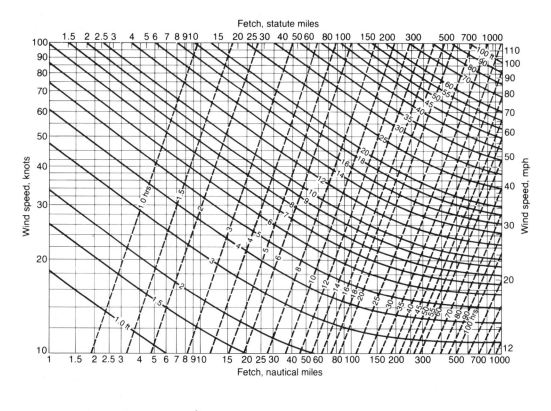

Fig. 13.2 Chart for forecasting the size (height) of deep-water waves.

Wave refraction

deep-water segment continues to move at a relatively high velocity. This causes the axis (crest line) of the wave to bend, or **refract,** which reorients the wave's energy more directly toward shore as it crosses the shallow-water zone.

Because refraction is controlled by the direction of wave approach and the bottom topography of the shallow-water zone, refraction patterns can be estimated based on deep-water wave direction and bathymetric maps. This can also be done by constructing lines called orthogonals perpendicular to the crest line of approaching waves as they appear on an aerial photograph. Assuming wave size (and therefore energy) is uniform along the entire wave crest in deep water, we see that any convergence or divergence of the orthogonals in shallow water represents a change in the relative

Wave energy distribution

distribution and the orientation of wave energy. Normally, refraction causes wave energy to become focused on headlands and the seaward sides of islands, and diffused in embayments and the leeward sides of islands. These are often the sites of erosion and deposition, respectively (Fig. 13.3).

In order for waves to modify shorelines, sediment must be picked up and moved from one location to another. For this to take place, sediment becomes waterborne as waves cross the shallow-water zone. On the outer edge of the shallow-water zone, transport is slight, especially in sand-sized particles, with movement limited to a to-and-fro motion with the passage of each wave. Nearer shore, this motion is combined with a lifting action that carries the particle into the wave and on a turbulent ride before settling back to bottom. Although the individual movements of particles can be in any direction, the net direction of movement after the passage of many waves is usually parallel to the shoreline.

Longshore transport

Two factors account for the parallel, or **longshore, transport** of sediment. One is that most waves approach and intercept the coast at an angle; therefore, the direction of wave force is oblique to the shoreline. Although waves refract into a more direct approach angle near shore, most retain a distinct angle as they cross the shallow-water zone. Thus a large component of the energy for sediment transport is set up parallel to the shoreline.

The second factor takes the form of a current that flows along the coast. This current, called a *longshore current,* moves parallel to the shoreline in the direction of wave movement at rates generally less than 1 meter per second. Longshore currents are driven by wave energy, increasing in velocity and size (volume) with wave size and

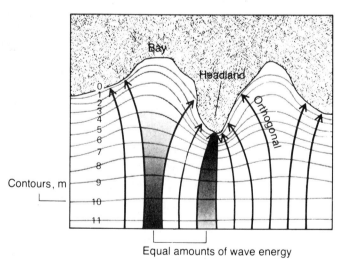

Fig. 13.3 Wave refraction around a headland and embayment. Notice that the distribution of energy wave is focused in one and diffused in the other.

duration. When sediment is churned up by waves, the longshore currents transport it downshore a ways before it settles back toward bottom.

Other types of currents also operate along the shore, and one of the most prominent is the rip current. Flowing seaward from the shore across the lines of approaching waves, rip currents are narrow jets of water that intercept the longshore train of sediments carrying part of it into deeper water. Together, rip currents, waves, and *Near shore circulation cells* longshore currents form **nearshore circulation cells,** moving both water and sediments toward, away from, and along the shore. These cells are in turn nested in larger circulation systems that transport sediments from *source areas,* such as river deltas, to *sinks,* which are deposition areas such as embayments (Fig. 13.4).

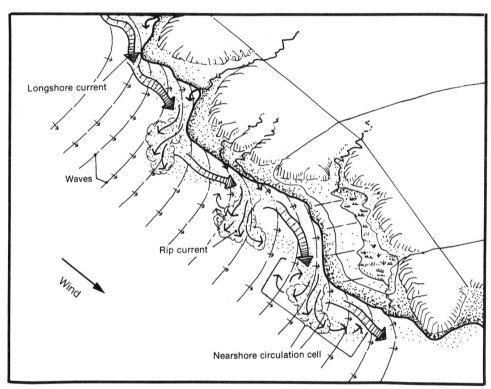

Fig. 13.4 Nearshore circulation showing waves, longshore currents, rip currents, and the transport of sediment from a source to a sink.

13.3 NET SEDIMENT TRANSPORT AND SEDIMENT MASS BALANCE

On most shorelines, waves and currents may change direction with the passage of storms or the seasons, which in turn causes reversals in the longshore transport. The same sediments may be transported past one point on the shore many times in one year. A measure of this quantity, the total amount of sediment moved past a point on *Gross and net sediment* the coast, is called **gross sediment transport.** For obvious reasons, it is not a good *transport* indicator of the balance of sediment at a place on the coast, because it tells us neither whether the shore is losing or gaining sediment, nor whether the beach is growing or shrinking. Therefore, another measure is used, called **net sediment transport.**

$$\text{Net } Q_t = Q_p - Q_s$$

Where

Net Q_t = net quantity of sediment/year
Q_p = longshore transport in the primary direction
Q_s = longshore transport in the secondary direction

Net sediment transport is the balance between the sediment moved one way and that moved the other way along the coast. If the longshore system is driven predominantly by waves from one quadrant of the compass, then net sediment transport can be large. By contrast, if the longshore system operates in both directions, then net transport may be small while gross transport may be large. Ultimately, it is the trend that we are concerned with, because it can tell us something about the development of the coastline.

Sediment mass balance   At a local scale of observation, where only a short segment of beach is concerned, we wound want to make a more detailed determination of the **sediment balance** (Fig. 13.5). This would include inputs from backshore slope erosion and runoff (R_i), losses (outputs) from wind erosion (W_o), onshore inputs from sand bar migration (O_i) in summer, and offshore outputs from bar migration (O_o) in fall and winter, as well as longshore input (L_i) and output (L_o). The mass of sediment on the beach for any period of time is equal to inputs minus outputs:

$$\text{Sediment mass balance: } L_i - L_o + O_i - O_o + R_i - W_o = O$$

A value greater than zero means that the reservoir of beach sediment has gained mass; less than zero, that it has lost mass. Generally, these trends are manifested in larger- and smaller-sized beaches. In most places, detailed data are not available for computation of the sediment mass balance, nor is there adequate time or resources in most planning studies to acquire the necessary data. Therefore, in site planning we must usually resort to an interpretation of local records and features such as vegetation, old maps, and land surveys to gain an idea of local trends.

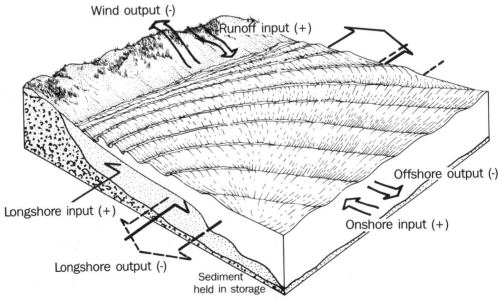

Fig. 13.5   Components in the sediment mass balance of a short segment of beach.

13.4 TRENDS IN SHORELINE CHANGE

Sediment sources   Rivers are the primary **source of sediment** for longshore transport, providing more than 90 percent of the total sediment supply yearly on the world's coasts. Where river sediments are abundant, virtually all available wave energy may be expended in transporting the sediment load along the coast. Where river sediments are scarce and wave energy is abundant, however, the body of beach sediment is often small and only a fraction of available wave energy is expended in moving it. Moreover, by virtue of its small volume, the sediment mass offers little protection for the *in situ* material under and behind the beach. Under such circumstances, the backshore can be severely eroded and the resulting debris incorporated into the longshore sediment system. As erosion takes place, the shoreline retreats landward. Such coastlines are characterized by features such as sea cliffs, bluffs, or wave-cut banks, and are referred to as *retrogradational,* because over the long run they retreat landward as they give up sediment.

Retreat and erosion   **Retreat** is defined as the landward displacement of the shoreline. It is usually caused by **erosion;** it may also be caused by a rise in water level, subsidence of coastal land, or any combination of the three. Where retreat is caused by erosion, the amount of *in situ* material actually lost can be computed by multiplying the retreat rate (R) times the back shore slope height (H) for a given length (L) of shoreline (Fig. 13.6):

$$\text{Erosion} = R \cdot H \cdot L$$

Deposition   At the other extreme are those coastlines that **collect sediments** and build seaward, called *progradational* coastlines. These coasts are characterized by low relief terrain in the form of various depositional features. The most common of these are beach ridges, broad fillets of sand at the heads of bays, and spits and bars near the mouths of bays and behind islands.

Most depositional features are prone to rapid changes in shape and volume; therefore, short-term trends should generally not be used as the basis for formulating land use plans in the coastal zone. In computing the volumetric change in a sand bar or a bayhead beach, for example, it is necessary to consider sediment added both above and below water level because the bulk of such features often develops under water. This is especially necessary if the rate of growth or decline of the feature is to be related to the net sediment transport rate over some time period.

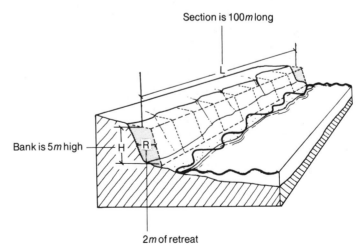

Section is 100 *m* long

Bank is 5 *m* high

2 *m* of retreat

Erosion = 5 *m* × 2 *m* × 100 *m* = 1000 cubic meters

Fig. 13.6 The erosion resulting from shoreline retreat is computed from the retreat rate (R), the back shore slope height (H), and the length of the shoreline (L).

13.5 SAND DUNE FORMATION AND NOURISHMENT

Another trend associated with active shorelines, especially prograding ones, is the formation of sand dunes. Sandy beach deposits formed by wave and current action are highly prone to wind erosion. Once entrained by wind, the sand may be heaped up into dunes and driven inland up to a mile or more. The fields of sand dunes that result represent a separate subsystem in the larger sediment system of the coastal zone.

Sand dunes are a common and integral part of every major coastline, including the Arctic. Their formation and maintenance are directly dependent on two key factors: (1) an ample supply of erodible sand; and (2) a source of wind energy to drive the sand landward. The source of sand for the vast majority of coastal dunes is the beach in front of them. Broad, sandy beaches with little or no plant cover are clearly the best sources. A second source of dune sand is wave-cut banks and cliffs of sandy composi-

Dune classes tion. These two sources give rise to two different **classes of coastal sand dunes:** (1) low-elevation dunes that begin near the backshore and rise gradually landward; and (2) perched dunes that begin above water level near the brow of a bluff or sea cliff (Fig. 13.7).

Coastal denodynamics The shore is a windier place than locations a little inland from it. The reason has to do with the movement of air at the base of the atmosphere, called the atmospheric boundary layer. This layer of air, which measures about 1000 feet deep, drags over the earth's surface and is slowed by the resulting friction. When the boundary layer moves over open water, a relatively smooth surface, it is less impaired by friction than it is over land; therefore, it is generally faster over water. In addition, as the air flows from water onto the land, it also tends to accelerate at the coastline. This is caused by the

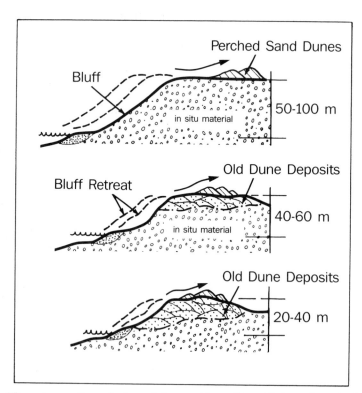

Fig. 13.7 Three types of perched sand dune settings. The old dune deposits in the lower diagram formed as low elevation sand dunes.

constriction of the boundary layer as the land rises in elevation at the coast. The air must be squeezed through a smaller space, and in order to maintain the continuity of flow, wind velocity increases, providing in turn more energy to erode and transport sand. This phenomenon is especially pronounced along high banks and sea cliffs where it may give rise to the formation of perched sand dunes (Fig. 13.8). It also accounts for the erosion of sand along high dune ridges located several hundred meters inland from the shore.

Dune origins

On most beaches, **dune formation** begins in the backshore zone with the development of a low ridge of sand paralleling the shore. As the ridge grows, blowouts form at selected spots from which tongues of sand migrate landward. These function as ramps for transport of sand wafted from the beach. The advancing edge of the dune deposit buries vegetation and soil as it moves inland. From the blowout to the leading edge of the dune, the form is one approximating an elongated U and in most places is called a hairpin dune (Fig. 13.9).

As the dune moves inland, it not only grows longer but deeper as sand is added to the main body of the deposit. At some distance from the shore, the available wind energy is insufficient to transport enough sand to overcome vegetation; therefore, the dune ceases to advance, and plants take over the surface. If the process of dune formation is repeated many times along a segment of coastline, the deposits tend to overlap and merge together forming a complex dune ridge called a *barrier dune*. The barrier dune generally marks the highest landward extent of the dunefield (the total mass of dune features landward of the beach). The barrier dune is usually steep on the leeward (inland) side, where wind deposits are held in place by vegetation, and gentle on the windward side where sand is transported upslope from the blowouts.

Management dilemma

Coastal sand dunes present difficult **management** and land use situations. They are extremely attractive to residential, resort, and recreational development by virtue of the open vistas, the juxtaposition of open sand, grass-covered, and wooded surfaces, and of course, the access to the shore. They are, however, very fragile environments where vegetation, sand deposits, and slopes may be so delicately balanced that only

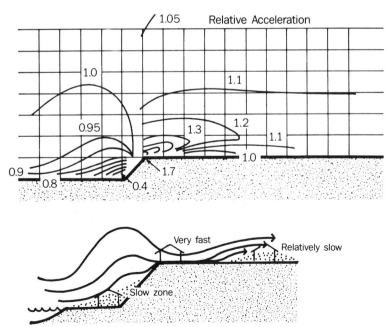

Fig. 13.8 Airflow over a coastal bluff or sea cliff. Velocity accelerates as much as fourfold from the toe to the brow of the slope. Below, corresponding development sites and wind streamlines.

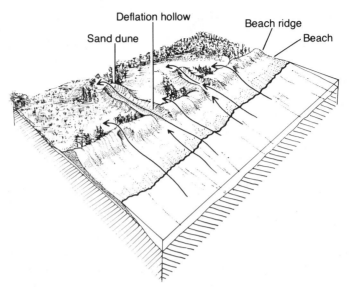

Fig. 13.9   The most common setting and forms associated with coastal sand dunes. The hairpin form of the dune follows the main line of airflow inland from the beach.

slight alterations in one can lead to a chain of changes such as renewed wind erosion, blowout formation, and dune reactivation.

What is often not clearly understood about coastal dunes is that they are themselves small sediment systems with source areas, transportation zones, and sediment sinks. In order for dune systems to maintain themselves, nourishment must be sustained. This requires maintenance of source areas as well as the flow of air from source *Development impacts* areas to sinks (deposition zones). When **development** takes place in dunefields, source areas may be reduced with the planting of groundcover on barren surfaces as a part of landscaping and erosion control programs. In addition, transportation zones may be disrupted with the building of roads and structures in the backshore and lower dune areas. In the area of the barrier dune complex, a favorite location for siting homes and resorts, construction inevitably requires alteration of metastable slopes held in place by vegetation. (See section 3.4 in Chapter 3 for a discussion of metastable slopes.)

Impacts on nourishment With respect to reductions in sand dune **nourishment,** the main problem is the weakening of the dune building and movement processes and the encroachment of vegetation over the dunefield. Successful erosion control programs that stabilize source areas may so limit the supply of sand that the interplay between geomorphic processes and vegetation—which gives the dunefield much of its special character—becomes largely one-sided and the dunefield becomes overgrown and inactive. In that case, the dunefield is transformed into sand hills, or what are sometimes called fossil dunes. Depending on management objectives, wind erosion, sand movement, and a changeable landscape may be the most desirable components of dune environments in the same way that wave action and beach dynamics are on shorelines.

13.6 APPLICATIONS TO COASTAL ZONE PLANNING AND MANAGEMENT

Proposals for development in the coastal zone today are subject to serious scrutiny in the United States and Canada. In order to evaluate a proposal, it is first necessary to know the makeup and dynamics of the coastline involved. This usually involves an

Inventory and mapping

inventory of coastal landforms and lithology (composition), and an assessment of recent erosion and disposition trends. Within this framework, more detailed studies can be carried out for the specific segment where the action is proposed. At the heart of such studies, especially when shoreline structures are involved, is an analysis of the sediment budget.

Analyzing net sediment transport

Two types of methods are available in **net sediment transport analysis** of the longshore system: shoreline change and wave energy flux. The most accurate method is based on measurements of volumetric changes in a shoreline. This usually involves comparing old charts and aerial photographs with newer ones, or making detailed measurements of sediment accumulation behind a shoreline barrier such as a breakwater. The latter necessitates making a topographic survey at the time of construction and one some years later, and then measuring the net change between the two. Where harbor entrances are maintained by sand bypassing, the amount of sediment scheduled to be transferred from one side of a barrier to the other each year is determined by this method (Fig. 13.10).

The second method is based on computations of wave energy and established correlations between wave energy flux and sediment transport rates. This method requires wave data for the location in question, and since such data are usually scarce, the wave energy computations are difficult to prepare.

Applications to land use questions

Upon completion of the coastal inventory and estimates of the sediment budget, two important questions can be answered: (1) What is the nature of the system we are dealing with in terms of the amounts of sediment being moved and the directions of movement? (2) What is the relationship among the features, processes, and trends of

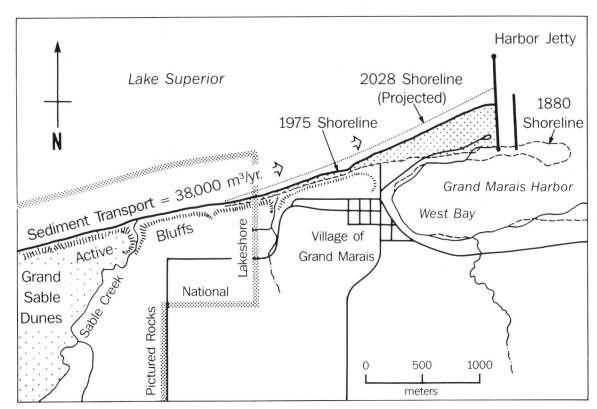

Fig. 13.10 Trends in shoreline change, 1880–1975 with a projection to 2028. Note change as a result of the harbor jetty (built in the 1960s) has been negative on the east and positive on the west. Net sediment transport is eastward.

the coast such as prograding shorelines, dunefields, and their nourishment? This information can then be used to test the feasibility of development schemes, evaluate community plans, or guide the formulation of coastal zone management plans. Among the problems commonly faced by private development is how to deal with "soft" environments such as sand dunes, wetlands, and erodible beaches. Coastal communities are faced with the problem of regulating private development as well as the problem of planning their own economic development schemes involving harbor improvements, marinas, and related facilities.

Site planning

Because the coastal zone is so attractive for residential development, it is necessary to examine briefly some of the problems of **site planning** near shorelines. In evaluating a site for development, it is important, as recommended above, to first examine the position of the site in the larger sediment system and determine whether it is in a retrograding, prograding, or stable part of the coastline. Next, it is necessary to determine the composition of the site and its topographic configuration. If it is comprised of bedrock, the site is usually safe from serious erosion, though the bedrock may pose significant problems in building construction, wastewater disposal, and stormwater drainage.

Seaward/landward fluctuation

Shorelines composed of unconsolidated materials should be treated carefully where development calls for permanent structures because most are prone to **seaward/landward fluctuations** over various time intervals. Minor fluctuations occur seasonally with winter/summer changes in the sediment mass balance. Over larger time periods, the magnitude of the fluctuations can be expected to increase with the average return period; that is, big changes occur with the lowest frequency. It is difficult to determine the proper setback distances for buildings because the magnitudes of the fluctuations are often different for different segments of a continuous shoreline and few if any data are available to help figure out trends. In some instances, however, vegetation can provide insight into trends and fluctuations. Exposed roots, tipped trees, and abundant driftwood are signs of shore erosion and retreat, whereas the establishment of numerous young plants on the back shore is a sign of progradation.

Vegetative indicators

If tree stands of different age classes can be identified on the backshore, they may reveal how far landward the sea or lake has advanced since the stands became established. In Fig. 13.11, for example, the presence of 75- to 100-year-old trees beginning at a distance of 100 meters from the shore indicates that the area beyond this point has been free of transgression by waves for at least 75 to 100 years. In contrast, at the 50

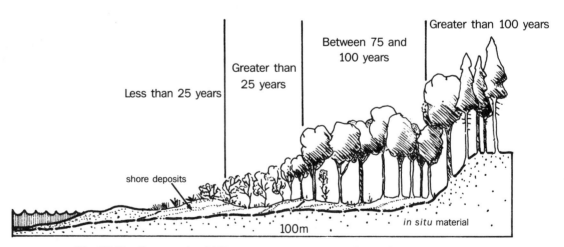

Fig. 13.11   Tree stands of different ages can sometimes be used as an indicator of the extent of past landward fluctuations in the shoreline.

meter distance the trees' ages tell us that the area has been eroded away in the last 75 to 100 years and reformed in the past 25 to 30 years. This technique is best suited to areas where one stand gives way sharply to another, because the absence of a transition between neighboring stands is a sign that the older stand has been cut back by erosion and the younger stand subsequently established on new deposits.

Soft shorelines   Despite their appeal as places to build and live, erodible, low-elevation coastal terrain is generally not suitable for development. Time and time again, nature demonstrates their unsuitability to us, particularly in areas exposed to the open sea. This suggests that such areas should best be left to open space, special easements, nature preserves and parks. Where commitments have already been made to development programs, the **planner's role** is to devise layout schemes in which structures are not only least prone to damage but themselves least interfere with coastal processes and seasonal changes. As a rule, this requires large setbacks not only because of the threat of wave erosion but also because of storm surges and flooding. The Atlantic and Gulf coasts of the southeastern United States are especially prone to hurricane surges, and development on islands and coastal plains are often severely damaged by large waves and high-water levels, as was demonstrated by Hurricane Hugo in 1989 (Fig. 13.12;

Planner's role

Fig. 13.12 Myrtle Beach, South Carolina, after Hurricane Hugo (1989) swept through a residential neighborhood situated along the shore.

also see Fig. 2.8). An important part of the federally supported coastal zone planning in such areas has been the development of evacuation plans that spell out a procedure for informing people of the danger level and providing directions for evacuation in the event of a hurricane.

High elevation sites

For development sites situated near the crest of a sea cliff or backshore slope, the threat of wave erosion may not be great; however, the effects of wind and slope instability may be significant. The pattern of onshore airflow over a coastal slope produces a zone of low velocity on the lower slope and high velocity on the upper slope relative to wind velocities at comparable elevations over flat ground. The velocity increase from the slope foot to the slope crest is about four times for slopes of 4:1 inclination or greater. In addition, as the air crosses the brow of the slope it appears to cling to the ground (or tree canopy) for some distance inland, and then the fast air separates from the surface. (Fig. 13.8).

Since the force of wind increases approximately with the cube of velocity, these zones are in reality more significant for site planning than raw wind data would lead us to believe. Sites situated near the brow of the slope are subject to severe wind stress during storms and, in cold climates, to high rates of heat loss and deep penetration of ground frost. Downwind from the brow, sand and snow accumulate where airflow separates; this zone is often the site of sand dune and snowbank formation. If the brow of the slope is forested, sand and snow accumulation often take place along the brow

Risk of the crestslope

(Fig. 13.8). Clearly, each zone presents limitations for development, and the nearer the crestslope, generally the more serious the limitations. Therefore, we can safely say that the placement of structures on or close to the brow of the slope is not advisable as a general practice. It is also necessary to add that development is feasible on stable sites only where proper site analysis and appropriate. engineering and architectural solutions have been worked out. This would necessitate slope analysis to determine stability against mass movement and erosion, soil assessment for stormwater and wastewater drainage, and wind velocity profiling to establish the aerodynamic conditions. Among many other things, the design of structures and landscaping on sites with exposures to strong winds should conform to the aerodynamic forces for best performance.

13.7 CASE STUDY

Documenting Coastal Change Using Aerial Photography

Roy Klopcic

Documenting change in the coastal zone has been facilitated greatly in the past 50 years by the use of vertical aerial photographs. In some instances, we can detect the amount and rate of change in shore erosion, sand dune development, and storm damage by comparing photographs of a specific location taken at different dates. This is done by measuring the relative distances between features such as houses and the shoreline over a known time interval.

As valuable as aerial photographs are as a source of data on the coastal environment, they are not without their problems when it comes to making precise measurements. Among them is an inherent geometric distortion caused by the photograph's single point perspective. In addition, every aerial photograph, owing to a variety of factors, has variation in scale. Failure to recognize and accommodate these factors when making measurements on aerial photographs can lead to erroneous answers and misleading conclusions.

One type of scale problem occurs in aerial photographs of terrain comprised of surfaces at different elevations. Those surfaces closer to the camera appear at larger scales, whereas those farther away appear at smaller scales.

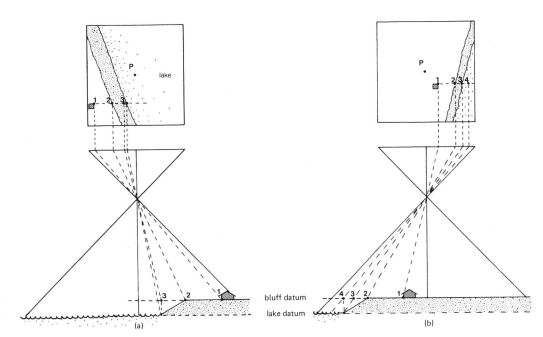

Differences in apparent locations of the shoreline and bluff using (a) lake datum and (b) bluff datum elevations.

This is often encountered in measuring shorelines because of the elevation differences between the top of a backshore slope or bluff and the beach near the toe of the slope. A simple solution to this problem involves making two sets of measurements: one for the lower datum and one for the upper datum. This requires that the photo scale used be specific to the datum where measurements are to be made.

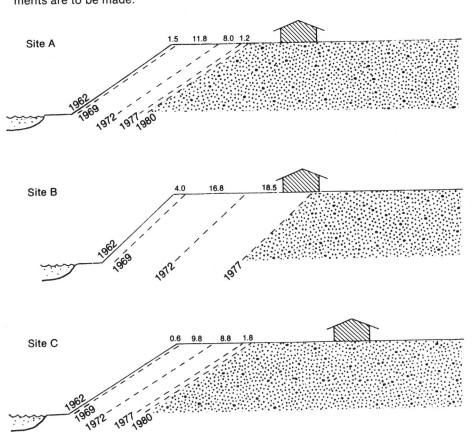

Pattern of bluff retreat from 1962 to 1977 (Site B) and 1980 (Sites A and C) based on measurements from aerial photographs. The accompanying aerial photograph shows the three sites (houses circled) in 1969.

To illustrate this measurement technique, a location was chosen on the Lake Michigan shoreline in an area that has experienced severe shore erosion, with considerable loss of and damage to property. The actual measurements were applied to three specific sites identified on aerial photographs flown on four separate dates; April 1962, April 1969, November 1972, and March 1977. The coastal zone in this area is comprised of two distinct topographic levels: one represented by the lake and the active shore and the other by an upper, terracelike surface 40 to 60 feet above lake level. The surfaces are separated by a steep bluff that is retreating because of wave erosion at its toe.

Because land use development is limited to the upper surface, measurements could be made by scaling the distance between the location of buildings and the edge of the bluff. The position of the shoreline could be extrapolated by constructing a model (profile) of the bluff at the appropriate angle and then measuring the distance to the shoreline on the horizontal axis of the model.

For major mapping projects, such as those undertaken by the U.S. Geological Survey or by private aerial mapping firms under contract to a planning agency, special machines are used to overcome distortion problems and improve the efficiency of interpretation. Stereoplotters and transfer scopes are commonly employed, not only to correct the distortion but also to remove scale variations by adjusting each photograph to fit an accurate planimetric base such as a topographic map. Consequently, it is a relatively routine matter to reconstruct whole coastal environments and make the desired measurements of the changes in selected features as they appear among photographs of different dates. The instruments involved in accomplishing this task are, however, expensive and do require special training if accurate results are expected.

Finally, when using aerial photographs, or any sort of landscape sampling or measurement procedure for that matter, it is necessary to realize that environmental change may be episodic, rather than continuous, and may thus escape detection because it falls between the sampling (overflight) dates. This is most likely to occur in river valleys and coastal zones where each event in a series of events produces change opposite that of its predecessor—for example, erosion, deposition, and erosion. The net change may be negligible while the gross change is great. If the frequency of overflights is such that photographs are taken only after the first and third events, then not only does it *appear* that no or little change has taken place, but an entire event or series of events crucial to understanding the behavior of the landscape has been masked out.

Roy Klopcic is a geographer at Central Michigan University and a specialist in remote sensing and natural resources. ∎

13.8 SELECTED REFERENCES FOR FURTHER READING

Allen, James R. "Beach Erosion as a Function of Variations in the Sediment Budget, Sandy Hook, New Jersey, U.S.A." *Earth Surface Processes and Landforms,* 6, 1981, pp. 139–150.

Bascom, W. N. *Waves and Beaches,* Garden City, N.Y.: Doubleday, 1964.

Bostwick, Ketchum N. *The Water's Edge: Critical Problems of the Coastal Zone.* Cambridge, Mass.: MIT Press, 1972, 393 pp.

Coastal Engineering Research Center. *Shore Protection Manual.* Washington, D.C.: U.S. Government Printing Office, U.S. Army Coastal Engineering Research Center, 1973.

Davies, J. L. *Geographical Variation in Coastal Development.* London: Longman, 1977.

Gutman, A. L., et al. *Nantucket Shoreline Survey.* Cambridge, Mass.: MIT Sea Grant Program, 1979, 51 pp.

Healy, R., C., and Zinn, J. A. "Enviornmental and Development Conflicts in the Coastal Zone." *Journal of the American Planning Association,* 51:3, 1985, pp. 299–311.

Inman, D. L., and Brush, B. M. "The Coastal Challenge." *Science* 181, 1973, pp. 20–32.

Jarrett, J. T., "Sediment Budget Analysis Wrightsville Beach to Kure Beach, North Carolina," Coastal Engineering Research Center Reprint 78–3, U.S. Army Corps of Engineers, 1978, pp. 986–1005.

Marsh, W. M., and Marsh, B. D. "Perched Dune Formation on High Lake Superior Bluffs". *Geografiska Annaler,* 1987, pp. 79–93.

Zenkovich, V. *Processes of Coastal Development,* trans. D. Fry. Edinburgh: Oliver and Boyd, 1967.

14

SUN ANGLES, SOLAR HEATING, AND ENVIRONMENT

14.1 INTRODUCTION

The energy crisis of the late 1970s brought the issue of solar energy squarely into the spotlight of public attention. Solar heating, solar energy, and solar collectors became "buzzwords" in virtually every sector of society as people debated energy alternatives, technologies, and policies. In the 1980s, the debate subsided as society was lulled by relaxed energy costs and ample supplies of gas, coal, and oil.

Energy issue   The urgency of the alternative **energy issue** remains with us, however, as we question the safety of nuclear energy, the environmental impacts of coal-burning power plants, and the dwindling world reserves of petroleum. Directions and alternatives actually pursued by nations are largely a matter of political policy, especially at the national level. Whatever the politics of energy, solar energy will have to be given serious attention in local planning and development and this in turn will require data on solar radiation for different locations and geographic settings. This brings with it an examination of sun angles, which, in addition to applications to energy problems per se, have an important bearing on microclimate, architecture, soils, and ecological conditions.

Solar considerations   In building architecture, sun angles are a traditional consideration because of the designer's concern with both heating and lighting problems. In fact, great debates may be waged among architects over window sizes, building orientation, roof pitches, exterior skin materials, and whether or not to "go solar." In recent decades, sun angles and solar factors in general have also gained status among planners and landscape architects, and today it is not uncommon to find such variables incorporated into the data base for a project along with soils, drainage, and topography. The translation of solar variables into meaningful information for planning decisions can be difficult exercise and, unfortunately, one that few practitioners are able to accomplish effectively. Approached properly, the problem often requires computation of the radiation balance and the heat balance, taking into consideration radiation gains and losses, surface reflection, ground materials, and energy flows in the form of ground heat, sensible heat, and latent heat. Our discussion here begins with rudimentary sun angle concepts and then goes on to solar heating of the landscape and its implications for local environments.

14.2 SUN ANGLE AND INCIDENT RADIATION

Sun angle   The angle formed between sunlight approaching the earth's surface and the surface itself is called the **sun angle**. To envision this angle, think of straight rays of light striking a flat surface such as an airfield. A more direct angle, one that is closer to 90 degrees, causes a greater concentration of solar radiation on the surface. Conversely, smaller angles have weaker solar intensities.

Understandably, sun angle is an important factor in heating the earth's surface. For example, visually compare the areas bombarded by the beam in diagrams (a) and (b) of Fig. 14.1. The beam in (a), which is the same strength as the beam in (b), spreads over more surface area because it strikes the surface at an angle. Since (a) spreads over more *Incident radiation*   area, its density or **incidence** is lower. We can show this with a simple computation that involves dividing the quantity of energy in the beam (S_i) by the area (A) that it strikes:

$$SI = \frac{S_i}{A}$$

where

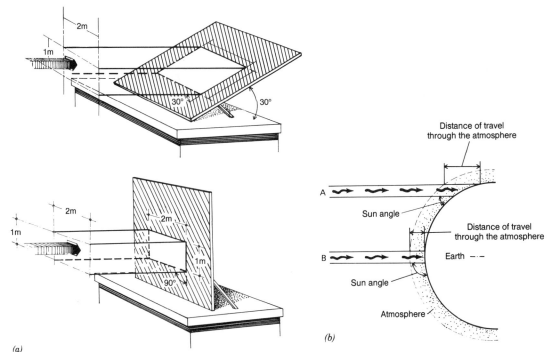

Fig. 14.1 (a) Variations in radiation intensity on an inclined surface, and a flat surface (b) shows the relationship between sun angle and the curvature of the earth including the relative thickness of the atmosphere to incoming solar radiation.

SI = solar radiation incident on the surface, cal/cm$^2 \cdot$ min
S_i = quantity of energy in the beam, cal/min
A = surface area intercepted by the beam, cm^2 or m^2

Because the earth is curved, most solar radiation enters the atmosphere and hits the surface at an angle. As one goes farther poleward, the angle becomes smaller and the beam of radiation becomes more diffuse. Figure 14.1b shows this by contrasting a beam at the equator (B) with one near the Arctic Circle (A). Beam A not only spreads over more surface area, but it also passes through a greater distance of atmosphere, thereby giving the atmosphere a greater opportunity to reflect and scatter radiation before it reaches the ground.

14.3 VARIATIONS IN SUN ANGLE WITH SEASONS AND TOPOGRAPHY

Seasonal change

To understand sun angles more completely, we must take some additional factors into account: one is **seasonal change** in the earths's tilt with respect to the sun. Because of the inclination of the earths's axis (23.5 degrees off vertical), the earth appears to tip toward and away from the sun as it orbits around the sun. This produces seasonal changes in sun angle for all locations on the earth.

Four seasonal sun angles are important at any location on the planet, and they tend to correspond to the seasons in the midlatitudes (Fig. 14.2). For the Northern Hemisphere, the highest and lowest angles occur each year on June 20 to 22 and December 20 to 22, respectively. These dates are called *summer* and *winter solstices*. In fall and spring the sun angles are intermediate, and there are two dates on which they are exactly intermediate, March 20 to 22 and September 20 to 22, called the *equinoxes*.

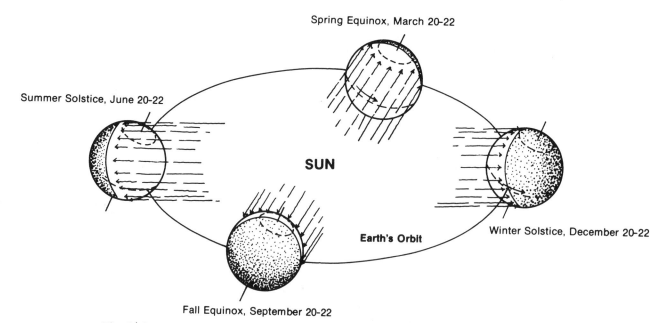

Fig. 14.2   Seasonal changes in sun angle and the orbital path of the earth about the sun.

From summer solstice to winter solstice, the sun angles for any location in the middle latitudes (defined, for convenience, as the zone between 23.5 degrees and 66.5 degrees latitude) vary by 47 degrees. Sun angle readings are normally given as the high noon position of the sun represented by the angle formed between one's outstretched arm pointed at the sun and the horizon on the landscape.[1] Figure 14.3 illustrates the principal sun angles in the year for 50 degrees north latitude.

Computing sun angle   **Computing the sun angle** for any latitude and date involves three basic steps. First, the declination of the sun must be known. This is the latitude on the earth where the sun angle is vertical (90 degrees) on a given date. For this information we consult the graph in Fig. 14.4a. Next, the zenith angle must be determined, which can be done by counting the number of degrees that separate the latitude of the location in question

---

[1] This would actually be an approximation because solar radiation is refracted (bent) somewhat as it passes through the atmosphere.

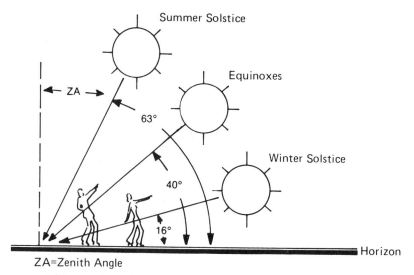

Fig. 14.3   The annual changes in sun angle for 50 degrees north latitude.

from the declination. The scale in Figure 14.4b may be helpful making this count. *Zenith angle* is the angle formed between a vertical line (perpendicular to the ground) and the position of the sun in the sky. In Fig. 14.3, it is the angle between the sun and the broken line, for the summer solstice. The last step is to subtract the zenith angle from 90 degrees. This gives us the sun angle. The following example shows the steps to be followed in computing a sun angle:

- Location = 50 degrees north latitude (given)
- Date = June 15 (given)
- Declination of sun = 23 degrees (Fig. 14.4a)
- Zenith angle, *ZA* = 27 degrees (Fig. 14.4b)
- Sun angle, *SA* = 90 degrees minus *ZA*
- *SA* = 90 degrees minus 27 degrees
- *SA* = 63 degrees

Landscape variations   Once the sun angle of a location is known, we can move to the local scale and examine the influence of the **landscape**—that is , how sun angle varies with hills, valleys, buildings, and the like. Hillslopes and roofs that face the sun are brighter and warmer than those that face away from the sun. In addition, the angle changes from dusk to dawn so that slopes with an eastward component to their orientations are favored by the morning sun and those with westward components are favored by the afternoon sun.

Ground sun angle   To compute the influence of an inclined surface on local sun angle (let us call it **ground sun angle**), we must first determine (1) the sun angle on flat ground for that latitude; (2) the direction in which the slope faces; and (3) the angle of the slope (that is, its inclination in degrees). If the slope faces the noon sun, the sun angle on the slope is equal to the flat ground angle plus the angle of the slope. If the product is greater than 90 degrees, then subtract if from 180 degrees to get the appropriate angle. For slopes that face away from the sun, the sun angle is equal to the flat surface sun angle minus the angle of the slope. If the product is negative, the slope is in shadow.

$$\text{Ground sun angle} = SA \pm \alpha$$

where

Ground sun angle = sun angle on slope face
SA = sun angle on flat ground
α = angle of slope in degrees

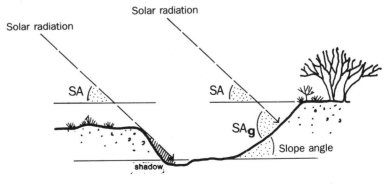

SAg = ground sun angle

SA = sun angle

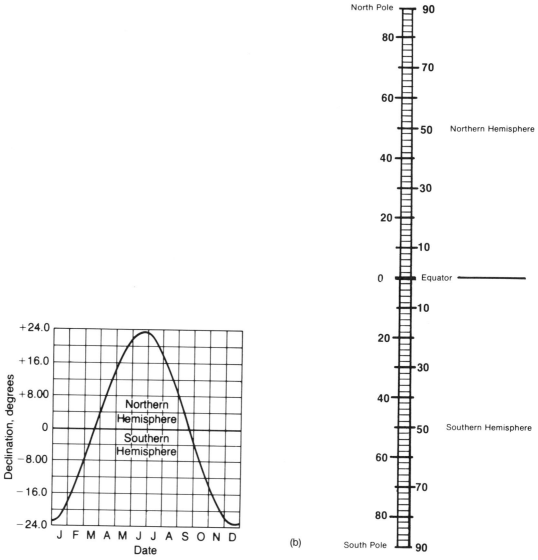

Fig. 14.4 (a) Sun declination chart. Read the chart by finding the date in question on the bottom line; then follow the nearest vertical line upward to the curved graph line. At that point, take the nearest horizontal line to the side of the chart and read the appropriate number. Be sure to read Northern or Southern Hemisphere. (b) Zenith angle chart. Find the latitude in question; then find the declination of the sun and count the number of degrees between the two. This will give you the zenith angle.

14.4 RADIATION BALANCE AND SOLAR HEATING

Albedo

To determine the amount of solar heating on a surface, it is first necessary to understand that at ground level solar radiation can be disposed of in only two ways: reflection and absorption. The reflective capacity of a surface, called **albedo**, is expressed as the percentage of incoming solar (shortwave) radiation rejected by the surface:

$$A = \frac{S_o}{S_i} \times 100$$

where

A = albedo
S_i = incoming shortwave (solar)
S_o = outgoing shortwave (solar)

All earth materials reflect a portion of the solar radiation that strikes them, but the values vary widely as Table 14.1 reveals.

Solar gain   The solar energy absorbed by a surface, let us call it **solar gain**, is equal to incoming shortwave (S_i) less the amount reflected (S_o):

$$\text{Solar gain} = S_i - S_o$$

This quantity represents energy added to the absorbing material in the form of heat, and it in turn will produce a rise in the material's temperature. The actual amount of temperature rise for a given amount of energy added will vary according to the material's composition. This means that equivalent amounts of heat in two different materials, say, water and soil, will not yield the same temperature. This is explained mainly by differences in a property called *volumetric heat capacity,* which for water is high compared to that for sand. (See Table 16.1 in Chapter 16.)

Taking into consideration the fact that solar radiation usually strikes surfaces in the

Table 14.1 Albedos for Various Surfaces

Material	Albedo, Percent
Soil	
Dune sand, dry	35–75
Dune sand, wet	20–30
Dark (e.g., topsoil)	5–15
Gray, moist	10–20
Clay, dry	20–35
Sandy, dry	25–35
Vegetation	
Broadleaf forest	10–20
Coniferous forest	5–15
Green meadow	10–20
Tundra	15–20
Chaparral	15–20
Brown grassland	25–30
Tundra	15–30
Crops (e.g., corn, wheat)	15–25
Synthetic	
Dry concrete	17–27
Blacktop (asphalt)	5–10
Water	
Fresh snow	75–95
Old snow	40–70
Sea ice	30–40
Liquid water	30–40
30° lat. summer	6
30° lat. winter	9
60° lat. summer	7
60° lat. winter	21

From William D. Sellers, *Physical Climatology* (Chicago: University of Chicago, 1974). Used by permission.

landscape at an angle, it is necessary to combine the concept of incident radiation flux (flow over the receiving area) with albedo to determine the solar heating for a surface. This can be done computationally using just three variables: the ground sun angle (based on latitude, date, and surface inclination or slope), the intensity of solar radiation, and the albedo of the surface:

$$SH = S_i (1 - A) \sin SA_g$$

where

SH = solar heating in cal/cm$^2 \cdot$ min
S_i = incoming solar radiation in cal/cm$^2 \cdot$ min
A = albedo ($1 - A$ gives the percentage absorbed)
SA_g = ground sun angle in degrees

Solar heating examples   It is instructive to see how important slope and albedo are in the solar heating of a varied landscape. For example, given the surfaces (at 45 degrees north latitude) represented by the profile in Fig. 14.5, the rates of solar heating at noon on the equinox would be as follows:

Building Roof

- slope = 45°
- orientation = south
- albedo = 10%
- SA_g = 90°
- S_i = .78 cal/cm$^2 \cdot$ min

$SH = .78 (1 - .10) \sin 90°$
$= .78 (.9) 1.0$
$= .70$ cal/cm$^2 \cdot$ min

Concrete Wall

- slope = 30°
- orientation = north
- albedo = 27%
- SA_g = 15°
- S_i = .78/cm$^2 \cdot$ min

$SH = .78 (1 - .27) \sin 15°$
$= .78 (.73) .26$
$= .15$ cal/cm$^2 \cdot$ min

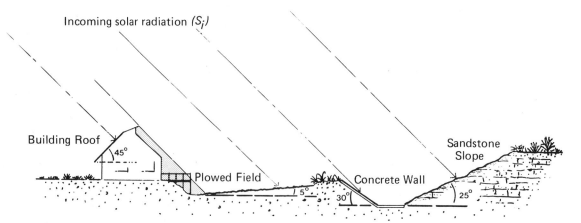

Fig. 14.5 Variation in solar heating related to slope and surface materials.

Plowed Field

■ slope = 5°

■ orientation = south

■ albedo = 22%

■ $SA_g = 50°$

■ $S_i = .78$ cal/cm² min

$$SH = .78 (1. - 22) \sin 50°$$
$$= .78 (.78) .77$$
$$= .47 \text{ cal/cm}^2 \cdot \text{min}$$

Sandstone Slope

■ slope = 25°

■ orientation = south

■ albedo = 40%

■ $SA_g = 70°$

■ $S_i = .78$ cal.cm² · min

$$SH = .78 (1 - .40) \sin 70°$$
$$= .78 (.60) .94$$
$$= .44 \text{ cal/cm}^2 \cdot \text{min}$$

The concrete wall gains the least energy, about one-third that of the field and slope and about one-fifth that of the roof.

Thermal microclimate   The influence of these variations on ground-level climate, called **micro-climate**, depends on many additional factors, including (1) how much of the solar energy absorbed is returned to the air over it as heat (either as sensible heat or by longwave (infrared) radiation, which in turn may heat the air); (2) local wind conditions (which account for the rate of flushing of heated air from surfaces); and (3) the size of the area covered by each heating surface (which determines the relative balance of thermal influences among the different surfaces in an area). Under calm air conditions, the layer of air over surfaces such as these will begin to develop a pattern of temperatures roughly corresponding to the pattern of solar energy absorbed. This may then induce differential air movement with the warm air rising or sliding upslope and the cool air draining downslope (Fig. 14.6) On some days this pattern may carry over well past the period of peak solar radiation and into the evening, given that regional weather systems do not obliterate it.

2:00 P.M.   3:00 P.M.   4:00 P.M.   5:00 P.M.

Fig. 14.6   Afternoon patterns of sunlight and shadow at Jordan Pond Valley, Acadia National Park, Maine, on August 1, based on a simulation model. The shadow slope will produce cool air drainage.

14.5 IMPLICATIONS FOR LAND USE, VEGETATION, AND SOIL

Assessing the impacts of land use

To gain an idea of the **impact of land use** change on the gain of solar energy by the landscape, we can compare the differences in slope (both angle and orientation) and surface materials before and after development. This would involve first mapping the predevelopment slopes of various angles, orientations, and compositions, measuring their areas, and then computing their total solar gain over some time period. These figures would be summed for the entire project area and compared to the parallel figure based on the same computation for the postdevelopment landscape. Although many additional factors would have to be taken into account to determine the climatic significance (that is, means and extremes in air temperature, wind, precipitation, humidity, and so on) of a change in solar gain, such a comparison does provide one measure of the realtive impact of different land uses and development schemes on the environment at ground level.

Vegetation patterns

Variations in incident radiation owing to differences in the orientation and inclination of slopes can have a profound influence on *vegetation* and ground conditions. In semiarid mountainous areas, such as parts of Colorado, New Mexico, and California, the more direct sun angles on south-facing slopes result in greater surface heating and, in turn, higher rates of soil moisture evaporation and plant transpiration than on north-facing slopes. The resulting difference in soil moisture is often great enough to cause marked differences in vegetation on north- and south-facing slopes. The photograph in Fig. 14.7a shows one such example from southern Colorado, where moisture stress limits trees to north-facing slopes.

Fig. 14.7 (a) Differences in vegetation on north- and south-facing slopes. The north-facing slopes sustain forest cover, whereas south-facing slopes are limited mainly to grasses. (b) Shadow zone along north-facing cliffs on Lake Superior helps creates a cool microclimate conducive to certain arctic and subarctic plants.

Runoff and erosion

In even drier areas, where only herbs and shrubs can survive, the plant cover on south-facing slopes is often measurably lighter than that on north-facing slopes. Because more ground is exposed, **erosion by runoff** may also be higher on south-facing slopes, resulting in higher densities of gullies and lower slope angles. In addition, there may be a difference in the abundance of certain species, with the more drought-tolerant species making up a higher percentage of the plant cover on south-facing slopes.

Plant species

Differences in **plant species** related to the influence of slope on incident radiation can also be found in humid regions, though the examples are rarely as obvious as those in dry areas. In the midlatitudes, combinations of heat and light may ensure the survival of certain plants on extreme slopes. For instance, north-facing cliffs along the south shore of Lake Superior harbor species of ferns and mosses that are separated by hundreds of miles from the main bodies of their populations in arctic and subarctic regions. (Fig. 14.7b). Apparently, the low light intensities and cool temperatures along these cliffs have favored the survival of these plants since the last continental glaciation.

14.6 IMPLICATIONS FOR BUILDINGS AND LIVING ENVIRONMENTS

The placement and size of buildings and trees in cities can seriously affect the reception of solar radiation. With rising concern over solar energy and building cooling, this issue has gained significance in urban planning and design. "Shadow corridors" and "solar windows" (or gaps) are two of the most common solar features of cities (Fig. 14.8).

Solar windows

Solar windows are narrow spaces between tall buildings through which the solar beam passes to ground level. Depending on the orientation and spacing of the buildings, the shaft of light may illuminate a patch of ground for only a short time each day, making it difficult to maintain street plants and virtually impossible to utilize solar radiation as a source of energy.

Shadow corridors

Shadow corridors are elongated zones, bordered by a continuous ridge of tall buildings that block the sun. In the most extreme situations, direct (beam) solar radiation is never received in such environments; the only light comes from diffused sky radiation and radiation reflected from nearby buildings.

Shadow length

The **length of a shadow** cast by a building or tree is a function of the height of the object and the sun angle; computations can be made using the formula:

$$S_l = \frac{h}{\tan SA}$$

where

S_l = shadow length
h = height of the object
SA = sun angle

tangents (tan) for angles $5° - 85°$	
5° = .087	45° = 1.0
10° = .176	50° = 1.19
15° = .268	55° = 1.43
20° = .364	60° = 1.73
25° = .466	65° = 2.14
30° = .577	70° = 2.75
35° = .700	75° = 3.73
40° = .839	80° = 5.67
	85° = 11.43

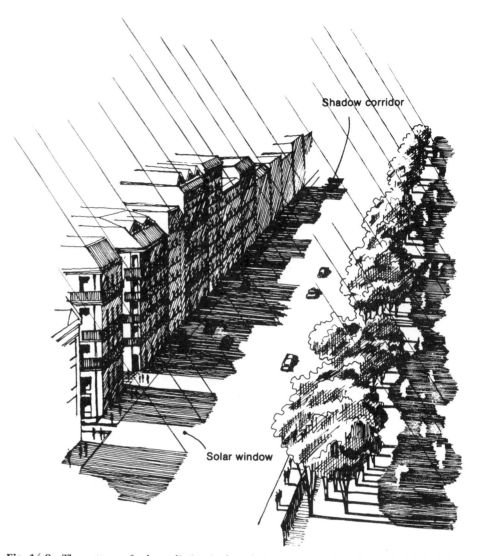

Fig. 14.8   The pattern of solar radiation in the urban environment as altered by tall buildings.

This formula is traditionally used in site planning in areas of excessive heat and intensive solar radiation because it is necessary to provide for shade in pedestrian areas, parking lots, on building faces, plazas, and the like. (See the case study. "Human Heat Syndrome in the City Center," in Chapter 15.) The need for shade is generally greatest in the hours between 11 a.m. and 4 p.m. when high solar intensities are coupled with high air ground temperatures (Fig. 14.9)

Urban microclimate

　　While the shade can be a distinct advantage for local pedestrians and residents of cities prone to frequent heat waves, in northern cities, such as Minneapolis, Detroit, Toronto, and Montreal, shadow corridors encourage the buildup of ice and snow, making foot travel hazardous. Moreover, the solar gain is very poor in these zones for living units with northerly exposures, resulting in somewhat cooler room temperatures and higher heating costs. This is especially significant in light of recent findings in Great Britain and the United States concerning illness and death among the elderly caused by hypothermia.

Accidental hypothermia

　　Accidental hypothermia, a disorder characterized by low body temperature (near 90°F), slowed heartbeat, lowered blood pressure, and slurred speech, can be brought on in persons over age 70 by room temperatures as modest as 65°F, inade-

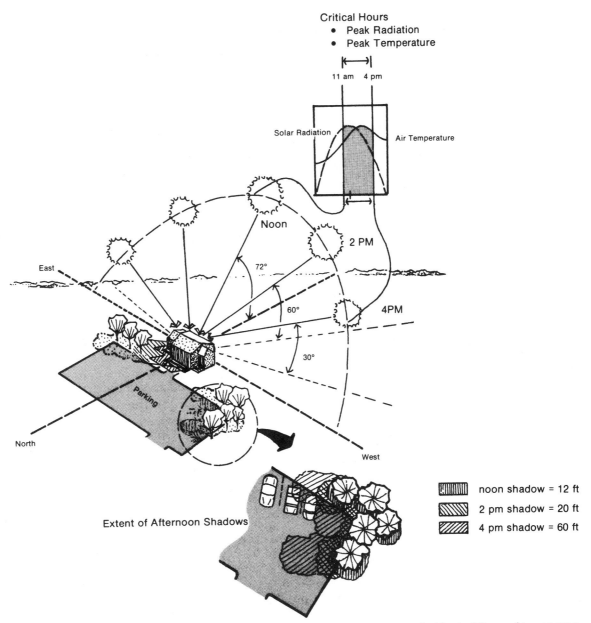

Fig. 14.9 Shadow patterns between noon and 4 p.m. associated with a building and trees near a parking lot. Shade is most critical between 11 a.m. and midafternoon, when air and ground temperatures are highest.

quate clothing, and prolonged periods of physical inactivity. Solar exposure may make a difference of several degrees in room temperatures, especially during cold spells, and in turn can tip the balance between hypothermia and a normal state of health in the elderly (Fig 14.10). The United States National Institutes of Health estimate that as many as 2.3 million elderly people in the United States are vulnerable to accidental hypothermia. Undoubtedly, many of these persons inhabit buildings whose orientation, design, and neighborhood exclude or greatly restrict access to direct solar radiation in living spaces. On the other hand, these same conditions may be an advantage during the summer in northern cities because they are not prone to excessive heating, a topic broached in Chapter 15.

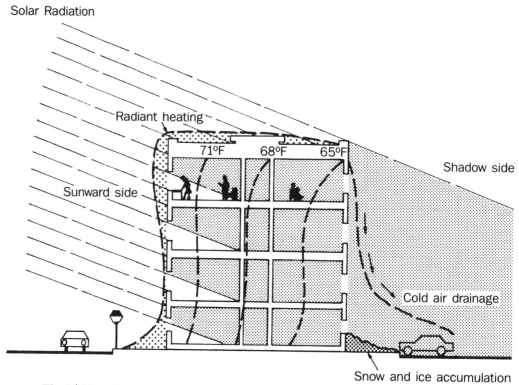

Solar Radiation

Radiant heating

71°F   68°F   65°F

Sunward side

Shadow side

Cold air drainage

Snow and ice accumulation

Fig. 14.10   Schematic diagram illustrating the effects of sun angle on winter living conditions in and around a northern apartment building.

14.7 CASE STUDY

Solar Considerations in Northern Residential Landscape Design

Carl D. Johnson

One of the primary objectives in residential and urban design is mitigation of the climatic extremes in spaces occupied by humans. In architecture the focus is on the internal climate of buildings, which is achieved through air conditioning, light control, and so on. In landscape architecture the primary concern is with outdoor spaces, and climatic modification is attained through the use of vegetation, siting of buildings, the use of different ground materials, and topographic features, either as they exist or as they could be constructed.

In the continental midlatitudes, discomfort from the cold poses a major restriction to the use and enjoyment of outdoor space. Therefore, in the design of modern residential complexes, it is desirable to achieve some modification of microclimate to encourage greater use of patio and yard space. Understandably, the level of modification that can be expected through landscape planning is relatively modest, particularly when set into a Minnesota or Quebec winter. On the other hand, small modifications of marginally cold or cool weather, such as that of spring and fall, are indeed possible, and days that would otherwise be uncomfortably cool can in fact be made to be quite pleasant through sensitive planning and design.

Newport West is a low-density townhouse development located on the northeast edge of Ann Arbor, Michigan. The development site is characterized by hilly terrain with a major swale running through it. The east-facing and south-facing slope of the swale, an old farmfield fringed by trees, was selected for the building site because it offered the greatest opportunity to optimize microclimate conditions and conserve building energy.

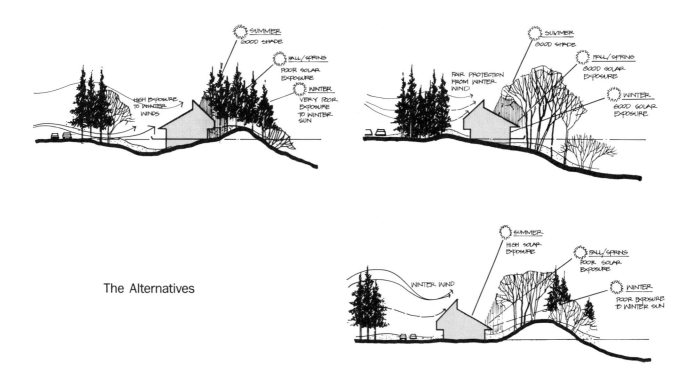

The Alternatives

The housing units were arranged in a series of clusters to form solar pockets and provide protective buffers from the cold, windy northern exposures. The sun pockets were designed to provide comfortable outdoor spaces in fall and spring, and to afford habitats for exotic plants such as azaleas and rhododendrons. The townhouses were constructed with large south-facing windows to receive solar radiation and augment interior heating in fall and winter. On the southwest sides of the units, facades were protected from excessive heating by the afternoon sun with full crown deciduous trees.

After construction and landscaping were completed and the units were occupied, a set of temperature readings were taken in early March to determine

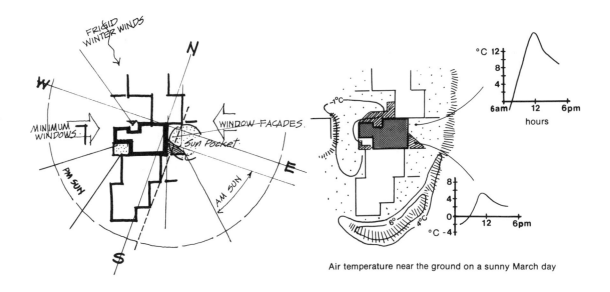

Air temperature near the ground on a sunny March day

The Layout   The Results

the effectiveness of the design in modifying microclimate. Ground temperatures varied substantially, depending on solar exposure, and were 7°C higher at the 5 cm depth on inclines near south-facing walls compared to surfaces near north- and northwest-facing walls. In the patio spaces, air temperatures varied with shade and beam radiation receipt; in the southeast-facing sun pocket the daily high temperature (at surface level) on one bright day was nearly 10°C higher than in permanently shaded areas nearby. On cloudy days and windy days the difference was negligible, however.

An examination of the climatic records shows that in the Midwest a total of 10 to 20 days in fall and spring can be classed as calm and sunny with uncomfortably cool ambient air temperatures. This brief study suggests that these sorts of conditions can be improved in near-building spaces through climate-oriented building design and siting. It also suggests that conditions for exotic plants are more favorable in sun pockets, although it should also be recognized that summer heat may be excessive, and protective shading with deciduous trees may be necessary. The study also implies that residential units that offer both warm and cool outdoor exposures are preferable to those with single exposures in the warm/cold climates because they increase the opportunities for the seasonal use of outdoor space. This consideration is growing increasingly important as people are faced with smaller residences situated in community or neighborhood clusters with limited yard space.

Carl D. Johnson of Johnson, Johnson and Roy, Inc., is a former professor of landscape architecture at the University of Michigan. ∎

14.8 SELECTED REFERENCES FOR FURTHER READING

American Institute of Architects Research Corporation. *Solar Dwelling Design Concepts.* Washington, D.C.: U.S. Department of Housing and Urban Development, 1976.

Buffo, John, et al. "Direct Solar Radiation on Various Slopes from 0 to 60 Degrees North Latitude." *U.S.D.A. Forest Service Research Paper PNW–142, 1972,* 74 pp.

City of Davis (California). *A Strategy for Energy Conservation.* Davis, Calif.: Energy Conservation Ordinance Project, 1974.

Land Design/Research, Inc. *Energy Conserving Site Design Case Study, Burke Center, Virginia.* Washington, D.C.: U.S. Department of Energy, 1979, 60 pp.

Marsh, William M., and Dozier, Jeff. "The Radiation Balance." In *Landscape: An Introduction to Physical Geography.* Reading, Mass.: Addison–Wesley, 1981, pp. 21–35.

National Institute on Aging. "A Winter Hazard for the Old: Accidental Hypothermia." Washington, D.C.: U.S. National Institutes of Health, Department of Health, Education and Welfare, 1981 (?), Pub. no. (NIH) 78–1464.

Sizemore and Associates. *Methodology for Energy Management Plans for Small Communities.* Washington, D.C.: U.S. Department of Enegy, 1978.

Sterling, Raymond, et al. *Earth Sheltered Community Design.* New York: Van Nostrand Reinhold, 1981, 270 pp.

Tuller, S. E. "Microclimatic Variations in a Downtown Urban Environment." *Geografiska Annaler 54A,* 1973, pp. 123–135.

15

MICROCLIMATE AND THE URBAN ENVIRONMENT

15.1 INTRODUCTION

Urbanization can cause significant changes in atmospheric conditions near the ground. In extreme situations, such as in the heavily build-up areas of larger cities, these changes extend hundreds of meters above the ground and are of such magnitudes that they produce a distinct climatic variant, the urban climate. Generally speaking, the urban climate is warmer, less well lighted, less windy, foggier, more polluted, and often rainier than the regionwide climate.

Within the urban landscape microclimatic variations can also be considerable: air quality may be exceptionally poor along transportation corridors and in industrial sectors; certain neighborhoods may be warmer than average in summer; and areas between tall buildings may receive little or no beam radiation, obtaining much of their energy instead from the heat loss of buildings.

These variations can be important considerations in urban planning and design. Documentation of the desirable climatic effects of vegetated areas, for example, helps provide a rationale for the inclusion of parks and greenbelts in master plans. Transportation planning today invariably includes air quality guidelines and goals. Proposals for industrial development must include forecasts on gaseous and particulate emissions and plume patterns under different atmospheric conditions.

15.2 THE URBAN HEAT ISLAND

Urban heat balance

Urbanization transforms the landscape into a complex environment characterized by forms, materials, and activities that are vastly different from those in the rural landscape. Not surprisingly, the flow of energy in the urban landscape is also different. As a whole, the receipt of solar radiation is substantially lower, while the generation of sensible heat at ground level is greater in cities compared to the neighboring countryside. Furthermore the rate of heat loss from the urban atmosphere through convective and radiant flows is lower. On balance, the increase in sensible heat coupled with lower rates of heat loss is more than enough to offset the thermal effects of the decrease in solar radiation, resulting in somewhat higher air temperatures in urban areas throughout most of the year and much higher temperatures on selected days. The spatial pattern of these temperatures is often concentric around the city center, producing a "heat island" in the landscape. The geographic extent and intensity of the urban heat island varies with city size (based on population) and with regional weather conditions. In general, large cities under calm, sunny weather produce the strongest heat islands.

Urban boundary layer

The overall structure of the urban atmosphere can be envisioned as a large dome centered over the urban mass. This body of air is called the **urban boundary layer.** Because of a heavy particulate content, it is highly efficient in back-scattering solar radiation, often effecting a reduction of 50 percent in the lower 1,000–2,000 meters above a city. A growing amount of research findings reveal that increased cloudiness and precipitation are associated with the urban atmosphere and that these trends carry downwind to neighboring areas in the urban region. Thus it appears that the domelike structure of the boundary layer is pronounced only during relatively calm atmospheric conditions, whereas during a steady airflow across the region, the dome is tipped downwind and develops a plume (Fig. 15.1).

At ground level the causes underlying the formation of the urban heat island, and indeed the urban climate in general, are many and complex. First, the materials of the urban landscape possess different thermal properties than those of the rural landscape. The volumetric heat capacities of street and building materials are appreciably lower than those of materials in the rural landscape (see Table 16.1 in Chapter 16). This

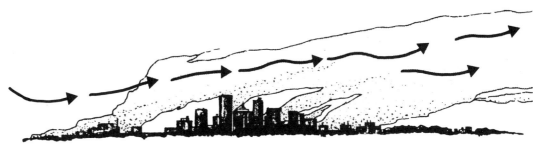

Fig. 15.1 Configuration of the urban "dust dome" during a cross wind. This plume may extend great distances downwind from the city, where it can produce a measurable increase in precipitation and cloudiness.

means that urban surfaces generally reach a higher temperature with the absorption of a given quantity of radiation and, in turn, heat the overlying air faster. Second, the Bowen Ratio, which is a measure of the heat released from a surface in the sensible form relative to the latent form, is much higher in cities owing to the limited areas of *Sensible and latent heat flux* open water, vegetation, and exposed soil. With a paucity of vapor sources, **latent heat flux** from the surface is relatively low; conversely, **sensible heat flux** is relatively high, giving rise to higher air temperatures. Added to this is the heat released from artificial sources (automobiles, buildings, etc.). In the midlatitudes, these sources typically contribute more energy to a city in mid-winter than the solar source does.

Heat inputs represent only one side of the system; the other is, of course, heat *Wind and heat loss* outputs, or losses, from the urban atmosphere. The principal consideration in this regard is wind speed. Overall, cities tend to have much lower wind speeds at ground level; therefore, heated air tends not to be flushed away as readily as it is in rural landscapes. Furthermore, the urban atmosphere retains more heat because of a higher carbon dioxide content. On balance, then, the urban landscape yields and retains more heat, thereby accounting for the heat island effect.

15.3 MICROCLIMATIC VARIATIONS WITHIN THE URBAN REGION

Although the climate of an entire city is an important issue for regional authorities, air pollution control boards, and increasingly those concerned with global climate change, climatic variations within the city have become important issues to the urban planner, landscape architect, and architect. Perhaps the easiest variation to visualize is that associated with solar radiation around tall buildings, but other parameters including temperature, wind, fog, and pollution also show considerable variation within the urban landscape (Fig. 15.2). The nature and significance of these variations is not well documented; however, experts seem to agree that extremes in these components of the urban climate do impair the health and safety of a significant number of people in most cities. There is also agreement that the urban climate can be improved through planning and management of land use activities and new approaches to urban design.

Solar Radiation Beam radiation is intercepted by buildings, and, depending on sun angle and building height, a shadow of some size is created. Where buildings are *Shadow corridors* closely spaced, a **shadow corridor** may form (see Fig. 14.8 in Chapter 14). For a single building site, incoming solar radiation varies with season, wall orientation, time of day, and the location and size of neighboring buildings. Pockets sheltered from beam radiation are illuminated by diffused and reflected radiation only, amounting to very small solar gains. (See Chapter 14 for more details on solar radiation in urban settings.)

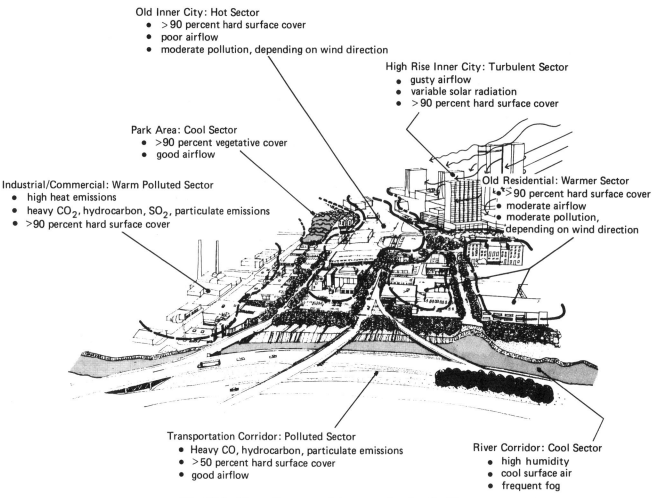

Old Inner City: Hot Sector
- \>90 percent hard surface cover
- poor airflow
- moderate pollution, depending on wind direction

High Rise Inner City: Turbulent Sector
- gusty airflow
- variable solar radiation
- \>90 percent hard surface cover

Park Area: Cool Sector
- \>90 percent vegetative cover
- good airflow

Industrial/Commercial: Warm Polluted Sector
- high heat emissions
- heavy CO_2, hydrocarbon, SO_2, particulate emissions
- \>90 percent hard surface cover

Old Residential: Warmer Sector
- \>90 percent hard surface cover
- moderate airflow
- moderate pollution, depending on wind direction

Transportation Corridor: Polluted Sector
- Heavy CO, hydrocarbon, particulate emissions
- \>50 percent hard surface cover
- good airflow

River Corridor: Cool Sector
- high humidity
- cool surface air
- frequent fog

Fig. 15.2 Microclimate conditions associated with different sectors of a city. Conditions vary with surface cover, solar radiation, airflow, and air pollution among other things.

Temperature Most cities are geographically diverse in surface materials, physical forms, and activities, and we would expect settings as different as people parks and industrial parks to develop markedly different temperature regimes. Studies show, however, that this is so only where thermal variations are not masked by strong regional weather systems or extreme local influences on climate. The latter is exemplified by a small park of vegetation in the midst of an inner city; whatever modification in temperature is achieved by the park is masked by the thermal umbrella of the surrounding mass of buildings.

Cool pockets　　Thermal modification of the urban heat island by a large park or greenbelt can be significant, however. For example, in a 90-acre Montreal park, a set of daytime temperature readings in summer showed the park interior to be 2°C cooler than the built-up area immediately surrounding it (Fig. 15.3). Other investigations have shown older residential areas with mature trees to be cooler than new residential areas and other urban surfaces. In Washington, D.C., it is not uncommon for the corridor of parks and water along the Potomac River Valley to be cooler during summer days and evenings than the heavily built-up areas on either side of it.

Heat island perimeter　　On the **perimeter** of the city the urban **heat island** may decline sharply where the urban landscape quickly gives way to the rural landscape. Pictured in a temperature profile, this sort of border is characterized by a "cliff" in the graph line. From a

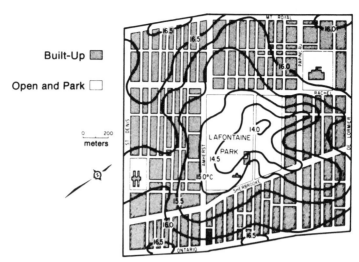

Fig. 15.3   A patch of cooler air associated with a large park in the midst of the Montreal heat island. The lower temperatures are related mainly to the vegetation, and the change is produced in latent heat flux and volumetric heat capacity.

planimetric perspective, the border configuration appears to be very irregular in detail with cool inliers represented by parks and river corridors and warm outliers represented by large shopping centers and industrial parks (Fig. 15.4).

Ground-level velocity   **Wind and Convective Mixing**   The general influence of a city on airflow is to reduce wind speed at levels near the ground. This can be illustrated by comparing the profiles of wind speed over urban and rural surfaces. The elevated topography of the urban environment displaces the profile upward, leaving a thicker layer of slow-moving air near the ground (Fig. 15.5). At a more detailed level of observation, however, large variations in wind speeds can be found within relatively small areas. Much of this *Airflow around buildings* variation is related to the size, spacing, and arrangement of **buildings.** Three examples are noteworthy. First, in the case of an individual building, the structure represents an obstacle to airflow and, in order to satisfy the continuity of flow principle, wind must

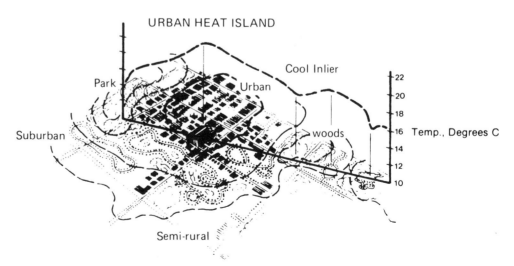

Fig. 15.4   A schematic diagram depicting the nature of the urban heat island and its boundary on the urban fringe.

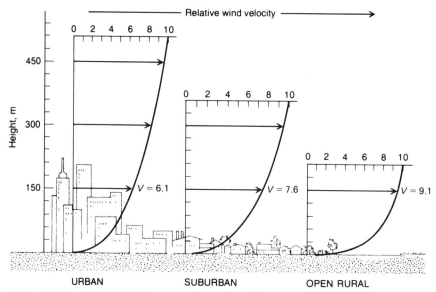

Fig. 15.5   Profile of wind velocity over urban and rural landscapes. Although ground-level wind velocities are markedly lower in cities, turbulence tends to be higher because of tall buildings.

speed up as it crosses the building. In a two-dimensional model the highest speeds are reached on the windward brow of the building and across the roof. Air is also deflected from the brow down the face of the building (labeled A in Fig. 15.6); on the leeward side, speeds decline and streamlines of wind spread out with some descending to the ground.

Where two tall buildings of similar heights are spaced close to each other, the streamlines of fast wind do not descend to the ground but are kept aloft by the roof of the second building. This gives rise to a small pocket of calm air between the buildings where mixing with the larger atmosphere of the city is limited (labeled "B" in Fig. 15.6). Depending on local conditions, the air in such pockets may be measurably different from the surrounding atmosphere.

The third example involves the alignment of buildings and streets. Streets bordered by a continuous mass of tall buildings have the topographic character of canyons

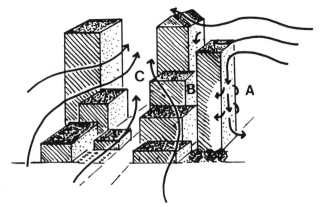

Fig. 15.6   Airflow over and around buildings. Highest velocities are reached on the windward brow and across the roof of the tallest building. A strong flow of air is also deflected down the building face (A), but a calm zone develops in the space between the buildings (B). C refers to accelerated flow associated with the canyon between large buildings.

and, if aligned in the direction of strong winds, tend to channel and constrict airflow. This produces higher wind velocities at street level, especially during gusts, and increased turbulence along the canyon walls (labeled "C" in Fig. 15.6).

Incidence and location

Fog The **incidence** of fog in cities may be twice that of surrounding country landscape. Most of this is usually attributed to the abundance of condensation nuclei from urban air pollution. Local concentrations of fog are common in **selected areas,** especially under calm atmospheric conditions coupled with strong night-time cooling at the surface. Several contributing factors can be identified besides air pollution, and one is related to the availability of water vapor near the ground. In low-lying coastal areas and in river valleys, the concentration of vapor may be appreciably higher than elsewhere in the city. In addition, cold air drainage into low-lying areas promotes fog development. Conversely, heated buildings and hard surfaces may locally reduce fog development because they tend to limit the normal rate of fall in night-time air temperatures.

Spatial variation

Air Pollution Although a body of heavily polluted air may blanket an entire urban region under certain atmospheric conditions, pollution levels are on the average higher in the inner city than in surrounding suburban areas (Table 15.1). In addition, pollution levels on many days vary sharply from one quadrant or sector of an urban area to another. Two factors account for this: (1) the site-specific nature of many pollution sources such as power plants, highway corridors, and industrial plants; and (2) short-term changes in the mixing and flushing capacity of the urban boundary

Weather influences

layer. During windy and unstable **weather,** pollutants are mixed into the larger mass of air over the city and flushed away, thereby limiting heavy concentrations, if any, to relatively small zones downwind of discharge points. During calm and stable conditions, however, pollutants tend to build up over source areas, and if these conditions are prolonged, the concentrations coalesce to form a composite mass over the urban region. An intermediate condition might be characterized by a light crosswind that draws plumes of polluted air from discharge points and areas. The behavior of individual pollution plumes depends on the thermal structure of the receiving atmosphere, wind direction and speed, and the height of release (Fig. 15.7).

Pollution mass balance

The **mass balance of pollutants** for a given volume of atmosphere can be estimated based on the total rate of pollutant emission and the rate of removal by airflow. Removal includes both lateral and vertical components; therefore, it is easy to imagine how heavy the buildup of pollution can become during a prolonged thermal inversion when airflow in all directions is negligible. Moreover, stagnation polluted

Table 15.1 Air Quality and Location in the Urban Region

Pollutant (μ/m^3)	Inner City		Suburb	Rural
Suspended particulates	102	(260)	40	21
Sulfur dioxide	65–80	(372)	60	40
Oxidants	125	(na)	na	na
Lead	0.21	1.11	0.09	0.02
Nitrate ion	1.4	2.4	0.8	0.4
Sulphate ion	10.0	10.1	5.3	2.5

μ/m^3 = micrograms per cubic meter
na = not available
(260) = peak value

From U.S. Council on Environmental Quality, *Environmental Quality: Third Annual Report,* Washington, D.C., 1972.

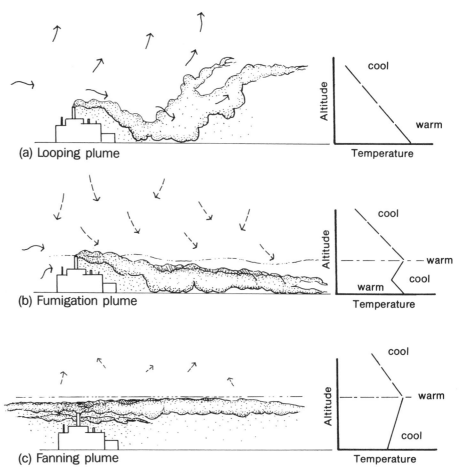

Fig. 15.7 Three basic types of stack exhaust plumes under different atmospheric conditions: (a) looping plume associated with unstable air; (b) fumigation volume associated with descending air; and (c) fanning plume associated with a thermal inversion.

Pollution events

air increases the prospects for oxidation and photochemical processes involving sulfur dioxide, nitrogen oxides, and hydrocarbons, leading to the formation of sulfuric acid, nitric acid, and noxious gases such as ozone. Under severe **episodes of air pollution,** the only realistic management option (other than regulating people's activities) is to reduce the rate of emission. In several instances, officials in American cities have actually restricted automobile traffic and industrial activity to avert a health disaster. Such decisions depend not only on the gross level of air pollution, but also on the levels of critical pollutants, especially hydrocarbons, oxides of nitrogen, sulfur dioxide, and airborne particles (Table 15.2)

Regional impacts

The plumes of polluted air generated from metropolitan areas are known to extend tens, hundreds, and in extreme cases, thousands of miles beyond their source areas (see Fig. 15.1). The effects on regional climate are not well documented, but it is known that they are more pronounced in certain regions and seasons and are characterized by increased cloudiness, precipitation, and turbulent weather. Another regional effect has recently been addded—**acid rain** in southeastern Canada and northeastern United States. Much of this is caused by the formation of sulfuric acid from the combination of atmospheric moisture and sulfur trioxide in polluted air. Because of the regional flow of weather systems across the Midwest, the acidic moisture is carried from industrial areas and precipitated in Ontario, Quebec, and New England where the

Acid rain

Table 15.2 Major Air Pollutants and Their Sources

Pollutant	Source	Effects
Carbon monoxide	• Gasoline-powered vehicles • Industry using oil and gas • Building heating using oil and gas	• Enters human bloodstream rapidly, causing nervous system dysfunction and death at high concentrations
Sulfur oxides (sulfur dioxide and sulfur trioxide)	• Industry using coal and oil • Heating using coal and oil • Power plants using coal, oil, and gas	• Irritates human respiratory tract and complicates cardiovascular disease • Damages plants, especially crops • Promotes weathering of building skin materials
Nitrogen oxides (nitric oxide and nitrogen dioxide)	• Gasoline-powered vehicles • Building heating using oil and gas • Industry and power plants	• Irritates human eyes, nose, and upper respiratory tract • Damages plants • Triggers development of photochemical smog
Hydrocarbons (compounds of hydrogen and carbon)	• Petroleum-powered vehicles • Petroleum refineries • General burning	• Toxic to humans at high concentrations • Promotes photochemical smog
Particulates (liquid or solid particles smaller than 500 micrometers)	• Vehicle exhausts • Industry • Building heating • General burning • Spore- and pollen-bearing vegetation	• Some are toxic to humans • Some pollens and spores cause allergic reactions in humans • Promotes precipitation formation

biota of thousands of lakes and ponds have been damaged by the increase in water acidity.

15.4 APPLICATIONS TO URBAN PLANNING

Utility of scientific models

Planners and designers widely recognize climate as an important ele▮▮▮ ▮▮ urban planning, but few have been able to incorporate climatic variables eff▮▮ information base for decision making. Several factors are responsible ▮▮ important being the level of scientific understanding of microclima▮▮ environment. Although architects and engineers understand many of the influences of climate on a building, for example, wind stress, solar exposure, and corrosion of skin materials, comparatively little is known about the influence of buildings on climate. In contrast to urban hydrology, for instance, technical planning is able to provide fewer models and less accurate forecasts to guide the urban planner in setting the heights of buildings, the balance between hard surfaces and vegetative surfaces, the widths of streets, and the like.

Planning regulations

A second factor is the general lack of **planning regulations** pertaining to climate. Although it is widely recognized that urban climate affects the health and well-being of people, resulting among other things in greatly increased medical costs, few ordinances have been enacted establishing climate performance standards for residential areas. Exceptions are in the area of air quality: national regulations on industrial and automotive emissions seek to improve living conditions in cities. In local transportation projects involving federal funds, a transportation master plan is required that takes air quality into consideration. In locales that are subject to severe episodes of air pollution, such as Los Angeles County, local agencies are responsible for regulating the outdoor activity of schoolchildren, and, under emergency conditions, for reducing automotive and industrial activity. Beyond examples related to air quality, however, planning agencies pay little attention to climatic parameters such as temperature, airflow, fog, and radiation. Prospects for change in this state of affairs are not good where a direct relationship to human safety or to capital costs is not apparent, that is, where direct savings to individuals, companies, agencies, or institutions are not evident. A case in point is the emergence of solar energy-oriented communities where ordinances on "solar rights" are beginning to appear because access to the sun can be given some economic value.

Climate in EIS   Climate is invariably addressed in **environmental impact statements,** but they usually consist of descriptions of existing conditions with some "forecasts" about potential changes given a proposed action. Only cases involving air quality changes are a source of serious concern and may be the basis for recommending against or altering a proposed action. As for changes in physical components of climate, no guidelines or performance standards have been established to aid planners in formulating plans and reviews. As a result, in most cases no one is quite sure how much importance should be ascribed to a suspected change in some aspect of physical climate. Thus the issue is often relegated to the bin of unused information.

15.5 CLIMATIC CRITERIA FOR URBAN PLANNING AND DESIGN

Modern cities in most countries appear to be undergoing almost constant physical change mainly in response to economic and political forces. This demands that the urban planner and designer be on constant watch for opportunities to improve pedestrian movement, commuter traffic, land use, air quality, wastewater disposal, and so on. The overriding challenge is to achieve a proper balance between the economic functions that are necessary to the city's existence and an environment that allows for the health and well-being of the populus. Planning to improve climate and the quality of the atmosphere is a good example of this challenge, judging from the struggle in the United States over whether to relax pollution emission standards in order to improve the industrial economy.

Five climatic factors influence the comfort and health of people in most urban environments: air temperature, humidity, solar radiation, wind, and air pollution. While little can be done in designing cities to combat regional atmospheric conditions, measures can be taken to minimize thermal extremes and high levels of air pollution associated with microclimates within the city. Basically, only four types of climatic controls or changes are possible through urban planning and design, given the goal of improving living conditions in cities prone to excessive heat and air pollution:

Planning and design objectives

1. Reduce solar radiation by shading critical surfaces, for example, pedestrian walks, waiting areas, and busy streets.

2. Reduce the abundance of concrete and asphalt, and increase the amount of vegetation and open water. This will create higher volumetric heat capacities and greater rates of latent heat flux, thereby lowering air temperatures.

3. Increase airflow at ground level to flush heated and polluted air away from the city.

4. Reduce pollution by decreasing emission rates, improving flushing rates, and locating discharge points to minimize impact on heavily populated sectors.

Scale considerations

In applying climatic factors to urban design, it is important first to consider the **scale of the problem.** For problems of citywide scope, the location, structure, and layout of streets, building masses, and industrial parks must be weighed against airflow patterns, sources of pollution (such as existing traffic corridors), and the ratio of open to developed space. In inland cities the maintenance of ground-level airflow in summer is very important; therefore, street corridors should be wide, aligned with prevailing winds, and kept free of major obstacles.

Where vacant land is available in and around built-up areas, it should be converted to vegetation, and, to as great an extent as possible, vegetation should be expanded into inner city areas along streets, in pocket parks, and on rooftops. Where pollution is a problem, seasonal patterns of airflow and weather should be considered in locating industry, power plants, and the like. In the midlatitudes, winter weather often produces plume patterns that direct polluted air toward the ground; where this is known to occur, polluting activities should be situated so as to minimize impact to residential areas.

At the scale of individual blocks of buildings, attention must be given to orientation with respect to airflow and solar radiation and to building sizes and forms. Building heights must be taken into account; to minimize the nuisance and danger of gusts to pedestrians, studies have shown that the taller of two adjacent buildings should not exceed the shorter by more than twofold.

Elevation considerations

In considering the vertical dimension of urban climate, it is important to ask what level (**elevation**) is most appropriate for different human activities. Clearly, ground level in the inner city has several distinct drawbacks, including severe heat, pollution, as well as competition with automotive traffic. Similarly, high elevations pose the hazard of high-speed winds that can damage structures and impair human safety. At the middle level, however, in the four- to ten-story range, air is generally cleaner than that at ground level but substantially less windy than that at higher elevations, providing a somewhat healthier and more comfortable climate. Therefore, where heat and pollution at ground level are a problem it seems that rooftop spaces and balconies in this zone offer promise for expanded human use if, as New Yorkers and others are finding,

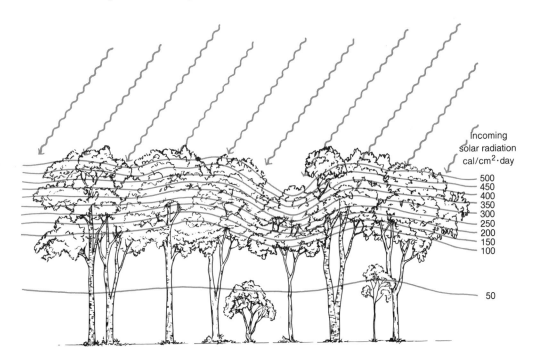

Fig. 15.8 Attenuation of solar radiation associated with a large forest.

appropriate landscaping can be introduced to ensure shade and safety. This concept is similar to the model of bioclimatic zonation in large, tropical forests where the middle level of the canopy is the optimum climatic zone for many creatures, the top being too windy and hot and the floor too humid and shaded. (Fig. 15.8).

Rooftop storage of stormwater may also be desirable in modifying the urban climate. Upon evaporation, large quantities of sensible heat are taken up and released with the water vapor, thereby cooling the roof surface and the air over it. In Texas, for example, as much as 80 inches of water can be evaported from open water surfaces in the average year, twice the average annual precipitation for most of the state. Therefore, it is easily possible to dissipate the total annual quantity of stormwater if the water can be held on rooftops.

Streetscapes   At the **street scale,** consideration must be given to the potential for thermal stress on people in waiting and walking spaces. This is especially critical in cities that record official temperatures above 90°F on many days per month in summer, because in thermal microclimates such readings translate into temperatures above 100°F. (Fig. 15.9). In addition to high temperatures, intensive solar radiation, poor airflow, high humidity, and physical exertion also contribute to heat syndrome. Thus, along pedestrian corridors with high solar exposures, poor air circulation, and long walking distances, the potential is great for heat syndrome among walkers. To avoid this, shaded rest stops with good ventilation should be provided at appropriate locations. The distribution and location of stops should be based on origin and destination patterns for different walkers, for example, elderly, disabled, and youth.

Finally, it is necessary to evaluate the performance of completed urban design

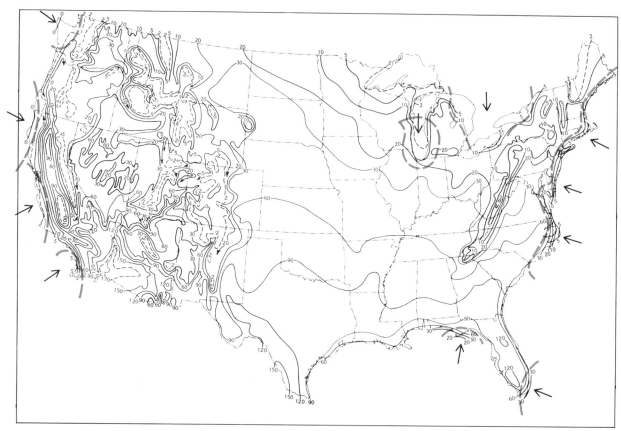

Fig. 15.9 The distribution of the average number of days per year with air temperature reaching 90° F or more. The arrows identify relatively cool coastal locations.

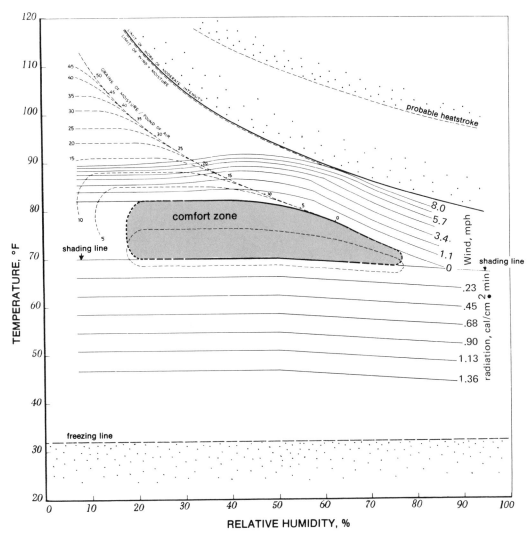

Fig. 15.10 Climate comfort chart that can be used to test urban environments for their suitability for humans.

projects based on microclimatic factors related to health (heat and pollution), safety (e.g., wind), energy costs, and aesthetics. With respect to heat syndrome, performance standards can be based on bioclimatic criteria such as those in Olgyay's bioclimatic chart, and would require field measurements of humidity, wind, temperature, and solar radiation in various types of space occupied by people (Fig. 15.10). Following design evaluation, modifications should be made to improve performance.

15.6 CASE STUDY

■ Human Heat Syndrome in the City Center

NOAA

In the period 1950–1967, more than 8000 persons were killed in the United States by the effects of heat and solar radiation. These were identified by health and medical authorities as direct casualties. How many deaths in the aged and infirm were encouraged by excessive heat or solar radiation is not known because medical records usually do not identify climatic factors as the cause of death in such cases.

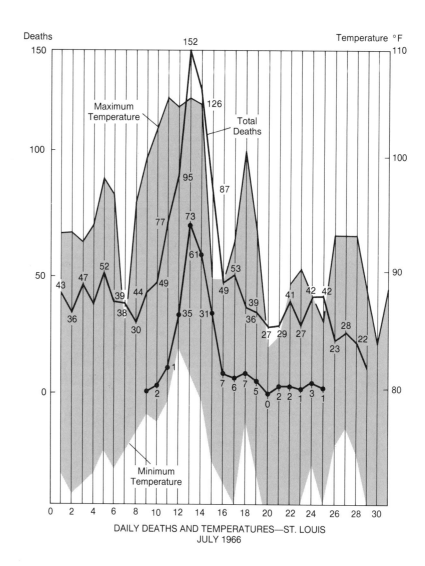

DAILY DEATHS AND TEMPERATURES—ST. LOUIS
JULY 1966

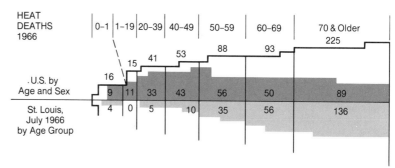

Heat syndrome refers to several clinically recognizable disturbances of the human thermoregulatory system. The disorders generally have to do with a reduction or collapse of the body's ability to shed heat by circulatory changes and sweating, or a chemical (salt) imbalance caused by too much sweating. Ranging in severity from the vague malaise of heat asthenia to the extremely lethal heat stroke, heat syndrome disorders share one common feature: the individual has been subject to overexposure and/or overexercise for his or her age and physical condition and the thermal environment.

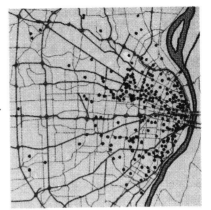

DISTRIBUTION
OF HEAT
DEATHS
ST. LOUIS, MO.
JULY 1966

Two climatic conditions are associated with most epidemics of heat syndrome: regional heat waves and thermal microclimates. Heat waves are usually accompanied by an increased mortality, especially among the elderly; this correlation can be expected without a complicating factor of high humidity or air pollution. Studies of heat syndrome show that it affects all ages of humans, but, other things being equal, the severity of the disorder tends to increase with age; heat cramps in a 17-year-old boy may be heat exhaustion in someone of 40 years, and heat stroke in a person over 60 years of age.

There is evidence that heat waves are worse in the brick and asphalt canyons of the "inner cities" than in the more open and better vegetated suburbs. The July 1966 heat wave in St. Louis is a case in point. Most of the 236 deaths attributed to excessive temperatures occurred in the more heavily built-up areas of the city. Records also show that the death rate soared when the daily high temperature exceeded 100°F and that the highest tolls lagged behind temperature peaks by about a day.

Thermal stress is worse for people with heart disease, than for others. In a hot, humid environment, impaired evaporation and water loss hamper thermal regulation, while physical exertion and heart failure increase the body's rate of heat production. The ensuing cycle is vicious in the extreme.

In a healthy person, the body acclimates to heat by adjusting perspiration-salt concentrations, among other things. In the midlatitude continental climates, this concentration changes in winter and summer just as it does when one moves from Boston to Panama. The body seeks an equilibrium in which enough water is lost to regulate body temperature without upsetting its chemical balance. Females appear to be better at this than males, because females excrete less perspiration and so less salt; therefore, heat syndrome usually strikes fewer females.

NOAA, The National Oceanic and Atmospheric Administration is the U.S. federal agency responsible for monitoring and forecasting weather and climate. ∎

15.7 SELECTED REFERENCES FOR FURTHER READING

American Society of Landscape Architects Foundation. *Landscape Planning for Energy Conservation.* Reston, Va.: Environmental Design Graphics, 1977, 224 pp.

Berry, Brian J. L., and Horton, F. E. *Urban Environmental Management: Planning for Pollution Control.* Englewood Cliffs, N.J.: Prentice–Hall, 1974, 425 pp.

Chandler, T. J. *The Climate of London.* London: Hutchinson and Co., 1965, 292 pp.

Ellis, F. P. "Mortality from Heat Illness and Heat-aggravated Illness in the United States." *Environmental Research* 5:1, 1972, pp. 1–58.

Federer, C. A. "Trees Modify the Urban Microclimate." *Journal of Arboculture* 2, 1976, pp. 121–127.

Landsberg, H. E. "The Climate of Towns." In *Man's Role in Changing the Face of the Earth.* Chicago: University of Chicago Press, 1956, pp. 584–606.

Marsh, William M., and Dozier, Jeff. "The Influence of Urbanization on the Energy Balance." In *Landscape: Introduction to Physical Geography.* Reading, Mass.: Addison–Wesley, 1981, 636 pp.

Oke, T. R. *Boundary Layer Climates.* New York: Halsted Press, 1978, 372 pp.

Oke, T. R. "Towards a Prescription for the Greater Use of Climatic Principles in Settlement Planning." *Energy and Buildings* 7, 1984, pp 1–10.

Olgyay, Victor, *Design with Climate.* 4th ed. Princeton, N.J.: Princeton University Press, 1973, 190 pp.

Thurow, C. *Improving Street Climate Through Urban Design.* Chicago: American Planning Association, Planning Advisory Service Report 376, 1983, 34 pp.

16

SEASONAL GROUND FROST, PERMAFROST, AND LAND DEVELOPMENT

16.1 INTRODUCTION

Practically everywhere in the landscape we can see the direct or indirect influences of ground heat. The germination of many seeds depends on ground temperature. Evaporation of soil moisture is influenced by soil heat. Permafrost, which occupies 25 to 30 percent of the land area of this planet, is a form of ground frost that can place severe stress on most modern land uses. In North America, the largest areas of permafrost lie in Canada and Alaska. The Trans-Alaska Pipeline and several similar projects in Canada have brought national attention to permafrost environments. Chief among the concerns is the impact of development on the tundra, one of the least disturbed of the major ecosystems on earth. This concern becomes more acute each decade with rising political and economic pressure to open up permafrost lands to oil, iron ore, and other extractive activities.

Though less serious than permafrost, seasonal ground frost can be an important consideration in planning and engineering facilities in the midlatitudes. In particular, water pipes and sewer lines must be laid below the frost line, and building foundations and roadbeds must be designed to minimize disruption and damage from frost.

16.2 DAILY AND SEASONAL VARIATIONS IN SOIL HEAT

Soil heat does not exist in a static state in the ground, but it is almost constantly changing in response to changes in heat at the surface. When the surface is relatively warm and the soil cool, then heat flows into the soil. When the soil is warmer than the atmosphere, heat flows out of the soil. Hardly ever are the soil and atmosphere at the same temperature, because the atmosphere is subject to such rapid, large temperature changes. The soil, on the other hand, is slow to change temperature, especially at depth.

Daily variation   We can examine soil heat flow in various time frames, beginning with a **day/night** period. On a summer day, for example, the soil surface may heat to a temperature of 35° to 45°C, while just 20 centimeters or so below, the ground temperature is only 20° to 25°C. The heat flow is downward, of course, but because soil is not a good conductor, it does not reach far into ground before the sun sets and the surface heat is lost. Later in the night the surface cools to a temperature even lower than that of the underlying soil, and the heat flow reverses as the heat gained during the day flows upward. The maximum depth at which the variability of day/night change is negligible is called *diurnal damping depth* (Fig. 16.1).

Seasonal variation   The ground temperature also varies with the **seasons.** If we examine the average surface temperatures for summer, fall, winter, and spring, it is apparent that from winter to summer the soil should be heating up, while from summer to winter it should be cooling down. The depth of the seasonal change is much greater than that of the daily change, so the seasonal damping depth is much greater, on the order of 3 meters in the midlatitudes. However, owing to the time it takes heat to reach to a depth of 3 meters the soil does not reach its maximum temperature until a month or more after the surface has. Thus the heat seasons in the soil do not coincide with the heat seasons on the surface; ground heat and surface heat are always out of phase with each other. In addition, because the soil acts as an insulation layer, it is always cooler in summer and warmer in winter than the surface. These facts have some important **implications for building** architecture and energy conservation. In regions with hot summers and cold winters, subterranean structures have a distinct thermal advantage over above-ground structures. Basements, for example, are cooler in summer, and in winter, a basement is less expensive to heat than a comparable structure above ground (Fig. 16.2).

Building implications

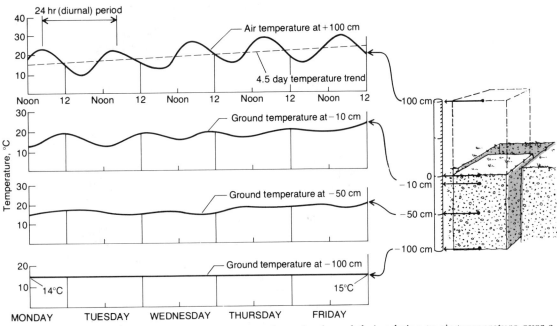

Fig. 16.1 Ground temperatures at three depths and their relation to air temperature over a 4.5-day period. The diurnal damping depth appears to lie close to 50 centimeters, for beyond that depth the daily variation in surface temperature is not apparent.

16.3 INFLUENCES ON SOIL HEAT AND GROUND FROST

Thermal conductivity

The rate at which heat flows into and out of the soil depends on two main factors: (1) the temperature differential between the soil at some depth and the surface; and (2) the composition of the soil, which determines its **thermal conductivity** (Table 16.1). In the first column of Table 16.1, the thermal conductivities are given for nine

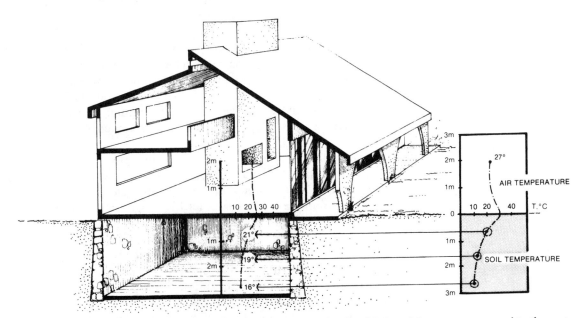

Fig. 16.2 Summer ground temperatures at depths of 1, 2, and 3 meters, compared to those at the same depths in the basement of a house.

Table 16.1 Thermal Properties of Some Common Earth Materials

Substance	Thermal Conductivity[a]	Volumetric Heat Capacity[b]
Air		
Still (at 10°C)	0.025	0.0012
Turbulent	3,500–35,000	0.0012
Water		
Still (at 4°C)	0.60	4.18
Stirred	350.00 (approx.)	4.18
Ice (at −10°C)	2.24	1.93
Snow (fresh)	0.08	0.21
Sand (quartz)		
Dry	0.25	0.9
15 percent moisture	2.0	1.7
40 percent moisture	2.4	2.7
Clay (nonorganic)		
Dry	0.25	1.1
15 percent moisture	1.3	1.6
40 percent moisture	1.8	3.0
Organic soil		
Dry	0.02	0.2
15 percent moisture	0.04	0.5
40 percent moisture	0.21	2.1
Asphalt	0.8–1.1	1.5
Concrete	0.9–1.3	1.6

[a] Heat flux through a column 1 m^2 in W/m when the temperature gradient is 1°K per meter.

[b] Millions of joules needed to raise 1 m^3 of a substance 1°K.

different earth materials. Notice that sand and clay conduct heat better than organic material, and conductivity increases with soil moisture content. Organic matter is a very poor heat conductor. As a result, it often serves as an effective thermal insulator, which helps explain why permafrost is particularly prominent and lasting in areas of muck and peat soils.

The rate at which a given temperature, such as the 0°C line, actually moves into the soil is somewhat different than is suggested by the conductivity value. This rate, called *thermal diffusivity*, is a product of the volumetric heat capacity, given in the second column of Table 16.1, and the conductivity of the soil. Diffusivity is highest at moisture contents between 8 and 20 percent. Thus, in saturated soils, frost penetration is usually not as great as it is in damp soils, owing to the higher heat capacity of wet soil (Fig. 16.3).

Ground cover   Other factors also play a part in ground frost penetration, in particular, **vegetation, snow cover,** and **land use.** Snow cover and vegetation tend to reduce soil heat loss in winter, whereas land use has a variable effect. For instance, a building reduces heat flow from the soil, whereas a barren highway usually serves to increase it. The combined effects of land use, vegetation, and snow cover can be dramatic. Where forest cover has been removed for agriculture or urban development, winds are able to blow most snow off the ground, which in turn facilitates soil heat loss. The graphs in Fig. 16.4 illustrate the influence of snow cover for a grass-covered site in Minnesota.

For most parts of North America, the depth of frost penetration is not well documented and is usually estimated from climatic records. The standard map of frost depth in the coterminous United States is based on representative winter temperatures and does not take into account factors such as snow cover or vegetation (Fig. 16.5). As

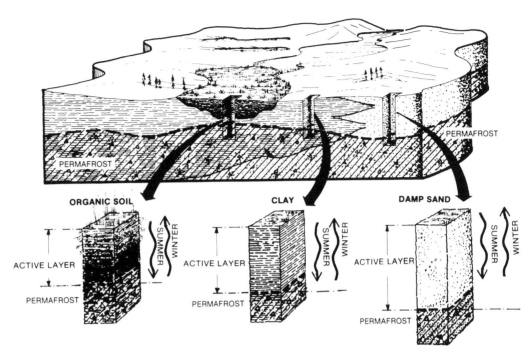

Fig. 16.3 Variations in the thickness of the active layer in permafrost can reflect the influence of soil composition and moisture content on heat flow. The directions and paths of seasonal heat flows are shown in the soil sections.

a result, field measurements of frost penetration will often show appreciable deviation from this map for any winter. A snow-covered swamp in Maine may receive no ground frost, whereas a nearby airfield may receive 2 meters or more.

Snow cover   When **snow cover** *is* taken into account, the following formula and graph can be used to estimate the depth of frost penetration in northern United States and southern

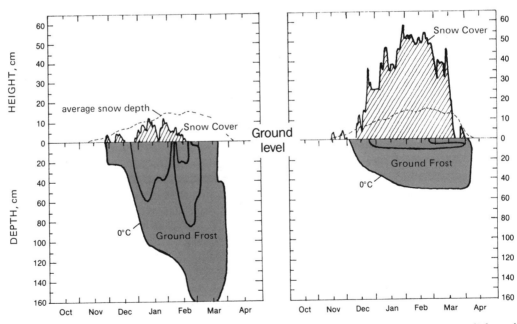

Fig. 16.4 Frost penetration related to snow cover. In the first graph snow cover was light and frost penetration great; the second illustrates the opposite condition.

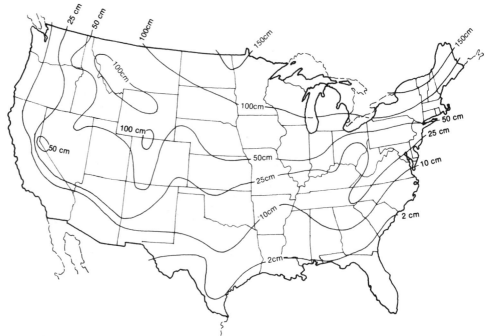

Fig. 16.5 Expected ground frost penetration by the end of winter. Departures from these values may be considerable, depending on the year and local snow, soil, and land use conditions.

Canada. The formula combines snow depth and heating degree days to give degrees temperature per inch (or centimeter). Taking the result of a computation using this formula, we find that the maximum depth of the zero-degree isotherm for the winter is read from the graph, in the manner illustrated for 20°F per inch (4.4°C/cm). For this example, the depth of the zero-degree isotherm would be about 105 cm.

$$T = \frac{\Sigma HDD_{OCT-MAR}}{\Sigma(S \cdot n)_{NOV-MAR}}$$

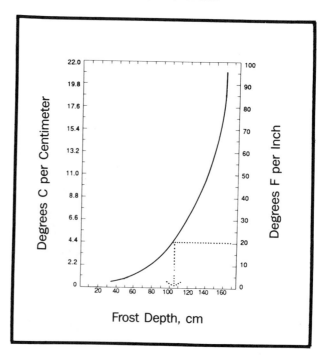

where

T	= degrees temperature per inch (or cm) (To find the frost depth, this figure is read into the vertical scale of the graph.)
HDD	= heating degree days, summed October through March
S	= average monthly snow depth, inches
n	= number of days with snow cover of 0.5 inch or more ($S \cdot n$ is computed month by month and summed November through March.)

Exposure In addition, the orientation and **exposure** of the ground can be critical; on barren slopes a southward exposure may make an appreciable difference in radiation receipts (see Fig. 14.7a in Chapter 14), whereas north-facing slopes may not only receive less radiation but also lose ground heat more rapidly because of exposure to northerly winds (Fig. 16.6).

On balance, then, we must take many factors into account when we attempt to forecast the pattern of ground temperature fluctuations and frost penetration, especially in areas of varied terrain. Unfortunately, mathematical models that integrate many variables are difficult to manipulate and require data from the field in order to be set up. In environmental inventories for impact studies, master planning, or constraint studies, we must instead often turn to simpler and less expensive methods in identi-

Mapping frost potential fying areas susceptible to heavy frost penetration. One of these is the **map overlay method** in which individual maps showing the influences of topography, vegetation, snow cover, exposure, and soils are superimposed on one another and the resulting combinations are designated high, medium, or low susceptibility. Each of the maps is usually broken down into categories that are numerically coded prior to overlaying; for example, soils might be classed as moist organic (1), moist mineral (2), and well-drained mineral (3), three being most susceptible to seasonal frost penetration. The results of this method do not indicate how deep frost penetration should be;

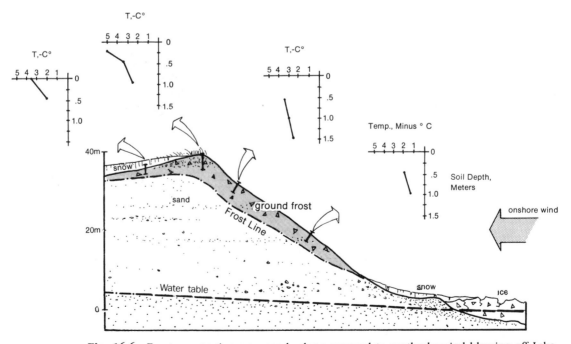

Fig. 16.6 Frost penetration on a sandy slope exposed to northerly wind blowing off Lake Superior. Wind velocity increases upslope, and heat loss increases, with wind velocity producing greatest frost penetration in the upper slope.

Table 16.2   Ground Frost Susceptibility

	Low	*Medium*	*High*
Soil type	Organic	Wet mineral (clay, loams, sand)	Well-drained mineral (loams, sand)
Soil moisture	Saturated	Moist (near field capacity)	Damp (less than field capacity)
Vegetative cover	Heavy forest	Grass	Barren
Wind exposure	Low exposure to cold, fast wind (usually S, SW, SE facing slopes)	Intermediate exposure (such as E, NE, W facing slopes)	High exposure to cold, fast wind (usually N, NW facing slopes)
Snow cover	>50 cm (Nov.–Mar.)	10–50 cm (Nov.–Mar.)	<10 cm; (intermittent cover throughout winter)
Solar exposure	South-facing slope > 20%	Flat ground or locally irregular terrain	North-facing, shaded

rather, they indicate only the relative penetration, and may be used to isolate areas where more detailed analysis can be carried out (Table 16.2).

16.4   PERMAFROST

Permafrost zones

From the southern border of the United States, the depth of ground frost penetration increases northward to a point in Canada where the inflow of summer heat is inadequate to melt the winter frost completely away. The layer of frozen ground that remains is permafrost. In varied terrain, **permafrost** first appears in isolated pockets on north-facing slopes where solar heating is weakest. In North America, such pockets of permafrost are reported as far south as 50° north latitude; in Asia they extend to 45° north latitude and beyond, into the Tibetan plateau and neighboring highlands. These areas mark the southern fringe of the *discontinuous zone* of permafrost.

Northward the pockets of permafrost grow much broader and thicker and are overlain by a layer of soil called the *active layer,* which freezes and thaws seasonally. Near the Arctic Circle, the discontinuous zone gives way to the *continuous zone* where permafrost extends uninterrupted over vast areas of land and reaches depths as great as 1000 meters. The thickness of the active layer also changes with latitude. In the discontinuous zone it is usually several meters thick, but poleward declines to a very thin layer or disappears altogether in the continuous zone (Fig. 16.7).

Seasonal heat flow

Nowhere is the **seasonal flow of soil heat** more apparent than in permafrost regions. In summer, the active layer develops with the penetration of heat from the surface (Fig. 16.8a). With the onset of cold weather in fall, the heat flow reverses in the upper active layer, and frost begins to penetrate the soil from the surface. Since the lower active layer is still thawed, heat flows both upward and downward from this

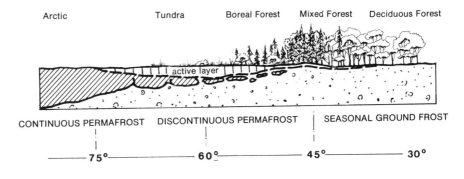

Arctic   Tundra   Boreal Forest   Mixed Forest   Deciduous Forest

active layer

CONTINUOUS PERMAFROST   DISCONTINUOUS PERMAFROST   SEASONAL GROUND FROST

—— 75° —— 60° —— 45° —— 30°

Latitude, Degrees North

Fig. 16.7 Ground frost zones between 30° and 80° N latitude, and the vegetation associated with each.

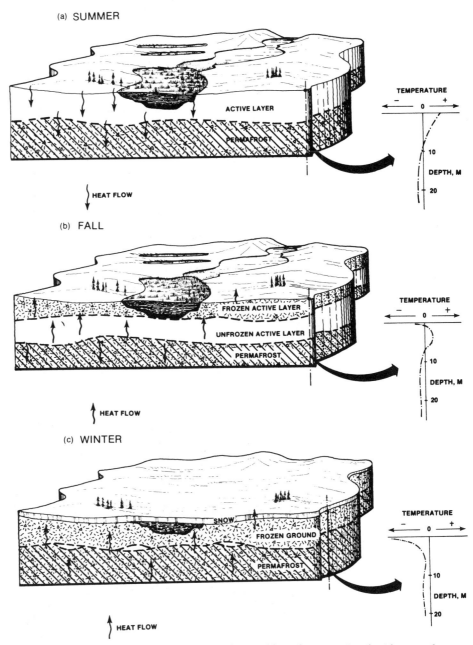

(a) SUMMER

ACTIVE LAYER

PERMAFROST

TEMPERATURE

− 0 +

10

DEPTH, M

20

HEAT FLOW

(b) FALL

FROZEN ACTIVE LAYER

UNFROZEN ACTIVE LAYER

PERMAFROST

TEMPERATURE

− 0 +

10

DEPTH, M

20

HEAT FLOW

(c) WINTER

SNOW

FROZEN GROUND

PERMAFROST

TEMPERATURE

− 0 +

10

DEPTH, M

20

HEAT FLOW

Fig. 16.8 The three seasonal models of ground heat flow associated with permafrost.

relatively warm zone (Fig. 16.8b). The temperature profile assumes a spoon shape at this time; but in the ensuing months of winter, when the active layer freezes out completely and surface temperatures fall far below 0°C, the thermal gradient is fully reversed from that of summer, and the heat flow is upward. Paradoxically, the permafrost layer is the primary source of heat for the landscape during winter (Fig. 16.8c).

16.5 LAND USE AND FROZEN GROUND

Ground subsidence

Modern land uses have proven to be problematic in most permafrost regions. In the past half-century many military installations, railroads, highways, and communities have been built in Alaska, northern Canada, and Russia, and they have provided ample evidence to illustrate the nature of the problem. The energy flow at ground level is altered first with the clearing of vegetation and surface grading. When a foreign material such as concrete or asphalt is placed on the ground, the thermal regime of the active layer is altered further, making it grow colder or warmer. In soils where ice comprises part of the soil bulk (in amounts greater than the volume of interparticle spaces at dry weight), thawing can **cause subsiding** in the permafrost (because of the volume reduction with change from ice to liquid water) and with it subsiding of the ground surface as well. When heated buildings, utility lines, or oil lines are set on the ground without adequate insulation to check the flow of heat into the active layer, subsiding can be dramatic (Fig. 16.9).

Drainage problems

Other problems experienced by land use in permafrost regions include **inadequate drainage** in summer, mass movement (such as mudflows and landslides) of surface material, and difficulties in procuring groundwater for water supplies. Faced with these problems, urbanization has been very limited in permafrost regions. In North America, the northern limit of urban development roughly coincides with the southern fringe of the permafrost zone.

Facility damage

Frozen ground is also a problem outside permafrost areas. In northern Europe, southern Canada and the northern United States, as well as in many other areas of the world, ground frost causes highway buckling, **damage** to building foundations, and freezing and breakage of water pipes (Fig. 16.10). In the United States and Canada,

Fig. 16.9 Subsiding caused by melting of the permafrost from the heat generated in this building. The structure was built in 1951 on a concrete basement heated by a furnace.

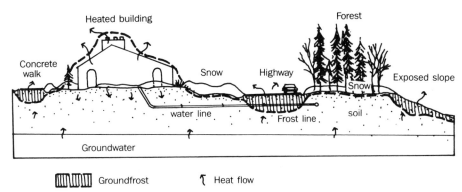

Fig. 16.10 Schematic diagram showing relative frost penetration as a function of soil, vegetation, land use, snow cover, and slope exposure.

building codes generally recommend that foundations be set below frost depth (usually given as 4 to 5 feet in the northern tier of states and in southern Canada) to minimize heaving and damage. In highway construction, frost heaving caused by the growth of ice lenses in the roadbed is a serious problem. To alleviate it, gravel-based roadbeds are required because gravel does not transmit capillary water upward from the underlying soil fast enough to allow ice lenses to form under the cold concrete or asphalt.

16.6 PLANNING APPLICATIONS

With the exception of engineering design standards, such as those previously mentioned, little formal attention has been given to ground frost in community planning outside permafrost regions. Within permafrost regions the picture is quite the opposite, though permafrost is by no means universally recognized and addressed in planning methodology and practice, even in the most hostile settings.

Review   In the Fairbanks, Alaska, planning region, the Soil Conservation Service (SCS) **reviews** development proposals with an eye to potential permafrost problems. The first level of evaluation involves checking the location of the proposed development against the distribution of soils known to have permafrost problems. Drawing on the results of permafrost research in the Fairbanks area, the SCS has been able to classify the soils of the Goldstream, Saulich, Ester, and Lemeta series as those with greatest susceptibility to permafrost (Fig. 16.11). For projects that would involve these soils, *Evaluation*   the review may be taken to a second level of **evaluation** and call for an examination of the types of activities and facilities actually proposed. In some cases the project may be compatible, because it is judged to be neither prone to damage from the environment nor itself of a significant threat to the environment. In other cases, modifications may be recommended, such as changes in building sites or the use of special engineering technology for footings and utility lines (Fig. 16.12). In still other cases, the project may be viewed as incompatible with the environment and not recommended for approval.

Planning recommendation   The SCS **recommendation** is then passed on to the staff of the planning agency in charge, where it is combined with recommendations from other technical fields and interest groups to form a general recommendation on the proposal. This statement is then studied and discussed by a decision-making body such as a planning commission, county board, or city council; a vote is taken; and the proposal is approved, denied, approved with specified reservations, asking the applicant to agree to certain changes, or sent back to the applicant or the reviewer for further work and documentation.

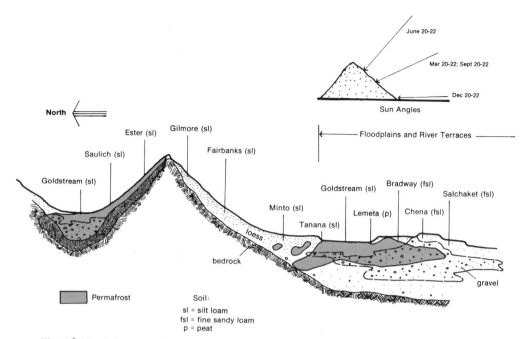

Fig. 16.11   Schematic diagram showing the locations of soils and their susceptibility to permafrost in the Fairbanks, Alaska, region.

Fig. 16.12   Design modifications in residential development in response to permafrost, Norman Well, Northwest Territory, Canada. Homes, water lines, and sewage lines are built above ground to minimize thermal disturbance of the permafrost.

16.7 CASE STUDY

■ Permafrost and the Trans-Alaska Pipeline

Peter J. Williams

Remarkable as it now seems, the earliest proposals in the Alyeska Oil Pipeline Project were to construct the pipeline in a conventional manner, burying it in the ground for virtually the entire distance of 800 miles from Prudhoe Bay to Valdez. In fact, the most basic problem was that the warm pipeline might thaw the underlying permafrost. Wherever the permafrost contained quantities of ice in addition to that within the soil pores, settlement or subsidence would inevitably follow thawing. At one planning stage serious consideration was given to using a chilled pipeline: cooling the oil so that the pipe could be buried without thawing the permafrost. This proposal was rejected because of the effect of low temperatures on the oil, which would not flow satisfactorily. The interaction of a chilled pipeline with the soil, which was to present problems for subsequently proposed gas pipelines, was apparently not foreseen.

Probably three-quarters of the proposed route overlay permafrost, and at least half of this was estimated to contain ice, which on melting would cause settlement. The effect of the warm pipeline was such that up to 10 m of soil could be expected to thaw in the first year. The amount would vary, of course, depending on the pre-existing ground temperatures and the type of soil.

Near Prudhoe Bay the permafrost is some 600 m thick. Southward it becomes generally thinner, although the thickness is very variable. Thawing around a buried, warm pipeline would progress downward, although at a decreasing rate, for many years. The degree of consequent settlement, or subsidence, would depend on the amount of "excess" ice in the thawed layer, but

Photo 1: Air view of service road and Alaska Pipeline under construction, 1975.

Photo 2:   Vertical support members with thermal devices (on top) to resist heat flow and keep footings frozen in the ground.

quite often there would be several metres displacement. Obviously, such effects left unchecked would cause great disruption of the pipeline. . . .

As soil surveys proceeded much more ground ice was discovered than was initially predicted. This, coupled with findings as to the amount of thaw that would occur, led gradually to the decision to build more and more of the pipeline above ground elevated on pile supports, rather than buried in the ground as first envisaged. The air passing beneath an elevated line would dissipate most of the heat from the pipe and greatly reduce the thawing of the permafrost. Furthermore, the pile supports, or "vertical support members" (known as VSMs), could be designed to permit lateral movements of the pipe as it expanded or contracted with temperature changes.

Raising the pipe above ground on the VSMs did not ensure that there would be no thawing of the ground. The disturbance inflicted on the ground during the course of construction was sufficient to initiate temperature changes in the soil which could result in thawing to a significant depth, in all except the coldest, most northern areas. Climatic change too, might in places initiate a continuing thawing.

Ultimately, the solution of the problem lay in the so-called thermal VSM. The thermal VSMs are equipped with devices known as heat pipes. These are sealed 2-inch diameter tubes within the VSMs. They extend below the surface and contain anhydrous ammonia refrigerant. In the winter months this evaporates from the *lower* end of the tube and condenses at the top where there are metallic heat exchanger fins. The evaporation process occurs because, during the winter months, the ground is *warmer* than the air outside. The evaporation process itself cools the lower end of the pipe and the surrounding ground, and this is the point of the device: by cooling the permafrost in winter its temperature is sufficiently lowered to prevent thaw during the summer. The mean ground temperature falls, the heat pipes preventing the warming that would otherwise occur following disturbance of the ground surface. About 610 km of pipe were built above ground, and about 80 percent of this length had thermal VSMs.

Peter J. Williams is Professor of geography and director of the Geotechnical Science Laboratories at Carleton University, Ottawa, and a specialist in prob-

lems of development in cold environments. (From Pipelines and Permafrost: Physical Geography and Development in the Circumpolar North, Longman, 1979. Used by permission of the author.)

16.8 SELECTED REFERENCES FOR FURTHER READING

Allen, L. J. The *Trans-Alaska Pipeline.* Alyeska Pipeline Service, 1977, 2 vols.

Baker, Donald G. "Snow Cover and Winter Soil Temperatures at St. Paul, Minnesota." *Water Resources Research Center Bulletin 37,* University of Minnesota, 1971, 37 pp.

Brown, R. J. E. "Influence of Climate and Terrain on Ground Temperatures in the Continuous Permafrost Zone of Manitoba and Keewatin District, Canada." *Third Conference of Permafrost Proceedings, 14*Edmonton, vol. 1, 1978, pp. 16–21.

Brown, R. J. E. *Permafrost In Canada,* Toronto: University of Toronto Press, 1970, 234 pp.

Ferrians, O. J., et al. "Permafrost and Related Engineering Problems in Alaska." U.S. Geological Survey Professional Paper 678, 1969, 37 pp.

French, H. M. *The Periglacial Environment.* New York: Longman, 1976, 309 pp.

Péwé, Troy L. "Effect of Permafrost on Cultivated Fields, Fairbanks Area, Alaska." In *Mineral Resources of Alaska, Geological Survey Bulletin* 989, 1951–1953, pp. 315–351.

Smith, M. W. "Microclimatic Influences on Ground Temperatures and Permafrost Distribution in the Mackenzie Delta, Northwest Territories." *Canadian Journal of Earth Science* 12:8, 1975, pp. 1421–1438.

U.S. Soil Conservation Service. *Soil Survey: Fairbanks Area, Alaska.* Washington, D.C.: U.S. Government Printing Office, 1963, 41 pp.

Washburn, A. L. *Periglacial Processes and Environments.* New York: St. Martin's Press, 1973, 320 pp.

Williams, Peter J. *Pipelines and Permafrost: Physical Georgraphy and Development in the Circumpolar North.* New York: Longman, 1979, 98 pp.

17

VEGETATION AND ENVIRONMENTAL ASSESSMENT

17.1 INTRODUCTION

Perhaps no component of the landscape is more directly related to land use and environmental change as vegetation. Besides being the most visible part of most landscapes, it is also a sensitive "thermometer" of conditions and trends in parts of the landscape that are otherwise not apparent without the aid of detailed observation and measurement. The loss of vigor in tree species near highways, for example, may be an indication of impaired drainage or heavy air pollution, thereby drawing attention to environmental impact problems that might otherwise be overlooked. In agricultural regions, changes in shrub and tree species in swales and floodplains may be a response to heavy sedimentation, pointing up the need for erosion control.

Vegetation also plays a functional role in the landscape since it is an important control on runoff, soil erosion, slope stability, microclimate, and noise. In site planning, plants are used not only for environmental control, but also to improve aesthetics, frame spaces, influence pedestrian behavior, and control boundaries. While other landscaping methods and materials can be used for the same purposes, few are as versatile and inexpensive as vegetation. Not surprisingly, much of the work of the landscape architect involves designing planting plans.

Although it is not widely recognized, there are also some negative aspects to vegetation. The most serious are probably the noxious plants that inhabit most metropolitan and suburban landscapes today. These are mainly weed plants, such as poison ivy and ragweed, that are poisonous (usually in the form of allergic reactions) to certain people. The plants causing the greatest difficulty appear to be certain wind pollinators that cause or exacerbate respiratory disorders such as hay fever, bronchitis, asthma, and emphysema.

17.2 DESCRIPTION AND CLASSIFICATION OF VEGETATION

Most projects involving planning or monitoring of land use and environment call for a description of vegetation. This may be combined with land use inventories to produce land cover maps or may be treated as an independent task. In either case, the objective is to document the distribution and makeup of the vegetative cover, and this requires the use of an appropriate plant or vegetation classification scheme. Detailed descriptions of vegetation are virtually a universal requirement of environmental impact statements, and the conscientious investigator typically provides vast inventories and descriptions that draw on several classification schemes.

Classification schemes   The **classification schemes** in greatest use today are: (1) the *floristic* (or Linnaean), which classifies individual plants according to species, genera, families, and so on, using the universally recognized system of botanical names; (2) the *form and structure* (or physiognomic) schemes, which classify vegetation or large assemblages of plants according to overall form (for example, forest and grassland) with special attention to dominant plants (largest and/or most abundant); and (3) the *ecological* schemes, which classify plants according to their habitat (for example, sand dunes, wetlands, lake shores) or some critical parameter of the environment such as soil moisture or seasonal air temperatures.

Selecting a scheme   Despite the conventions of the environmental impact methodology (that is, wholesale inventory and cross-classification), the type of description and classification used in a project should be governed by the nature of the problem and the form and variety of information that are called for. In many cases this requires using some mix of floristic, form and structure, and ecological schemes because in planning problems vegetation must be understood not only as a biological phenomenon tied to other biological phenomena such as animals and insects, but also as a physical component of the landscape having height, volume, texture, color, and functional ties with soil, water, air, and land use.

A five-level scheme   The scheme given in Table 17.1 is organized into **five levels**, each addressing a different classification element. Level I is based on overall structure, level II on dominant plant types, level III on plant size and density, level IV on site and habitat, and level V on significant species. Level V is included to provide for rare, endangered, protected, and highly valued species, a standard requirement of environmental assessments and impact statements, as well as plants of value in landscaping for a proposed or existing land use.

17.3 TRENDS IN VEGETATION CHANGE

Most of the major trends in vegetation change in North America are related to three land use activities: agriculture, lumbering, and urbanization. Forest clearing for agriculture over large parts of the Midwest, South, and East has resulted in the loss of virtually *Agricultural impact* all the original forest cover over vast areas and in the formation of a landscape that is best described as agricultural parkland. Only in nonarable sites such as swamps and deep stream valleys has the forest and related vegetation escaped complete destruction. But even these sites have been dramatically reduced and altered. In the United States (less Alaska), more than 50,000 square miles of wetland have been destroyed since settlement, and since 1950, agriculture has accounted for 70 to 90 percent of the losses. In addition, the remaining patches of vegetation are often quite different floristically from the original plant cover because increased runoff, sedimentation, and other sorts of disturbances from the surrounding lands have caused the elimination of certain tree species and ground plants (Fig. 17.1).

A second trend has been the contraction of the agricultural landscape as the bulk of the rural population has shifted to the cities over the past five decades. With the *Abandonment of farmland* **abandonment of the small farms**, much cultivated land has reverted back to natural, or unmanaged, vegetation. The second growth species, however, are often weedy plants; herbs, shrubs, and trees, such as thistles, sumac, and hawthorn, that are of limited aesthetic and economic value. On the other hand, these plants are effective ground stabilizers and, as such, have helped to reduce rates of runoff and soil erosion. They are also important small-game habitat, especially bird habitat.

Urban sprawl   The trend toward urbanization after World War II has led to massive **urban sprawl** with the development of freeway systems, residential subdivisions, and shopping centers. Initially, much of this growth was absorbed by abandoned farmland, but as the development rate accelerated and land values increased, active farmland was also absorbed (Fig. 17.2). Nearly everywhere that urban sprawl has taken place it has resulted in wholesale destruction of existing vegetation including the fencerows, woodlots, and orchards of active farmland as well as the second-growth woodland of abandoned farmland. Large tracts of habitat such as woodland corridors along stream valleys have been fragmented and reduced in area. Only in the past few decades have developers begun seriously to consider existing vegetation for its role as animal habitat and as a landscape amenity with dollar value.

Maturation of   As landscapes go, most of **suburbia** is new and the vegetative **cover** is still *suburban cover* developing, meaning that it is undergoing comparatively rapid change as it adjusts to this new environment. In most areas, street trees are one or more decades from maturity, hedgerows are still being planted, and property owners are still in the process of making adjustments in yard plants by replacing exotic species with poor survival records with hardier species. One measure of the level of maturity of suburban

Table 17.1   Vegetation Classification

Level I (vegetative structure)		Level II (dominant plant types)	Level III (size and density)	Level IV (site and habitat or associated use)	Level V (special plant species)
Forest (trees with average height greater than 15 ft with at least 60% canopy cover)		E.g., oak, hickory, willow, cottonwood, elm, basswood, maple, beach, ash	Tree size (diameter at breast height) Density (number of average stems per acre)	E.g., upland (i.e., well-drained terrain), floodplain, slope face, woodlot, greenbelt, parkland, residential land	Rare and endangered species; often ground plants associated with certain forest types
Woodland (trees with average height greater than 15 ft with 20–60% canopy cover)		E.g., pine, spruce, balsam fir, hemlock, douglas fir, cedar	Size range (difference between largest and smallest stems)	E.g., upland (i.e., well-drained terrain), floodplain, slope face, woodlot, greenbelt, parkland, residential land	Rare and endangered species; often ground plants associated with certain forest types
Orchard or plantation (same as woodland or forest but with regular spacing)		E.g., apple, peach, cherry, spruce, pine	Tree size; density	E.g., active farmland, abandoned farmland	Species with potential in landscaping for proposed development
Brush (trees and shrubs generally less than 15 ft high with high density of stems, but variable canopy cover)		E.g., sumac, willow, lilac, hawthorn, tag alder, pin cherry, scrub oak, juniper	Density	E.g., vacant farmland, landfill, disturbed terrain (e.g., former construction site)	Species of significance to landscaping for proposed development
Fencerows (trees and shrubs of mixed forms along borders such as road, fields, yards, playgrounds)		Any trees or shrubs	Tree size; density	E.g., active farmland, road right-of-way, yards, playgrounds	Species of value as animal habitat and utility in screening
Wetland (generally low, dense plant covers in wet areas)		E.g., cattail, tag alder, cedar, cranberry, reeds	Percent cover	E.g., floodplain, bog, tidal marsh, reservoir backwater, river delta	Species and plant communities of special importance ecologically and hydrologically; rare and endangered species
Grassland (herbs, with grasses dominant)		E.g., big blue stem bunch grass, dune grass	Percent cover	E.g., prairie, tundra, pasture, vacant farmland	Species and communities of special ecological significance; rare and endangered species.
Field (tilled or recently tilled farmland)		E.g., corn, soybeans, wheat; also weeds	Field size	E.g., sloping or flat, ditched and drained, muckland, irrigated	Special and unique crops; exceptional levels of productivity in standard crops

Adapted from W. M. Marsh, *Environmental Analysis for Land Use and Site Planning*, by W. M. Marsh. Copyright © 1978, McGraw–Hill, New York. Used with the permission of McGraw–Hill Book Company

Fig. 17.1 Vegetation destroyed by burial of wind blown sand. This sort of impact can be initiated by agricultural activity in areas prone to wind erosion.

vegetation is the diversity and abundance of wildlife such as squirrels, songbirds, and raccoons; generally, animal habitat improves with the density and diversity of the plant cover.

A fourth trend in vegetation is the establishment of noxious weed plants in disturbed areas. Though small by geographic standards, this trend represents a major health hazard. Again, there seems to be an association with urbanization, but not so *Urban decay* much with sprawl as with **urban decay**. With the decline of inner cities, industrial areas, and old residential neighborhoods, the ground is taken over by weeds. Many of these plants yield huge amounts of pollen to the atmosphere which, when inhaled, causes allergic reactions in many people. A similar trend may be found on the suburban fringe where land is taken out of use and/or cleared and then held for several years before development. In some communities, by contrast, inner city decline is offset with streetscape restoration (Fig. 17.3).

Two additional trends in vegetation change are also noteworthy. One is the *Special environments* increased use and destruction of **special plant environments**, such as wetlands, sand dunes, mountain slopes, and shorelands. Wetlands have generally been treated badly

Fig. 17.2 The loss of farmland to urban development is illustrated by these photographs of the Valley Stream area, Long Island, New York. Photographs taken in 1933 and 1959.

Fig. 17.3 The introduction of vegetation to commercial districts has become a common practice in programs to renew the attractiveness of inner cities.

by all varieties of land use, mainly because they were (and still are in many quarters) viewed as health hazards, barriers to development, or unproductive land. The second trend is the change in forest cover associated with lumbering. This has resulted not only in the harvesting of most of the original forests in the coterminous United States and southern Canada, but also in the formation of new types of forests. Forests managed for a sustained yield of timber based on the selective cutting concept are usually comprised of multiple stories representing different tree ages. By contrast, planted forests that represent a complete replacement of some original cover consist of even-aged stands of floristically uniform trees (Fig. 17.4).

17.4 THE CONCEPT OF SENSITIVE ENVIRONMENTS

Minority environments

The concept of sensitive environments in planning has grown in part from a reaction to the wholesale mistreatment of what we might call **minority environments**, such as wetlands, stream valleys, and sand dunes, whose value cannot be measured accurately by standard economic criteria, that is, how much the land is worth on the open market. It has also grown from improved understanding of the role of such environments in the maintenance and quality of the larger landscape. Wetlands are often important ground-

Fig. 17.4   Aerial photograph showing planted stands of conifers.

water recharge areas, and small stream valleys are important in the maintenance of river water quality. Today it is not uncommon to find communities incorporating special provisions for sensitive environments into their master plans based on economic rationale (because it costs more to build in and manage such environments), social rationale (because these environments are valued by people for their scenic and general aesthetic value), and scientific rationale (because they are often necessary to the maintenance of larger environmental systems). Wetlands and shorelands are examples of landscapes that are widely recognized as sensitive environments.

Wetland impacts   **Wetlands**   Prior to the midtwentieth century, wetlands were generally viewed as third-rate landscapes of limited economic value. As a result, they were indiscriminately altered and destroyed on a wholesale basis to provide cropland, improve agricultural production, improve navigation, control pests, and provide land for urban development. Wetlands are now widely recognized for their roles as hydrologic, ecologic, recreational, forestry, and agricultural resources.

   The definition and mapping of wetlands, which is taken up in detail in the next chapter, is generally based on three sets of criteria: vegetation, soils, and hydrology. Although hydrologic processes are usually the controlling force in the origin and formation of wetlands, the definition of wetlands based on hydrologic criteria has proven difficult for a variety of reasons. Vegetation, on the other hand, has provided a more useful set of criteria, especially indicator species.

Shores and dunes   **Shorelands**   Coastal areas have long been attractive places to visit, but in the past 50 years development for residential and commercial purposes has increased substantially. This has been facilitated by the growth of highway and road systems, increased availability of land with the decline of agriculture, and the rising popularity of water-oriented living. The development has led to widespread alteration of coastal environments, especially the "softer" ones such as barrier beaches, beach ridges, sand dunes, and backshore slopes where prized plant communities are often found (Fig. 17.5). Because of the delicate balance that typically exists between plants, such as dune grasses, and environment, the imposition of roads and houses often leads to loss of entire plant communities and in turn the decline of an environment valued by many for ecological and aesthetic reasons.

17.5 VEGETATION AS A TOOL IN ENVIRONMENTAL PLANNING

The place of vegetation as a planning tool has improved signifcantly in the past several decades. Among other things, the costs of land clearing and landscaping alone have motivated developers to incorporate more existing (predevelopment) vegetation into

Dollar values   site plans. In residential areas, a mature shade tree may have an estimated **value** of $1000 to $10,000 (1985 dollars), and the composite assemblage of plantings may improve the real estate value of an average residential lot by $5000 to $10,000.

Visual   Beyond its direct economic value, vegetation is also recognized for its functional or environmental value in land use planning. In site planning, for example, it is

Screening   regularly used to **screen** certain land use activities and features, abate noise, modify microclimate, and stabilize slopes. As a visual barrier, hedgerows and border trees can help separate conflicting land uses such as residential, commercial, industrial, and institutional. In this capacity, the density and permanency of the foliage is critical because it controls the transmission of light (Fig. 17.5).

Noise   Vegetation can also be used to help control noise. Under barrier-free conditions, the level (magnitude) of sound from a point source decreases at a rate of six

Decibel change   **decibels** with each doubling of travel distance. (From a linear source such as a highway, the decay rate is nearer three decibels per doubling distance.) Placed in the path of sound, vegetation absorbs and diverts energy, and is somewhat more effective

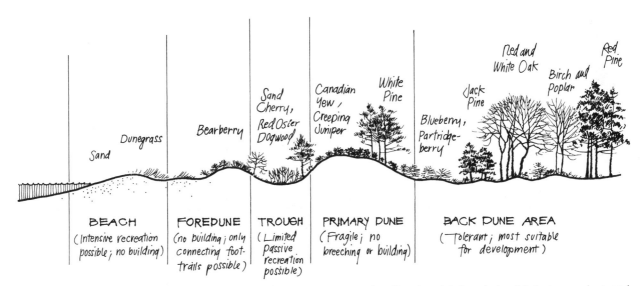

Fig. 17.5 A profile across a belt of sandy shoreline showing the relationship between plants and landforms including an assessment of the relative resistance of microenvironments to disturbance.

for sound in the high frequency bands (those above 1000–2000 hertz). In forests the litter layer (decaying leaves and woody materials) appears to be most effective in sound absorption. Table 17.2 gives an example of the reduction in locomotive noise associated with a 250-foot-wide belt of forest. For the most effective use of vegetation in noise reduction, it is best to combine plantings with a topographic barrier such as a berm or an embankment.

Ground-level climate

Microclimate   The influence of vegetation on **ground-level climate** can be very pronounced. A plant cover effectively displaces the lower boundary of the atmosphere upward from the ground onto the foliage. A microclimate of some depth is thus formed between the foliage (for example, under the tree canopy) and the ground where solar radiation, wind, and surface temperatures are lower than those over a nonvegetated surface. Heat exchange between the landscape and atmosphere is also influenced by vegetation. The Bowen Ratio (sensible heat to latent heat flux) is lower because of transpiration, producing somewhat lower air temperatures over vegetated than non-vegetated surfaces (see Fig. 15.3).

Effects on airflow

As a barrier to **airflow**, vegetation tends to force wind upward, thereby increasing the depth of the zone of calm air (called the boundary sublayer) over the ground. The taller and denser the vegetation, the thicker the sublayer; under a mature fir forest it is usually around 2.5 meters deep, whereas in grass it is a hundred times less at 2.5 centimeters (Fig. 17.6). A related effect can be found on the downwind side of a vegetative barrier where a calm zone forms under the descending streamlines of wind. The breadth of this sheltered zone also varies with the height and density of the barrier; however, significant wind reduction can generally be expected over a distance of 10 to 20 times the height of the barrier (Fig. 17.7). In snowfall areas, this zone is subject to the formation of snow drifts, the length of which can be estimated using this formula:

$$L = \frac{36 + 5h}{K}$$

where

L = snow drift length in feet
h = barrier height in feet
K = barrier density factor (50 percent density is equal to 1.0, and 70 percent is
   equal to 1.28.

Air Pollution   The influence of vegetation in reducing contaminants in polluted air is not well documented for urban areas, but the existing evidence suggests that it is relatively small. Plants are known to absorb certain gaseous pollutants, for example, carbon dioxide, ozone, and sulfur dioxide, but it is apparently limited to the air immediately around the leaf and thus has only miniscule effects on these pollutants in the larger urban atmosphere. Heavy herb covers and dense stands of shrub and *Catchment*   tree-sized vegetation with full covers of foliage act as sinks (**catchments**) for airborne particulates, but their net effectiveness is questionable because a sizable percentage of particulates initially caught appears to reenter the atmosphere within hours or days. Overall, vegetation appears to be most effective in trapping large particles in air moving laterally within several meters of the ground.

Plant impact

In areas of heavy air pollution, a more pressing question may be that of the **impact** of pollutants on the health and survival of vegetation. Ozone and sulfur dioxide are the pollutants causing greatest damage to woody plants; other pollutants such as fluorides, dust, and chlorine are also known to cause damage, but it is usually localized around the point of emission.

Table 17.2 Locomotive Noise Reduction With and Without a 200-Foot-Deep Forest

Frequency, Hertz	Noise at 250 ft without Forest	Noise at 250 ft with Forest
31.5 Hz	39 dB	39 dB
63	57	56
125	63	61
250	68	65
500	73	69
1000	74	68
2000	72	64
4000	68	56
8000	61	41
	79 dBA	73 dBA

dB = decibel; unit of measurement of sound magnitude based on pressure produced in air from a sound source

dBA = decibel scale adjusted for the sensitivity of the human ear; a correction factor applied to dB units that takes into account the pattern of sound frequencies perceived by the human ear

Frequency = the pitch of sound measured in cycles per sound; higher pitches have higher frequencies (more cycles per second)

Hertz (Hz) = cycles per second

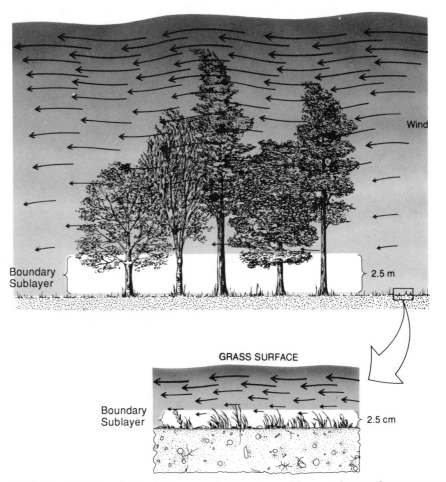

Fig. 17.6 The difference in the thickness of the boundary sublayer under coniferous trees and grass. This layer is important to the formation of ground-level microclimates.

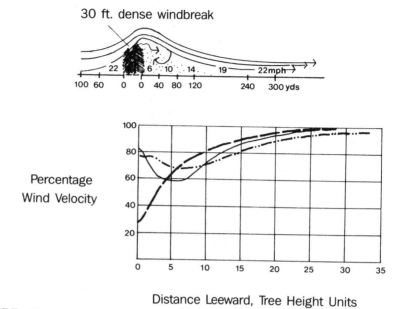

Fig. 17.7 Above, pattern of wind velocity across a barrier. Below, curves representing the percentage change in wind velocity downwind from a tree barrier.

Social preference **Social Value** People have long recognized the desirability of vegetation in neighborhoods, towns, and cities. This is related not only to the perceived role of plants in climate control, noise abatement, and the like, but also to sociocultural norms that place value on living plants and the habitats they create. Residential **preference** surveys bear this out when people identify parks and green spaces as important reasons for choosing one neighborhood or community over another. Real estate data also support this because wooded and landscaped lots consistently bring higher prices than those without vegetation or with unkempt vegetation.

17.6 APPROACHES TO VEGETATION ANALYSIS

In most landscapes the distribution of plants can be highly variable, even at the local scale. The reasons for the variation are often complexly tied to existing environmental conditions, past events such as fires and land use, and the geographic availability of species to inhabit the area. Which of these myriad of variables exerts the greatest control is usually a difficult question to answer.

Spatial correlations In searching for explanations for the distributions of plants, three basic types of studies or approaches are used. One approach is to map the distribution of plant types and environmental features and then examine the two distributions to see what **correlations** can be ascertained. For example, a comparison of topography and plant species may show that certain species consistently appear in stream valleys. What such a relationship means is not revealed by the correlation, but it may provide clues about what questions should be raised for analysis. The floors of stream valleys are usually wetter, subject to more flooding, and comprised of more diverse soils than other settings. Plants must spend much of the year under conditions of very wet soil and/or standing water. Moisture tolerance may thus prove to be a good candidate for detailed analysis of plants that are found in stream valleys, especially if the other settings that support different vegetation in the study area are appreciably drier (Fig. 17.8).

A second approach begins with an examination of the environment in an effort to

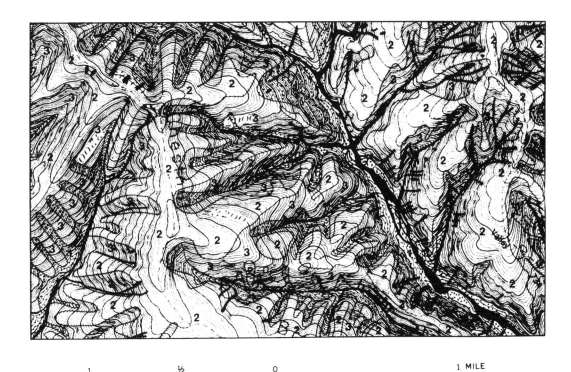

1 ½ 0 1 MILE

Fig. 17.8 The relationship of forest types to landforms in a section of the central Appalachian Mountains. Certain events (the cloudburst flood of 1949) and soil moisture conditions associated with these landforms are suggested by the authors as the basis for the distribution.

Chutes and channels created by the cloudburst flood of June 1949: Ground generally bare rock or soil; young trees abundant

Unit 1   Northern Hardwood Forest Type: Characteristic of hollows, channelways, and flood-plains

Unit 2   Yellow Pine Forest Type: Characteristic of noses (ridges)

Unit 3   Oak Forest Type: Characteristic of side slopes

Search for controls

identify those features and processes that may influence plant distributions. The purpose here is to document the forces and processes that could **control** the plants and then propose where certain plants or groups of plants should and should not be found. The analytical part of this approach involves testing the proposed or expected distributions by making measurements in the field and then investigating the detailed relations between the affected plant(s) and the environmental variable (Fig. 17.9).

Plants as environmental indicators

The third approach uses key **plants as indicators** of environmental conditions and events. Based on existing knowledge of the habits and tolerance levels of selected plants, the controlling forces in the environment can often be identified according to which plants are found in an area. At the simplest level, this entails determining the presence or absence of certain types of vegetation over an area. For instance, in a region where forests are the predominant natural vegetation, the absence of forest cover at a site is an indication that (1) levels of stress (light, water, heat, and carbon dioxide) are too great for trees; (2) the resources of the site, for example, soil cover and water supply, are limited; and/or (3) a recent disturbance such as a tornado destroyed the forest at the site and it has not grown back yet. Table 17.3 lists a number of site conditions in different bioclimatic regions that can be interpreted from vegetation.

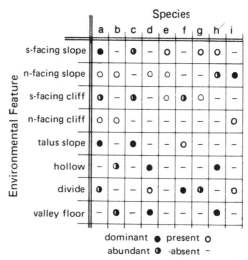

Fig. 17.9 A simple matrix showing the expected correlation between selected plant species and selected processes and features of the environment.

17.7 SAMPLING VEGETATION

Rationale

Whether our objective is to inventory and describe vegetation for the environmental impact and assessment studies, analyze vegetation for scientific purposes, or use vegetation as an indicator of site conditions and past events, it is usually necessary to sample vegetation in some way. Sampling is a means of selective observation that enables us to estimate various aspects of a plant population or vegetation community based on measurements of only a small portion of it. Sampling is attractive because it saves time and money; however, the proper use of sampling techniques can be difficult. Among the techniques used in vegetation studies are: quadrat sampling, stratified sampling, transect sampling, systematic sampling, and windshield-survey sampling.

Preparation

In any sampling problem the first task is to define the relevant population. In the case of vegetation this is usually accomplished by defining the geographic area occupied by the vegetation under study. This area(s), which may be a development site or particular environmental zone, is outlined on a large-scale map. The vegetation within it can then be sampled, using either the quadrat or transect method.

Quadrat sampling

Quadrats are small plots, the size of which varies with the type of vegetation being sampled. In **quadrat sampling** the first step involves subdividing the whole area into grid squares. For small study areas, individual squares may be used as a sample quadrat, whereas for large areas, it may be necessary to use some fraction of a square as a quadrat depending on the type of vegetation. Generally speaking, a 1- to 2-square meter quadrat would be used for grasslands and marshes, 4 to 6 square meters for low shrub covers, 15 to 30 square meters for brushland, and 30 to 100 square meters for woodland and forest.

Stratified sampling

Stratified sampling involves subdividing the population or study area into subareas or sets prior to drawing the sample. These are coherent subdivisions based on observable characteristics or prior knowledge of the area. A typical subdivision for many areas involves three strata: floodplains, valley slopes (walls), and uplands. Within these strata, quadrats are chosen on a random basis. Stratified sampling is widely used today with remote sensing imagery to define regional vegetation patterns. Indeed, aerial photographs are almost indispensable in modern vegetation studies, and more technically sophisticated remote sensing systems, such as line scanners, are showing promise for discriminating major types of vegetation. A form of stratified sampling is

Table 17.3 Vegetation Indicators of Site Conditions

Climatic Region	Absence of Plant Cover	Sparse Herb and Shrub Cover	Thick Herb and Shrub Cover	Brush and Small Trees	Blade and Reed Plants	Highly Localized Tree Cover
Humid (Eastern North America, Pacific Northwest, South)	• Bedrock at or very near surface • Active dunes • Recent human use, cultivation, etc. • Recent fire • Recent loss of water cover	• Bedrock near surface • Recent or sterile soils—dunes, fill • Recently disturbed (fallow, fire, flood) • Active slopes/erosion	• Recently logged or burned • Too wet for trees • Managed grazing • Organic soil • Old field regrowth	• Landslide/fire, flashflood scars • Old field or woodlot regrowth • Shale/clay substrate • Organic soil • Moisture deficiency	• Organic soil • Standing water • High ground-watertable • Springs, seepage zones	• Wet depression, organic soil, steep • Slopes in agricultural areas • Flood-prone areas
Semiarid (High Plains, S. California)	• Caliche or salt pan (playa) at or very near surface • Desert pavement	• Localized water sources • Eolian erosion • Overgrazing	• Overgrazing • Free from burning • Too dry for trees	• Channels of available moisture • Aquiferous substrate	• (Same as above)	• Aquiferous substrate • Seepage zone or spring • Stream valley (galleria) forest • Plantation
Arid (Southwest, Great Basin)	• Rock surface • Unstable ground such as dunes or rockslides • Too dry			• Protected pockets • Favorable (moist) slopes • Logged/burned		
Arctic and Alpine (N. Canada, Alaska, Rockies)	• Rock surface • Active slopes • Semipermanent ice or snow cover • Ponded water during growing season	• Above tree line • Semipermanent ice or snow cover • Active slopes • Periglacial processes active	• Above tree line • Ice, snow, and wind pruning • Mildly active slopes • Wet depressions	• Wind/ice pruning • Avalanche, landslide scars, fire • Recent logging near tree line permafrost near surface	• (Same as above)	• Protection pockets

Beyond this sort of exercise, the particular types of plants, their densities, and physiological conditions (health) can be examined to learn about the detailed nature of the environment and its forces.

From W. M. Marsh, *Environmental Analysis for Land Use and Site Planning* (New York: McGraw–Hill, 1978). Used by permission.

also used in soil mapping for land use projects where the strata are defined and sampling points assigned according to development and use zones.

Random sampling   In **random transect sampling** the study area is divided into a number of strips, called transects. The width of the transects should vary with the type of vegetation; 5 to 10 meters would, for example, be appropriate for most forests. Of the transects selected for sampling, the entire transect may be sampled, or individual quadrats may be selected for sampling within the transect.

Systematic sampling   **Systematic sampling** requires no prior knowledge of the population or area under consideration. A grid is drawn over the area, and a sample is taken at each intersect in the grid. Quadrats can be used as the sample unit, and it is generally recommended that, together, the quadrats cover a minimum of 20 percent of the study area.

Windshield survey   The **windshield survey** is the quickest and least expensive sampling technique. Though more commonly employed in land use surveys than in vegetation studies, it can be helpful in gaining an overview of vegetation types. We should be aware, however, that roadside vegetation may not be representative because it may be planted, cut back in road construction or maintenance, or atypical of the area owing to the establishment of second-growth trees and weedy plants in the road right-of-way.

17.8 VEGETATION AND ENVIRONMENTAL ASSESSMENT

Finally, let us comment on vegetation as it relates to environmental assessment and impact analysis. As we mentioned earlier, few components of the landscape lend themselves to identification of environmental stress and change as does vegetation. At least five parameters or measures of impact related to vegetation can be highlighted in this context for evaluating a proposed action.

Measurement parameters   First, the sheer loss of cover, measured, for example, by the area of vegetation lost to development, is a very significant indication of impact because of its implications with respect to runoff, microclimate, aesthetics, and so on. Second, the loss of valued species, communities, and habitats is a critical measure of environmental impact as mandated by law at various levels of government. Third is the economic loss represented by the loss of merchantable vegetation such as timber and the longer term loss of profitable production areas. Fourth, vegetation is often an integral part of larger environmental systems such as microclimate, soils, and hydrology, and alteration or loss of plant cover can spell serious decline in these systems. Fifth, it is important to remember that natural vegetation is adjusted to a certain set of environmental conditions, and changes in these conditions, even subtle ones, are often reflected in changes in the vigor, reproduction capacity, and makeup of plant communities. Therefore, plants serve as valuable "thermometers" of environmental performance, giving us warnings when things are not working well.

17.9 CASE STUDY

Wildlife Habitat Considerations in Residential Planning, Central Texas

Jon Rodiek and Tom Woodfin

In southcentral Texas, as in many other parts of the country, urbanization has promoted habitat fragmentation. Fragmentation is characterized by compartmentalization of otherwise large, spatially continuous areas of habitat. It has two negative impacts on wildlife: (1) reduction in total habitat area, which primarily affects population size; and (2) subdivision of the remaining area into disjunct patches, often separated by barriers, which primarily affect dispersal and migration routes. According to recent studies, temperate ecological communities appear to be more resistant to the effects of fragmentation than are tropical communities. Among the reasons cited are that temperate species tend to occur in higher densities, are more widely distributed, and have better dispersal powers. On the other hand, it can be argued that the effects of fragmentation only *seem* less severe in temperate zones because most of the habitat damage there was done long before basic documentation of original landscapes and wildlife could be recorded. Such is likely the case in the region of College Station, Texas, where much of the clearing in the floodplains and woodlands took place around the 1860–1900 period. In the past 50 years, however, the trend toward fragmentation has actually reversed in many rural areas with the regeneration of small woodland and riparian patches following the abandonment of farming. Near cities this recovery process is interrupted by conventional suburban sprawl.

In one 2800-acre drainage area, which was analyzed for cover change over a 47-year period (1940–1987), losses were measured in the following cover types: pastureland, old fields, young stands of upland hardwoods, cultivated fields, shrub-grasslands, hardwood-shrub lands, and mature bottomland hardwoods. Increases were measured in grasslands, mature upland hardwoods, savannahs, and riparian woodlands. Drainage lines changed little judging from a slight decrease in the total lengths of first-, second-, and third-order streams. Roads and houses increased significantly, however. Roads increased from 7.96 miles to 22.6 miles, and houses and other buildings increased from 30 to 124.

On balance, the trend in land cover change can be characterized by a three-phase sequence: floodplain/riparian woodland to agrarian land to mixed suburban/urban/agrarian land. This is, of course, typical of land use changes in and near urban regions across the United States and Canada, and it has serious implications for wildlife. As agrarian ecotones (or their remnants) are converted to residential tract development, they become segmented and reduced in size. The challenge for environmental planners and landscape architects is to devise more creative styles of land conversion which increase habitat areas and geographic continuity.

In this particular case, an experiment was set up to design a residential landscape that incorporates basic biogeographic principles for wildlife habitat improvement. The effort was organized around two objectives: (1) to lay out two single-family residences on 15 acres of land, and if the layout proved successful (2) to extend the site design concept over a larger, remaining residential tract.

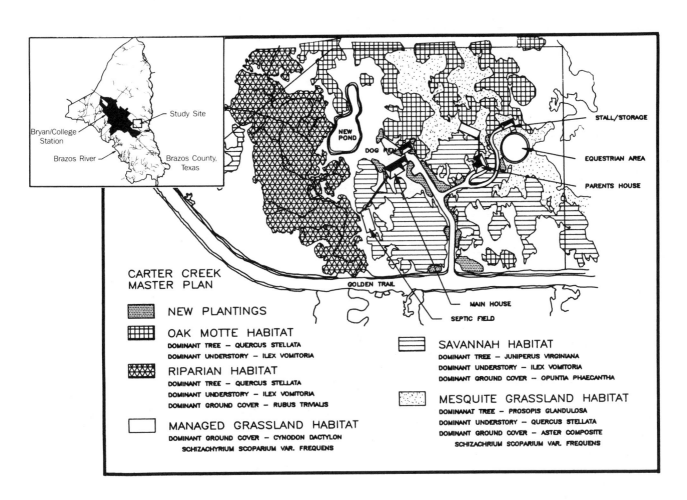

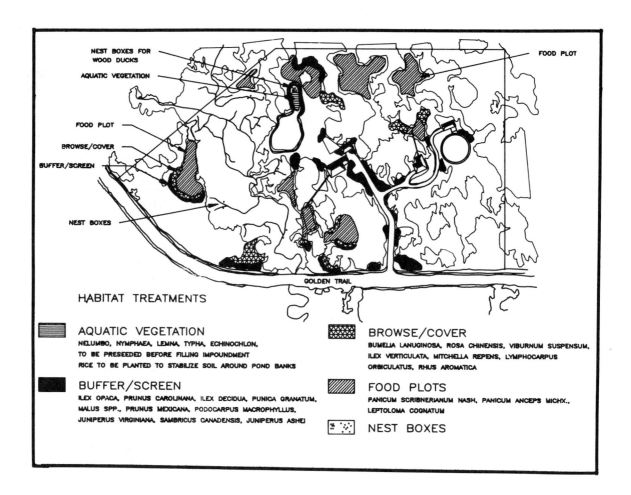

HABITAT TREATMENTS

AQUATIC VEGETATION
NELUMBO, NYMPHAEA, LEMNA, TYPHA, ECHINOCHLON,
TO BE PRESEEDED BEFORE FILLING IMPOUNDMENT
RICE TO BE PLANTED TO STABILIZE SOIL AROUND POND BANKS

BUFFER/SCREEN
ILEX OPACA, PRUNUS CAROLINANA, ILEX DECIDUA, PUNICA GRANATUM,
MALUS SPP., PRUNUS MEXICANA, PODOCARPUS MACROPHYLLUS,
JUNIPERUS VIRGINIANA, SAMBRICUS CANADENSIS, JUNIPERUS ASHEI

BROWSE/COVER
BUMELIA LANUGINOSA, ROSA CHINENSIS, VIBURNUM SUSPENSUM,
ILEX VERTICULATA, MITCHELLA REPENS, LYMPHOCARPUS
ORBICULATUS, RHUS AROMATICA

FOOD PLOTS
PANICUM SCRIBNERIANUM NASH, PANICUM ANCEPS MICHX.,
LEPTOLOMA COGNATUM

NEST BOXES

The ultimate goal would be to apply this approach to an entire watershed habitat reserve, a network made up of subregion habitat reserves tied together with a large number of site-scale habitat reserves.

In the first phase of the project, plant cover associations and related land uses were analyzed at three essential scales: watershed, subregion, and sites. Oak mottes, riparian woodlands, managed grasslands, and savannah were found to be common at all three scales. Mesquite grassland habitats were common to only the subregion and site level.

The initial planning task involved formulating a framework plan that attempted to integrate a residential complex and wildlife habitat. This plan first calls for the siting of facilities, including two residences, drives, storage facilities, and an equestrian area, in a configuration that least impacts existing woodland habitat. Vegetation was then added to provide screening, browse, and cover in selected areas, mainly along drives, open areas, and the riparian corridor. To further diversify habitat, a pond was added adjacent to the riparian habitat area. Finally, feed areas were added to the site in the form of winter and summer pasture.

The ultimate goal of this project is to mitigate the impacts of fragmentation of wildlife habitat brought on by urbanization. The strategy employed is based on the idea of establishing a skeletal corp of wildlife habitat along the riparian woodland and bottomland-hardwood landscapes. These habitats are most critical to the resident wildlife in the region. Although wooded landscapes are increasing in acreage, they currently represent only 6 percent of the subregion total. Protective zoning and enhancement of these landscapes, especially edges and linking segments, are seen as the most effective means of improving the balance between wildlife and residential development in this area.

Jon Rodiek and Tom Woodfin are landscape architects at Texas A&M University who specialize in wildlife habitat planning as a part of landscape design. ∎

17.10 SELECTED REFERENCES FOR FURTHER READING

Carpenter, Philip L., et al. *Plants in the Landscape.* San Francisco: W. H. Freeman, 1975, 491 pp.

Davis, Donald D. "The Role of Trees in Reducing Air Pollution." In *The Role of Trees in the South's Urban Environment* (Symposium Proceedings), University of Georgia, 1970.

Grey, Gene W., and Deneckie, F. J. *Urban Forestry,* New York: Wiley, 1978, 279 pp.

International Union of Forestry Organizations. *Trees and Forests for Human Settlements.* Toronto: University of Toronto Centre for Urban Forestry Studies, 1976.

McBride, J. R. "Evaluation of Vegetation in Environmental Planning." *Landscape Planning* 4, 1977, pp. 291–312.

Marsh, George Perkins. *Man and Nature; or Physical Geography as Modified by Human Action.* New York: Chas. Scribner, 1864.

Mooney, P. F. *Plants: Their Role in Modifying the Environment; A Selected and Annotated Bibliography.* Mississanga, Ontario: Landscape Ontario Horticultural Trades Formation, 1981.

Schmid, J. A. *Urban Vegetation: A Review and Chicago Case Study.* Chicago: University of Chicago, Department of Geography Research Paper 161, 1975.

Thurow, Charles, et al. *Performance Controls for Sensitive Lands.* Washington, D.C.: American Society of Planning Officials, Reports 307 and 308, 1975, 156 pp.

U.S. Forest Service. *Better Trees for Metropolitan Landscapes.* Washington, D.C.: U.S. Government Printing Office, USDA Forest Service General Technical Report NE–22, 1976, 256 pp.

U.S. Forest Service. *National Forest Landscape Management* (Agricultural Handbook No. 478). Washington, D.C.: U.S. Government Printing Office, 1974.

18

WETLANDS, HABITAT, AND LAND USE PLANNING

18.1 INTRODUCTION

Much of environmental planning has to do with edges—the lines and ribbons in the landscape where one environment gives way to another. No edge is more important than that between land and water. More than a billion people live on this edge, and the most productive ecosystems on earth are found there. Among these ecosystems are wetlands which occupy the shallow-water environments.

Long regarded as fringe environments of marginal utility for land use, wetlands have been the object of severe misuse for centuries. In the United States (less Alaska), it is estimated that since about 1800 as much as 50 percent of the original area of wetlands has been destroyed. In the past few decades, however, wetlands have found a solid place in the environmental agendas of the United States, Canada, and other countries. Laws have emerged calling for their protection against the pressures of land

Environmental rationale

development. The **environmental rationale** behind these laws is basically twofold: (1) wetlands are important habitat necessary to the survival of a host of aquatic and terrestrial species; and (2) wetlands are integral parts of the hydrologic system necessary for the maintenance of water supplies and water quality.

Practical rationale

Besides the environmental quality rationale, there are a number of purely **practical reasons** for respecting wetlands in land use planning. First, the places in the landscape where wetlands form are characterized by drainage conditions that are extremely limiting to most land uses. The sources of these conditions usually extend over an area larger than the wetland itself, and in most instances the conditions do not simply disappear by scraping the wetlands away. Therefore, attempts to build in wetland sites may significantly increase overall development costs because of the need for special allowances for site drainage, flood protection, and facility maintenance. Second, most wetlands are usually underlain by organic soils that are unstable for most forms of development. To use such soils often requires special and often elaborate engineering schemes, or the soils must be removed by excavation and replaced with stable fill material. In either case costs are increased significantly. Third, wetlands are landscape amenities and, like lakes and streams, can improve land values and design opportunities for the insightful developer. For many land uses, wetlands clearly enhance property values if they are properly integrated into land use planning schemes.

Wetlands cover such a wide spectrum of physical conditions and ecological characteristics that it is difficult to arrive at a succinct definition of them. Scientists generally agree, however, that all wetlands have three characteristics, and these serve

Wetland definition

as a general **definition**:

■ The presence of water on the surface, usually relatively shallow water, all or part of the year.

■ The presence of distinctive soils, often with high organic contents, which are clearly different from upland soils.

■ The presence of vegetation composed of species adapted to wet soils, surface water, and/or flooding.

The regulatory agencies responsible for environmental policies have formulated various definitions of wetlands. The U.S. Fish and Wildlife Service uses the following definition, which planners have widely accepted:

Wetlands are lands transitional between terrestrial and aquatic systems where the water table is usually at or near the surface or the land is covered by shallow water. . . . Wetlands must have one or more of the following three attributes: (1) at least periodically, the land supports predominantly hydrophytes, (2) the substrate is predominantly undrained hydric soil, and (3) the substrate is nonsoil and is saturated with water or covered by shallow water at some time during the growing season of each year.

In Canada, the following definition is used in the Canadian Wetland Registry:

> Wetland is defined as land having the water table at, near, or above the land surface or which is saturated for a long enough period to promote wetland or aquatic processes as indicated by hydric soils, hydrophylic vegetation, and various kinds of biological activity which are adapted to the wet environment.

18.2 WETLAND HYDROLOGY

Water is the most fundamental component of wetlands. Although vegetation is usually the most visible component of the wetland environment and is conventionally used to define them for regulatory purposes, water is decidedly the driving force behind the origin and maintenance of wetlands. Indeed, the practice of wetland eradication almost always involved draining the problem area and limiting the influx of the normal water supply.

Hydrologic regime

Each wetland can be described as a hydrologic system with inflows and outflows of water. For most wetlands there is a particular pattern or **regime** to the inflows and outflows which is manifested in rises and falls in the internal water level. These fluctuations have a wide variety of periods depending on wetland setting, water sources, and climatic situation. Some are rhythmical as in the daily flux of water in tidal marshes; others are seasonal as in stream valleys which flood in the spring; and still others are sporadic as in isolated locales where water comes anytime with the runoff from rainfall events. In all cases the hydrologic regime is essential to understanding and managing wetlands. Among other things, plant productivity and animal life cycles are adjusted to it.

Water sources and losses

There are four possible **sources of water** for the wetland system: (1) direct *precipitation*, (2) *runoff* from surrounding lands including inflowing streams, (3) *groundwater* inflow, and (4) ocean *tide water* (Fig. 18.1). All wetlands receive precipitation, and virtually all receive runoff of some sort in the form of streamflow, stormwater, and/or overland flow. Depending on the geologic conditions controlling subsurface water, however, only certain wetlands receive groundwater, and of course only coastal wetlands receive ocean water or lake water. On the water loss side, wetlands lose water to evapotranspiration, seepage into the ground, stream discharge, and tidal outflow. Taken together, the inputs and outputs of water define the wetland's water balance (Fig. 18.1).

Storage water

In order to maintain most wetlands, the water balance cannot fluctuate so radically that there are long periods without substantial inputs of external water. To buffer against such deteriorating events, wetlands usually hold a large reserve of **storage water** in the form of soil moisture and groundwater. Organic soils, which form the substratum of most wetlands, have a very high moisture-holding capacity. At full saturation, organic matter such as muck and peat can hold more than 6 inches of water for each foot of soil. In addition, these materials have a high moisture transfer capacity whereby moisture is readily conducted from depth to the root zone by capillary action. These two hydrologic conditions account for the survival of many terrestrial wetlands— particularly those not attached to a major source of water such as a stream, or lake, or an aquifer—during prolonged periods of summer drought.

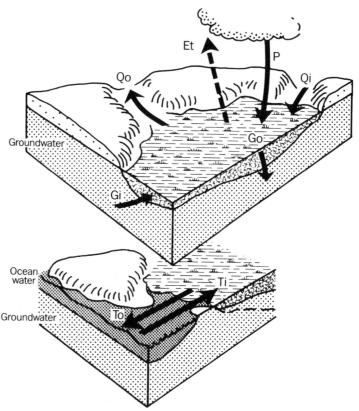

Fig. 18.1 Three-level classification of wetlands and deepwater habitats, showing systems, is precipitation, Et is evapotranspiration, Qi is stream inflow, Qo is stream outflow, Ti is tidal inflow To is tidal outflow, Gi is groundwater inflow and Go is groundwater outflow.

18.3 THE WETLAND ECOSYSTEM

Wetlands are attractive habitats for many plants and animals. The diversity of species is often higher in wetlands than in nearby upland landscapes, and where species diversity is not great, the population of individual species may be great. Biomass (the total weight of living matter per square meter of surface) is usually greater in wetlands than in adjacent deep-water habitat or upland areas, and the productivity of the wetland vegetation, measured by the amount of new organic material produced each year, is typically greater than that of other habitats.

Wetland ecosystem   Ecological character and function are clearly the ranking attributes of wetlands in today's planning and management agendas. Among other things, wetlands are often cited as model ecosystems. An **ecosystem** is a biological energy system made up of food chains along which energy is passed from one group of organisms to another. The ecosystem's basic source of energy is the solar radiation, heat, and other essential resources taken up by plants in photosynthesis and converted into organic energy in the form of organic compounds (sugars and carbohydrates). Within the plant itself this energy is moved along two paths; some is used in respiration (plant maintenance processes) and some in growing new tissue (leaves, seeds, etc.). The total amount of new tissue manufactured in a year is termed *primary productivity*, and it is the source of energy on which *all* other organisms in the ecosystem depend, either directly or indirectly, beginning with the herbivores and ending with the specialized predators (Fig. 18.2).

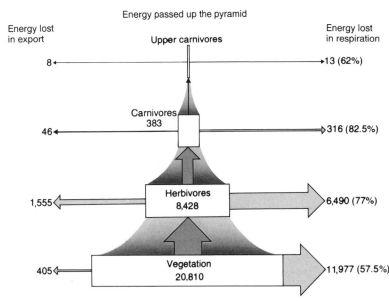

Fig. 18.2 Model of an ecosystem, called an energy pyramid, showing the four basic levels of organization, Silver Springs, Flordia. All units in kilocalories per square meter per year.

Productivity   Wetland **productivity**, which is measured in grams of organic matter generated per square meter of surface per year, may typically be twice that of hearby upland vegetation. A salt marsh along the Gulf of Mexico, for example, may average close to 2000 grams (per m²) per year compared to 1000 to 1500 grams per year in a neighboring subtropical forest. Many factors influence wetland productivity. Obviously, climatic conditions are important; northern bogs average only 500 to 600 grams per year because of growing season limitations. Hydrology is also important as it

Nutrient supply   apparently influences the **supply of nutrients**. Wetlands with the highest productivity are those with a moderate but continuous flow of water; stagnant wetlands, by contrast, generally have low productivities. Wastewater can also affect productivity. Wetlands receiving enriched waters from stormwater and sewage treatment facilities usually show accelerated productivites, whereas those receiving pollutants such as heavy metals and petroleum residues not only show a decline in productivity but a decline in species diversity as well.

If wetlands are capable of producing large amounts of organic matter, they must also have the means of disposing of it. The balance between productivity and disposal or loss determines the *organic mass balance* of the wetland. Changes in the organic mass balance are reflected in changes in the reserve of organic matter in the wetland substratum, that is, the muck and peat deposits. When the mass balance is negative, loss exceeds productivity and this reserve declines.

Organic loss processes   The processes responsible for the **loss of organic matter** in wetlands are decompostion by microorganisms, consumption by herbivores, erosion by surface waters, and leaching to groundwater. Export of organic matter by erosion and leaching varies greatly depending on the local setting and hydrology; for tidal wetlands such as mangrove swamps and salt marshes it may be as great as 40 to 50 percent of annual productivity. In wetlands that tend to be hydrologically closed, however, export is usually negligible, and decomposition is virtually the sole means of loss of organic

Organic decomposition   matter. Among the controls on **decomposition**, water depth is the most critical because it, along with the mixing motion of the water, governs the availability of oxygen to many of the decomposing organisms. Under fully flooded conditions, little oxygen is available in the organic deposits and decomposition is slow, especially in stagnant water. If water is drained away to the point where the organic deposits are exposed to the atmosphere, decomposition rates rise dramatically. This is a principal reason for the decline in wetlands when they are artifically drained.

Marshes

In a general way the ecology of a wetland is also reflected in the character of its plant cover. Traditionally, wetlands are described according to the structure (or form) and composition of the plant cover. Various terms, such as swamp, marsh, and bog, have been used over the years, and although their meanings tend to vary somewhat from place to place, these terms are still meaningful and still widely used. **Marshes** are dominated by herbaceous vegetation, typically bladeleaf plants such as cattails, reeds, and rushes (Fig. 18.3). Although these plants may reach a height of 6 feet of more, marshes often have the look of a grassland or meadow; indeed, some marshes are called wet meadows. Soils are typically rich with relatively high (alkaline) pH levels, which has made marshes attractive to agriculture in many areas.

Swamps

Swamps are dominated by trees and shrubs (Fig. 18.3). There are many varieties of swamps in the United States and Canada. At the climatic extremes, for example, are cypress swamps in the American South and northern conifer swamps in the U.S. North and Canada. Northern conifer swamps may be dominated by various tree covers: spruce, tamarack, cedar, or balsam fir, and these may occur in various associations with other trees and shrubs. Owing to the short growing season and persistently wet (or flooded) soils, the trees of the northern conifer swamps are often stunted and at full maturity may reach heights of only 10 to 20 feet.

Bogs

Bogs are northern wetlands containing a wide diversity of vegetation. They are characterized by deep organic deposits, typically peat, and tend to be acidic. Bogs often form in small lakes where the vegetation is organized in concentric bands ranging from trees in the outer band to emergent and floating vegetation near the middle (Fig. 18.3).

18.4 WETLAND TYPES AND SETTINGS

Physiographic factors

Wetlands can be classified in a variety of ways—for example, on the basis of vegetative cover (as described above), hydrologic regime, or geographic (or physiographic) setting. The most basic control in shaping the wetland system is its **physiographic** setting. This includes the topographic situation, the proximal landscape (surrounding land use and vegetation), soils, and subsurface conditions (deposits and bedrock). Some combination of these factors produces a state of impeded (slow) drainage and/or abundant water supply that gives rise to wetland habitat.

Learning to recognize the physiographic conditions that produce wetlands is the first step in understanding their function and maintenance because setting is critical to wetland hydrology. In many instances, the relationship between setting and hydrologic function is readily apparent from casual field observation as in cases of shallow waters along the shore of a pond or estuary. In other settings, however, it is not so apparent because sources of water or the conditions responsible for regulating water loss may be hidden underground or tied to sporadic hydrologic events.

Surficial sites

We can define four general classes of wetlands based on physiographic setting and hydrologic conditions: (1) surficial, (2) groundwater, (3) riparian, and (4) composite. **Surficial wetland sites** are dependent on surface sources of water, mainly direct precipitation, and local runoff in the form of overland flow, ephemeral channel flow, and interflow (Fig. 18.4). These waters collect in shallow swales, closed depressions, and disturbed places where drainage has been blocked by deposits, tree throws, construction, or farming activity. The wetland begins with the establishment of a plant

Coastal salt marsh (Estuarine)

Inland freshwater (Lacustrine)

Deciduous swamp (Palustrine)

Conifer swamp (Palustrine)

Shrub swamp (Palustrine)

Bog (Palustrine)

Aquatic bed (Lacustrine)

Open stream (Riverine)

Fig. 18.3 Photographs showing examples of marshes, swamps and bogs.

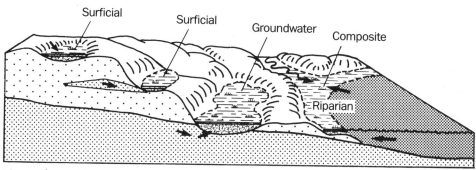

Fig. 18.4   A schematic diagram showing some types of physiographic and hydrologic conditions associated with surficial, groundwater, riparian, and composite wetland sites.

cover over the wet spot, which is followed by two changes that help to stabilize the site as a wetland environment: (1) accumulation of organic debris and mineral sediments leading to the formation of a wetland soil; and (2) sealing of the wetland floor with fine sediments. These changes improve the wetland's overall water balance by increasing its water-retention capacity.

Surficial wetlands also include those supported by perched groundwater. These are lenses of groundwater that lie near the surface above the main groundwater body (Fig. 18.4). Where perched lenses intercept the surface, water seeps out saturating the overlying soil giving rise to wetland conditions. In certain northern bogs where sphagnum moss is the dominant plant cover, the wetland may actually expand upward and outward beyond the limits of the seepage zone. This is attributed to the rise of water by capillary flow within the organic mass.

Groundwater sites   **Groundwater wetland sites** are usually found at lower elevations in the landscape such as on the floors of stream valleys, sinkholes, and glacial kettles. These sites lie at or below the water table of the main groundwater body, and as low-pressure points in the groundwater system, they receive groundwater discharge. Because the supporting aquifers are often large, the water supply to the wetland is substantial and, unlike surficial wetlands, is not subject to radical fluctuations with variations in precipitation and alterations in the surrounding land cover and surface drainage patterns (Fig. 18.4). Nevertheless, some groundwater wetlands are subject to water-level fluctuations in the range of several feet on a seasonal and longer term basis as the water table rises and falls around them.

Riparian sites   **Riparian wetland sites** are those in and around major water features such as lakes, large streams, and estuaries (Fig. 18.4). These wetlands usually show a strong gradation in habitat with water depth from deep-water aquatic on the wet side to upland mesic on the terrestrial side. As the principal source of water, the controlling water feature governs the wetland's hydrologic regime. This is a two-sided coin, however, because the water feature is also the source of destructive processes such as storm waves, floodflows, and ice movements that can cut wetlands back and in some instances obliterate them entirely (Fig. 18.5).

Composite sites   **Composite wetland sites** are those supported by two or more major sources of water. Most large, enduring wetlands fall into this class. For example, cypress swamps in river floodplains are dependent on both floodwaters and groundwater. Coastal marshes are often supported by a combination of tidal water, stream discharge, and groundwater. Because each source has a different regime, the principal supply of water to the wetland may change from season to season. For example, in the Great Lakes, stream discharge peaks in spring, whereas the lakes themselves reach their highs in late summer. Therefore, as the streamflows feeding coastal marshes subside in late summer, the Great Lakes often augment the wetland's shrinking water budget. Understandably, the composite class of wetlands is often the most complex of the wetland systems and

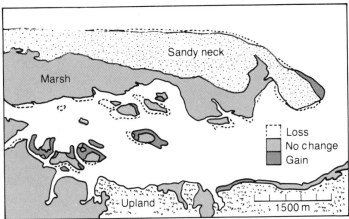

Fig. 18.5 Wetland changes in an estuarine marsh on the Atlantic Coast, 1859–1957. This illustrates a characteristic of wetlands that is not widely appreciated, namely, that wetlands can decline as well as grow under natural conditions.

therefore the most difficult to manage because alterations may have compound effects on its various sources of water, mechanisms for internal water transfer, and water discharge. This is often illustrated with the construction of roads, canals, navigational facilities, and flood control structures where the impact on the wetland may initially appear to be minor but leads to gradual change that builds into substantial impact in the long run. One of the most controversial management dramas of this sort is currently being played out in the Florida Everglades.

18.5 COMPREHENSIVE WETLAND CLASSIFICATION SYSTEM

Regulatory agencies
Among the many governmental **agencies** concerned with wetlands, the U.S. Fish and Wildlife Service, the U.S. Environmental Protection Agency, and the U.S. Army Corps of Engineers are at the heart of the regulatory review process. They are responsible for wetland interpretation as well as the review of porposals for permitting projects in wetland areas. To facilitate the review process, these regulatory agencies have adopted a wetland classification system that is comprehensive in scope and part of the recent National Wetlands Survey (Fig. 18.6).

Deep-water limits
In this system, both wetlands and deep-water habitats are addressed. Deep-water habitats are permanently flooded lands that lie below the deep-water boundary of wetlands. In saltwater settings, deep-water habitat begins at the extreme low water of low spring tide. In other waters, the boundary line is at 2 meters (6.6 feet) below the low water mark. This is taken as the maximum depth of growth of emergent aquatic plants. Landward of the deep-water line is wetland.

Wetland systems
The classification scheme is organized into three basic levels beginning with systems (Table 18.1). Five **wetland systems** are recognized: marine, estuarine, riverine, lacustrine, and palustrine. The *marine system* consists of the deep-water habitat of the open ocean and the adjacent marine wetlands of the intertidal areas along the mainland coast and islands. The *estuarine system* is associated with coastal embayments and drowned river mouths and includes salt marshes, brackish tidal marshes, mangrove swamps as well as deep-water bays. The *riverine system* is limited to freshwater stream channels, and the *lacustrine system* is limited to standing water-bodies, mainly lakes, ponds, and reservoirs. Both the riverine system and the lacustrine system include deep-water habitat. By contrast, the fifth system, the *palustrine system*, includes only wetland habitat. It is also the major system because it encompasses the vast majority of North America's wetlands, namely, inland marshes, swamps, and bogs.

Beyond the system level, *subsystems* are defined for all but the palustrine system.

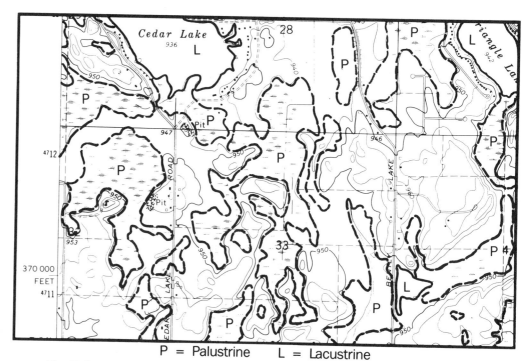

P = Palustrine   L = Lacustrine

Fig. 18.6   A portion of a map from the National Wetlands Survey. The base map is a standard U.S. Geological Survey topographic contour map. The code refers to wetland classification.

Wetland classes   At the third level, *wetland classes* are defined, and they represent either basic habitat types or wetland types based on vegetation. Among the palustrine wetlands, the three major classes are (1) emergent wetland, (2) scrub-shrub wetland, and (3) forested wetland. Emergent wetlands are dominated by herbaceous vegetation including grasses, cattails, rushes, and sedges. Scrub-shrub wetlands are dominated by short, woody vegetation (shrubs and trees less than 20 feet high), and forested wetlands are dominated by trees taller than 20 feet.

18.6   WETLAND MAPPING

Wetland mapping has become one of the most important inventory activities in environmental planning. No matter the nature of the project, it is essential not only to identify wetlands but to define their geographic limits as well. As with virtually all efforts to map landscape features, three problems must be faced at the outset: (1) the criteria or indicators to be used as the basis for boundary delineation; (2) the sources of data; and (3) the mapping resolution, that is, the level of geographic detail required.

Vegetation   Three criteria are consistently named in ordinances for wetland mapping purposes: vegetation, soils, and hydrology. Depending on state and local guidelines, all three, two, or just one criterion may be required to define a wetland. **Vegetation** is the most commonly used criterion in wetland mapping. Many wetland edges can be identified by a relatively abrupt change in the *vegetative structure*, especially where the lowland/upland transition is sharp. This border may also be marked by a third vegetative form, a belt of shrub-sized plants fringing the wetland. Whereas structure is useful in wetland mapping, *floristic composition* of the plant cover is considered more reliable for boundary demarcation. Certain plants can be used as wetland indicator species, and their dominance may be taken as sound evidence of wetland habitat. Indicator species vary from region to region, and in most locales, a preferred list of

Table 18.1 Three-level classification of wetlands and deepwater habitats, showing systems, subsystems, and classes. The Palustrine system does not include deepwater habitats.

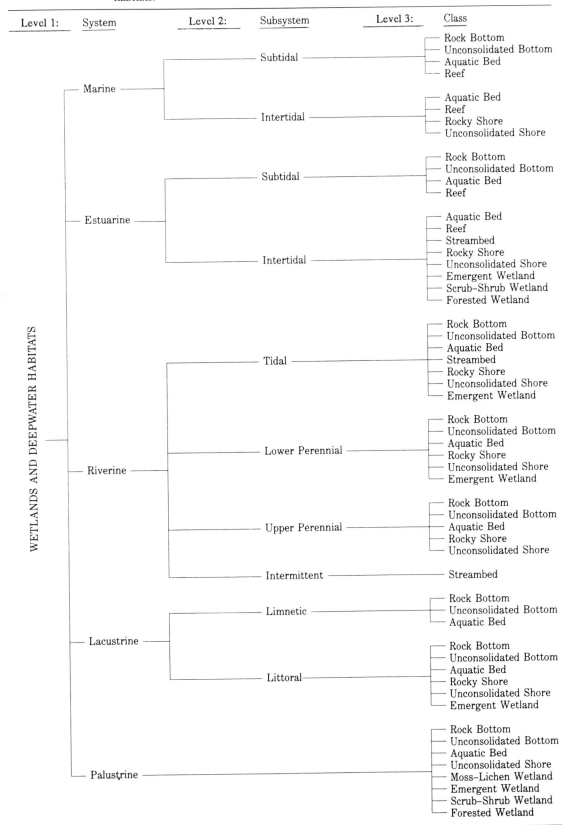

Soil

indicator species can be obtained from environmental agencies, university botanist, or environmental organizations (also see Appendix E).

The second criterion is **soil**. The term *hydric* is widely used to describe wetland soils. These are mainly organic soils, such as muck or peat, but may also include saturated mineral soils. Soils are generally used as a secondary indicator after vegetation. Care should be taken in using published soil maps to corroborate wetland borders initially mapped on the basis of vegetation patterns because many of the original soil boundaries were based in part on vegetation. Thus discovery of a strong correlation between hydric soils, as shown, for example, on U.S. Soil Conservation Service maps, and wetland vegetation may constitute circular reasoning. Field checks of soils are usually advisable in wetland mapping.

Flooding

The third criterion is **flooding**. If an area is periodically or frequently flooded and lies in a flood zone such as a designated floodplain, it is also taken as evidence of wetland. Whereas flood-prone areas such as floodplains are readily identifiable, the boundaries of such areas are usually inexact because they are normally defined by hydrological calculations rather than by field measurement of floodwater coverage. Therefore, the delineation of wetlands in terms of fixing a boundary line should usually be based more on vegetation and soils than on flood zones.

Data sources

Topographic and soil maps

The **sources of data** and information for wetland mapping fall into two classes: (1) published sources in the form of topographic maps, aerial photographs, and soil maps, and (2) field surveys. Large-scale **topographic contour maps,** published in the United States by the U.S. Geological Survey and in Canada by the National Mapping Branch, mark wetland areas larger than 10 acres or so. These areas are mapped from aerial photographs on the basis of visible surface water, vegetation patterns, topographic trends, and proximity to water features such as lakes and streams. **Soil maps** such as those published by the U.S. Soil Conservation Service, do not necessarily show wetlands, but they do depict hydric soils. As noted above, however, the original placement of the soil borders that appear on the SCS maps was often guided by vegetation and topographic lines. Therefore, these borders cannot always be taken as reliable independent indicators at the local scale. Field verification is usually necessary when using soils for wetland delineation.

Aerial imagery

Aerial photographs are especially helpful in wetland mapping. Stereoscopic models afford an exaggerated view of the vegetation structure and forms, and textural differences in forest cover and bladeleaf vegetation, for example, help in distinguishing wetland areas. In addition, infrared imagery provides enhanced scenes in which water, different vegetation types, and exposed soil contrast more sharply with each other than they do on standard aerial photographs.

Field verification

In cases calling for development or alteration of sites containing wetland, **field verification** and border refinement of wetlands are usually advisable. This involves walking the border, taking note of indicator plants, soils, and evidence of high water. The evidence of high water includes water marks on trees, debris stranded on low branches and foliage, stranded driftwood on the ground, and shallow and exposed tree roots. As the border is identified, it should be flagged so that it can be fixed by field survey and plotted on site maps.

18.7 MANAGEMENT AND MITIGATION CONSIDERATIONS

Wetland mitigation begins not on the development site or at the water's edge, but with programs dealing with public attitudes and information on wetlands. As with many environmental problems, the first steps toward solutions involve improved public awareness followed by understanding of the value of wetlands in the environment. In other words, society has to know enough about something and feel strongly enough

The national agenda

about it to make a place for it in the great **agenda** of environmental problems. That has already happened with wetlands in a general way, and it has led to enforcement of wetland protection laws such as Section 404 of the Federal Clean Water Act as well as the enactment of new laws at the state and local levels.

How to balance society's need to use land and the need to protect wetlands, however, requires the attention of planners and scientists working at the level of individual land use sites. This involves two levels of activity: (1) management of existing land uses and (2) planning future land uses. The principal challenge is with existing land uses that continue to damage and destroy wetlands. Chief among these is agriculture, which in the United States has been responsible for 70 to 90 percent of the wetland loss since the 1950s. Limiting future wetland loss to agriculture is important, but mitigation of damage from existing operations is also needed. Unfortunately, few if any wetland ordinances apply to agricultural activities, and until they do, wetland protection policy will remain somewhat hollow. This is not the case, however, with new urban development; residential, industrial, and commerical land use plans are carefully scrutinized for wetland conflicts by federal, state, and local agencies.

Wetland mitigation

The search for land use compatibility with wetlands may be approached along two lines: mitigation and management planning. **Mitigation** involves taking certain actions to counterbalance wetland losses or damage. Three types of mitigation are usually practiced: (1) restoration of damaged environments; (2) creation of new wetlands; and (3) control of potentially damaging actions. The third type usually includes various means of controlling construction activity, stormwater runoff, soil erosion, sedimentation, and building encroachment, but it may also involve various land protection arrangements such as deed restrictions and environmental easements. The case studies at the end of the chapter describe two wetland restoration projects.

Management planning

The concept of **management planning** goes beyond site-limited mitigation by addressing the larger system of which the wetland is a part. This entails defining the principal sources of water and the controls on the water flow system, and evaluating the vulnerability of the flow system to alterations from land use that could affect the wetland. In the case of the wetland in Fig. 18.7, for example, the principal sources of water happened to be vegetated swales heading up in the surrounding upland. According to the state regulations governing the site, a buffer zone of fixed width was to be designated around the entire wetland to protect it against land use encroachment. Because of the character of the topography and drainage patterns around the wetland, however, such a buffer definition did not offer adequate protection for the sources of runoff. Therefore, an alternative buffer concept was devised based on the configuration of the swale drainage system. The total area of buffer remained about the same, but the performance of the buffer in terms of the inflow of water and the long-term maintenance of the wetland improved with the functional based concept.

Hydrologic system approach

The main point of wetland management planning is to approach wetlands in much the same way as we would an inland lake, that is, to treat the contributing **watershed** as the main vehicle for managing the waterbody. This includes understanding not only the extent and nature of the water sources, but also the role of water storage and the controls on water release in the overall maintenance of the wetland. As with lake watersheds, the sources of water have to be evaluated in terms of the directness of their linkage to the wetland, their relative contributions, and whether they tend to fall into the manageable or nonmanageable class. Nonmanageable sources are those beyond the reasonable reach of management such as precipitation and deep sources of groundwater. For manageable sources that make significant contributions to the wetlands, care should be taken to insure that the availability of water is maintained and the delivery system is not impaired by structures, grading, or stormwater diversion.

Stormwater management

The use of wetlands in **stormwater management** is widespread today, and while generally encouraged, the practice is seriously questioned for wetland habitats prone

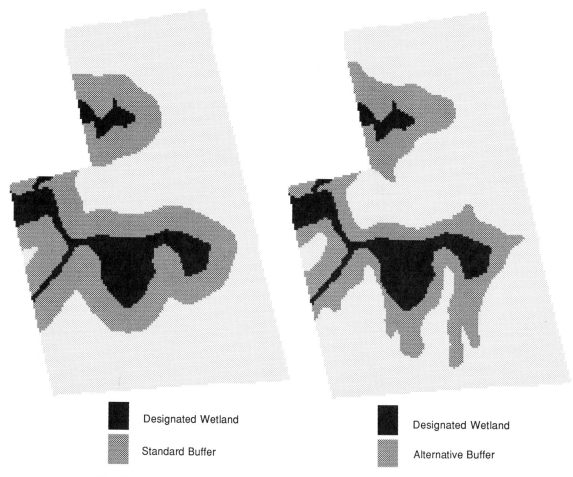

Designated Wetland

Standard Buffer

Designated Wetland

Alternative Buffer

Fig. 18.7   Maps showing (a) a standard 100-foot wetland buffer and (b) a buffer adjusted to the configuration of the drainage patterns around the wetland.

to damage from changes in water regime and water quality. Marshes polluted by many years of urban and industrial runoff, for example, have been discovered to decline sharply in species diversity, eventually reaching a state described as a monoculture. The levels of permissible pollutant loading in wetlands are clearly a matter of much uncertainty, which at this writing awaits further research.

18.8 CASE STUDIES

Wetland Mitigation: Creating a Salt Marsh in Long Island, New York

David Salvesen
Ron Abrams

The number and scope of federal and state laws designed to protect wetlands has increased dramatically in the past decade. Under Section 404 of the Clean Water Act, for instance, developers must first get a permit from the U.S. Army Corps of Engineers (Corps) before building in wetlands. The Corps usually issues a permit on the condition that the developer mitigates any adverse impacts on a wetland stemming from the development. In addition, a growing number of states have adopted wetland protection laws that are more stringent than federal laws; in the Northeast, many towns have adopted even stricter regulations. Ten years ago, only a few states had laws protecting wetlands. Now over half the states do, and the list is growing. In densely populated regions, where property values are high, the municipal restrictions on developers have become quite severe.

Before receiving a permit to develop in wetlands, developers must first demonstrate that, for so-called nonwater-dependent uses such as a mall or a housing development, no practicable, nonwetland sites exist. (Water-dependent uses include, for example, marinas and ports.) Furthermore, both the Corps and local regulators generally require developers to minimize adverse impacts on a wetland and to compensate for any wetland loss by restoring or creating a wetland nearby preferably in the same watershed as their project. This is generally referred to as wetland mitigation.

Wetland mitigation, particularly wetland creation, has become the subject of scientific debate and is very controversial. Wetlands are complex, dynamic ecosystems, and attempts to create them have yielded mixed results. Environmentalists argue that constructed wetlands can scarcely be considered adequate substitutes for natural wetlands. Developers counter that wetland creation allows development to occur in wetlands, particularly where fill is unavoidable, while improving the quality and quantity of wetlands overall. Each side of what has become an impassioned debate can point to wetland creation failures and successes to support its argument. There are no easy answers. It appears that some wetlands, such as tidal marshes, can be created successfully but others, such as bogs and bottomland hardwood forests, are more problematic due to the time required for their establishment (50 to 100 years). Given the uncertainties, regulatory agencies have grown increasingly reluctant to allow developers to exchange built wetlands for natural ones. As a result, developers are beginning to shy away from development in wetlands.

In East Patchogue (pronounced patch-hog), Long Island, a small coastal marsh lies along an estuarine stream that enters Patchogue Bay. Originally a cordgrass marsh, the hydrology of this 55-acre wetland was severely altered when a canal, constructed during the 1950s as part of a building craze on Long Island, was cut through the marsh to the bay. As in wetlands which have been drained by excavation for canals or mosquito ditches, common reed quickly moved in and covered the site.

In exchange for building a dock on the canal and a walkway through the marsh connecting a new residential subdivision to the dock, a local developer agreed to restore a portion of the former cordgrass marsh. The restoration plan, devised by Dru Associates, called for creating a crescent-shaped cordgrass marsh along the canal bed. The first task was to remove the thick stand of common reed that blanketed the site and to take steps to prevent its return. Typically, herbicides are used to kill unwanted plants like common reed, but state and local regulators balked at this method, fearing contamination to Long Island's precious and vulnerable groundwater and the adjacent Great South Bay environment. Instead, an excavator was brought in to physically remove the reed grass down to a depth below the root mat. Once the reed grass was removed, the area was filled with sandy loam from a nearby construction site, graded to the proper elevation, and prepared for planting. The key to success was identifying the grade at which cordgrass would prosper, while common reed would not. In addition to removing the reed grass, a narrow, 12-foot-wide channel was dug along the inner curve of the new wetlands site to keep the invasive reed grass at bay.

Creating a salt marsh typically involves hand-planting thousands of young cordgrass plants and scheduling the work around the tides. In this project, workers could only plant for four to five hours per tidal cycle. Thirty-one thousand cordgrass sprigs in peat plugs were hand-planted at 18-inch staggered centers and supplemented with time-release fertilizer. A crew of five people took 15 days to complete the hand-grading and planting. While waiting to be planted, the cordgrass sprigs, stored on site, had to be protected from pre-

Site preparation

Planting

Growth

Establishment

dation by geese and muskrats, and also prevented from drying out in the hot July sun. The plants were soaked daily with freshwater from a nearby construction site. Only about 1 percent of the plants died in storage.

After planting was completed, a crew of two to four people closely monitored the site for three months until the end of the growing season. Throughout the winter one or two people visited the site every two to three weeks to maintain goose fences and tend to drainage. They checked for predation, for debris that might impair drainage, and for any remaining clumps of common reed that would allow it to gain a foothold in the new marsh. Initially, geese preyed heavily on the young cordgrass, but relatively few plants died. By the end of September, the cordgrass was 3 feet high and covered roughly 90 percent of the site. By early spring of the second year, the cordgrass had sent out runners joining the first year clumps. Some of the plants, perhaps 20 percent, went to seed in the first year. The total cost for the restoration, including planning, obtaining government approvals, site preparation, planting, and two years of monitoring and maintenance, was about $160,000. In the second year, an additional $10,000 was expended on supplemental plantings and labor in the areas where propagation was weak. Routine maintenance will be carried out throughout a third season to ensure ultimate success.

David Salvesen is a senior associate with the Urban Land Institute, Washington, D.C.
Ron Abrams is principal ecologist and president of Dru Associates Inc., an ecological consulting firm.

18.8 CASE STUDY

■ **The Saga of an Urban Marsh, San Francisco Bay**

Peter Grenell

Most of this country's coastal wetlands have been lost—filled or dredged for farms, towns, and ports. Around San Francisco Bay only remnants remain of the once-great marsh system that European settlers found when they arrived a little over 200 years ago. Here, briefly, is the story of how one of these marsh remnants is being brought back to life.

The 11-acre Redwood High School Marsh is located in the suburban city of Larkspur, a few miles north of San Francisco in environmentally conscious Marin County. Only a remnant of a larger coastal wetland, the marsh has been reduced by tens of acres over the years because of incremental draining, filling, and construction. Today levees and streets border the marsh on two sides, and one of the adjacent filled areas was recently developed as a community athletic field.

The marsh, however, continues to receive water from both terrestrial and marine sources. Drainage culverts bring freshwater from the land to the west, and saltwater is received via tide gates from the Bay to the east. The combination of freshwater and saltwater produces a brackish water environment that is habitat for plants such as California cordgrass, pickleweed, and coyote brush. Near the tide gates, on the Bay side, the wetland is dominated by salt marsh species. Sheltered marshes are important refuge, feeding, and resting places for migratory ducks and shorebirds.

Over the years, the value of the Redwood High School Marsh as a habitat for a variety of birds, fish, insects, and microorganisms has been drastically reduced and degraded. Filling and construction activities have reduced the area of the marsh, and the wetland habitat has been degraded in some large part by the constriction of tidal water flows, and by the influx of stormwater discharge from nearby developed lands. In addition, the city of Larkspur uses the marsh as a flood control basin, which has caused further damage to habitat and wildlife.

Like many other wetland remnants around San Francisco Bay, this small marsh was considered by resource agencies to be too insignificant and isolated to be worth restoring and managing. A 1985 study of Bay Area marshes,

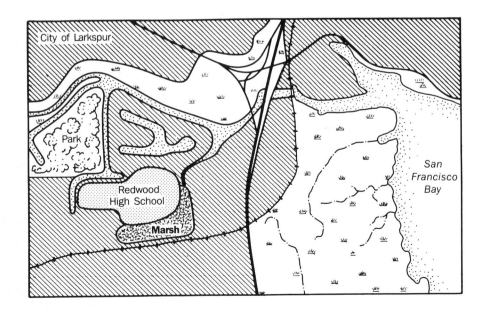

however, suggested that small marsh "islands" in the urban settlement "sea" are still vitally important to the Bay's wildlife and should be saved. Of direct interest to the local people, too, was the opportunity provided by the Redwood High School Marsh for a unique educational experience.

As with most environmental restoration efforts, there were technical, political, and financial problems. Among them were:

- How to restore the marsh to health and how to resolve the potential conflict between the needs of marsh habitat and those of the city for flood control.
- How to provide public access without damaging the fragile marsh plants and wildlife areas.
- How to design an appropriate and meaningful educational program.
- How money could be raised to implement the restoration program.

The Coastal Conservancy, a state government agency with funds and powers to work with local governments and nonprofit groups, agreed to provide money and technical assistance for the preparation and implementation of a marsh plan. Other money for the project came from private foundations through local fund-raising efforts, the Marin Audubon Society, and most recently from U.S. EPA through its San Francisco Estuary Project.

The planning program was launched with studies of the marsh's ecology, hydrology, and water quality. These studies provided data and guidelines for designing the various engineering, landscape, and human use features. The design program included tidal flow structures to combat the ill effects of stagnant water without upsetting the delicate balances required to maintain wildlife habitat; enlarged and improved feeding areas for shore and wading birds; and additional plant cover for wildlife along the drainage channel banks and flat areas. All these changes had to be worked out without eliminating the marsh's role in local flood control for the city of Larkspur.

In addition, a system of pathways was designed for public access to the marsh which would encourage interest and observation but discourage intrusion into sensitive habitat areas. Especially important was access for high school students who would use the marsh as a study area. To match this opportunity, the high school biology curriculum had to be modified to include the special opportunities for new field studies in wetland biology.

After a three-year effort, the plan was completed and presented to the city of Larkspur, its citizens, and the Coastal Conservancy for review. The plan was approved, and implementation funding from the Coastal Conservancy authorized. Work is now underway: dredging, planting, trail-building, fencing, and so on. Following the construction program, the marsh and its wildlife will be continuously monitored. Through this monitoring, local project participants will follow the progress of the marsh's rejuvenation. Students will be able to study the whole process of biological restoration as it proceeds, and the general public will be able to enjoy the blessings of some of the last open space available to them on the Bay shore.

Peter Grenell is the executive officer of the California State Coastal Conservancy.

18.9 SELECTED REFERENCES FOR FURTHER READING

Cowardin, L. M., et al. *Classification of Wetlands and Deepwater Habitats of the United States.* Washington, D.C.: U.S. Government Printing Office, 1979, 131 pp.

Frayer, W. E., et al. *Status and Trends of Wetlands and Deepwater Habitats in the Coterminous United States, 1950s to 1970s.* St. Petersburg, Fla.: Fish and Wildlife Service, U.S. Department of the Interior, 1983, 32 pp.

Mitsch, W. J., and Gosselink, J. G. *Wetlands.* New York: Van Nostrand, 1986, 539 pp.

National Wetlands Policy Forum. *Protecting America's Wetlands: An Action Agenda.* Washington, D.C.: Conservation Foundation, 1988, 69 pp.

Salvesen, David. *Wetlands: Mitigating and Regulating Development Impacts.* Washington, D.C.: Urban Land Institute, 1990, 117 pp.

Sather, J. H., and Smith, R. D. *An Overview of Major Wetland Functions and Values.* Washington, D.C.: Fish and Wildlife Service, U.S. Department of the Interior, 1984, 69 pp.

Tiner, R. W., Jr. *Wetlands of the United States: Current Status and Recent Trends.* Washington, D.C.: U.S. Government Printing Office, 1984, 59 pp.

U.S. Fish and Wildlife Service. *National Wetlands Priority Conservation Plan.* Washington, D.C.: U.S. Department of the Interior, 1989, 58 pp.

GLOSSARY

Acid rain Precipitation with pH levels much below average as a result of the integration of oxides in polluted air with moisture.

Active layer The surface layer in a permafrost environment, which is characterized by freezing and thawing on a seasonal basis.

Aggradation Filling in of a stream channel with sediment, usually associated with low discharges and/or heavy sediment loads.

Albedo The percentage of incident radiation reflected by a material. Usage in earth science is usually limited to shortwave radiation and landscape materials.

Alluvial fan A fan-shaped deposit of sediment laid down by a stream at the foot of a slope; very common features in dry regions, where streams deposit their sediment load as they lose discharge downstream.

Angiosperm A flowering, seed-bearing plant. The angiosperms are presently the principal vascular plants on earth.

Angle of repose The maximum angle at which a material can be inclined without failing. In civil engineering the term is used in reference to clayey materials.

Aquifer Any subsurface material that holds a relatively large quantity of ground-water and is able to transmit that water readily.

Atterberg Limits Test A test used to determine a soil's response to the addition of water based on its changes in the physical state, as from plastic to liquid.

Backscattering That part of solar radiation directed back into space as a result of diffusion by particles in the atmosphere.

Backshore The zone behind the shore—between the beach berm and the back-shore slope.

Backshore slope The bank or bluff landward of the shore that is comprised of *in situ* material.

Backswamps A low, wet area in the floodplain, often located behind a levee.

Bankfull discharge The flow of a river when the water surface has reached bank level.

Baseflow The portion of streamflow contributed by groundwater. It is a steady flow that is slow to change even during rainless periods.

Bay-mouth bar A ribbon of sand deposited across the mouth of a bay.

Berm A low mound that forms along sandy beaches; also used to describe elongated mounds constructed along water features and site borders.

Biomass The total weight of organic matter within a prescribed surface area, usually 1 square meter.

Bog A cool/cold climate wetland characterized by peat deposits, an acidic pH, and often a diverse plant cover.

Boreal forest Subarctic conifer forests of North America and Eurasia; floristically homogeneous forests dominated by fir, spruce, and tamarack. In Russia, it is called *taiga.*

Boundary layer The lower layer of the atmosphere; the lower 300 meters of the atmosphere where airflow is influenced by the earth's surface.

Boundary sublayer The stratum of calm air immediately over the ground which increases in depth with the height and density of the vegetative cover.

Bowen Ratio The ratio of sensible-heat flux to latent-heat flux between a surface and the atmosphere.

Buffer The zone around the perimeter of a wetland or lake where land use activities are limited in order to protect the water features.

Buildable land units Parcels of various size within a designated project area that are suitable for development as defined by a prescribed development program.

Capillarity The capacity of a soil to transfer water by capillary action; capillarity is greatest in medium-textured soils.

Carrying capacity   The level of development density or use an environment is able to support without suffering undesirable or irreversible degradation.

Choropleth map   A map comprised of areas of any size or shape representing qualitative phenomena (e.g., soils) or quantitative phenomena (e.g., population); often has a patchwork appearance.

Climate   The representative or general conditons of the atmosphere at a place on earth. It is more than the average conditions of the atmosphere, for climate may also include extreme and infrequent conditions.

Closed forest   A forest structure with multiple level of growth from the ground up; a forest in which undergrowth closes out the area between the canopy and the ground.

Coastal dune   A sand dune that forms in coastal areas and is fed by sand from the beach.

Coefficient of runoff   A number given to a type of ground surface representing the proportion of a rainfall converted to overland flow. It is a dimensionless number between 0 and 1.0 that varies inversely with the infiltration capacity; impervious surfaces have high coefficents of runoff.

Colluvium   An unsorted mix of soil and mass-movement debris.

Concentration time   The time taken for a drop of rain falling on the perimeter of a drainage basin to go through the basin to the outlet.

Conditional stability   A condition in the landscape in which stability is dependent on one or two essential factors, such as plants holding an oversteepened slope in place; also called metastability.

Conduction   A mechanism of heat transfer involving no external motion or mass transport. Instead, energy is transferred through the collision of vibrating molecules.

Conveyance zone   The central route of drainage, usually a channel and valley, in a drainage basin.

dBA   Decibel scale that has been adjusted for sensitivity of the human ear.

Decibel   Unit of measurement for the loudness of sound based on the pressure produced in air by a noise; denoted dB.

Declination of the sun   The location (latitude) on earth where the sun on any day is directly overhead; declinations range from 23.27°S latitude to 23.27° N latitude.

Degradation   Scouring and downcutting of a stream channel, usually associated with high discharges.

Density   *See* **Development density.**

Depression storage   Rainwater and overland flow held in shallow, low spots in the terrain.

Design storm   A rainstorm of a given intensity and frequency of recurrence used as the basis for sizing stormwater facilities such as stormsewers.

Detention   A strategy used in stormwater management in which runoff is detained on site to be released later at some prescribed rate.

Development density   A measure of the intensity of development or land use; defined on the basis of area covered by impervious surface, population density, or building floor area coverage, for example.

Discharge   The rate of water flow in a stream channel; measured as the volume of water passing through a cross-section of a stream per unit of time, commonly expressed as cubic feet (or meters) per second.

Discharge zone   An area where groundwater seepage and springs are concentrated.

Disturbance   An impact on the environment characterized by physical alteration such as forest clearing.

Diurnal damping depth   The maximum depth in the soil which experiences temperature change over a 24-hour (diurnal) period.

Drainage basin   The area that contributes runoff to a stream, river, or lake.

Drainage density   The number of miles (or km) of stream channels per square mile (or km^2) of land.

Drainage divide   The border of a drainage basin or watershed where overland separates between adjacent areas.

Drainage network   A system of stream channels usually connected in a hierarchical fashion. *See also* **Principle of stream orders.**

Drainfield   The network of pipes or tiles through which wastewater is dispersed into the soil.

Ecosystem   A group of organisms linked together by a flow energy; also a community of organisms and their environment.

Ecotone   The transition zone between two groups, or zones, of vegetation.

Emergent wetland   Wetland dominated by herbaceous vegetation growing in shallow water.

Energy balance   The concept or model that concerns the relationship among energy input, energy storage, work, and energy output of a system such as the atmosphere or oceans.

Environmental assessment   A preliminary study or review of a proposed action (project) and the influence it could have on the environment; often conducted to determine the need for more detailed environmental impact analysis.

Environmental impact statement   A study required by U.S. federal law for projects (proposed) involving federal funds to determine types and magnitudes of impacts that would be expected in the natural and human environment and the alternative courses of action, including no action.

Environmental inventory   Compilation and classification of data and information on the natural and human features in an area proposed for some sort of planning project.

Ephemeral stream   A stream without baseflow; one that flows only during or after rainstorms or snowmelt events.

Erodibility   The relative susceptibility of a soil to erosion.

Erodibility factor   A value used in the universal soil loss equation for different soil types representing relative erodibility; called the *K*-factor by the U.S. Soil Conservation Service.

Erosion   The removal of rock debris by an agency such as moving water, wind, or glaciers; generally, the sculpting or wearing down of the land by erosional agents.

Estuarine wetland   Coastal wetlands associated with bays and estuaries of the ocean.

Eutrophication   The increase of biomass of a waterbody leading to infilling of the basin and the eventual disappearance of open water; sometimes referred to as the aging process of a waterbody.

Evapotranspiration   The loss of water from the soil through evaporation and transpiration.

Exchange time   See Residence time.

Facility   Any part of the built environment, especially structures and mechanical systems.

Facility planning   Planning for facilities such as power-generating stations or sewage treatment plants; usually carried out by engineers.

Feasibility study   A type of technical planning aimed at identifying the most appropriate use of a site.

Fetch   The distance of open water in one direction across a waterbody; one of the main controls of wave size.

Floodway fringe   The zone designated by U.S. federal flood policy as the area in a river valley that would be lightly inundated by the 100-year flood.

Floristic system   The principal botanical classification scheme in use today. Under this scheme the plant kingdom is made up of divisions, each of which is subdivided into smaller and smaller groups arranged according to the apparent evolutionary relationships among plants.

Formation   A structural unit of vegetation that may be considered a subdivision of a biochore; a formation may be made up of several communities. In the traditional terminology, it is called a physiognomic unit; in geology, a major unit of rock.

Frequency   The term used to express how often a specified event is equaled or exceeded.

Frost wedging   A mechanical weathering process in which water freezes in a crack and exerts force on the rock, which may result in the breaking of the rock; a very effective weathering process in alpine and polar environments.

Geographic information system (GIS)   Computer mapping system designed for ready applications in problems involving overlapping and complex distributional patterns.

Geomorphic system   A physical system comprised of an assemblage of landform linked together by the flow of water, air, or ice.

Geomorphology   The field of earth science that studies the origin and distribution of landforms, with special emphasis on the nature of erosional processes; traditionally, a field shared by geography and geology.

Global coordinate system   The network of east-west and north-south lines (parallels and meridians) used to measure locations on earth; the system uses degrees, minutes, and seconds as the units of measurement.

Grafting   The practice of attaching additional channels to a drainage network. In agricultural areas new channels appear as drainage ditches; in urban areas, as stormsewers.

Gravity water   Subsurface water that responds to the gravitational force; the water that percolates through the soil to become groundwater.

Greenbelt   A tract of trees and associated vegetation in urbanized areas; may be a park, nature preserve, or part of a transportation corridor.

Groin   A wall or barrier built from the beach into the surf zone for the purpose of slowing down longshore transport and holding sand.

Gross sediment transport   The total quantity of sediment transported along a shoreline in some time period, usually a year.

Ground frost   Frost that penetrates the ground in response to freezing surface temperatures.

Ground sun angle   The angle formed between a beam of solar radiation and the surface that it strikes in the landscape.

Groundwater   The mass of gravity water that occupies the subsoil and upper bedrock zone; the water occupying the zone of saturation below the soil-water zone.

Gullying   Soil erosion characterized by the formation of narrow, steep-sided channels etched by rivulets or small streams of water. Gullying can be one of the most serious forms of soil erosion of cropland.

Habitat   The environment with which an organism interacts and from which it gains its resources. Habitat is often variable in size, content, and location, changing with the phases in an organism's life cycle.

Hardpan   A hardened soil layer characterized by the accumulation of colloids and ions.

Hazard assessment   Study and evaluation of the hazard to land use and people from environmental threats such as floods, tornadoes, and earthquakes.

Heat island   The area or patch of relatively warm air which develops over urbanized areas.

Heat syndrome   Various disorders in the human thermoregulatory system brought on by the body's inability to shed heat or by a chemical imbalance from too much sweating.

Heat transfer   The flow of heat within a substance or the exchange of heat between substances by means of conduction, convection, or radiation.

Hillslope processes   The geomorphic processes that erode and shape slopes; mainly mass movements such as soil creep and landslides and runoff processes such as rainwash and gullying.

Horizon   A layer in the soil that originates from the differentiation of particles and chemicals by moisture movement within the soil column.

Hydraulic gradient   The rate of change in elevation (slope) of a groundwater surface such as the watertable.

Hydraulic radius   The ratio of the cross-sectional area of a stream to its wetted perimeter.

Hydric soil   Soil characterized by wet conditions; saturated most of the year; often organic in composition.

Hydrograph   A streamflow graph that shows the change in discharge over time, usually hours or days. *See also* **Hydrograph method.**

Hydrograph method   A means of forecasting streamflow by constructing a hydrograph that shows the representative response of a drainage basin to a rainstorm; the use of "normalized" hydrograph for flow forecasting in which the size of the individual storm is filtered out. *See also* **Hydrograph.**

Hydrologic cycle   The planet's water system, described by the movement of water from the oceans to the atmosphere to the continents and back to the sea.

Hydrologic equation   The amount of surface runoff (overland flow) from any parcel of ground is proportional to precipitation minus evapotranspiration loss, plus or minus changes in storage water (groundwater and soil water).

Hydrometer method   A technique used to measure the clay content in a soil sample that involves dispersing the clay particles in water and drawing off samples at prescribed time intervals.

Hypothermia   A physiological disorder associated with cold conditions and characterized by the decline of body temperature, slowed heartbeat, lowered blood pressure, and other symptoms.

Impervious cover   Any hard surface material such as asphalt or concrete which limits infiltration and induces high runoff rates.

Infiltration capacity   The rate at which a ground material takes in water through the surface; measured in inches or centimeters per minute or hour.

Inflooding   Flooding caused by overland flow concentrating in a low area.

Infrared film   Photographic film capable of recording near infrared radiation (just beyond the visible to a wavelength of 0.9 micrometer), but not capable of recording thermal infrared wavelengths.

Infrared radiation   Mainly longwave radiation of wavelengths between 3.0–4.0 and 100 micrometer, but also includes near infrared radiation, which occurs at wavelengths between 0.7 and 3.0–4.0 micrometers.

In situ   A term used to indicate that a substance is in place as contrasted with one, such as river sediment, that is in transit.

Interception   The process by which vegetation intercepts rainfall or snow before it reaches the ground.

Interflow   Infiltration water that moves laterally in the soil and seeps into stream channels. In forested areas this water is a major source of stream discharge.

Isopleth map   A map comprised of lines, called isolines, that connect points of equal value.

Lacustrine wetland   Wetland associated with standing waterbodies such as ponds, lakes, and reservoirs.

Land cover   The materials such as vegetation and concrete that cover the ground. *See also* **Land use.**

Landscape   The composite of natural and human features that characterize the surface of the land at the base of the atmosphere; includes spatial, textural, compositional, and dynamic aspects of the land.

Landscape design   The process of laying out land uses, facilities, water features, vegetation, and related features and displaying the results in maps and drawings.

Landscape planning   The decision making, technical, and design processes associated with the determination of land uses and the utilization of terrestrial resources.

Landslide   A type of mass movement characterized by the slippage of a body of material over a rupture plane; often a sudden and rapid movement.

Land use   The human activities that characterize an area, for example, agricultural, industrial, and residential.

Latent heat   The heat released or absorbed when a substance changes phase as from liquid to gas. For water at 0°C, heat is absorbed or released at a rate of 2.5 million joules per kilogram (597 calories per gram) in the liquid/vapor phase change.

Leachate   Fluids that emanate from decomposing waste in a sanitary or chemical landfill.

Leaching   The removal of minerals in solution from a soil; the washing out of ions from one level to another in the soil.

Levee   A mound of sediment that builds up along a river bank as a result of flood deposition.

Life form   The form of individual plants or the form of the individual organs of a plant. In general, the overall structure of the vegetative cover may be thought of as life form as well.

Lineament   Straight features in the landscape marked by slopes segments of stream channels, soil patterns, or vegetation.

Line scanner   A remote sensing device that records signals of reflected radiation in scan lines that sweep perpendicular to the path (flight line) of the aircraft.

Littoral drift   The material that is moved by waves and currents in coastal areas.

Littoral transport   The movement of sediment along a coastline. It is comprised of two components: longshore transport and onshore–offshore transport.

Loess   Silt deposits laid down by wind over extensive areas of the midlatitudes during glacial and postglacial times.

Longshore current   A current that moves parallel to the shoreline. Velocities generally range between 0.25 and 1 m/sec.

Longshore transport   The movement of sediment parallel to the coast.

Magnetic declination   The deviation in degrees east or west between magnetic north and true north.

Manning formula   A formula used to determine the velocity of streamflow based on the gradient, hydraulic radius, and roughness of the channel; an empirical formula widely used in engineering for sizing channels and pipes.

Marsh   A wetland dominated by herbaceous plants, typically cattails, reeds, and rushes.

Mass balance   The relative balance in a system, based on the input and output of material such as sediment or water; the state of equilibrium between the input and output of mass in a system.

Mass movement A type of hillslope process characterized by the downslope movement of rock debris under the force of gravity; includes soil creep, rock fall, landslides, and mudflows; also termed *mass wasting*.

Meander A bend or loop in a stream channel.

Meander belt The width of the train of active meanders in a river valley.

Metastability See Conditional stability.

Microclimate The climate of small spaces such as an inner city, residential area, or mountain valley.

Mitigation A measure used to lessen the impact of an action on the environment.

Model Any device including conceptual constructs, mathematical formulas, or hardware apparatus, used in problem solving and analysis.

Montmorillonite A type of clay that is notable for its capacity to shrink and expand with wetting and drying.

Moraine The Material deposited directly by a glacier; also, the material (load) carried in or on a glacier. As landforms, moraines usually have hilly or rolling topography.

Mudflow A type of mass movement characterized by the downslope flow of a saturated mass of clayey material.

Nearshore circulation cell The circulation pattern of water and sediment formed by the combined action of rip currents, waves, and longshore currents.

Net sediment transport The balance between the quantities of sediment moved in two (opposite) directions along a shoreline.

Nonpoint source Water pollution that emanates from a spatially diffuse source such as the atmosphere or agricultural land.

Nutrients Various types of materials that become dissolved in water and induce plant growth. Phosphorus and nitrogen are two of the most effective nutrients in aquatic plants.

Ogallala Aquifer The largest aquifer in North America stretching from Nebraska to Texas.

Open forest A forest structure with a strong upper one or two stories and limited undergrowth; a forest that is largely open at ground level.

Open space Term applied to underdeveloped land, usually land designated for parks, greenbelts, water features, nature preserves and the like.

Open system A system characterized by a throughflow of material and/or energy; a system to which energy or material is added and released over time.

Opportunities and constraints A type of study often carried out in planing projects to determine the principal advantages and drawbacks to a development program proposed for a particular site.

Outflooding Flooding caused by a stream or river overflowing its banks.

Outwash plain A fluvioglacial deposit comprised of sand and gravel with a flat or gently sloping surface; usually found in close association with moraines.

Overdraft A condition of groundwater withdrawal in which the safe aquifer yield has been exceeded and the aquifer is being depleted.

Overland flow Runoff from surfaces on which the intensity of precipitation or snowmelt exceeds the infiltration capacity; also called Horton overland flow, for hydrologist Robert E. Horton.

Oxbow A crescent-shaped lake or pond in a river valley formed in an abandoned segment of channel.

Ozone One of the minor gases of the atmosphere; a pungent, irritating form of oxygen that performs the important function of absorbing ultraviolet radiation.

Palustrine wetland   Wetlands associated with inland sites which are not dependent on stream, lake, or oceanic water.

Parallels   The east-west-running lines of the global coordinate system. The equator, the Arctic Circle, and the Antarctic Circle are parallels; all parallels run parallel to one another.

Parent material   The particulate material in which a soil forms. The two types of parent material are *residual* and *transported.*

Passive solar collector   A solar collector that operates without the aid of powered machinery.

Peak annual flow   The largest discharge produced by a stream or river in a given year.

Peak discharge   The maximum flow of a stream or river in response to an event such as a rainstorm or over a period of time such as a year.

Peak flow. *See* **Peak discharge.**

Pedon   The smallest geographic unit of soil defined by soil scientists of the U.S. Department of Agriculture.

Percolation rate   The rate at which water moves into soil through the walls of a test pit; used to determine soil suitability for wastewater disposal.

Percolation test   A soil-permeability test performed in the field to determine the suitability of a material for wastewater disposal; the test most commonly used by sanitarians and planners to size soil-absorption systems.

Perennial stream   A stream that receives inflow of groundwater all year; a stream that has a permanent baseflow.

Performance concept   The concept of setting standards on how an environment or land use is expected to perform; includes formulation of goals, standards, and controls.

Periglacial environment   An area where frost-related processes are a major force in shaping the landscape.

Permafrost   A ground-heat condition in which the soil or subsoil is permanently frozen; long-term frozen ground in periglacial environments.

Permeability   The rate at which soil or rock transmits groundwater (or gravity water in the area above the watertable); measured in cubic feet (or meters) of water transmitted through a specified cross-sectional area when under a hydraulic gradient of 1 foot per 1 foot (or 1 m per 1 m).

Photopair   A set of overlapping aerial photographs that are used in stereoscopic interpretation of aerial photographs.

Photosynthesis   The process by which green plants synthesize water and carbon dioxide and, with the energy from absorbed light, convert it into plant materials in the form of sugar and carbohydrates.

Physiography   A term from physical geography traditionally used to describe the composite character of the landscape over large regions; today used mainly in planning and landscape architecture to describe the physical, mainly natural, character of a site or planning region.

Piping   The formation of horizontal tunnels in a soil due to sapping that is, erosion by seepage water. Piping often occurs in areas where gullying is or was active and is limited to soils resistant to cave-in.

Plane coordinate system   A grid coordinate system designed by the U.S. National Ocean Survey in which the basic unit is a square measuring 10,000 feet on a side.

Planned unit development (PUD)   A planning strategy aimed at reducing urban sprawl and related impacts by clustering development into carefully planned units.

Plant production   The rate of output of organic material by a plant; the total amount of organic matter added to the landscape over some period of time, usually measured in grams per square meter per day or year.

Plume   The stream of exhaust (smoke) emanating from a stack or chimney.

Point source   Water pollution that emanates from a single source such as a sewage plant outfall.

Pollutant loading   The amount of pollution released to runoff from different land uses measured in pounds or kilograms per acre or square kilometer.

Pollution   Contamination of the environment from foreign substances or from increased levels of natural substances.

Porosity   The total volume of pore (void) space in a given volume of rock or soil; expressed as the percentage of void volume to the total volume of the soil or rock sample.

Primary productivity   The total amount of organic matter added to the landscape by plant photosynthesis, usually measured in grams per square meter per day or year.

Principal point   The center of an aerial photograph, located at the intersection of lines drawn from the fiducial marks on the photo margin.

Principle of limiting factors   The biological principle that the maximum obtainable rate of photosynthesis is limited by whichever basic resource of plant growth is in least supply.

Principle of stream orders   The relationship between stream order and the number of streams per order. The relationship for most drainage nets is an inverse one, characterized by many low-order streams and fewer and fewer streams with increasingly higher orders. *See also* **Stream order.**

Progradation   The process of seaward growth of a shoreline.

Pruning   In hydrology the cutting back of a drainage net by diverting or burying streams; usually associated with urbanization or agricultural development.

Quadrat sampling   A field sampling technique in which small plots, called quadrats, are laid out in the landscape and from which the sample is drawn.

Radiation   The process by which radiant (electromagnetic) energy is transmitted through free space; the term used to describe electromagnetic energy, as in infrared radiation or shortwaves radiation.

Radiation beam   The column of solar radiation flowing into or through the atmosphere.

Rainfall erosion index   A set of values representing the computed erosive power of rainfall based on total rainfall and the maximum intensity of the 30-minute rainfall.

Rainfall intensity   The rate of rainfall measured in inches or centimeters of water deposited on the surface per hour or minute.

Rainshadow   The dry zone on the leeward side of a mountain range of orographic precipitation.

Rainsplash   Soil erosion from the impact of raindrops.

Rainwash   Soil erosion by overland flow; erosion by sheeets of water running over a surface; usually occurs in association with rainsplash; also called *wash.*

Rating curve   A graph that shows the relationship between the discharge and stage of various flow events on a river. Once this relationship is established, it may be used to approximate discharge using stage data alone.

Rational method   A method of computing the discharge from a small drainage basin in response to a given rainstorm. Computation is based on the coefficient of runoff, rainfall intensity, and basin area.

Recharge   The replenishment of groundwater with water from the surface.

Recharge zone   An area where groundwater recharge is concentrated.

Recurrence   The number of years on the average that separate events of a specific magnitude, for example, the average number of years separating river discharges of a given magnitude or greater.

Regime   The characteristic pattern of a process or system over time as in the seasonal regime of streamflow or the wet/dry regime of precipitation in California.

Regulatory floodway   A zone designated by the U.S. federal flood policy as the lowest part of the floodplain where the deepest and most frequent floodflows are conducted.

Relief   The range of topographic elevation within a prescribed area.

Residence time   The time taken to exchange the water in an aquifer or a lake for new water. Also called exchange time.

Retention   A strategy used in stormwater management in which runoff is retained on site in basins, underground, or released into the soil.

Riparian wetland   Wetland that form on the edge of a major water feature such as a lake or stream.

Rip current   A relatively narrow jet of water that flows seaward through the breaking waves. It serves as a release for water that builds up near shore.

Riprap   Rubble such as broken concrete and rock placed on a surface to stabilize it and reduce erosion.

Riverine wetland   Wetlands associated with streams and stream channels.

Runoff   In the broadcast sense the flow of water from the land as both surface and subsurface discharge; in the more restricted and common use, surface discharge in the form of overland flow and channel flow.

Safe well yield   The maximum pumping rate that can be sustained by a well with lowering the water level below the pump intake.

Sapping   An erosional process that usually accompanies gullying in which soil particles are eroded by water seeping from a bank.

Scatter diagram   A graph characterized by a series of plotted points showing the relationship between two quantitative variables.

Scattering   The process by which minute particles suspended in the atmosphere diffuse incoming solar radiation.

Scrub-scrub wetland   Wetland dominated by shrubs and short trees.

Sediment sink   A coastal environment that favors the massive accumulation of sediment.

Seepage   The process by which groundwater or interflow water seeps from the ground.

Sensible heat   Heat that raises the temperature of a substance and thus can be sensed with a thermometer. In contrast to latent heat, it is sometimes called the heat of dry air.

Sensitive environment   Special environments such as wetlands or coastal lands that require protection from development because of their aesthetic and ecological value.

Septic system   Specifically, a sewage system that relies on a septic tank to store and/or treat wastewater; generally, an on-site (small-scale) sewage-disposal system that depends on the soil to dispose of wastewater.

Septic tank   A vat, usually placed underground, used to store wastewater.

Setback   A term used in site planning to indicate the critical distance that a structure or facility should be separated from an edge such as a backshore slope or lake shore.

Shoreland   The discontinuous belt of land around a waterbody that is not drained via stream basins.

Side-looking airborne radar   The radar system used in remote sensing; so named because the energy pulse is beamed obliquely on the landscape from the side of the aircraft.

Sieve method   A technique used to separate the various sizes of coarse particles in a soil sample.

SLAR   *See* **Side-looking airborne radar.**

Slope failure   A slope that is unable to maintain itself and fails by mass movement such as a landslide, slump, or similar movement.

Slope form   The configuration of a slope, for example, convex, concave, or straight.

Sluiceway   A large drainage channel or spillway for glacier meltwater.

Slump   A type of mass movement characterized by a back rotational motion along a rupture plane.

Small circle   Any circle drawn on the globe that represents less than the full circumference of the earth. Thus the plane of a small circle does not pass through the center of the earth. All parallels except the equator are small circles.

Soil-absorption system   Small-scale wastewater disposal system that relies directly on soil to absorb and disperse sewage water from a house or larger building.

Soil creep   A type of mass movement characterized by a very slow downslope displacement of soil, generally without fracturing of the soil mass. The mechanisms of soil creep include freeze-thaw activity and wetting and drying cycles.

Soil-forming factors   The major factors responsible for the formation of a soil: climate, parent material, vegetation, topography, and drainage.

Soil-heat flux   The rate of heat flow into, from, or through the soil.

Soil material   Any sediment rock, or organic debris in which soil formation takes place.

Soil profile   The sequence of horizons, or layers, of a soil.

Soil structure   The term given to the shape of the aggregates of particles that form in a soil. Four main structures are recognized: blocky, platy, granular, and prismatic.

Soil texture   The cumulative sizes of particles in a soil sample; defined as the percentage by weight of sand, silt and clay-sized particles in a soil.

Solar constant   The rate at which solar radiation is received on a surface (perpendicular to the radiation) at the edge of the atmosphere. Average strength is 1372 joules/m^2 · sec, which can also be stated as 1.97 cal/cm^2 · min.

Solar gain   A general term used to indicate the amount of solar radiation absorbed by a surface or setting in the landscape.

Solar heating   The process of generating heat from absorbed solar radiation; a widely used term in the solar energy literature.

Solifluction   A type of mass movement in periglacial environments, characterized by the slow flowage of soil material and the formation of lobeshaped features; prevalent in tundra and alpine landscapes.

Solstice   The dates when the declination of the sun is at 23.27°N latitude (the Tropic of Cancer) and 23.27°S latitude (the Tropic of Capricorn)—June 21-22 and December 21-22, respectively. These dates are known as the winter and summer solstices, but which is which depends on the hemisphere.

State plane coordinate system   *See* **Plane coordinate system.**

Stereoscope   A viewing device used to gain a three-dimensional image from a photopair.

Stormflow   The portion of streamflow that reaches the stream relatively quickly after a rainstorm, adding a surcharge of water to baseflow.

Stratified sampling   A sampling technique in which the population or study area is dividedd into sets or subareas before drawing the sample.

Stream order   The relative position, or rank, of a stream in a drainage network. Streams without tributaries, usually the small ones, are first-order; streams with two or more first-order tributaries are second-order, and so on.

Subarctic zone   The belt of latitude between 55° and the Arctic and Antarctic circles.

Subbasin   A small drainage basin within the watershed of a lake or impoundment.

Sun angle   The angle formed between the beam of incoming solar radiation and a plane at the earth's surface or a plane of the same altitude anywhere in the atmosphere.

Sun pocket   A small space designed especially to take advantage of solar radiation and heating.

Surficial wetland   A wetland originating from impaired local drainage, usually surface or near surface runoff.

Surge   A large and often destructive wave caused by intensive atmospheric pressure and strong winds.

Suspended load   The particles (sediment) carried aloft in a stream of wind by turbulent flow; usually clay- and silt-sized particles.

Swamp   A wetland dominated by trees and/or shrubs. There are many varieties including cypress, mangrove, and conifer.

Taxon   Any unit (category) of classification system, usually biological.

Technical planning   Data collection, analysis, and related activities used in support of the decision-making process in planning.

Temperate forest   A forest of the midlatitude regions that could be described as climatically temperate, for example, broadleaf deciduous forests of Europe and North America, comprised of beeches, maples, and oaks.

Temperature inversion   An atmospheric condition in which the cold air underlies warm air. Inversions are highly stable conditions and thus not conducive to atmopsheric mixing.

Thermal gradient   The change in temperature over distance in a substance; usually expressed in degrees Celsius per centimeter or meter.

Thermal infrared system   Line scanner capable of recording thermal infrared energy at wavelengths of 3–5 and 8–14 micrometers.

Threshold   The level of magnitude of a process at which sudden or rapid change is initiated.

Tolerance   The range of stress or disturbance a plant is able to withstand without damage or death.

Topsoil   The uppermost of the soil, characterized by a high organic content; the organic layer of the soil.

Township and range   A system of land subdivision in the United States which uses a grid to classify land units. Standard subdivisions include townships and sections.

Transect sampling   A field sampling technique in which the sample is drawn from strips or transects laid out across the study area.

Transmission   The lateral flow of groundwater through an aquifer; measured in terms of cubic feet (or meters) transmitted through a given cross-sectional area per hour or day.

Transpiration   The flow of water through the tissue of a plant and into the atmosphere via stomatal openings in the foliage.

Transported soil   Soil formed in parent material comprised of deposits laid down by water, wind, or glaciers.

Tree line   The upper limit of tree growth on a mountain where forest often gives way to alpine meadow.

Tundra   Landscape of cold regions, characterized by a light cover of herbaceous plants and underlain by permafrost.

Turbidity   A measure of the clearness or transparency of water as a function of suspended sediment.

Turbulent flow   Flow characterized by mixing motion in which the primary source of flow resistance is the mixing action between slow-moving and faster-moving molecules in a fluid.

Universal Soil Loss Equation   A formula for estimating soil erosion by runoff based on rainfall, plant cover, slope, and soil erodibility.

Urban boundary layer   A general term referring to the layer of air over a city that is strongly influenced by urban activities and forms.

Urban canyon   City street lined with tall buildings; an urban terrain feature that has a pronounced effect on airflow, radiation, and microclimate as a whole.

Urban climate   The climate in and around urban areas, it is usually somewhat warmer, foggier, and less well lighted than the climate of the surrounding region.

Urban design   An area of professional activity by architects, landscape architects, and urban planners dealing with the forms, materials, and activities of cities.

Urbanization   The term used to describe the process of urban development, including suburban residential and commerical development.

Vascular plants   Plants in which cells are arranged into a pipelike system of conducting, or vascular, tissue. Xylem and phloem are the two main types of vasular tissue.

Water table   The upper boundary of the zone of groundwater. In fine-textured materials it is usually a transition zone rather than a boundary line. The configuration of the watertable often approximates that of the overlying terrain.

Wave refraction   The bending of a wave, which results in an approach angle more perpendicular to the shoreline.

Wavelength   The distance from the crest of one wave to the crest of the next wave.

Wetland   A term generally applied to an area where the ground is permanently wet or wet most of the year and is occupied by water-loving (or tolerant) vegetation such as cattails, mangrove, or cypress.

Wetted perimeter   The distance from one side of a stream to the other, measured along the bottom.

Windshield survey   A rapid and general sampling method for vegetation and land use based on observations from a moving automobile.

Zenith   For any location on earth, the point that is directly overhead to an observer. The zenith position of the sun is the one directly overhead.

Zenith angle   The angle formed between a line perpendicular to the earth's surface (at any location) and the beam of incoming solar radiation (on any date).

APPENDIX A

U.S. AND CANADIAN SOIL CLASSIFICATION SYSTEMS

Table A.1 USDA Comprehensive System (Orders and Suborders)

Order	Outline Description	Rapid Recognition Characteristics	Suborders	
Alfisols	Argillic horizon present; base content moderate to high	All mineral horizons present except oxic	With gleying	Aqualfs
			Others in cold climates	Boralfs
			Others in humid climates	Udalfs
			Others in subhumid climates	Ustalfs
			Others in subarid climates	Xeralfs
Aridisols	Semidesert and desert soils	Ochric or argillic horizon present, no oxic or spodic horizon; usually dry	With argillic horizon	Argids
			Others	Orthids
Entisols	Weakly developed, usually azonal	No diagnostic horizon except ochric, anthropic, albic, or agric	With gleying	Aquents
			With strong artificial disturbance	Arents
			On alluvial deposits	Fluvents
			With sandy or loamy texture	Psamments
			Others	Orthents
Histosols	Developed in organic materials	30% or more organic matter	Rarely saturated, 75% fibric	Folists
			Usually saturated, 75% fibric	Fibrists
			Usually saturated, partly decomposed	Hemists
			Usually saturated, highly decomposed	Saprists
Inceptisols	Moderately developed; not listed elsewhere	Cambic or histic horizon present; no argillic, natric, oxic, or petrocalcic horizon, no plinthite	With gleying	Aquepts
			On volcanic ash	Andepts
			In tropical climates	Tropepts
			With umbric epipedon	Umbrepts
			With plaggen epipedon	Plaggepts
			Others	Ochrepts
Mollisols	With dark A horizon and high base status	Mollic horizon present; no oxic horizon	With albic argillic horizon	Albolls
			With gleying	Aquolls
			On highly calcareous materials	Rendolls
			Others in cold climates	Borolls
			Others in humid climates	Udolls
			Others in subhumid climates	Ustolls
			Others in subarid climates	Xerolls
Oxisols	With oxic horizon	Oxic horizon present	With gleying	Aquox
			With humic A horizon	Humox
			Others in humid climates	Orthox
			Others in drier climates	Ustox
			Usually dry	Torrox
Order	Outline Description	Rapid Recognition Characteristics	Suborders	
Spodosols	With spodic horizon	Spodic horizon present	With gleying	Aquods
			With little humus in spodic horizon	Ferrods
			With little iron in spodic horizon	Humids
			With iron and humus	Orthods

(Continued)

Table A.1 (*Continued*)

Order	Outline Description	Rapid Recognition Characteristics	Suborders	
Utisols	Argillic horizon present; base status low	Mean annual temperature 8°C or above; soils not listed elsewhere	With gleying With humic A horizon In humid climates Others in subhumid climates Others in subarid climates	Aquults Humults Udults Ustults Xerults
Vertisols	Cracking clay soils	30% or more clay, with gilgai or other signs of up-and-down movement	Usually moist Dry for short periods Dry for long periods Usually dry	Uderts Usterts Xererts Torrerts

Mountain Soils These vary greatly over short distances; with many steep slopes.

Table A.2 Canadian Soil Classification System (Orders and Great Groups)

Order, Great Group	General Description
Chernozemic Brown Dark brown Black Dark gray	Soils of the semiarid and subhumid grasslands of the Manitoba, Saskatchewan, and Albert. Typically, rich organic accumulation in A horizon and parent material made up principally of silt and clay deposits. Calcium carbonate content is high, and pH is consistently above 7. Soils support the great wheat-growing area of Canada.
Solonetzic Solonetz Solodized solonetz Solod	Soils developed in salinized material mainly within the area of chernozemic soils of the Interior Plains. Very limited geographic coverage (less than 1 percent of Canada) and low agricultural potential owing to the abundant salt.
Luvisolic Gray brown luvisol Gray luvisol	Soils with silicate clay accumulation in the B horizon and fairly strong organic accumulation in A horizon. Found in forested areas and in loamy glacial deposits originally of calcareous composition. In southern Ontario and Quebec, they have been extensively cultivated.
Podzolic Humic podzol Ferro-humic podzol Humo-ferric podzol	Soils with a strong B horizon comprised of iron and aluminum oxides. Characterized by heavy leaching favored by humid climate and sandy parent material. A horizon usually contains significant organic accumulation. Found throughout Canada, covering a total of 15.6 percent of the country.
Brunisolic Melanic brunisol Eutric brunisol Sombric brunisol Dystric brunisol	Soils with a brownish-colored B horizon and a substantial organic accumulation in the A horizon. They form under forest covers in the humid subarctic of northern British Columbia and southern Yukon. Often rocky and thin with a pH around 5–6.
Regosolic Regosol Humic regosol	Soils of recent sandy deposits and active geomorphic environments. Horizons are absent or very weak. They are found with all sorts of climates and vegetation.
Gleysolic Humic gleysol Gleysol Luvic gleysol	Soils of mineral composition that are saturated all or part of the year and characterized by reducing conditions. Gleyed horizons of gray or bluish color are a common trait. Occur in all regions as poorly drained counterpart of other soils.

(*Continued*)

Table A.2 (*Continued*)

Order, Great Group	General Description
Organic Fibrisol Mesisol Humisol Folisol	Soils composed of largely organic matter. Found in areas of prolonged saturation and swamp and bog vegetation. Most are underlain by permafrost; located in large area on southern Hudson Bay and prominent within areas of luvisols.
Cryosolic Turbic cryosol Static cryosol Organic cryyosol	Soils with permafrost within 1–2 m of surface and mean annual soil temperature under 0°C. Vegetation and texture are highly variable; surface drainage is often poor, and frost action induces mechanical mixing of the active layer. The most extensive soil order in Canada, covering 40 percent of the country.

Source: The Canadian System of Soil Classification, Ottawa, 1978.

Table A.3 Unified Soil Classification System

Letter	Description	Criterion	Further Criteria
G	Gravel and gravelly soils (basically pebble size, larger than 2 mm diameter)	Texture	Based on uniformity of grain size and the presence of smaller materials such as clay and silt
S	Sand and sandy soils	Texture	W Well graded (uniformly sized grains) and clean (absence of clays, silts, and organic debris)
			C Well graded with clay fraction, which binds soil together
			P Poorly graded, fairly clean
M	Very fine sand and salt (inorganic)	Texture; composition	Based on performance criteria of compressibility and plasticity
C	Clays (inorganic)	Texture; composition	L Low to medium compressibility and low plasticity
O	Organic silts and clays	Texture; composition	H High compressibility and high plasticity
P_t	Peat	Composition	

APPENDIX B

U.S. RAW SURFACE WATER STANDARDS FOR PUBLIC WATER SUPPLIES

	Surface-Water Criteria, mg/liter	
Substance	*Permissive Criteria*	*Desirable Criteria*
Coliforms (MPN)	10,000	<100
Fecal Coliforms (MPN)	2,000	<20
Inorganic chemicals (mg/l)		
Ammonia-N	0.5	<0.01
Arsenic[a]	0.05	Absent
Barium[a]	1.0	Absent
Boron[a]	1.0	Absent
Cadmium[a]	0.01	Absent
Chloride[a]	250	250
Chromium[a] (hexavalent)	0.05	Absent
Copper[a]	1.0	Virtually absent
Dissolved oxygen	≥4	Near saturation
Iron	0.3	Virtually absent
Lead[a]	0.05	Absent
Manganese[a]	0.05	Absent
Nitrate[a]−N	10	Virtually absent
Selenium[a]	0.01	Absent
Silver[a]	0.05	Absent
Sulfate[a]	250	<50
Total dissolved solids[a]	500	<200
Urany ion[a]	5	Absent
Zinc[a]	5	Virtually absent
Organic chemicals (mg/l)		
ABS		
Carbon chloroform extract[a]	0.15	<0.04
Cyanide[a]	0.20	Absent
Herbicides		
2,4 − D + 2,4,5 − T + 2,4 − TP[a]	0.1	Absent
Oil and gases[a]	Virtually absent	Absent
Pesticides[a]		
Adrian	0.017	Absent
Chlordane	0.003	Absent
DDT	0.042	Absent
Dieldrin	0.017	Absent
Endrin	0.001	Absent
Heptachlor	0.018	Absent
Lindane	0.056	Absent
Methoxychlor	0.035	Absent
Toxaphene	0.005	Absent
Phenols[a]	0.001	Absent

[a]Substances that are not significantly affected by the following treatment process: coagulation (less than about 50 mg/liter of alum, ferric sulfate, or copperas, with alkali addition as necessary but without coagulant aids or activated carbon), sedimentation (6 hours or less), rapid sand filtration (3 gpm/ft² or less), and disinfection with chlorine (without consideration to concentration or form of chlorine residual).

Source: "Raw Water Quality Criteria for Public Supplies," National Technical Advisory Committee Report (U.S. Department of the Interior, issued by the Federal Water Pollution Control Administration, 1968).

APPENDIX C

U.S. NATIONAL AIR QUALITY STANDARDS

Pollutant	Primary Standard, Micrograms Per Cubic Meter	Secondary Standard, Micrograms Per Cubic Meter
Particulate Matter		
Annual geometric mean	75	60
Maximum 24-hour concentration[a]	260	150
Sulfur Oxides		
Annual arithmetic mean	80 (0.03 ppm)	—
Max. 24-hour concentration[a]	365 (0.14 ppm)	—
Max. 3-hour concentration[a]	—	1,300 (0.5 ppm)
Carbon Monoxide		
Max. 8-hour concentration[a]	10 (9 ppm)	10
Max. 1-hour concentration[a]	40 (35 ppm)	40
Ozone		
Max. hourly avg. concentration[a]	235 (0.12 ppm)	235
Nitrogen Dioxide		
Annual arithmetic mean	100 (0.05 ppm)	100
Hydrocarbons		
Max. 3-hour concentration[a]	160 (0.24 ppm)	160
(6–9 A.M.)	160 (0.24 ppm)	160
Lead		
Max. arithmetic means (average over calendar quarter)	1.5	1.5

[a] Not to be exceeded more than once a year per site.

Note: ppm indicates parts of pollutant per million parts of air.

Source: Environmental Protection Agency Regulations on National Primary and Secondary Ambient Air Quality Standards.

APPENDIX D
U.S. NOISE STANDARDS

Table D.1   EPA Noise Criteria and Standards and Risks

Sound Levels (decibels)	Source	Risk from Exposure
140	Jet engine (25 m distance)	Harmful to hearing
130	Jet takeoff (100 m away)	
	Threshold of pain	
120	Propeller aircraft	
110	Live rock band	Chance of hearing loss
100	Jackhammer/pneumatic chipper	
90	Heavy-duty truck	
	Los Angeles, 3rd floor apartment next to freeway	
	Average street traffic	
80	Harlem, 2nd floor apartment	Damage possible with prolonged exposure
70	Private car	—
	Boston row house on major avenue	
	Business office	
	Watts—8 mi. from touchdown at major airport	
60	Conversational speech or old residential area	
50	San Diego—wooded residential area	—
40	California tomato field	
	Soft music from radio	
30	Quiet whisper	
20	Quiet urban dwelling	—
10	Rustle of leaf	
0	Threshold of hearing	

Source: U.S. Environmental Protection Agency.

Table D.2   OSHA Noise Exposure Limits

Noise (dB$_A$)	Permissible Exposure (hours and minutes)
85	16 hrs
87	12 hrs 6 min
90	8 hrs
93	5 hrs 18 min
96	3 hrs 30 min
99	2 hrs 18 min
102	1 hr 30 min
105	1 hr
108	40 min
111	26 min
114	17 min
115	15 min
118	10 min
121	6.6 min
124	4 min
127	3 min
130	1 min

Exposures above or below the 90 dB limit have been "time weighted" to give what OSHA believes are equivalent risks to a 90 dB eight-hour exposure. From U.S. Federal Register.

APPENDIX E

COMMON AND SCIENTIFIC NAMES OF NORTH AMERICAN WETLAND PLANTS

Scientific name	Common name
Acer rubrum L.	Red maple
Alisma plantago-aquatica L.	(Water plantain)
Alnus spp.	Alders
A. rugosa (DuRoi) Spreng.	Speckled alder
A. tenuifolia Nutt.	Thinleaf alder
Alopecurus aequalis Sobol.	Foxtail
Andromeda glaucophylla Link	Bog rosemary
Arctophila fulva (Trin.) Anderss.	Pendent grass
Aristida stricta Michx.	(Three-awn)
Ascophyllum spp.	(Rockweeds)
A. nodosum (L.) LeJol.	Knotted wrack
Aulacomnium palustre (Hedw.) Schwaegr.	(Moss)
Avicennia germinans (L.) L.	Black mangrove
Azolla spp.	Mosquito ferns
Baccharis halimifolia L.	Sea-myrtle
Beckmannia syzigachne (Steud.) Fernald	Slough grass
Betula nana L.	Dwarf birch
B. pumila L.	Bog birch
Brasenia schreberi J. F. Gmel.	Water shield
Calamagrostis canadensis (Michx.) Beauv.	Bluejoint
Calopogon spp.	Grass pinks
Caltha palustris L.	Marsh marigold
Campylium stellatum (Hedw.) C. Jens	(Moss)
Carex spp.	Sedges
C. aquatilis Wahlenb.	(Sedge)
C. atherodes Spreng.	Slough sedge
C. bipartita All.	(Sedge)
C. lacustris Willd.	(Sedge)
C. lasiocarpa Ehrh.	(Sedge)
C. lyngbyei Hornem.	(Sedge)
C. paleacea Schreb. *ex* Wahlenb.	(Sedge)
C. pluriflora Hulten	(Sedge)
C. ramenskii Kom.	(Sedge)
C. rariflora (Wahlenb.) J. E. Smith	(Sedge)
C. rostrata J. Stokes	Beaked sedge
Cassiope tetragona (L.) D. Don	Lapland cassiope
Caulerpa spp.	(Green algae)
Cephalanthus occidentalis L.	Buttonbush
Ceratophyllum spp.	Coontails
Chamaecyparis thyoides (L.) B.S.P.	Atlantic white cedar
Chamaedaphne calyculata (L.) Moench	Leatherleaf
Chara spp.	(Stoneworts)
Chenopodium glaucum L.	(Goosefoot)
Chiloscyphus fragilis (Roth) Schiffn.	(Liverwort)
Chondrus crispus Stackhouse	Irish moss
Cladina spp.	Reindeer mosses
C. rangiferina (L.) Harm	(Reindeer moss)
Cladium jamaicense Crantz	Saw grass
Colocasia esculenta (L.) Scott	Taro
Conocarpus erectus L.	Buttonwood
Cornus stolonifera Michx.	Red osier dogwood
Cymodocea filiformis (Kuetz) Correll	Manatee grass
Cyperus spp.	Nut sedges
Cyrilla racemiflora L.	Black ti-ti
Decodon verticillatus (L.) Elliott	Water willow

(Continued)

Scientific name	Common name
Dendranthema arcticum (L.) Tzvel.	Arctic daisy
Dermatocarpon fluviatile G. H. Web) Th. Fr.	(Lichen)
Distichlis spicata (L.) Greene	(Salt grass)
Drepanocladus spp.	(Moss)
Dryas integrifolia Vahl	(Dryas)
Echinochloa crusgalli (L.) Beauv.	Barnyard grass
Eichhornia crassipes (Mart.) Solms	Water hyacinth
Eleocharis sp.	(Spike rush)
E. palustris (L.) Roem. & J. A. Schultes	(Spike rush)
Elodea spp.	Water weeds
Elymus arenarius L.	(Lyme grass)
Empetrum nigrum L.	Crowberry
Enteromorpha spp.	(Green algae)
Eriophorum spp.	Cotton grasses
E. russeolum Fr.	(Cotton grass)
E. vaginatum L.	(Cotton grass)
Fissidens spp.	(Moss)
F. julianus (Mont.) Schimper	(Moss)
Fontinalis spp.	(Moss)
Fraxinus nigra Marshall	Black ash
F. pennsylvanica Marshall	(Red ash)
Fucus spp.	Rockweeds
F. spiralis L.	(Rockweed)
F. vesiculosus L.	(Rockweed)
Glyceria spp.	Manna grasses
Gordonia lasianthus (L.) J. Ellis	Loblolly bay
Habenaria spp.	(Orchids)
Halimeda spp.	(Green algae)
Halodule wrightii Aschers.	Shoal grass
Halophila spp.	(Sea grass)
Hippuris tetraphylla L.f.	(Mare's tail)
Hydrilla verticillata Royle	(Hydrilla)
Ilex glabra (L.) Gray	Inkberry
I. verticillata (L.) Gray	Winterberry
Iva frutescens L.	Marsh elder
Juncus spp.	Rushes
J. gerardii Loiseleur	Black grass
J. militaris Bigel.	Bayonet rush
J. roemerianus Scheele	Needlerush
Kalmia angustifolia L.	Sheep laurel
K. polifolia Wangenh.	Bog laurel
Kochia scoparia (L.) Schrad.	Summer cypress
Languncularia racemosa (L.) C. F. Gaertn.	White mangrove
Laminaria spp.	(Kelps)
Larix laricina (DuRoi) K. Koch	Tamarack
Laurencia spp.	(Red algae)
Ledum decumbens (Ait.) Small	Narrowleaf Labrador tea
L. groenlandicum Oeder	Labrador tea
Lemna spp.	(Duckweeds)
L. minor L.	Common duckweed
Leucothoe axillaris (Lam.) D. Don	Coastal sweetbells
Ligusticum scothicum L.	Beach lovage
Lithothamnion spp.	Coralline algae
Lycopodium alopecuroides L.	Foxtail clubmoss

(Continued)

Scientific name	Common name
Lyonia lucida (Lam.) K. Koch	Fetterbush
Lythrum salicaria L.	Purple loosestrife
Macrocystis spp.	(Kelps)
Magnolia virginiana L.	Sweet bay
Marsupella spp.	(Liverworts)
M. emarginata (Ehrenberg) Dumortier	(Liverwort)
Myrica gale L.	Sweet gale
Myriophyllum spp.	Water milfoils
M. spicatum L.	(Water milfoil)
Najas spp.	Naiads
Nelumbo lutea (Willd.) Pers.	American lotus
Nitella spp.	(Stoneworts)
Nuphar luteum (L.) Sibth. & J. E. Smith	(Yellow water lily)
Nymphaea spp.	(Water lilies)
N. odorata Soland. in Ait.	(White water lily)
Nyssa aquatica L.	Tupelo gum
N. sylvatica Marshall	Black gum
Oncophorus wahlenbergii Brid.	(Moss)
Panicum capillare L.	Old witch grass
Pedicularis sp.	(Lousewort)
Peltandra virginica (L.) Kunth	Arrow arum
Pelvetia spp.	(Rockweeds)
Penicillus spp.	(Green algae)
Persea borbonia (L.) Spreng.	Red bay
Phragmites australis (Cav.) Trin. *ex* Steud.	Reed
Phyllospadix scouleri Hook.	(Surfgrass)
P. torreyi S. Wats.	(Surfgrass)
Picea mariana (Mill.) B.S.P.	Black spruce
P. sitchensis (Bong.) Carriere	Sitka spruce
Pinus contorta Dougl. *ex* Loudon	Lodgepole pine
P. palustris Mill.	Longleaf pine
P. serotina Michx.	Pond pine
Pistia stratiotes L.	Water lettuce
Plantago maritima L.	Seaside plantain
Podostemum ceratophyllum Michx.	Riverweed
Polygonum spp.	Smartweeds
P. amphibium L.	Water smartweed
P. bistorta L.	Bistort
Pontederia cordata L.	Pickerelweed
Potamogeton spp.	Pondweeds
P. gramineus L.	(Pondweed)
P. natans L.	Floating-leaf pondweed
Populus balsamifera L.	Balsam poplar
P. deltoides W. Bartram *ex* Marshall	Cottonwood
Potentilla anserina L.	Silverweed
P. fruticosa L.	Shrubby cinquefoil
P. palustris (L.) Scop.	Marsh cinquefoil
Puccinellia grandis Swallen	(Alkali grass)
Quercus bicolor Willd.	Swamp white oak
Q. lyrata Walter	Overcup oak
Q. michauxii Nutt.	Basket oak
Ranunculus pallasii Schlecht.	(Crowfoot)
R. trichophyllus D. Chaix	White water crowfoot
Rhizophora mangle L.	Red mangrove

(Continued)

Scientific name	Common name
Rhododendron maximum L.	Great laurel
Rhynchospora spp.	Beak rushes
Rubus chamaemorus L.	Cloudberry
Rumex maritimus L.	Golden dock
R. mexicanus Meisn.	(Dock)
Ruppia spp.	Ditch grasses
R. maritima L.	Widgeon grass
Sagittaria spp.	Arrowheads
Salicornia spp.	Glassworts
S. europaea L.	(Samphire)
S. virginica L.	(Common pickleweed)
Salix spp.	Willows
S. alaxensis (Anderss.) Coville	Feltleaf willow
S. fuscescens Anderss.	Alaska bog willow
S. ovalifolia Trautv.	Ovalleaf willow
S. planifolia Pursh	Diamondleaf willow
S. reticulata L.	Netleaf willow
Salvinia spp.	Water ferns
Sarcobatus vermiculatus (Hook.) Torr.	Greasewood
Scirpus spp.	Bulrushes
S. acutus Muhl. *ex* Bigel.	Hardstem bulrush
S. americanus Pers.	Common threesquare
S. robustus Pursh	(Bulrush)
Scolochloa festucacea (Willd.) Link	Whitetop
Solidago sempervirens L.	Seaside goldenrod
Sparganium hyperboreum Laest.	(Bur-reed)
Spartina alterniflora Loiseleur	Saltmarsh cordgrass
S. Cynosuroides (L.) Roth	Big cordgrass
S. foliosa Trin.	California cordgrass
S. patens (Ait.) Muhl.	Saltmeadow cordgrass
Sphagnum spp.	Peat mosses
Spiraea beauverdiana C. K. Schneid.	Alaska spiraea
S. douglasii Hook.	(Spiraea)
Spirodela spp.	Big duckweeds
Stellaria spp.	(Chickweed)
Suaeda californica S. Wats.	(Sea blite)
Tamarix gallica L.	Tamarisk
Taxodium distichum (L.) L. C. Rich.	Bald cypress
Thalassia testudinum K. D. Koenig	Turtle grass
Thuja occidentalis L.	Northern white cedar
Tolypella spp.	(Stoneworts)
Trapa natans L.	Water nut
Triglochin maritimum L.	Arrow grass
Typha spp.	Cattails
T. angustifolia L.	Narrow-leaved cattail
T. latifolia L.	Common cattail
Ulmus americana L.	American elm
Ulva spp.	Sea lettuce
Utricularia spp.	Bladderworts
U. macrorhiza LeConte	(Bladderwort)
Vaccinium corymbosum L.	Highbush blueberry
V. oxycoccos L.	Small cranberry
V. uliginosum L.	Bog blueberry
V. vitis-idaea L.	Mountain cranberry

(*Continued*)

Scientific name	Common name
Vallisneria americana Michx.	Wild celery
Verrucaria spp.	(Lichens)
Wolffia spp.	Watermeals
Woodwardia virginica (L.) J. E. Smith	Virginia chain-fern
Xanthium strumarium L.	(Cocklebur)
Xyris spp.	Yellow-eyed grasses
Xyris smalliana Nash	(Yellow-eyed grass)
Zannichellia palustris L.	Horned pondweed
Zenobia pulverulenta (W. Bartram) Pollard	Honeycup
Zizania aquatica L.	Wild rice
Zizaniopsis miliacea (Michx.) Doell & Aschers.	Southern wild rice
Zostera marina L.	Eelgrass
Zosterella dubia (Jacq.) Small	Water stargrass

Source: U.S. Department of Agriculture, National List of Scientific Names, 1982.

Note: Common names that refer to a higher taxon (category) and common names that are not widely used or generally agreed upon are given in parentheses.

APPENDIX F

UNITS OF MEASUREMENT AND CONVERSIONS

F.1 LENGTH, AREA, AND VOLUME

Length

- 1 micrometer (μm) = 0.000001 meter = 0.0001 centimeter
- 1 millimeter (mm) = 0.03937 inch = 0.1 centimeter
- 1 centimeter (cm) = 0.39 inch = 0.01 meter
- 1 inch (in) = 2.54 centimeters = 0.083 foot
- 1 foot (ft) = 0.3048 meter = 0.33 yard
- 1 yard (yd) = 0.9144 meter
- 1 meter (m) = 3.2808 feet = 1.0936 yards
- 1 kilometer (km) = 1000 meters = 0.6214 mile (statute) = 3281 feet
- 1 mile (statute) (mi) = 5280 feet = 1.6093 kilometers
- 1 mile (nautical) (mi) = 6076 feet = 1.8531 kilometers

Area

- 1 sqaure centimeter (cm^2) = 0.0001 square meter = 0.15550 square inch
- 1 square inch (in^2) = 0.0069 square foot = 6.452 square centimeters
- 1 square foot (ft^2) = 144 square inches = 0.0929 square meter
- 1 square yard (yd^2) = 9 square feet = 0.8361 square meter
- 1 square meter (m^2) = 1.1960 square yards = 10.764 square feet
- 1 acre (ac) = 43,560 square feet = 4046.95 square meters
- 1 hectare (ha) = 10,000 square meters = 2.471 acres
- 1 square kilometer (km^2) = 1,000,000 square meters = 0.3861 square mile
- 1 square mile (mi^2) = 640 acres = 2.590 square kilometers

Volume

- 1 cubic centimeter (cm^2) = 1000 cubic millimeters = 0.0610 cubic inch
- 1 cubic inch (in^3) = 0.0069 cubic foot = 16.387 cubic centimeters
- 1 liter (1) = 1000 cubic centimeters = 1.0567 quarts
- 1 gallon (gal) = 4 quarts = 3.785 liters
- 1 cubic ft (ft^3) = 28.31 liters = 7.48 gallons = 0.02832 cubic meter
- 1 cubic yard (yd^3) = 27 cubic feet = 0.7646 cubic meter
- 1 cubic meter (m^3) = 35.314 cubic feet = 1.3079 cubic yards
- 1 acre-foot (acft) = 43,560 cubic feet = 1234 cubic meters

F.2 MASS AND VELOCITY

Mass (Weight)

- 1 gram (g) = 0.03527 ounce[*] = 15.43 grains
- 1 ounce (oz) = 28.3495 grams = 437.5 grains
- 1 pound (lb) = 16 ounces = 0.4536 kilogram

- 1 kilogram (kg) = 1000 grams = 2.205 pounds
- 1 ton* (ton) = 2000 pounds = 907 kilograms
- 1 tonne = 1000 kilograms = 2205 pounds

Velocity

- 1 meter per second (m/sec) = 2.237 miles per hour
- 1 km per hour (km/hr) = 27.78 centimeters per second
- 1 mile per hour (mph) = 0.4470 meter per second
- 1 knot (kt) = 1.151 miles per hour = 0.5144 meter/second

F.3 ENERGY, POWER, FORCE, AND PRESSURE

Energy Units and Their Equivalents

- *joule* (abbreviation J): 1 joule = 1 unit of force (a newton) applied over a distance of 1 meter = 0.239 calorie
- *calorie* (abbreviation cal): 1 calorie = heat needed to raise the temperature of 1 gram of water from 14.5°C to 15.5°C = 4.186 joules
- *British Thermal Unit* (abbreviation BTU): 1 BTU = heat needed to raise the temperature of 1 pound of water 1°Fahrenheit from 39.4° to 40.4°F = 252 calories = 1055 joules

Power

- *watt* (abbreviation W): 1 watt = 1 joule per second
- *horsepower* (abbreviation hp): 1 hp = 746 watts

Force and Pressure

- *newton* (abbreviation N): 1 newton = force needed to accelerate a 1-kilogram mass over a distance of 1 meter in 1 second squared
- *bar* (abbreviated b): 1 bar = pressure equivalent to 100,000 newtons on an area of 1 square meter
- *millibar* (abbreviation mb): 1 millibar = one-thousandth $\left(\dfrac{1}{1000}\right)$ of a bar
- *pascal* (abbreviation Pa): 1 pascal = force exerted by 100,000 newtons on an area of 1 square meter
- *atmosphere* (abbreviation Atmos.): 1 atmosphere = 14.7 pounds of pressure per square inch = 1013.2 millibars

ILLUSTRATION
AND PHOTO CREDITS

Chapter 1
Fig. 1.1 Royal Institute of British Architects.
Fig. 1.2 Bettman/Hulton.
Fig. 1.3 Photo by Winston Vargas.
Fig. 1.4 Greenpeace (photo by Geering).
Fig. 1.7 Harley Ellington Pierce Yee Associates.
Fig. 1.8 U.S. Army Corps of Engineers.

Chapter 2
Figs. 2.1 to 2.5 W. M. Marsh, *Earthscape: A Physical Geography* (John Wiley & Sons, 1987).
Fig. 2.6 U.S. Soil Conservation Service.
Figs. 2.7 to 2.13 W. M. Marsh, *Earthscape: A Physical Geography* (John Wiley & Sons, 1987).

Chapter 3
Figs. 3.1 and 3.3 U.S. Air Force.
Fig. 3.2 Nina L. Marsh.
Fig. 3.4 Photo by F. J. Swanson.
Fig. 3.5 Nina L. Marsh.
Fig. 3.6 U.S. Soil Conservation Service.

Chapter 4
Fig. 4.1 Nina L. Marsh.
Figs. 4.4 and 4.7 James G. Marsh.
Fig. 4.8 U.S. Soil Conservation Service.
Fig. 4.9 W. M. Marsh, *Earthscape: A Physical Geography* (John Wiley & Sons, 1987).

Chapter 5
Figs. 5.1 and 5.4 W. M. Marsh, *Earthscape: A Physical Geography* (John Wiley & Sons, 1987).
Fig. 5.3 James G. Marsh.
Figs. 5.6, 5.8, and 5.9 Nina L. Marsh.
Fig. 5.10 U.S. Soil Conservation Service.

Chapter 6
Fig. 6.4 Stock, Boston, photo by Daniel S. Brady.
Fig. 6.5 W. M. Marsh, *Earthscape: A Physical Geography* (John Wiley & Sons, 1987).
Fig. 6.7 U.S. Soil Conservation Service.

Chapter 7
Figs. 7.1, 7.2, 7.4, and 7.6 W. M. Marsh, *Earthscape: A Physical Geography* (John Wiley & Sons, 1987).
Figs. 7.3 and 7.7 U.S. Geological Survey.
Figs. 7.5 and 7.9 Nina L. Marsh.

Chapter 8
Fig. 8.3 Based on U.S. Department of Agriculture data.
Fig. 8.8 Adapted from H. Deardorff and R. Chipman.
Fig. 8.9 U.S. Soil Conservation Service.

Chapter 9
Fig. 9.6 Adapted from Peter Van Dusen.
Fig. 9.7 L. B. Leopold, U.S. Geological Survey Circular 554.

Chapter 10
Fig. 10.1 James G. Marsh.
Fig. 10.2 W. M. Marsh, *Earthscape: A Physical Geography* (John Wiley & Sons, 1987).
Fig. 10.5 Data from T. Dunne and L. B. Leopold, *Water in Environmental Planning* (San Francisco: Freeman, 1978).
Fig. 10.6 Data from U.S. National Weather Service.
Fig. 10.8 U.S. Water Resources Council.

Chapter 11
Fig. 11.1 From W. M. Marsh and R. Hill-Rowley, "Water Quality, Stormwater Management and Development Planning on the Urban Fringe," *Journal of Urban and Contemporary Law,* 1989.
Fig. 11.5 From J. M. Omernick, *Non-point Source–Stream Nutrient Level Relationships: A Nationwide Study* (U.S. Environmental Protection Agency, 1977).
Fig. 11.6 Nina L. Marsh

Chapter 12
Fig. 12.1 U.S. Soil Conservation Service.
Fig. 12.2 From M. G. Wolman, "A Cycle of Sedimentation and Erosion in Urban River Channels," *Geografiska Annaler,* 1967.
Fig. 12.3 U.S. Soil Conservation Service, *Cropland Erosion,* 1977.
Fig. 12.4 From U.S. Soil Conservation Service.
Fig. 12.5 After F. Hjulstrom, 1939.
Fig. 12.7 Howard Deardorff.

Chapter 13
Figs. 13.1, 13.3, 13.5, and 13.9 W. M. Marsh, *Earthscape: A Physical Geography* (John Wiley & Sons, 1987).
Fig. 13.2 U.S. Army Corps of Engineers.
Figs. 13.7 and 13.10 W. M. Marsh, "Nourishment of Perched Sand Dunes and the Issues of Erosion Control on the Great Lakes," *Journal of Environmental Geology and Water Science,* 1990.
Fig. 13.12 Reuters/Bettmore.

Chapter 14
Fig. 14.4a W. M. Marsh and J. Dozier, *Landscape: An Introduction to Physical Geography* (Addison–Wesley, 1981).
Fig. 14.6 Williams and Woo, Inc.
Fig. 14.7b Jeff Dozier.
Fig. 14.8 Antonio Tellez.
Case Study First set, Brian Larson.

Chapter 15
Fig. 15.2 Base drawing adapted from Johnson, Johnson and Roy
Fig. 15.3 T. R. Oke, "Evapotranspiration in Urban Areas and Its Implication for Urban Climate Planning" in *Teaching the Teachers on Building Climatology* (Stockholm: Swedish National Institute for Building Research, 1972).
Fig. 15.9 U.S. Weather Service.
Fig. 15.10 Adapted from V. Olgyay, *Design With Climate: Bioclimatic Approach to Architectural Regionalism* (Princeton: Princeton University Press, 1963).

Chapter 16

Fig. 16.1 W. M. Marsh and J. Dozier, *Landscape: An Introduction to Physical Geography* (Addison–Wesley, 1981).

Fig. 16.2 Antonio Tellez.

Fig. 16.4 Donald G. Baker, "Snow Cover and Winter Soil Temperatures at St. Paul, Minnesota," *Water Resources Center Bulletin 37* (University of Minnesota, 1971).

Fig. 16.6 Data from W. M. Marsh.

Figs. 16.9 and 16.10 Troy W. Péwé.

Case Study Photos by Troy W. Péwé.

Chapter 17

Fig. 17.1 Photos by W. M. Marsh and Soil Conservation Service (inset).

Fig. 17.2 Long Island State Park and Recreation Commission.

Fig. 17.3 Korab Photography.

Fig. 17.5 From C. Johnson; rendered by R. Chipman.

Fig. 17.7 W. M. Marsh and J. Dozier, *Landscape: An Introduction to Physical Geography* (Addison–Wesley, 1981).

Fig. 17.7 From U.S. Department of Agriculture.

Fig. 17.8 From J. T. Hack and J. L. Goodlet, "Geomorphology and Forest Ecology of a Mountain Region in the Central Appalachians," *U.S. Geological Survey Professional Paper 347,* 1960.

Chapter 18

Fig. 18.1 Nina L. Marsh.

Fig. 18.2 Data from H. T. Odom, 1957.

Fig. 18.3 All photos by Frank C. Golet, The University of Rhode Island.

Fig. 18.4 Nina L. Marsh.

Fig. 18.5 Adapted from A. C. Redfield, "Development of a New England Saltmarsh," *Ecological Monographs 42:*2, 1972.

Fig. 18.6 U.S. Fish and Wildlife Service.

Fig. 18.7 Laboratory for Land and Water Management, University of Michigan-Flint.

Case Study Photos by Ron Abrams.

Case Study Photo by P. Grenell; map by Nina L. Marsh.

INDEX